W9-ADZ-959

WHY MILTON MATTERS

ALSO BY JOSEPH WITTREICH

BOOKS

Angel of Apocalypse: Blake's Idea of Milton (Madison and London: University of Wisconsin Press, 1975)

Visionary Poetics: Milton's Tradition and His Legacy (San Marino: Huntington Library, 1979).

"Image of that Horror": History, Prophecy, and Apocalypse in "King Lear" (San Marino: Huntington Library, 1984).

Interpreting "Samson Agonistes" (Princeton: Princeton University Press, 1986). [Winner of the James Holly Hanford Award presented by the Milton Society of America, December, 1987]

Feminist Milton (Ithaca, N.Y.: Cornell University Press, 1987).

Shifting Contexts: Reinterpreting "Samson Agonistes" (Pittsburgh: Duquesne University Press, 2002).

EDITIONS

The Romantics on Milton: Formal Essays and Critical Asides (Cleveland and London: Press of Case Western Reserve University, 1970).

ANTHOLOGIES

Ed. Joseph Wittreich, *Calm of Mind: Tercentenary Essays in Honor of John S. Diekhoff* (Cleveland and London: Press of Case Western Reserve University, 1972).

Ed. with Stuart Curran, *Blake's Sublime Allegory: Essays on "The Four Zoas," "Milton," and "Jerusalem"* (Madison and London: University of Wisconsin Press, 1973).

Ed. Joseph Wittreich, *Milton and the Line of Vision* (Madison and London: University of Wisconsin Press, 1975).

Ed. with Richard S. Ide. *Composite Orders: The Genres of Milton's Last Poems* (Pittsburgh: University of Pittsburgh Press, 1983), a special issue of *Milton Studies*, XVII.

Ed. with C. A. Patrides, *The Apocalypse in English Renaissance Thought and Literature* (Manchester and Dover, NH: Manchester University Press, 1984).

Edited with Peter E. Medine, *Soundings of Things Done: Essays in Early Modern Literature in Honor of S. K. Heninger, Jr.* (Newark University of Delaware Press and London: Associated University Presses, 1997).

Ed. with Mark R. Kelley, *Altering Eyes: New Perspectives on "Samson Agonistes"* (Newark: University of Delaware Press and London: Associated University Presses, 2002).

PAMPHLETS

William Blake's Illustrations for "Paradise Regained" (Cleveland: Rowfant Keepsake, 1971).

WHY MILTON MATTERS: A NEW PREFACE TO HIS WRITINGS

Joseph Wittreich

palgrave
macmillan

First published in 2006 by
PALGRAVE MACMILLAN™
175 Fifth Avenue, New York, N.Y. 10010 and
Houndmills, Basingstoke, Hampshire, England RG21 6XS
Companies and representatives throughout the world.

PALGRAVE MACMILLAN is the global academic imprint of the Palgrave Macmillan division of St. Martin's Press, LLC and of Palgrave Macmillan Ltd. Macmillan® is a registered trademark in the United States, United Kingdom and other countries. Palgrave is a registered trademark in the European Union and other countries.

ISBN-13: 978–1–4039–7229–3
ISBN-10: 1–4039–7229–X

Library of Congress Cataloging-in-Publication Data

Wittreich, Joseph Anthony.
   Why Milton matters : a new preface to his writings /
by Joseph Wittreich.
      p. cm.
   Includes bibliographical references and index.
   ISBN 1–4039–7229–X (alk. paper)
      1. Milton, John, 1608–1674—Criticism and interpretation. I. Title.

PR3588.W58 2006
821′.4—dc22   2006043418

A catalogue record for this book is available from the British Library.

Design by Newgen Imaging Systems (P) Ltd., Chennai, India.

First edition: November 2006

10 9 8 7 6 5 4 3 2 1

Printed in the United States of America.

CITATIONS

Most of the citations of Milton's poetry, unless otherwise indicated, are from *The Complete Poetry of John Milton*, ed. John T. Shawcross, rev. ed. (Garden City, NY: Doubleday, 1971), sometimes for clarity referred to as CP. Most of the citations of Milton's prose writings are from *Complete Prose Works of John Milton*, gen. ed. Don M. Wolfe, 8 vols. (New Haven: Yale University Press, 1953–82), referred to as YP. Occasionally citations are from *The Works of John Milton*, gen. ed. Frank Allen Patterson, 18 vols. (New York: Columbia University Press, 1931–40), referred to as CM.

CONTENTS

Citations   viii

Illustrations   x

Preface   xi

1   "Reading" Milton: The Death (and Survival) of the Author   1

2   Horizons of Expectations: Repressions, Receptions, and the Politics of Milton's Last Poems   61

3   Questioning and Critique: The Formation of a New Milton Criticism   141

Notes   195

Index   241

for
VINCENT NEWTON
1917–2005

just, skillful, magnanimous

[I]n the context of what appears to be a crisis . . . in the late twentieth-century university, the question of how, and still more why, *we should still be reading [Milton] . . . seems to deserve a larger scrutiny.*

—Annabel Patterson

ILLUSTRATIONS

1.1   *Lycidas* (the first page of the poem) in *Poems of
      Mr. John Milton* (1645)   5
1.2   The Table of Contents for *Poems upon Several
      Occasions* (1673)   6
1.3   The Frontispiece to *Poems of Mr. John Milton* (1645)   8
1.4   The Frontispiece to *The History of Britain* (1670)   12
1.5   The Frontispiece to *Art of Logic* (1672)   13
1.6   The Frontispiece to *Paradise Lost* (1674)   14
1.7   The Title Page to *Poems of Mr. John Milton* (1645)   17
2.8   The Marked Ending of *Poems of
      Mr. John Milton* (1675)   65
2.9   The Frontispiece to *Paradise Lost*, 4th ed. (1688)   83
2.10 John Baptist Medina's Illustration to Book I of
      Paradise Lost ("Satan Calling up His Legions")   85
2.11 Title Page No. 2 to *Paradise Lost* (1668)   89
2.12 Title Page No. 2 (variant) to *Paradise Lost* (1668)   90
2.13 The Title Page to *Paradise Lost* (1725)   94
3.14 Richard Westall's Illustration for *Samson Agonistes*
      ("The Messenger Reporting the Catastrophe")   153
3.15 The Title Page for the 1671 Poetic Volume   158
3.16 The Separate Title Page for *Samson Agonistes* in
      the 1671 Poetic Volume   159

PREFACE

Today, nearly three and a half centuries after Paradise Lost *was first published, it is more influential than ever. . . . It will not go away.*

—Philip Pullman

For what is "Paradise Lost"—and, for that matter, Milton's other masterpiece in verse "Samson Agonistes"—if not a highly idiosyncratic appropriation of Hebrew scripture? It is impossible to understand not only Milton but a great deal of the greatest literature, art and music produced in the English-speaking world . . . without grasping that the English saw themselves as the new Israel. . . . [And] what has all this to do with present-day politics? Quite a lot, actually.

—David Johnson[1]

If, as Harold Bloom remarks, "Milton was out of season, from 1660 until his death in 1674,"[2] it is high time to say that Milton is back in season (and still fair game) today. His last poems are appropriated not just by America but other nations, both East and West, and they are no longer confined to Jewish and Christian cultures, though they might have been earlier. In the later years of the twentieth century, *Paradise Lost* was the text the Hell's Angels packed away in their hip pockets; that (in the Harvard Classics version) Malcolm X read in prison and therein discovered the fundamental teachings of the Muslim religion. It is the poem that enabled a *Washington Post* editorialist to wax eloquently on the *whys* of the Iranian hostage crisis and, subsequently, a *New York Times* correspondent to wonder, *What kind of God is this?* Yet it is also a poem that gets no mention in a *New York Post* column on the lost canon of English literature but that, even if not explicitly cited, seems to be a touchstone to Toni Morrison's thinking about paradises lost, and perhaps not recoverable, until there is a seismic change in how we go about instantiating utopian ideals. If *Paradise Lost* was the poem over the centuries adapted for children, most recently by Nancy Willard, and now popularized into graphic novels by Neil Gaiman, it is also the poem from which the so-called great generation took messages for democracy in time of war and from which America, during the Cold War years, learned about the evil empires of the world, sometimes in newly fictionalized forms like Steven Brust's *To Reign in Hell*.[3]

Correspondingly, *Samson Agonistes* was illustrated by Albert Decaris in 1939, when, in self-induced blindness, part of the world seemed to be rushing back to tyranny and when Milton's tragedy, within the historical context of World War II, was pointedly invoked as an example of "political art" with a powerful "lesson" for history: "Nazi Germany had already seized Austria and moved into Czechoslovakia. Europe was under a red alert."[4] *Samson Agonistes* once again seemed to matter. The world, full of rage, was fast becoming a mirror of the eyeless world of *Samson Agonistes*. Sixty two years later, in the aftermath of 9/11, Milton's tragedy is being invoked yet again, as Aldous Huxley once did it through the title-phrase, "Eyeless in Gaza" (41), to figure "political unrest and confrontation," government deception, its policies of blindness practiced in a world, all of whose "principal players are blind"—and their "faces without eyes."[5] *Samson Agonistes* is the poem, in these post–9/11 years, repeatedly cited in the journalistic press, both in England and America, and even invoked as a handbook on terrorists and terrorism, although there is some heated dispute over the lessons this poem would teach. Nevertheless, as much as Milton's poems were yesterday, they remain today part of the crisis, still (as Nigel Smith might say) situated "at its epicentre."[6] Milton's poems are thus given "new currency" as "a vital living part of contemporary culture," which also paves way "to a plurality of interpretations, freed to be used in multiple [and I would add, *shifting*] contexts."[7]

The issue, finally, is whether Milton's last poems—*Paradise Lost, Paradise Regain'd*, and *Samson Agonistes*—are vehicles for timeless or timely truths and, more largely, whether the standards of permanent interest and steady value are typically met by canonical authors. With reference to *Paradise Lost*, Michael Bérubé, asking the right question, responds incisively to it:

> What are these spiritual lessons, these timeless truths? Lately we've noticed that our antagonists get uncharacteristically tongue-tied when we ask them what specific truths they have in mind: Is *Paradise Lost* a 10,000 word version of "just say no?" Likewise they begin to bluster when we ask them who they mean by us, and they get downright sullen

when we ask whether these great works say the same thing every time
they speak.

That's why nothing outrages the Right quite like the current academic interest in attempting to understand what literary works did and
didn't say to their contemporary readers and audiences, and for what
reasons. From the Right's perspective, inquiring into the historical
production and reception of cultural artifacts is the most subversive
enterprise of all, for it threatens to undo the very notion of artistic
autonomy and timelessness. . . .

Generally, when the Right complains that we're reading ideologically,
it means that we're reading historically.[8]

The alternative side in the debate, then, often reading historically, also
reads critically, and, attuned to complexity, is both alert to and appre-
ciative of conflict and contradiction, the conspicuous features of
Milton's poems and the very features some think are there to impel a
revolutionary outcome. For anyone troubled by collapsing hierarchies
and by subversive maneuvers, or by notions of oppressive traditions
and political transformations, Milton's last poems are bound to make
for unsettling reading. This is so in part because, within the boundaries of canonical literature, those poems are the surest reminder that
texts used to serve elitist ideologies are not necessarily based upon,
much less biased toward them; that religious poems are not necessarily in possession of coherent or dogmatic creeds.

It is revealing to pair Milton's last poems with their biblical counterparts and then to examine the hermeneutics accruing to each of their
stories. If critical tradition strives for a monologic discourse that would
fix interpretation, Milton's poetry yields a dialogic discourse of floating
interpretations, its objective being not to reify existing commentary but
to infuse it with greater intricacies and thus imbue it with more nuanced
insight. Philip Pullman drives home a similar point when he declares
that "however many times . . . [Milton's story] is told in the future, and
however many interpretations are made of it, I don't think that the version created by Milton . . . will ever be surpassed."[9] Pullman's message
is obvious: Milton raised the bar of both scriptural storytelling and biblical exegesis to new heights. Still at the core of Milton criticism is the
question—and the ensuing controversy—over what precisely is *the version created by Milton* and just how Milton's version of the story is to be
interpreted. These issues sit at the core of *Paradise Lost*, Books 6, 7, and
8, which are as much about the struggle for interpretation as about its
necessity. As Victoria Kahn shows, the struggle for interpretation,
together with its necessity, dominates *Samson Agonistes* as well.[10]

Though it may be generally true that hermeneutical traditions strike a monologic relationship with their scriptural texts in contrast to literary works, which, on the contrary, relate dialectically to their pretexts and often antithetically to existing interpretations, it is a truth actively complicated by the unsettling of received interpretation during the seventeenth century. The hermeneutical project of the Age of Milton is given chiseled definition by numerous commentators whose agenda is to disturb, not confirm, venerable interpretations of key biblical stories with the consequence that, as Milton's century progresses, interpretation becomes increasingly conflicted. There is no *single* Samson hermeneutic and, correspondingly, no *one* hermeneutic either for the Creation/Fall story or for the tale of Jesus tempted in the wilderness. Any poem of Milton's century faithful to hermeneutic tradition in its seventeenth-century phase will necessarily array competing interpretations of a given story or myth and (to the extent that the poem captures the intricacy of either) will produce a subtle mapping of rival discourses, marking contradictions both within and between them, even perhaps marbleizing inherited contradictions within newly perceived ones.

What is true of *Paradise Lost* pertains equally to Milton's 1671 poetic volume. *Paradise Regain'd* and *Samson Agonistes* will not (in the words of the first epigraph to this Preface) "go away" either. In Book 3 of *Paradise Lost*, addressing Uriel as "Interpreter" (657) and then himself proffering interpretation (670–76), Satan alerts us to the essential nature of Milton's last poems, each of which is rippling with interpreters, rife with interpretations. Interestingly, when Milton refers to the act of interpretation in his last poems, it is to bracket the frustrations and difficulties *especially* of human interpretation: "let mee / Interpret for him," says the Son in Book 11 (32–33), now acutely aware of man's propensity for misinterpreting—for seeing "A" and calling it "B" (see *Samson Agonistes*, 790–91). Apparently, the "Dialect of Men," even when exalted to an art that would tell all "*if* Art could tell" (4.236; my italics), is an insufficiently refined device for interpretation and becomes less so after the Fall when Art is sometimes "calumnious" and often a haven for "counterfeted truth" (5.770–71).

Not even the artful tongue of angels is a perfectly tuned instrument for interpretation, in part because the angels no more than mankind are privy to certain of God's secrets, if even God can be trusted to reveal them. While the Almighty declares that the Son is "Equal to God," the hymning angels, according to the narrator of *Paradise Lost*, perceive the Son as sitting "Second" to God (3.306, 409). All the characters in Milton's last poems are interpreters: human and divine, angels and demons, God as well as Satan. Most notably, the narrator is an interpreter, both moralistic and prophetic; and if it can still be said that "we have misconstrued the poem by ignoring the role of the narrative voice," "the role of the narrator as interpreter to the fallen reader,"[11] that is so because we continue to forget, one, that the narrator is himself a fallen figure and, two, that his moral observation and prophetic insight (sometimes at odds) are therefore filtered through a fallen consciousness. We see what we want to see, or are able to see, and thus, like the hymning angels of Book 3 of *Paradise Lost*, do not always see as God sees. Yet, with altering eyes, with an ever-expanding consciousness, we see more and more as Milton's poems proceed, their magnificent complexity yielding a drama of ideas through which a vision of an indefinite future becomes increasingly a detailed blueprint for one.

Divine and human, heavenly and earthly analogies tease us into uncertainties and often into unexpected conclusions. What in the seventeenth century was more subversive than for women to think themselves superior to men, much less assert their felt superiority? This wish may belong to Eve in the temptation scene, but it is fostered by Satan who, thinking woman less, touts her as greater than man, but only as a part of his own desire for revenge and his own will to domination. In *Paradise Lost*, Milton lays bare the sexism engrained in the courtly love tradition and its idolatry of woman, for example in the early modern love-sonnet. The real reason for man's extolling woman as more, Milton implies, is his wish for her to become less than he is— the desire, which is Satan's, that she be his subject. And it is Satan's way throughout this poem to subjugate others by feigning submission, to undo Creation by upside-downing its hierarchies. If God is reported to have created the animals as man's subjects, Satan claims in his temptation of Eve that God has "Subjected to . . . [mankind's] service Angel wings" (9.155), then tells Eve that she "shouldst be seen / A Goddess among Gods, adorn'd and serv'd / By Angels numberless, thy daily Train" (9.546–48). Satan's confusion becomes Adam's when, once fallen into a state of subjection, he asserts at the end of Book 9 his preeminence and dominion over Eve, Eve having just declared herself, even before God's curse, to be Adam's subject. Rigid patriarchy—male supremacy, female subjection—is registered emphatically in this poem as an aspect and manifestation of fallen existence.

What we learn from *Paradise Lost* is that mind/body, head/ heart dichotomies are no way of conceiving human relationships, only demonic ones, with Satan's "armie of Fiends" serving as "fit body to fit head" (4.953) and, more, that this "sly hypocrite" (4.957) only seems a patron of liberty and only feigns submission as a way of dispossessing all, then reigning. Feigned submission, the way of those who themselves disdain subjection, has the subjugation of others as its motive (4.50, 96). Submission and subjection are opposites, not contraries, in *Paradise Lost* with subjection defining but two sets of relationships—those between man and animals (8.343–45), and those between Satan and his fiends—which, in turn, become models for how Satan would relate to all others in the poem, placing them in lowly servitude. Mankind "should have rul'd," Satan tells his legions, as he now would rule over God's Creation (10.492–93). Satan has distorted the world of Paradise, then teased us into seeing it as a replication of his own world in which there is coy submission with the intention of promoting self-interest; where hierarchy is a way of leveling everyone into submission to his tyranny. As Satan argues his cohorts into subjection to order and degree, inadvertently he argues Adam and Eve into equality; for they are "equals" who are "In freedom equal" (5.796–97). The equality Satan feigns with God is the actual equality the Son enjoys with his Father and that Adam and Eve should have enjoyed—and eventually do enjoy—with one another.

A poem that enfolds hierarchies, *Paradise Lost* is equally a poem that destabilizes them. The very fact that some biblical commentators argued for, and others against, a hierarchy in hell comparable to the one in heaven allows Milton certain latitude. Thus the devils in the catalogue to Book 1 may seem to exist in hierarchy, even if, in the council scene of Book 2, there seem to be just two classes and if, still later, because their names are used so confusedly, the devils all blur into one. The unsettling of the infernal hierarchy finds precedent in a tradition which claims that, at the time of the Harrowing of Hell, Beelzebub displaces Satan as prince of the devils. That is, an asymmetrical parallelism between Hell and Heaven shows Satan unwillingly surrendering his scepter in contrast with God who, at the end of time, willingly gives his scepter to the Son. To what extent, others have wondered, does this same parallelism, symmetrically or asymmetrically, apply to Adam, Eve, and life in this world? Does Milton's blurring of hierarchies, both in Heaven and Hell, prove paradigmatic for what occurs on earth? Just how accurate is the contention that "The Hierarchical idea . . . is the indwelling life of the whole work, . . . foam[ing] or burgeon[ing] out of it at every moment"? Just how "neat, dainty, . . . fastidious" is this "man" supposedly "enchanted" by "the Hierarchical principle"?[12]

If Satan's early impressions of the new creation match with Pauline interpretation, Satan's is also an interpretation that *Paradise Lost* would refine out of existence. Mary Ann Radzinowicz states the case exactly: Milton's "political instances involving scriptural scenarios in *Paradise Lost*" are all the same: "In them Scripture is history and not authority; no interpretation is coercive; no . . . policy comes with God's fiat behind it to overrule freedom. . . . Scripture is a datum for interpretation and not a set of given precedents."[13] *Paradise Lost* is a compendium of contradictory interpretations. The reader's task is to distinguish the true from the false, the more from the less adequate interpretations and then, in accordance with the hidden logic of the poem, to privilege this interpretation over that one, while never forgetting the partiality and incompleteness of all interpretations.

It is no accident that the exchange of speeches between Adam and Eve in Book 4, just after Satan's soliloquy, should invoke the competing hermeneutics, feminist and masculinist, that by Milton's time had attached to Genesis 1 and 2—and no small irony that the feminist reading should be assigned to Adam and the masculinist (Pauline) reading to Eve. By Adam's account Eve is privy to the interdiction: "for well thou knowst / God hath pronounc't it death to taste that Tree" (4.426–27). She shares in "Dominion," the "power and rule / Conferrd upon us" (4.429–30). By Adam's reckoning, which follows the particulars of Genesis 1, Eve is his equal. By Eve's account, which exhibits its allegiance to what we recognize as Pauline interpretation, she is but Adam's "image" (4.472), her beauty "excelld" by his "grace / And wisdom" (4.490–91). Adam is her "Guide / And Head" (4.442–43), "Author and Disposer" (4.635). The warring hermeneutics here are replicated in Books 7 and 8 in which Raphael follows Genesis 1 and Adam Genesis 2 and, again no accident, Milton positions between their different accounts of Creation, differing explanations of cosmology—Ptolemaic and Copernican—thus juxtaposing choices that must be made with those that need not be made. Still, even in matters of cosmology, tentative interpretations are not only implied but urged, especially when one theory is uttered by Adam, then Satan, and an altogether different one by Raphael. After all, the debate between the sexes, no less than between competing cosmologies, "raged full tilt through the sixteenth and seventeenth centuries,"[14] and to that debate Milton adds his own distinct and sometimes surprising inflections. There is no significant feature of early modern Genesis commentary unaccommodated to *Paradise Lost*. Nor are rival interpretations of Jesus in the wilderness or of Samson at the prison house excluded from either of Milton's last poems.

Yet, whether the point of reference is Milton *or* the Bible, the same observation holds true: "a revisionist dynamic inheres in the whole project"; or, as Herbert Schneidau also says: the intellectual processes at work here are "mythoclastic . . . because they are critical, dissolvent, and revisionist."[15] Milton's project is *biblical* in the strictest sense—is to interrogate, often with the intention of disposing of, the cherished commonplaces of his culture, and to do so by using his stories not to elaborate or dramatize fixed "truths," nor to expose them as simply lies, but to reveal them instead as concepts both partial and sometimes stultifying. In their transgression of biblical stories and their timeworn interpretations, in the interpolations they provide for the one and in the revisions they force upon the other, Milton's narratives, whether they involve the stories of Creation and Fall, the Temptations in the Garden or in the Wilderness, the tales of Jesus on the pinnacle or of Samson at the pillars—those narratives cut across the grain of the many orthodoxies long associated with, and hence subtended by, these stories. Yet they also bring scriptural into alignment with current history, nowhere more strikingly than in what would, in its second edition, become Book 8 of *Paradise Lost*.

The lessons learned from studying Milton's final poems in relation to the Bible and its hermeneutic traditions are strikingly similar to those garnered from reading each poem within the context of literary imitations inspired by it, or within the context of the poems' emerging interpretive traditions. In the simple formulation of Christopher Hill, Milton is "not an orthodox reader"[16] or interpreter of Scripture, his project involving less the reproduction of biblical tales than the reimagining of their myths in the light of current politics and contemporary history. As much as their scriptural counterparts, these poems are inspired with contradictions sufficiently unsettling that the typical tendency in criticism, as well as the enterprise of both poet-imitators and book-illustrators, has been to contradict both texts (biblical no less than Miltonic) out of their contradictions. Generic invention and transformation may both be hallmarks of Miltonic poetics, imprints of internal confusions and ideological equivocations, left upon that poetics by national crisis.[17]

Founded upon the notion that the voices of many great writers ring out against cultural orthodoxies—aesthetic, political and religious—a new Milton criticism, as Nancy Armstrong and Leonard Tennenhouse intuit, is poised to see this poet among those few who wrote "their way through the death of one historical moment and the birth of another"[18] and among those, too, who burst the boundaries of the very culture that produced their major poems, which, in Milton's case, are both part of and apart from his own world. For example, Milton's last poems are *part of* their world in the sense that their discontinuities and disjunctions are evidence, first, of the contradictions within a culture and its various traditions and second, and quite secondarily, of the contradictions within a mind shaped by that culture. Milton is *apart from* that world in as much as the poet's mind eventually breaks free of certain contradictions (yet not every one of them) in which his culture is mired and, in its freedom, moves here to cancel and there to resolve some of the conflicts that are a chief token of the early modern era and a crucial aspect of its poetics.

Rather than fogging over its meanings, the clashing perspectives in Milton's poetry and its different arenas of conflict are the transmitters of meaning, not simple but subtle, sophisticated, often stinging consciousness into a new state of awareness. Themselves a field of contending forces and competing paradigms, Milton's poems contain but are not contained by the frustrating contradictions and ambiguities that, a goad to truth, are also these poems' defining features. If as Gerald Graff contends, "the most influential trend in today's politically oriented academic criticism is to see works of art not as simple ideological statements but as scenes of ideological and psychological conflict,"[19] then *Paradise Lost, Paradise Regain'd*, and now *Samson Agonistes*—battlegrounds for a culture's contending viewpoints and ideologies—testify to the enduring value of discussion, debate, dispute, dissent. To move from Milton's prose writings to these poems is not to move from politics to poetry but from the writings of a feisty polemicist to those of a wily politician who knows that inscribing contradictions leads to debating alternatives—a debate, in its turn, that witnesses to the positive potentiality of controversy. Without contraries is no progression, and without progress no paradise will ever be brought into being by a poem.

Poets are the unacknowledged architects of the world until the moment, still in the offing for Milton, when their ideals and values are concretized in history. Then they can be specially acknowledged. In a very special as well as in a much more exacting sense, then, Milton may be the poet of the twenty-first century and perhaps will be that only if Miltonists reawaken to their own mission, having now become cognizant of its risks. Increasingly an international poet, Milton is memorialized, with lines from a poem by Alexander Pushkin engraved on the reverse side of a Russian Bronze Medal that was released to commemorate the 375th anniversary of Milton's birth,[20] at a time when the collapse of the Soviet Union was imminent: "In the evil days of hurt, blindness and poverty he banded all his strength and dictated

Paradise Lost."[21] Yet Milton remains, no less, an "emphatically *American*" poet because, as Margaret Fuller (initially quoting Mr. Griswold) told her own century, in Milton is expressed so much of the thought from which this nation was born: "He understood the nature of liberty, of justice. . . . He is one of the Fathers of the Age, of that new Idea which agitates the sleep of Europe. . . . But the Father is still far beyond the understanding of his child."[22] In this same spirit, Milton is invoked by Gabriel Conroy, in James Joyce's "The Dead," as an example to those living in "a less spacious age," in "a skeptical . . . and thought-tormented age," in the "hope" that renewal, individual and national, will come with "the memory of those dead and gone great ones whose fame the world will not willingly let die."[23]

It is true that Milton promised a work that its recipients would not willingly let die and true, too, that he addressed himself to a future generation—a generation yet to come but, one hopes, now in the smithy, ready for forging and just as ready to resist a cultural imperialism that, as Jack Lang observes, instead of grabbing territory, "grabs consciousness, ways of thinking, ways of living,"[24] thus betraying us as much as it menaces those would-be makers of a new consciousness. In its avoidance of conflict and contradiction, Old paved the way for New Historicism, which, working in concert with revisionist history, interrogates received opinions and official explanations. Such revisionism, as Arthur M. Schlesinger, Jr., explains, "is an essential part of the process by which history," literary no less than cultural, "through the posing of new problems and the investigation of new possibilities, enlarges its perspectives and enriches its insights."[25] This is one item the culture wars place on an agenda for literary criticism; and if we use its past failures to escape instead of excuse our own failings, we begin to reconstruct the historical past of Milton's life and writings, of their reception, of the enormous body of criticism that has accrued to them, if I may borrow one of Schlesinger's formulations, "according to its own pattern, not according to ours."[26] Too often our obsession has been with the paucity of a reception for Milton's poetry, which sometimes translates into a complete lack, whereas our attention might better be directed toward receptions hitherto neglected, even sometimes suppressed, hence still unstudied, yet to be decoded.

If we look to one faction in the culture wars, we encounter an innovation that is "the salient energy" and, looking to another, discover, as Ralph Waldo Emerson did in a different context, "the pause on the last moment" before, it is to be hoped, setting a foot forward in the interest of reform.[27] What needs reforming on both sides is a fundamental premise concerning the nature of Milton's poetry and poetics.

Toward the end of *Illiberal Education*, Dinesh D'Souza laments that "Somehow the intended symphony has become a cacophony."[28] In Milton criticism, the problem is otherwise: the spirit of contradiction that marked Milton's poetry from the beginning (certainly perceived as early as John Dryden) and that is remarked upon in the eighteenth century by John Dennis and the Jonathan Richardsons—by critics who tabulate the inconsistencies in Milton's poetry even as they attempt to resolve them—this spirit of contradiction is subdued and silenced within Milton's supposedly harmonious vision or within such subsuming strategies as the temptation or harassment of the reader. Too often hiding disputes and divisions, Milton criticism, for over three centuries, would diminish conflicts, disguise inconsistencies, downplay contradictions, which once were a measure of Milton's artistry, but are, since the advent of New Criticism, evidence of its failures.

If at the midpoint of the last century, there was a war among Milton's critics, it was a war over differing perceptions waged by *men* usually adhering to the same system of values. When C. S. Lewis announced "the recovery of a true critical tradition" for Milton,[29] he did no more than inaugurate a modern—fundamentally conservative—phase of criticism by reinstating the gag rule lifted from Milton criticism during the Romantic era. The key sentence of Romanticism is Blake's "he was a true Poet and of the Devils party without knowing it"[30]—not because of its implied Satanism but because of its open acknowledgment of conscious versus unconscious meanings in *Paradise Lost*, its admission of inconsistencies and contradictions, which an earlier criticism nearly succeeded in silencing. Lewis may have for a while prevailed but not before inciting successive reactions from A. J. A. Waldock, John Peter, and J. B. Broadbent—all of whom underscore the presence in Milton's poetry of the very qualities that Lewis, for the most part, would conceal: unbearable stresses, perplexing ambiguities, nagging inconsistencies, unsettling contradictions, mystifying imperfections, narrative presentation and narrator's commentary pulling oppositely, a language and a style both of which seem more like "a screening haze than a lucid medium"[31] and finally, broken, often difficult, sometimes mysterious, narrative sequences with menacing undercurrents.

No wonder that Broadbent, perhaps as a spokesman for them all, declares: "We want to avenge ourselves on the gaunt patriarch for exposing us on the mountainside of his work"[32]—to the splits and chasms; to his disparate, never unified, ideals; to the sustained antagonisms, polar oppositions, irreconcilable modes, and unbridgeable gaps of his poetry; to its "duplicity" and "doubletalk."[33]

Waldock and the Miltonoclasts see differently from Lewis and the bardolaters and, though observing the same value system (unity, coherence, consistency), judge differently. Witness Broadbent for whom "the Miltonic 'ideal' " is flawed because it is "not unified": "we expect art to reconcile the poles. . . . *Paradise Lost* does not do this."[34] Yet others say it exemplifies precisely these features, on a grand scale subduing disorder, ordering chaos. Critical problems are thus shelved, not settled. They await a resolution that perhaps will come with our committing what is for John Peter the unpardonable sin of praising a poem's supposed faults as if they were successes.

Milton's poetry is marked, not marred, by contradictions—the contradictions within his poems finding their counterparts in the conflicts both within the scriptural texts and hermeneutic traditions on which they are based and the critical tradition they found. Yet the understanding of Milton criticism, especially of late, has been paralyzed, indeed impoverished, by the suppression of such conflicts or just plain avoidance of them. To set the critical understanding free again we may have to reclaim Milton's last poems as proliferating contradictions, restore a conflict model to our criticism, and then remember these poems for what, historically, they have always been: the battleground for competing intellectual paradigms and clashing critical methodologies. Milton criticism, in the process of "rethinking" itself (as John T. Shawcross urges) is cusping toward something new as is boldly evident in Peter C. Herman's "destabilizing" of Milton with a "Poetics of Incertitude," in Michael Bryson's deployment of once discredited models (like William Empson) and in their jointly— and effectively—switching to a revised paradigm or new critical approach.[35] Alternative models, new foundational principles, an expanding knowledge base, and an enlarging critical consciousness— these will be the salient features of a new Milton criticism, the watchwords of which, despite protests to the contrary, will be "conflict, ambivalence, and open-endedness"; the models for which (because Milton is the ultimate model) will be "take[n] . . . further than they themselves had ever thought to go."[36] And finally, because the first principle of this new criticism is that "Milton is continually in dialogue with himself," this principle, as set forth by Stanley Fish, will at every turn subvert another of Fish's propositions, namely that "everything has changed—everything, that is, but Milton."[37] As Herman Melville remarks with specific reference to Milton, "He who thinks for himself never can remain of the same mind."[38] As we move toward a fullness of perception, Milton's changing rather than changeless mind will become increasingly the object of our study, producing a criticism that involves not just validation of the past but often correction of it.

As in Milton's poetry, so with Milton criticism generally and so with the unending culture wars: the temptation is always to choose sides when the wiser recourse may be to choose not to choose, locating significance in the conflict and wresting meaning from the contradiction. That may also be the wiser course for a new Milton criticism, which, instead of confronting opposing points of view in order to silence one of them, might be both empowered and emboldened by competing interpretations to produce finer honings of its own readings. Criticism of the highest order unfetters—it does not restrain— the mind; it may correct but does not coerce. When it cries up liberty, it means liberty, not license, the latter concept sometimes sponsoring a meanness of spirit that practices retaliation and perpetuates censorship and the former, testing the values it posits, tolerating ambiguities, as well as differences of opinion, and as a matter of course, it seems, hosting conflicting systems of thought.

Milton's last poems may not settle, but they do bring and keep under scrutiny the nagging questions, the thorny issues of theology and politics, reminding us of the enormous barriers to changing entrenched structures and ideas as well as the imminent dangers in remaining sexually and culturally blind. As much about what unites as about what divides us; acutely sensitive to the interconnectedness of science and religion, of politics and poetry—their interdependency and mutuality; in its global reach uniquely poised for global challenges and in its vast learning seemingly addressed to knowledge-based societies still in our future; here threatened by the Right and there scorned by the Left—in all these ways, Milton's epics and his tragedy are at once harbingers of cultural transformations and preparations for them. From their perspective, Milton's final poems form a perspective on history—on the politics as well as the poetry of a history seething with contradictions, yet rife with possibilities.

A poet of the seventeenth century, Milton with his future gaze and soaring vision may prove to be (singularly among the triumverate of Chaucer, Shakespeare, and Milton) the poet *for* the new millennium— the poet *for* the twenty-first century. Milton will be so to the extent that through him we see the upheavals in the humanities as deriving not from a revision of the canon but rather, as Bill Readings insists, from "a crisis in the *function* of the canon"[39] and, then, to the extent that Milton shocks us into the recognition that poets sometimes deliver messages at odds with those with which they are credited. As Herman Melville reminds us of a doubting Milton, of Milton as "an

Infidel," he also alerts us to a poetry full of "many profound atheistical hits"; of a poetry "Put into Satan's mouth, but spoken with John Milton's tongue" in ways that convey "strong controversial meaning." Thus, Milton's is a poetry with what Melville calls "a twist"[40]—a poetry in which, increasingly, answers come in the form of questions. It is also a poetry in which Milton's imprints can be found everywhere—a poetry in which, as has been said of Abraham Lincoln, "his personal mythology [becomes] our national mythology . . . calling us to our destiny."[41] As we write about *Paradise Lost* (and so Gordon Teskey attests), "we end up writing about our modernity"; and alternatively, as we "write about our modernity we feel it necessary to conduct that writing through the text of *Paradise Lost*"[42]—and increasingly through the text of *Samson Agonistes* as well.

Why Milton Matters, the title of this book and the abiding concern of each of its chapters, is a question initially put to me—repeatedly, persistently so—during the 1960s by my students at the University of Wisconsin, Madison. Jacqueline DiSalvo, then a student, now my colleague at the Graduate Center, was particularly relentless in her pursuit of that question. But the two people who pressed this topic as a book were Vincent Newton, to whom this book is dedicated, and Annabel Patterson, whose friendship over the years has been steady and nourishing. Over the last five years or so, Albert C. Labriola, Roy C. Flannagan, Sharon Achinstein, and, subsequently, John Mulryan, Robert Wickenheiser, Diana Trevino Benet, Matthew Mauger, Richard Rambuss, and my students here at the Graduate Center from Esther Khana Mendora and Tali Naoimi to Laurence Lowe, Bill, Goldstein, and Zach Davis have provided occasions for the development and refinement of this topic. My research assistant, John Harkey, has been a huge help and so, too, my colleagues, especially Eddie Epstein, Tom Hayes, Rich McCoy—and again Jackie DiSalvo.

Still, it was a fellowship at the Henry E. Huntington Library that launched this project as a book, and timely grants from the Professional Staff Congress of the City University of New York enabled its completion. Parts of each chapter of the book have been previously published, and I am grateful to their publishers for initial encouragement, as well as kind permission now to republish some of my work within the broader context of this book. Chapter 1 is an expansion of " 'Reading' Milton: The Death (and Survival) of the Author," in *Milton Studies* 38 (2000): 10–46 (a special issue edited by Albert C. Labriola and Michael Lieb and entitled *John Milton: The Writer in His Works*), ©2000 by the University of Pittsburgh Press and used here with its permission. Parts of both Chapters 1 and 2 assimilate materials from " '*More and More Perceiving*': Paraphernalia and Purpose in *Paradise Lost*, 1668, 1669," in *"A Poem Written in Ten Books": "Paradise Lost" 1667*, ed. Michael Lieb and John T. Shawcross (Pittsburgh, PA: Duquesne University Press, 2007), forthcoming. Parts of this essay are reprinted here (with special thanks to Susan Wadsworth-Booth and Al Labriola) by permission of Duquesne University Press. Chapter 2 is a significant enlargement of " 'Under the Seal of Silence': Repressions, Receptions, and the Politics of *Paradise Lost*," in *Soundings of Things Done: Essays in Early Modern Literature in Honor of S. K. Heninger Jr.*, ed. Peter E. Medine and Joseph Wittreich (Newark: University of Delaware Press and London: Associated University Presses, 1997), 293–323. Permission is granted to use this material by Associated University Presses, with special thanks to Julien Yoseloff. Finally, chapter 3 includes a huge expansion of two previously published essays: "Why Milton Matters," in *Milton Studies* 44 (2005): 22–39; and " 'The Ramifications of Those Ramifications': Compounding Contexts for *Samson Agonistes*," in *Milton Studies* 45 (2006), forthcoming, both essays © by the University of Pittsburgh Press and here greatly enlarged with the permission of the University of Pittsburgh Press.

My debts are legion, especially to Julia Cohen, Maran Elancheran, and Elizabeth Sabo who oversaw the production of this book and to Stuart Curran who joins me in the salute this book makes (all too belatedly) to Vincent Newton. More than just our friend, the late Vincent Newton was dear friend also to Cynthia Newton Berena, . . . Carla and Leigh McCloskey, as well as Marjorie and Joe Perloff, Reid Austin and Bill Houston and the Osmans of Istanbul and New York City. Surrogate father (and sometimes mother) to Stuart and me, Vincent had also been an astonishing role model not just to us but to many of our friends, including Joe Boone and Dale Wall, James Bristol and Troy Fernandez, Robert Cather and that very special man from Santa Fe, Damon Laemmle, as well as the now deceased Roger Horwitz, Richard Ide, and Paul Monette. Together, we became another family to Vincent Newton, this one by election, and we wish (as one) that, when Vincent's ashes are scattered in the fields of the Massachusetts farm he once owned, its pastures will dance with lambs.

Joseph Wittreich
New York City
February 14, 2006

CHAPTER 1

"READING" MILTON: THE
DEATH (AND SURVIVAL)
OF THE AUTHOR

*John Milton himself is in every line of the Paradise Lost. . . . There
is a subjectivity of the poet, as of Milton, who is himself before himself
in every thing he writes. . . . In the Paradise Lost—indeed in every
one of his poems—it is Milton himself whom you see; his Satan, his
Adam, his Raphael, almost his Eve—are all John Milton; and it is
a sense of this intense egotism that gives me the greatest pleasure in
reading Milton's works. The egotism of such a man is a revelation of
spirit.*

—Samuel Taylor Coleridge

*The author's consciousness is the consciousness of a consciousness, that
is, a consciousness that encompasses the consciousness and the world
of a hero—a consciousness that encompasses and* consummates *the
consciousness of a hero . . . . The author not only sees and knows
everything seen and known by each hero individually and by all the
heroes collectively, but he also sees and knows more than they do;
moreover, he sees and knows something that is in principle inaccessible
to them.*

—Mikhail M. Bakhtin[1]

Nowhere are poet and poem so irrevocably involved as in the
writings of John Milton, so much so that poet and poem—Milton
and *Paradise Lost*—can be used metonymically each for the other.
Milton would be no stranger to such an observation inasmuch as, in

An Apology against a Pamphlet, he insists that the poet "ought him selfe to bee a true Poem" (YP, 1:890); in *Areopagitica*, urges that "a good Booke is the pretious life-blood of a master spirit" (YP, 2:493); and then, using a poet's name in lieu of a title, in *Of Education* speaks of reading about sublimity "in *Horace*" (YP, 2:204).[2] Book and author, Horace and his epistles, are one for Milton, inseparably so. Indeed, as one critic remarks, in Milton's view "the spirit of the author is held within the printed volume as within a vial."[3] So intertwined are they that, for the Milton of *Areopagitica*, killing a good book is tantamount to killing its author (YP, 2:492).

Henry Fuseli, responsible for the much acclaimed Milton Gallery of 1799, acknowledges as much when he remarks that Milton says some praise the work, some the master, indicating that at least some regard the work and its master as indistinguishable from one another;[4] that reading *Paradise Lost* is "reading" Milton. Nor, as this rhetoric might imply, is this a particularly masculinist tradition, or understanding, for Fuseli's intimate friend, Mary Wollstonecraft, in her very first novel allowed as how the only compositions with a power to delight are those in which "the soul of the author is exhibited, and animates the hidden springs" of a work with one character now echoing the mind and another reflecting the soul of the author who himself or herself, a composite of his or her characters, may thus assume the role of protagonist/hero in the tale.[5] In Wollstonecraft's novel, the heroine, rambling in a paradise of her own making, takes her early lessons from *Paradise Lost*, which is to say from Milton and which is then but to acknowledge that Woelstoneraft, like another of her contemporaries, this time William Blake, sees in Milton's last poems the Foucauldian moment when "stories of heroes" give way to the "author's biography"; the founding moment for "the fundamental critical category of 'the man and his work.' "[6]

Milton's presence in his poetry is a presumption that, encouraged by the poet as well as his Romantic followers, survives as a core concept in much modern criticism, both its theory and its practice. Yet where to locate Milton's presence, where it is most keenly felt, and the intricacies of that presence, remain a mystery, if not solvable, at least now more readily explicable, through advances in literary theory coupled with ruminations in Milton criticism. Theory and criticism together afford complicating perspectives on a matter unwittingly posed by Milton in his *Defense of Himself* (and still very much with us, and with us as a postmodern concern): "what now becomes of the author?" (YP, 4:746).[7] "Now you see him, now you don't," writes J. Martin Evans who, reading through Milton's poetry from the

"Nativity Ode" to *Paradise Regain'd*, finds Milton "gradually materializ[ing] before our eyes." In Evans's account, the poet is initially an absence, obtruding briefly in "The Passion" in which Milton writes about himself writing, and more pervasively in *L'Allegro* and *Il Penseroso* in which as "an authorial presence" he is "split into two competing selves." In *Lycidas*, having "virtually ceased to be a presence," the poet disappears (as it were) only to reappear in the poem's final stanza, here as a "new author" who, emerging again in *Paradise Lost*, has not fully evolved until *Paradise Regain'd*.[8]

This chapter tells another more gnarled story that, like the one told by Evans, is prompted by Milton himself and, largely because of Milton's promptings, has a different outcome. If Milton leaves his own imprint on the emerging genre of autobiography, it is by tilting this genre toward apologia and inflecting it with self-defense; then by converting the story from the details of everyday life to an autobiography of the human psyche. In this way, Milton the author, even when supposed dead, preserves a presence in his writings. Yet that presence, highly elusive, is found in sometimes unexpected places.

AUTHORIAL PRESENCE

The autobiographical impulse, notoriously strong in Milton's writings, poetry and prose alike, evident as early as his Prolusions and no less conspicuous in the early poems, becomes so pervasive both in his prose writings and later poems that, as William B. Hunter avers, autobiography of the spiritual kind, minus the conversion experience, "seems explicitly or implicitly meant in everything that . . .[Milton] wrote."[9] Indeed, Milton wrote at a time when the autobiographical impulse, impressively developed during the seventeenth century, was asserting itself everywhere, almost as if it were an expression of the spirit of the age. Milton's writings, as it happens, afford examples of autobiography both as factual narrative and as spiritual chronicle, as memoir as well as *apologia*, with those writings, along with notebooks and personal correspondence, in their turn, producing materials for a handful of biographies in Milton's own century as well as a belatedly constructed autobiography of the twentieth century, aptly titled *Milton on Himself*.[10]

Milton's early poems, containing many fragments of self-portraiture, and his prose works, rife with autobiographical reference and reflection, create the expectation of a persisting authorial presence in the late poems. Reading them, it has often seemed, is "reading" Milton: discovering him in those poems, then reading them as revelations of the poet's mental life and spiritual experience. However, a check is placed on such easy inferences, especially by the 1645 *Poems of Mr. John Milton*. Despite the various elements asserting authorial presence, including a frontispiece portrait and other front matter, plus epistles, headnotes, and endnotes to individual poems, the poems themselves seem to suggest that, often in hiding, the author must be sought out in unexpected places and sometimes will be found in curious postures, modifying earlier attitudes and correcting previously stated opinions, and even found in the interstices of a text in the guise of craftsman. At best, the poems offer flickering images in contrast with, and subversive of, both the stabilizing image of the frontispiece portrait and title-page message, each by insinuation aligning Milton with a royalist, cavalier line of poetry, while the accompanying poems effect a realignment of Milton with the traditions of prophecy and a poetics of both transgression and discovery. Alternative traditions of poetry, this time of epic and prophecy, will be foregrounded again in the dedicatory poems accompanying the second edition of *Paradise Lost* and yet again in the pairing of genres, now brief epic and tragedy, in the 1671 poetic volume.

If in "On the Morning of Christs Nativity" the poet pleads that his Muse rush to the manger, beating other gift-bearers there with the present of a "humble ode" (24), by the time he composes *Lycidas* (some eight years later), Milton forces a distinction, powerfully evident in *Paradise Lost* as well, between two poets (the one who sings the elegy, the other who speaks its final words), this distinction emerging from the wrenching conclusion to the monody, a distancing operation, "Thus sang the uncouth swain" (186). That conclusion is a stunning reminder that "the 'I' of written discourse," as Louis A. Renza argues, "can never in itself signify the writer's self-presence."[11] Moreover, the forced distinction is then reinforced by the headnote elaborated from the *Lycidas* manuscript and added to *Lycidas* in its 1645 printing, one sentence of which will later appear in "The Table of the *English* Poems" as part of the poem's title (see figures 1.1 and 1.2). One poet is inside the poem looking out, the other outside the poem looking in. Even as Milton the author or Milton the man seems to acknowledge a knit of identity with the uncouth swain, in effect saying "Been there! Done that!" he forces a distinction that he creates here, and throughout *Paradise Lost* maintains, thus developing a twin consciousness or what Wordsworth in *The Prelude* describes as "Two consciousnesses"—a consciousness of oneself and of some other being (2.32–33).[12] To adapt words from *Tetrachordon*, he creates a consciousness of "*another self, a second self, a very self it self*" (YP, 2:600).

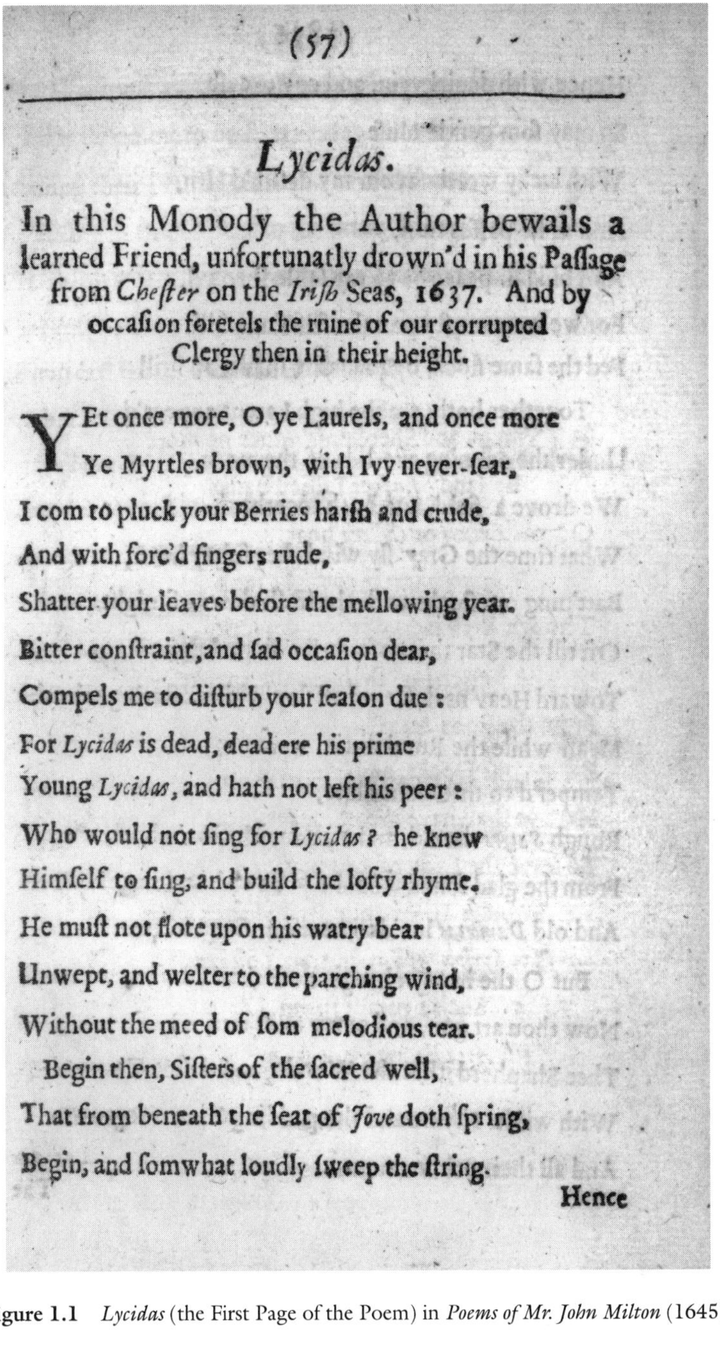

(57)

Lycidas.

In this Monody the Author bewails a
learned Friend, unfortunatly drown'd in his Paſſage
from *Cheſter* on the *Iriſh* Seas, 1637. And by
occaſion foretels the rnine of our corrupted
Clergy then in their height.

Et once more, O ye Laurels, and once more
  Ye Myrtles brown, with Ivy never-ſear,
I com to pluck your Berries harſh and crude,
And with forc'd fingers rude,
Shatter your leaves before the mellowing year.
Bitter conſtraint, and ſad occaſion dear,
Compels me to diſturb your ſeaſon due :
For *Lycidas* is dead, dead ere his prime
Young *Lycidas*, and hath not left his peer :
Who would not ſing for *Lycidas* ? he knew
Himſelf to ſing, and build the lofty rhyme.
He muſt not flote upon his watry bear
Unwept, and welter to the parching wind,
Without the meed of ſom melodious tear.
  Begin then, Siſters of the ſacred well,
That from beneath the ſeat of *Jove* doth ſpring,
Begin, and ſomwhat loudly ſweep the ſtring.

Hence

Figure 1.1   *Lycidas* (the First Page of the Poem) in *Poems of Mr. John Milton* (1645)

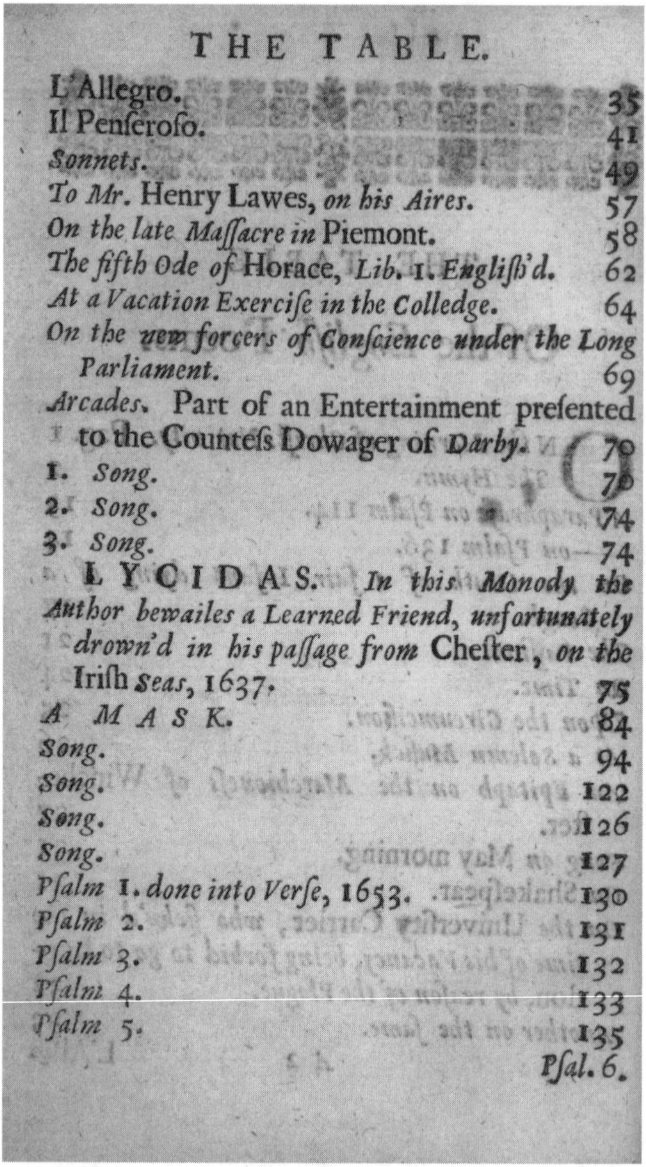

6

THE TABLE.

L'Allegro.   35
Il Penserofo.   41
Sonnets.   49
To Mr. Henry Lawes, *on his Aires.*   57
On the late Maffacre in Piemont.   58
The fifth Ode of Horace, *Lib.* 1. *Englifh'd.*   62
At a Vacation Exercife in the Colledge.   64
On the new forcers of Confcience under the Long
   Parliament.   69
Arcades. Part of an Entertainment prefented
   to the Countefs Dowager of Darby.   70
1. Song.   70
2. Song.   74
3. Song.   74
   LYCIDAS. *In this Monody the
Author bewailes a Learned Friend, unfortunately
drown'd in his paffage from* Chefter, *on the*
Irifh *Seas,* 1637.   75
A MASK.   84
Song.   94
Song.   122
Song.   126
Song.   127
Pfalm 1. done into Verfe, 1653.   130
Pfalm 2.   131
Pfalm 3.   132
Pfalm 4.   133
Pfalm 5.   135
                                                        Pfal. 6.

Figure 1.2 The Table of Contents for *Poems upon Several Occasions* (1673)

In the Nativity Ode, the poet is distinct from and subordinate to the Muse, at least until the conclusion of the poem when "thy . . . ode" (24) becomes "our . . . Song" (239). In *Lycidas*, two poets emerge: one is the piper and the other the bard; one is the poet's former and the other a new self; or as the poem implies, the one is the natural, the other the spiritual man, who emerges from this crisis lyric—a shipwreck of faith, over-tossed, without haven or shore—as the oracle of a better time. In *Paradise Lost*, one poet is the bardic narrator and the other the controlling consciousness of the poem; the one experiences an apocalypse of mind and the other effects an apocalypse of mind in his readers. Both poems, nonetheless, pit the gathering awareness of the poet within the poem against the enlarged consciousness of the poet who authors it with the consequence that we see, as Blake saw in Wordsworth, the natural man continually rising up against the spiritual man.

This distinction asserts itself not only within the 1645 *Poems* but on its more than ornamental frontispiece, in which the mature poet of the main frame looks out upon the young poet in the window frame; in which bard beholds piper, the poet at age thirty seven (it is sometimes suggested) beholding the poet in his twenty-first year (see figure 1.3). More probably, however, the frontispiece is an example of illustration as much as portraiture in the tradition, let us say, of Chaucer depicted among his pilgrims or of John on Patmos attended by an eagle and taking in his vision, in which case the portrait/ illustration is better read as emblematizing the double consciousness of *L'Allegro* and *Il Penseroso* with the withered face of the portrait depicting the poet with a full acquist of experience, now in "weary age" (167) "attain[ing] / To something like Prophetic strain" (173–74). In this instance, it is not so much what John T. Shawcross calls the "performing self" and the "real self" but rather two different versions of the performing self that are pitted against one another.[13]

The mental progress inscribed within the frontispiece of the 1645 *Poems* is the progression mapped in the twin lyrics, encapsulated within *Lycidas*, and encompassed by the poetic volume itself. We can profitably think of this progress as an embedded narrative within the 1645 *Poems* and, doing so, will want to remember with Marshall Grossman that these narratives of the self relate not to the author as he "always essentially was," or even to the author as he now is, but rather to "the person he . . . will become by the story's end."[14] Moreover, these words encourage a refinement of what we have already said about *Lycidas*: the two poets within the poem, the singer of the elegy and the speaker of the epilogue, are different versions of

Figure 1.3 The Frontispiece to *Poems of Mr. John Milton* (1645)

the performing self, both distinct from the author who speaks through the title and headnote to his poem.

In *Paradise Lost*, the situation is altogether more complicated with the prologues to individual books presenting different versions of the performing self, all of which bear similarity to and display difference from the poet's real self, and with the poem itself (in its own wily maneuverings) compounding these selves (again to use Shawcross's terms) with "hidden" and "inferred" selves.[15] Just as there are blurrings of characters, protagonists with antagonists, so in the four prologues, with autobiographical detail as the agent, there are repeated blurrings of the poem's narrator and its author, then of the author with various of his characters, even Galileo who, John Guillory proposes, is "a cryptic self-portrait" of Milton himself and whose portrayal, with this implicit self-portrait, takes its point from the fact that Galileo himself had become, in the words of Adrian Johns, "a Protestant hero of free thought."[16] Additionally, from the author's perspective, as Robert Durling explains, "the figure of the narrator is a role in which the author casts himself . . . [as] a dramatic projection," with the work itself revealing "the author . . . [as] it dramatizes or projects the structure of his consciousness." Harbored in this insight is the realization that when the author, through a persona, tells a story, he is not "on the same level with the other characters. He exists above that level" because he is omnipresent in a narration, "the fabric of . . . [which] is the *Author's* act of narration."[17]

The subtlety of Durling's comment, lost within the simplifications of Robert McMahon's observations, is caught nicely by Balachandra Rajan when he describes the epic voice of *Paradise Lost* as "the voice of the imperial imagination":

> of sumptuous orchestration, of metaphorical opulence, the encyclopaedic, outreaching, all-encompassing voice, the voice of the unifying imperative. No one articulates this voice more resplendently than Milton; and no one struggles against it more insistently.[18]

Very simply, throughout *Paradise Lost* there is an entanglement of characters and voices, with Milton here hinting at a knit of identity, while always maintaining distinctions—a point (as we shall see) that is equally pertinent to what is supposedly Milton's most autobiographical poem, *Samson Agonistes*. In the latter poem, the point can only be grasped once we uncover a hidden self that forges unexpected alliances with others engaging the same materials and writing within the same traditions, with emphasis falling not on sameness but on difference and not on continuities with but departures from those traditions.

Within its fabric of narration, details of autobiography like blindness, fearful circumstances, and treacherous enemies link the narrator of *Paradise Lost* and its author; and as if to underscore the autobiographical impulse within this poem, autobiography (as Barbara Lewalski has shown) is invented by Eve, perfected by Adam, and parodied by Satan. It is also autobiography inflected "as exemplum, a moralizing life" in the case of Eve and as "spiritual autobiography" in the instance of Adam,[19] but with the paradox that by the end of the poem Adam is the moralizing figure and Eve much more the spiritual presence. Jesus in *Paradise Regain'd* and Samson in Milton's tragedy will similarly use autobiography to relate their experiences, some details of which have led to the speculation that especially Samson is a projection of Milton. "Here Milton in the person of Samson," writes Thomas Newton, "describes exactly his own case, what he felt, and what he thought," particularly in the years after the Restoration.[20] A century later, David Masson follows suit: "The story of Samson must have seemed to Milton a metaphor or allegory of much of his own life in its later stages."[21]

Indeed, what for the most part had been read as a political and patriotic poem is, by Masson, reinflected toward the personal and the autobiographical: "Samson is Milton," "Milton himself."[22] The undercurrent of personal allusion, emphasizing "the parallelism between the history of Samson and [Milton] himself," eventually yields the conclusion that Milton is "the true protagonist of the drama"; that Milton Agonistes, "the counterpart of his hero" is himself the hero of his own work.[23] Indeed, the nineteenth century cements the view that *Samson Agonistes*, a poem of "sublime despair," both "dark" and "passionate," is an autobiographical poem, as well as a drama, in which a defeated, yet defiant Milton, uncompromising in his principles and, as Louis Raymond de Véricour puts it, in "eloquent revcenge," "eloquent invective" and "bloody melee," triumphs over his adversaries.[24] For these critics, it is almost as if, like Benvenuto Cellini with his Perseus, Milton has inscribed his own self-portrait on the back of the head of his Samson. But even if so, this yoking invites the question: why does the self-portrait exist? To mark similarity or to enforce difference? Does Milton mean to reinforce or, as others do in the same century, to challenge the supposed autobiographical connections?

One conclusion seems irresistible. What Andrew Marvell implied concerning *The Second Defense* applies to most of Milton's writings. As Marvell confides in a letter dated June 2, 1654, they are "imboss'd" with Milton's presence—so much so that in her fictional biography

Ann Manning will have Deborah Milton report that her father's "Mind . . . too often ran upon Things around him, and made his Poem [she speaks specifically of *Samson Agonistes*] the Shadow and Mirrour of himself."[25] This conclusion would seem confirmed, even flagged, by the different frontispiece portraits (see figures 1.3, 1.4, 1.5, and 1.6) to *The Poems of Mr. John Milton* (1645), *The History of Britain* (1671) and *Art of Logic* (1672), plus the frontispiece portrait that is now a fixed feature of the second edition of Milton's epic prophecy (1674). Traditionally memorializers, the frontispiece portraits, as used in these books, function instead as definers and aggrandizers of the artist, perhaps even sometimes as gestures toward laureateship. Yet even here, Milton implies, these portraits fall short of their supposed function of indexing the poet's mind, his distinctive character, of deciphering the inner man, his heart and soul, his moral attitudes and ethical values.

It is as if these frontispiece portraits, facing title pages and casting Milton's image across them into the book, announce the interchangeability of the author and the work while declaring, first, that the author, now a felt presence, runs surveillance over his works and, second, that the works themselves, more than representations of physical likeness, are portraits of the artist altogether more nuanced and shaded than the picture portraits of Milton accompanying them, which, if we are to believe John Aubrey, "are not *at all* like him."[26] Or as Jonathan Richardson, Sr., had complained, because there are "so Few Good Pictures" of Milton, indeed so many "a Bad Picture," he is presenting this account of the poet's life: "This Picture of the Mind of *Milton*, Drawn by Himself Chiefly."[27] That is, not pictures drawn by others but word pictures crafted by Milton himself afford the best portraiture. Paradoxically, then, Milton's frontispiece portraits drive home the point that less the portraits than the compositions they preface, as well as exhibiting the soul of the author, show that soul to be the animating force of a work in which the author, echoed by this character, reflected by that one, becomes the hero of his own tales.

That is surely an inference to be drawn from the infamous legend accompanying the portrait to the 1645 *Poems*, with the implication that, like a poem, the poet may be a pattern of honor and virtue, hence doctrinal to a nation and able, potentially, to turn an entire civilization into a nation of visionaries; that, again like a poem, he may figure a process of change—a transformed self, an expanding consciousness—with the emphasis falling not on physical likeness but on the mental life of the poet, his spiritual form. No less so than a poem, the poet is an arena of forces, tensions, and contradictions; and

Figure 1.4 The Frontispiece to *The History of Britain* (1670)

Figure 1.5 The Frontispiece to *Art of Logic* (1672)

Figure 1.6   The Frontispiece to *Paradise Lost* (1674)

it is in the gaps created by such that we are most likely to find him, not in the frontispiece portraits, which, if Milton's later remarks in *Eikon Basilike* are any indication, are too often pieces of "conceited portraiture" that are there only "to befool the people" (YP, 3:342–43). Indeed, it is as if Milton were saying that how an author acts upon a work, especially its narrative, is of more consequence and ultimately is more revelatory of him than how, hidden in characters, he acts within the work.

In 1645 Milton addresses his audience, "This image was drawn by an untaught hand, / you might perhaps say, looking at the form of the original. / But since here you do not recognize the modelled face, friends, / laugh at a bad imitation by a worthless artist" (CP, 200). Rather than discouraging the practice of assuming too close a relationship between portrait and poems, established by the legend to the Abraham Cowley portrait in the 1633 edition of *Poetical Blossomes*, Milton here denies any relationship between the poet and this portrait. His point is not, as has recently been proposed, to use his epigram to assert his authorship, "and his alone,"[28] but, instead, to insist that he is a better definer and revealer of himself than any portrait artist and then to assert his own presence, as well as the reader's presence, at this portal to his poems by transgressing the tradition of having another speak the legend. Rather, the words of this legend are Milton's own, the poet's comment on himself. Even if this frontispiece portrait were not a poor likeness, it would always take second place to the poems, which are articulations of their author's spiritual rather than physical form. Thomas Cross's epigram, appended to the frontispiece portrait of Hugo Grotius, which accompanies his *Sophompaneas*, affords an analogy through which Milton's point can be made clear:

> His outward figure heere you find
> Of Grotius who hath drawne the mind,
> Whose Counterfeits how they agree
> With the Originalls, read and see.[29]

The *originals*—the self-portraits—of the poems by Grotius and Milton exhibit an accuracy unrivaled by, indeed unavailable in, the counterfeit portraits of both writers drawn by others.

The works of Milton, taken together, create a serial portrait of their author in analogy with the sixty-some self-portraits by Rembrandt, which imply, as do Milton's word pictures, that the artist, "never satisfied," says Georges Gusdorf, "acknowledges no single image as his definitive image." As Gusdorf goes on to suggest, such portraits, images of a changing self (from mop-headed young man to old man with double chin and bulbous nose, like those of Rembrandt) possess an authenticity unmatched by portraits of the painter by other artists, the true image of which seems always to elude them. Both a means of self-definition and aggrandizement and a vehicle for self-defense, as well as of self-knowledge, the serial portrait, never finished, always an ever expanding array of fragments, diagrams a life in motion, a mind evolving. As Gusdorf might say, these portraits are "a revenge on history,"[30] and on one's enemies, quite literally so in the case of John Milton, in which the poems present less a body than body-parts and less a physical than a mental and spiritual form.

One thinks immediately of the previously mentioned Greek epigram below the William Marshall portrait—of what has been called a "crude, Samson-like jest"[31]—rebuking the artist for the poor likeness of Milton, a more accurate and complex image of whom appears in the word pictures of the accompanying poems, especially *Lycidas* and *Damon's Epitaph*, and later of the *Defense of Himself*. Through the last of these titles, Milton identifies the driving force behind the inlays of autobiography in poetry and prose works alike: apologia (or in the words of Milton's Preface to *Samson Agonistes*) "self defence, or explanation." One should at the same time remember that, calculatedly, the 1645 *Poems* segregate (as will *not* be the case in 1673) the efforts of Milton's right hand from those of his left, although, if only for an instant, Milton's two identities, as poet and polemicist, merge in the newly added headnote to *Lycidas*, which "*foretells* [prophesies] *the ruin of our corrupted Clergy then in their height*" (see figures 1.1 and 1.2). Furthermore, the Virgilian epigraph on the title page, as Barbara Lewalski urges, "explicitly refus[es] the construction laid upon . . .[Milton] by Moseley's apparatus,"[32] even as it seems to refer to early receptions of Milton the polemicist by promising the predestined bard protection against the slanderous tongues likely to malign him (see figure 1.7). The Virgilian epigraph here, moreover, may anticipate what many in our own century regard as a similar mark of "Virgilian debt" in the twelve-book structure of the second edition of *Paradise Lost*, where, in the words of John K. Hale, Milton is even busier in "self-presentation" and altogether more elaborate in "self-explaining" and more expansive in his "Virgilianizing."[33]

If Milton taunted Marshall about the 1645 frontispiece portrait (and one can never be sure that Marshall himself was not "in" on the joke), Alexander More taunted Milton with it: "would I reproach with blindness . . . or with deformity," More asks in *The Public Faith*

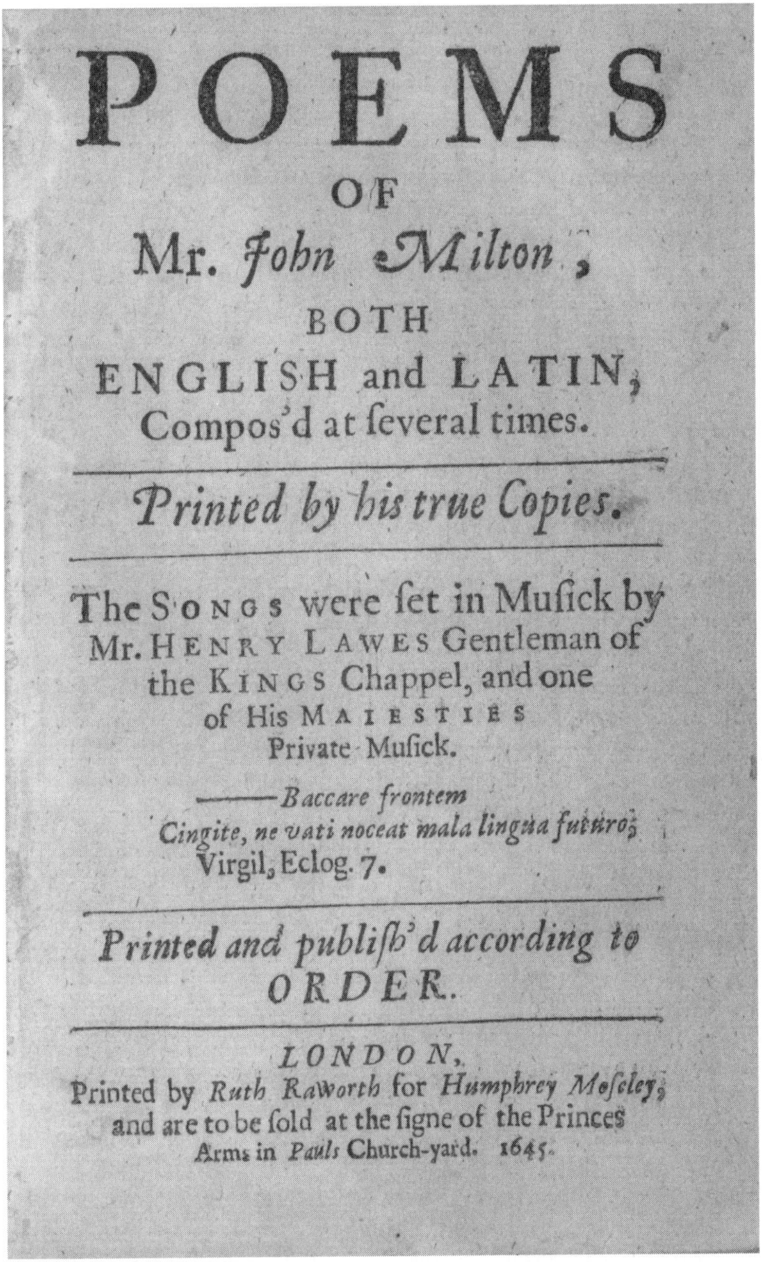

POEMS

OF

Mr. *John* *Milton*,

BOTH

ENGLISH and LATIN,

Compos'd at several times.

Printed by his true Copies.

The S o n g s were set in Musick by
Mr. H E N R Y L A W E S Gentleman of
the K I N G S Chappel, and one
of His M A I E S T I E S
Private Musick.

——*Baccare frontem*
Cingite, ne vati noceat mala lingua futuro,
Virgil, Eclog. 7.

Printed and publish'd according to
ORDER.

LONDON,
Printed by *Ruth Raworth* for *Humphrey Moseley*,
and are to be sold at the signe of the Princes
Arms in *Pauls* Church-yard. 1645.

Figure 1.7 The Title Page to *Poems of Mr. John Milton* (1645) "who even believed you handsome, especially after I saw that elegant picture prefixed to your Poems?" (YP, 4:1097) This comment provokes Milton's bitter complaint in his *Defense of Himself*: "I did not wish to be a Cyclops, though you so depicted me, and because you have seen a picture totally unlike me 'prefixed to my poems' . . . at the suggestion and solicitation of a bookseller" (YP, 4:750–51). Milton's presence in the form of a frontispiece portrait is another's doing, a point he makes himself by removing that portrait from the 1673 edition of his *Poems* and perhaps by inciting others to remove the portrait from the 1645 Poems. However, Milton's presence through the legend accompanying the portrait is his own doing. The legend, its authentic voice, rather than canceling authorial presence in the 1645 *Poems*, instructs the reader to look for that presence outside the portrait: in the accompanying legends and iconography, in other of the front matter (especially the Virgilian epigraph), in the poetry and annotation thereof that complete the volume, even in the elongated title accorded *Lycidas* on the contents page of the 1673 *Poems* (see figures 1.1 and 1.2).

Portrait and legend, Marshall and Milton, relate to one another here as contentious biography relates to self-serving autobiography. Milton's complaint about the Marshall portrait finds its analogue in John Singer Sargent's quip: "A portrait is a likeness in which there is something wrong about the mouth."[34] It is just that, from Milton's point of view, the whole face is wrong; and it is the face, after all, that is an index to the mind. In portraiture, as Richard Brilliant explains, the face is "the primary field of expressive action"[35] with the portrait itself reflecting social expectations, if not realities, that seem at odds with Milton's conception of himself as both poet and man of virtue. The portrait missing from some copies of the 1645 *Poems*, its removal from the 1673 *Poems*, speaks to Milton's displeasure with a portrait, not to his—or anyone else's—feeling that he is no presence in these poems. That others thought differently is suggested by the fact that where frontispiece portraits are missing, either because of mutilation or exclusion, they are often tipped into the book. Sometimes they are tipped in because of a powerful sense created by Milton and shared by his readers that he is a presence in his poetry. The note written in one of two copies of the 1673 *Poems* in the Huntington Library speaks provocatively: "It is *erroneously* stated . . . that this edition should be accompanied by a portrait of Milton."[36]

Portraits are idealizations. Yet Marshall and Milton are worlds apart when it comes to imagining the ideal, which for Milton has little to do with social trappings and aristocratic bearing and everything to do with greatness of mind, loftiness of spirit, and high intelligence, features unattended to in the facial iconography of the Marshall portrait, which is missing the traditionally large cranium of, let us say, Albrecht Durer's *Philip Melanchthon* (1526) or Martin Droeshout's *William Shakespeare* (1623). The seemingly contrary claims and competing signals of Marshall's portrait and Milton's legend anticipate the grounds of contestation involving later prose works, particularly the three Defenses, in which Milton as represented by others and then by himself is surrounded by a confusing range of contradictory images. For every action there is a reaction: whenever Milton is represented by another, he counters with a self-representation as if to say that he knows himself and in self-portraiture is better revealed than in representations by the William Marshalls of the world. Over time, Milton's self-representations become so numerous that they constitute, as Brilliant might say, "a figural record of the subject over the years, providing, in the ensemble, a sense of the whole being as a changing constant."[37]

Indeed, by the time of Milton's three Defenses, the autobiographical impulse is so strong, his presence so powerful, that in *The Public Faith* More chides him for delivering "windy panegyric . . . by yourself upon yourself," in virtually the same breath suggesting as an alternative title for *The Second Defense, Milton upon His Own Life* (YP, 4:1097)—a proposal Milton leaps at as he proceeds to fashion *Pro Se Defensio*, his *Defense of Himself,* but which works, taken together, suggest the entanglement of self-defense and defenses of the English people, the interdependency and interchangeability of all these works. "*John Milton, Englishman*"—the poet's preferred signature, and part of the inscription in the oval surrounding the 1645 Marshall portrait, another indication of authorial collaboration in the design of this frontispiece, is reminiscent of scriptural convention in which Abraham and Samson stand for both individual and nation, their reputations and national destiny irrevocably involved.

If there is any shock to be registered, it comes with the recognition that the conclusions Milton invites, the very contentions he elicits from his critics, then and now, concerning his seeming omnipresence in his poetry, are ones he himself challenges in terms that anticipate those used in our own time by Roland Barthes to question similar claims of authorial presence. As the theorist who proclaimed the "Death of the Author," who would subvert the very notion of authorship, has said, the "dead" writer still survives in characters who, though not the author, are "a secondary, derived fragment" of him. The author survives in the text not as host but as guest, "inscribe[d]. . . as one of his characters, drawn as a figure in the carpet; his inscription is no longer privileged . . . : he becomes, one can say, a paper author . . . a paper *I*."[38]

That is just how the Milton of both *An Apology against a Pamphlet* and *The First Defense* would have it. In the first instance, he declares that "the author is ever distinguisht from the person he introduces" (YP, 1:880); and in the second:

> we should consider not so much what the poet says, as who in the poems says it. Various figures appear, some good, some bad, some wise, some foolish, each speaking not the poet's opinions but what is appropriate for each person. (YP, 4:439)

Then quoting a passage from Seneca's *Hercules Furens*, Milton complicates, even confounds, this idea with the proposal that some voices in a poem or a play may be privileged over others:

> if you take these as the words of Hercules, in whose mouth they are placed, they show the judgment of the greatest Greek of his time; if you take them as the words of the poet who lived in Nero's age—and it is the custom of great poets to place their own opinions in the mouths of their great characters—he indicates what he himself and all good men in Nero's time thought should be done with tyrants; how righteous, how pleasing to the gods they held tyrannicide to be. (YP, 4:446)

The proposition set forth in this last statement reminds us that Milton's poetry regularly exposes the limitations in critical systems, which would contain and explain it; that there is never in Milton's poetry an easy one-to-one correspondence between the poet and his persona.

In the first two of the previously quoted passages, Milton formulates the proposition that a line of critics (which includes Anne Ferry, Robert Durling, Harry Berger, William Riggs, Boyd Berry, John Mulder, John Steadman, John Shawcross, and Robert McMahon) has been driving home: "What the poem says at its various points and what its historical author thought or believed are not necessarily the same."[39] The usually unacknowledged progenitor of this line of criticism is William Blake whose "Annotations to Swedenborg's *Heaven and Hell*" includes this observation:

> Thus Fools quote Shakespeare The Above is Theseus's opinion Not Shakespeares You might as well quote Satans blasphemies from Milton & give them as Miltons Opinions [.][40]

Yet Milton also pushes further than his critics, as if to ask of them the questions such as Barthes asks of Balzac: "Who speaks this way? Is it the hero of the tale"[41] (if we think we know who he or she is)? Is it Milton's poetic persona, Milton the author, or Milton the man? Does he speak universal wisdom? Or the politics and theology of his time? Or, rather, does he try to articulate a newly emerging (but still shared) understanding, or one unique to himself as a sect of one? As an early modern writer, does Milton support or subvert the empire (some would say the tyranny) of the author? And if he is engaged in subversion, is it simply a gesture of iconoclasm effecting the removal of the author? Or does Milton make league with the reader—in the process, repressing the author in order to rescue the reader?

If it can be said that Milton's poetic career begins with the publication of the 1645 *Poems*, in which his emergence as an author is, according to Humphrey Moseley, "*as true a birth, as the Muses have brought forth since . . . Spencer wrote,*"[42] then it should also be acknowledged that Milton's poetic career, culminating in the publication of *Samson Agonistes*, ends with the removal and death of the author effected by the lifting of a narrative frame and consequent annihilation of a narrative voice. Still, the author may say *no* to death, thereby announcing his survival, in the case of *Samson Agonistes*, within the recesses of the poem's epistle, as well as in the shadows of this poem's protagonist, although one must always ask if in Samson we behold Milton's current or a former self, a real or a fabled image of the author. A poetic career that begins with a conspicuous authorial presence ends with a rather more elusive one.

Milton discourages easy correlations of himself with his personae or between the author and various personalities of his characters. Simultaneously, he lays down hints concerning where marks of his presence can be found; where that presence, unprecedentedly strong, yet highly amorphous, can be most completely felt and best observed. And doing so by steering us from pictures to the word, from portraits to poems, and then to the writer writing, Milton displays his greatest affinity with postmodern theory. The New York artist Frank J. Boros is responsible for a whole series of portraits, some of them self-portraits, that, never depicting a human figure, instead map character by figuring the space the person or artist inhabits: by what is there and not there, by relative order and disorder—by accouterments. Revelations emerge from delineations of personal space, not persons, and by extension from poems by, not portraits of, the artist. Boros's conception, thus translated from painting into literature, suggests that authors do not so much write themselves into their works as, through their very lives, afford a model for their new work, in Milton's case the poem.

Inlays of autobiography, rather than digressions, are integral to the prose and poetry alike. As Margaret Bottrall explains, they are aspects of "self-assertion, self-scrutiny, self-revelation" and, just as important, "pertinent replies to the abuse that had been flung at [Milton]. . . by political adversaries."[43] Yet these inlays, especially in the poetry, do not mean that Milton, even if blind and a prisoner like Samson, is writing autobiography. Rather, as Northrop Frye has said of the last published of these poems: "the link between Samson and Milton does not mean that *Samson Agonistes* is an autobiographical poem: it simply means that Milton was the only man who could have written it."[44]

The Author as Collaborator

We are in process of recovering what seems to have been a widely held understanding in the seventeenth century: "books were not the product of an isolated individual operating autonomously" but instead, as Stephen B. Dobranski observes, part of "a complex, dynamic, cooperative process"—a collaborative process between the writers of books and the makers of them.[45] Moreover, it seems self-evident to recent students of early modern texts that, in the 1645 *Poems*, Milton asserts a collaborative relationship with William Marshall, Henry Moseley, and typographers, the likes of which he maintains in his later publications, quite remarkably so in both editions of *Paradise Lost*. As an author, Milton may not direct but he does participate in the publication process; he has his say in the design of the book. On the 1645 frontispiece, through the devices of a legend in the oval frame of the portrait, an epigram beneath it, and iconographic embellishments in its margins, Milton, even as he hints that collaboration may be more extensive than we have supposed, that Marshall himself may be privy to Milton's joke, contests the authorial identity projected through a portrait, the figure in academic regalia and aristocratic pose. At the same time, Milton uses such devices to begin the construction of an alternative identity hinted at in other of the front matter and confirmed by the poems themselves. Indeed, those poems contradict the claims of the frontispiece and title page (see figures 1.3 and 1.7), which would place Milton in the courtly tradition of Waller, and situate him instead within the Spenserian tradition claimed for him by Humphrey Moseley and, more broadly, the Virgilian tradition insinuated through epigraphs on both the main title page and the 1637 title page for *A Mask*.

Since Milton never specifies, we will never know the extent of his collusion with printers or their compositors concerning the makeup of his books, much less their title pages. Still, it becomes evident in *An Apology against a Pamphlet*, then *Areopagitica* and *Eikonoklastes*, and finally in his *Defense of Himself* that during the seventeenth century others as well as Milton scrutinize both titles and title pages (YP, 1:876, 877; 3:343, 597; 4:733–34). As he worries over what is an apt title in *Areopagitica*, Milton notices how "Sometimes 5 *Imprimaturs* are seen together dialogue-wise in the Piatza of one Title page, complementing and ducking each to other" (YP, 2:504) and thereby seems to acknowledge that the imprimatur is evidence of thought control and a mark of a book's conformity to cultural orthodoxies. Yet in *Areopagitica*, Milton also speaks of "shrewd books, with dangerous Frontispices" (YP, 2:524). In the *Defense of Himself*, moreover, Milton admits to collusion concerning the frontispiece portrait to the 1645 *Poems of Mr. John Milton* as he explains that the picture "prefixed" to this volume is there "at the suggestion and solicitation of a bookseller" with whom he "suffered" to cooperate (YP, 4:750–51) and then specifically praises the title page to his *Second Defense of the English People* as "veracious and in all respects proper to the book" (YP, 4:734).[46]

Additionally, title pages, loose, as Adrian Johns reminds us, were often "set out as advertisements" in book stores, in this way serving as announcements of a book's availability[47] and as invitations to a preliminary reading. The presentation of a book and of its author obviously affects how both are perceived: how books are made and displayed may afford evidence of sedition, blasphemy, or obscenity; may alienate a readership or, alternatively, entice it. Nor were portraits the only way of creating and controlling images of an author, for what eventually gets rejected from the front matter of a book, for instance, may be as revelatory as what is initially included or what eventually appears there. Thus emendations included in a first edition may engender errata lists in subsequent editions, Milton's initial gesture opening the way and functioning as a precedent, however tardily, for later editors.

The best surmise, when it comes to the title pages of *Paradise Lost*, is that, besides providing the poet with a way of mediating his work to a readership, they constitute part of a collaboration between poet and printer and hence should be regarded both as implicit commentary by Milton on his poem and as an early reception, indeed as a way of anticipating and shaping reception and thus as an integral part of this poem's reception history. These title pages, like seventeenth-century title pages generally, are themselves, and imply that so too are the texts they accompany, sites for mediation between poet and printer and between both and a book's readership, often with the author himself taking the lead. Furthermore, if John Phillips (in his "Response") is a reliable guide (see YP, 4:905), Milton was fully aware of the circumstances in which an author may publish anonymously, or nearly so, as Milton did with his poem "*On Shakespear*," the 1637 edition of *A Mask*, the 1638 publication of *Lycidas*, the first edition of *The Doctrine and Discipline of Divorce*, and two (yet not the first two) issues of *Paradise Lost*, each with a 1668 title page.[48] Given this history, what is remarkable is that *The Reason of Church-government Urg'd against Prelaty* By Mr. *John Milton* (1641) is Milton's first signed publication and that by 1644, owing to the notoriety of the divorce tracts, Milton is an international figure embroiled in fierce dispute.

In Milton's case, the most striking evidence of literary collaboration and poetic competition comes early, in the Edward King memorial volume, *Justa Edovardo King Naufrago* (1638), in which *Lycidas* seems to be in continuous dialogue with the poems it succeeds, in both halves of the volume, and in strident competition with some of those poets, most notably Henry King, Samson Briggs, and Thomas Norton. It is folly to forget that "typographically sophisticated" elements in texts, whether Spenser's or Milton's, whether *Lycidas* or the later *Paradise Lost* are in the words of Mark Bland, "more likely to have come from an author or a party acting on the author's behalf, rather than the printer" and a mistake, too, to overly credit Flannagan's contention that "[t]he blind Milton obviously exerted less control on the printing of what he wrote than the sighted Milton."[49] This first point is illustrated powerfully by the title page of *Areopagitica*. If the printer has suppressed his own name, Milton fearlessly showcases his own identity, incorporating it into the subtitle of this work. The second point, earlier challenged (as we have seen) by Richardson, finds its best illustration in the expanding front matter for *Paradise Lost* as that poem moves through different issues and eventually into a second edition, this front matter implying that the two editions of Milton's poem are decidedly different from one another, perhaps exaggeratedly so, in this way warding off the presumption that different editions of a work are all the same. Indeed, in the instance of *Paradise Lost*, what as a second edition may have seemed a taming of the first edition is, instead, a centering and highlighting of its revolutionary content, quite literally the moment of civil war and revolution, including the Copernican Revolution, as each is focused in

Book 6 and what will eventually become Books 7 and 8 of *Paradise Lost*. This strategy is evident as early as *Lycidas*, in which an epigraph not included in the first printing is added to the second, thus underscoring that this oracular poem, a monody, features a prophetic center.

Milton's name, it has been said, is "an indispensable part of his poetry,"[50] as well as of his prose writings. Signatures of authorship become marks of honor for Milton as he complains, in his *Second Defense*, about engaging in polemic with those who, publishing "furtively and by stealth," choose to remain "nameless" and who, doing so, are neither "devoted enough . . . nor loyal enough" to their cause. By contrast, Milton says of himself: "I was so far from being ashamed either of myself or my cause that I considered it disgraceful to attack so great a theme without openly acknowledging my identity" (YP, 4:561, 560–61). Any argument that the later Milton is hiding out when he publishes nearly anonymously, with only initials ("J. M."), the second edition of *The Readie and Easie Way*, as well as two early issues of *Paradise Lost*, needs to keep in mind that earlier titles of both works bear his full signature and that similarly anonymous works, or works nearly so, like *The Doctrine and Discipline of Divorce*, *Tetrachordon*, and *A Treatise of Civil Power*, even if their title pages bear no signature, or no more than an initialed signature, carry prefaces (in all instances addressed "To The Parlament") with a full signature: John Milton. For example: *The Doctrine and Discipline of Divorce* . . . The Author *J. M.* (1644) carries a preface "To the Parlament of England, with the Assembly," signed "Iohn Milton." Or, in analogy with *Paradise Lost*, of the two issues of *Accedence Commenc't Grammar*, both published in 1668, on one title page Milton's name is spelled out; on the other, only his initials are given, as they are again on the title page of *Of True Religion* (1673). These arguments are not conclusive, but they are important checks on any explanation of Milton's anonymous—or nearly anonymous—publication, whether it is explained in terms of social pressure or political caution. And more: such arguments enjoy the pedigree of Milton's own thinking on such topics, as well as his literary practice.

If often not enough has been made of Milton's signatures, too much should not be made of them either. But that said, it is worth mentioning that trust invested in a book by its readership depends majorly on both its prior knowledge and current opinion of the book's author, and then worth noticing that the very idea of authorship appears on the title pages to *Paradise Lost* at precisely the moment when "The Author," according to some, goes into hiding behind his initials. The designation of "The Author" from this time forward is a

constant on title pages for the first and second editions of *Paradise
Lost*. Furthermore, the appearance of this phrase on the title pages
makes abundantly clear that here J[OHN] M[ILTON] either claims,
or is credited with, authorship; that there is no effort to shift the
responsibility of authorship from the poet to the printer and every
effort, in the second edition, to identify the poet as his own revisionist,
enlarger, editor, and commentator: "The Second Edition / Revised
and Augmented by the / *same* Author" (my italics).

This notation is doubly important, because, first, it forces us to see
the poet as revisionist and the revisionist, in turn, as interpreter.
Milton himself is engaged in the activity of interpretation in which he
engages his narrators and his characters, along with his readers, in
Paradise Lost, and where there is interpretation there is always the
possibility of error: "thus they relate / Erring" (2.746–47). Milton
himself may err, and it is in such moments (as John Leonard
remarks[51])—it is in the midst of his inaccuracies—that we see the
author in his works. Moreover, when we remember the errata list
included in some issues of the first edition, and its remark—"Other
literal faults the Reader of himself may Correct" ([a4v])—the remark
itself invites Milton's readership to collaborate with him in the editorial job of proofreading even as, in comparison with Milton's note to
the second edition—"Revised and Augmented by the / same
Author"—restrictions seem to be imposed on a collaboration wherein
we may proofread and correct but *not* revise and augment. We are not
licensed to add—or to subtract—from his words. The Richard
Bentleys of the world of Milton scholarship have been thus anticipated
and admonished. An errata list is not only a reminder of error, authorial or otherwise, but an invitation to readers to give their attention to
an author's words and his revisions of them. That no errata list accompanies the second edition of *Paradise Lost* may be as noteworthy as the
fact that such a list is appended to the first edition. And Milton leaves
it to his readers to discover, and then account for, the additional fifteen lines of poetry that make a poem of 10,550 lines into one of
10,565 lines.

Some thought—and many continue to think—that the very name
of "John Milton" ensured a resistant readership, some of whom,
remembering Milton's prose writings and hence withholding their
trust, would recoil from *Paradise Lost* in disgust if its author's identity
were known. In this context, it needs to be remembered, further, that
not Milton's name, only his initials were given to the licenser of
Paradise Lost; and that as early as 1638 when *Lycidas* was published
nearly anonymously (simply initialed "J. M."), if politics was at issue,

it was probably first the politics of the poem's author, especially in view of the fact that other poets in the Edward King memorial volume revile just the sort of questioning of providence, just the sort of critique of religion that Milton composes within his own poem. Relevant, too, is the fact that as Peter Levi relates, "Dr Bastwick of Colchester, with the Revd Mr Burton of Friday Street, who had been railing against bishops since 1624, went to prison in 1637 and had their ears cut off in the pillory; Prynne," having already had his ears cut off, now "had the stumps . . . sawn off."[52] Prynne's punishment is a poignant reminder that authorial responsibility and culpability extend beyond what is actually written to interpretations inferred from or fixed upon a published text, especially if the medium is prose.

This may also explain why the manuscript (sub)title, "November 1637," was deleted, if one supposes that the first particle of that title, accompanying a pastoral elegy, would invoke *The Shepheardes Calender*, together with the story of its printer's involvement with John Stubbs where the author lost his right hand and his printer, Hugh Singleton, nearly did. When it comes to *Paradise Lost*, that someone—either poet or printer—felt threatened, and thus sought a shield of protection, would seem confirmed by the fact that only after Milton's signature is restored to the title page and the printer of the poem identified (in Edition 1, Issue 4, dated 1669) is the title-page announcement "Licensed and Entred according to Order" dropped. Only then, presumably, is the text also safe from the licenser's interference, which, were he provoked, could have taken the form of either erasure or emendation. *Paradise Lost* had finally averted the eye of the censor.

It is certainly possible that the strategy implicit in the initialed signature, as David Masson remarked long ago, is to save a poem like *Paradise Lost* by saving its reputation from that of its author. For, it is likely that Milton's name, as well as any poem he produced, would be suspected of bearing political meanings and seems to have been thus suspected by friends and associates from John Phillips to Theodore Haak and H. L. Benthem and even, if only because he protests too much to the contrary, by Andrew Marvell.[53] On the other hand, it is even more likely that the two initialed title pages of *Paradise Lost* (Edition 1, Issues 3A and 3B, dated 1668) reveal not a poet hiding from his prospective readers, but a printer concealing his associations with and wanting to avoid the same fate as the poem's beleaguered author, who admits to having "fall'n on evil dayes, / . . . and evil tongues" and, in fear of his life, complains of now being blind, "In darkness, and with dangers compast round" (7.25–26, 32–39, 27).

After all, no printer's name is given on the title pages of *Paradise Lost* dated 1667, nor on those for two of three issues dated 1668. Moreover, if we should seek a precedent, we find one in *Areopagitica* in which Milton argues that "no book be Printed, unlesse the Printers and the Authors name, or *at least the Printers be register'd*" (YP, 2:569; my italics), this directive coming in the peroration of a work in which Milton boldly wraps his own name within the title of the work and in which the title page itself bears the name of no printer at all.

Sometime later, Adrian Vlacq complained that the printer of Milton's *First Defense of the English People*, "as is his wont, . . . was unwilling to have his name attached to it" (YP, 4:1089). And Milton himself argues in the *Defense of Himself* that, in the absence of an author's name, "he who published [the book] . . . must be considered its author" (YP, 4:701). Printing houses were sometimes seen as sites of sedition, and the printers themselves, as well as booksellers, as engineers of rebellion. Thus, on the one hand, both could lend a book integrity and veracity but also, depending upon their reputations, could implicate a book in controversy, even conspiracy. Indeed, if as Adrian Johns contends, the names of printers and booksellers on title pages "could tell a prospective reader as much about the contents [of a book] as could that of the author,"[54] especially so with radical books, then *Paradise Lost* seems to have been in double jeopardy and, as a poem, would deploy all the subterfuges of its art in order to deliver its message, even if in disguise.

When after the fall of the Protectorate, as Nicholas von Maltzahn reports, "Milton went from publishing with the government printer to the Baptist bookseller Livewell Chapman, at the centre of radical religious politics,"[55] he made a choice, which would not have gone unobserved and which thus might have consequences both for him and for the printers and booksellers of his later poems. At some time, all were likely to be caught in a web of suspicion. From a family of dissenting printers and booksellers, Samuel Simmons, whose name appears on three (but *not the first three*) title pages of *Paradise Lost*, on ones dated 1668 and 1669, and whose signature ("S. Simmons") is appended to the addition, "The Printer to the Reader," already had one encounter with the government in the very year Milton's poem was published and, in consequence, had been arrested.[56] Simmons would obviously be leery of another encounter with the authorities and would want to avoid yet another arrest. Poet and printer are equally vulnerable and, evidently, similarly cautious. Booksellers perhaps less so. Yet Robert Boulter, named as one of the booksellers on five of the seven title pages, had been hauled into court to explain two hundred copies of a pirated almanac in his bookshop.[57] And such issues, not restricted to *Paradise Lost*, come to mind again with the publication of *Paradise Regain'd* and *Samson Agonistes*. John Starkey, for whom these poems were printed, is known to have participated in the tactic whereby multiple printing houses were deliberately involved in the production of risky texts as a way of neutralizing responsibility for a book, the contents of which any one printer knew only piecemeal.[58] Indeed, as Annabel Patterson reports in conversation, by 1671 John Starkey had become an icon for radical publication.

From the sixteenth century onward, censorship was used as a check on political sedition and religious heresy; and anonymity, as Robert J. Griffin perceives, often "an officially tolerated form of sanctuary," was not only an author's safeguard against detection and sometimes assertion of humility but evidence of "anxiety over public exposure, fear of prosecution, hope of an unprejudiced reception," as well as a "desire to deceive" (even to hide from) one's printer or publisher.[59] Milton had something to lose, then, but so too did Simmons, although poetry itself was an ideal mechanism that, because a convenient subterfuge, could hide discord in its basement while maintaining an impression of harmony on its surface. Nevertheless, to focus on just two of the seven title pages for *Paradise Lost* is, finally, to ignore the virtual parity established on all the other title pages for the first, as well as the second, edition of *Paradise Lost* between author and title, poet and poem, and thus to resist the clear implication from three of these title pages, also as it happens the ones bearing the name of Simmons, that reading *Paradise Lost* is "reading" Milton. If there are to be recriminations, then, Milton takes the first hits.

It is abundantly evident from the printer's note to the reader in two issues of the first edition of *Paradise Lost* that printer collaborates with poet to produce both the note on "why the Poem Rimes not" (*A2*) and the Arguments to its individual books, each reminding us that there is a poet behind this poem, overseeing, orchestrating the whole performance even to the point of revising it. The nature of the revisions (especially with regard to poetic structure) is revelatory,[60] no less so than inclusions as well as exclusions (preliminary poems by Samuel Barrow and Andrew Marvell in the first instance, and in the second the absence of a dedicatory page). When *Paradise Lost* goes into a second edition, this point is reinforced by the acknowledged revision of a ten- into a twelve-book poem; then punctuated by the expansion of the front matter to include the preliminary—and mediatorial—poems by Barrow and Marvell. Now the Arguments, once preliminary matter, are assimilated to the poem and printed as headpieces to the twelve books even as some fifteen lines of new poetry, some of them carefully calibrated for their bracketing power, are silently added.

With the disappearance of the printer's note from the second edition, Milton himself, through his note on "The Verse," acts as mediator even as he now seems to enlist Barrow and Marvell, through their preliminary poems, as additional negotiators with his readers. Taken together, this front matter constitutes a negotiation strategy probably crafted by Milton, who is, in this way, seen at the portal to his poem quite apart from the frontispiece portrait added to this second edition. He is also seen in his revisions to poems (witness the title-page acknowledgment for the second edition of *Paradise Lost*, previously cited), with the "Omissa" to *Samson Agonistes* further illustrating the point, as if flagging Milton's presence and thereby driving home Anne Middleton's proposition that "the author's labors as maker also situate the author himself within . . . [a poem's] reception history as reviser."[61] In the very act of mediating a poem to its audience, the author himself becomes a crucial player in the drama of its reception with Milton, in the second edition of *Paradise Lost*, usurping from his printer direct responsibility for mediating his verse form to the public, and, while acknowledging revisions, except for the shift from a ten- to a twelve-book poem, specifies none. This circumstance leads Gordon Teskey to quip that "*Redistributed*" would be a better term for describing what happens in the change from the first to the second edition of *Paradise Lost*—far better than Milton's own title-page acknowledgment, "*revised and augmented.*"[62] (As previously noted, there is no errata sheet for the second as there had been for the first edition.)

Particularly remarkable about Milton's title pages, together with the accumulating front matter, is that poet and poem, poem and reader are bound inextricably in single compact so as to insist upon the poet's presence in a poem that completes itself in the mind of the reader, establishing outside the poem the dialectical relationship between poet and reader that is at its core. In his note, "The Printer to the Reader," Samuel Simmons addresses Milton's "*Courteous Reader*"— an address occasioned by those "many" readers who have enquired about the "reason . . . why the Poem Rimes not" (*A2*). Through his own note entitled "The Verse" and then through the Arguments for the individual books of the poem, Milton responds to these concerns of his readership. As earlier remarked, the table labeled "ERRATA" similarly prompts the reader: "Other literal faults the Reader of himself may Correct" ([a4v])—just as the errata sheet for the 1673 *Poems, &c. upon Several Occasions*, will again instruct readers to correct errors. Yet in "The Verse," in the very moment he acknowledges his readership, Milton differentiates between "vulgar Readers," apt to construe the absence of rhyme as "a defect" ([a4]), and those he eventually designates in his poem as "fit audience . . . though few" (7.31)—those alert to the politics encoded in rhymelessness, a politics (as we have seen) that Milton may have found enunciated by his contemporary John Spencer in the very year, 1665, that Milton allegedly completed *Paradise Lost*.

Yet it is a politics Milton would, in other ways, rescind by presenting *Paradise Lost* as a prophecy to a world from which Spencer would rid such *"Seditious"* writings; and to a world from which, unlike Milton, Spencer scuttled the idea of all the Lord's people becoming prophets on the grounds that prophecy was not a gift bestowed upon *all*, certainly not upon "ruder minds" or the "ignorant Multitude."[63] Nowhere is the point made more emphatically than in the final book (eventually books) of *Paradise Lost*, which take as their subject these verses from the prophecy of Joel:

> And it shall come to pass afterward, *that* I will pour out my spirit upon all flesh: and your sons and your daughters shall prophesy, your old men shall dream dreams, your young men shall see visions.
>   And also upon the servants and the handmaids in those days Will I pour out my spirit. (2:28–29)

Those words recall the ones Milton earlier echoes from the Book of Numbers: "If there be a prophet among you, *I* the Lord will make myself known unto him in a vision, *and* will speak to him in a dream" (12:6). The visionary, prophetic dimensions of Milton's poem, this poem's radical aesthetic and revolutionary politics gestured toward in Milton's note on "The Verse," explains the erasure, the trimming away, of this "aesthetically- and politically-packed paragraph in Spanish translations of *Paradise Lost*, starting from its greatly delayed first translation by Canon Juan Escoiquiz in 1812 to its later popular prose translation by Cayetano Rosell"—an erasure, a suppression, that Jorge Louis Borges strives to recover.[64]

As we proceed from some title pages to *Paradise Lost* in which Milton's name (in initials only) is nearly anonymous to later ones (still belonging to the first edition) in which the poet's name, even if muted by comparison with other elements of the title page, is nevertheless spelled out, and then onward to the second edition of *Paradise Lost*, in which the poet's image is flashed across the title page by virtue of its frontispiece status—when we take all this into account, the conclusion seems obvious. In 1668, at any rate, Milton mutes his presence through a practiced self-effacement as explained by John Phillips in his earlier cited "Response" to John Rowland as he perhaps borrows on Milton's wisdom. To Rowland's remark, "it is by no means unusual for worthy men to withhold their names . . . [as does] St. Paul in the Epistle to the Hebrews," Phillips retorts, "He did, to be sure, write anonymously, but to a people bitterly hostile to his name about matters quite new and little credited" (YP, 4:905), the emphasis now falling not so much on the author as subject as on the subject matter of the author's discourse, which itself requires a shield of protection. We may continue to look for Milton in his writings and, doing so, discover him as a disruptive presence in the folds of a torn text, there discoursing on things unattempted yet, thus not before written of. Such tears are first evident in conspicuous omissions, then in marked revisions, and finally in differences (however slight) between the various issues of the first edition of *Paradise Lost* and the separate texts of the poem's first and second editions, as well as the discrepancies that exist between what some of the Arguments to books of *Paradise Lost* promise and what individual books, in contradistinction, then provide. Here we will want to sort our way through two opposing perspectives: one that views inaccuracies and discrepancies as often just that, yet, paradoxically, as sites within his work in which the writer is found in all his vulnerability; and another from which such sightings of Milton have less to do with inaccuracy and error and far more to do with this poet's evolving thinking, shifts of attitude, developing and even corrective interpretation (is it the serpent or rather Satan in the serpent?) or changing inflection, often to provide more theological coloring or to register a theological fine point.[65]

ENTERING THE BREACH

One of the most provocative and, simultaneously, misguided claims of late twentieth-century Milton criticism is that there is a "sequential principle" operating in and between Milton's epic-prophecies and that it operates so rigidly as to privilege the second over the first poem, and later books of *Paradise Lost* over earlier ones. What comes last, according to one critic, qualifies and corrects what precedes it; that is, "later utterances can modify earlier ones, but earlier ones cannot modify later ones."[66] By such calculation, coming late in Book 12, Adam's embrace of the *felix culpa*—"O goodness infinite, goodness immense! / That all this good of evil shall produce" (469–70)—would constitute the poem's final, definitive word on this topic.

Calculating interpretation by this sequential principle, of course, evades Milton's own concept of privileged voices. Adam's voice, according to one critic, takes precedence over God's, which earlier repudiates a doctrine that *fallen* Adam eventually embraces: "Happier, had it suffic'd him to have known / Good by it self, and Evil not at all" (11.88–89). The whole notion of a happy fall, even before these concluding books, is eroded by the narrator's declaration, "O yet happiest if ye seek / No happier state, and know to know no more" (4.774–75), and then by Raphael's insistence that no one needs to fall in order to rise. Rather, "body [will] up to spirit work, in bounds / Proportiond to each kind" (5.478–79), Raphael says, while explaining that the time will "come when men / With Angels may participate" (5.493–94). Then comes the acknowledgment of *unfallen* Adam that "In contemplation of created things / By steps we may ascend to God" (5.511–12) and his later admission to God that "[thou] Canst raise thy Creature to what highth thou wilt / Of Union or Communion, deifi'd" (8.430–31). Only the voice of the fallen Satan upholds the doctrine to which *fallen* Adam subscribes: "From this descent / Celestial vertues rising, will appear / More glorious and more dread then from no fall" (2.14–16) and, later, "happie though thou art, / Happier thou mayst be" (5.75–76). Milton's opinions, if they are to be found in his poetry, are, by his own admission, to be found in the mouths of his *great* characters, whose independence of mind steers clear of theological trivia—and commonplaces.

Milton's opinions are also to be found, it would seem, in sites of contestation like the following. These are the words of Milton's sometimes Pauline narrator who declares that, although Eve is "much deceav'd" (9.404), Adam is "*not* deceav'd, / But fondly overcome with Femal charm" (9.998–99; my italics; cf. 1.34–36), his words contradicting those of God: "Man falls deceiv'd / By the other first: Man therefore shall find grace, / The other none" (3.130–32). God's words, moreover, are echoed here by Satan and there by Adam and Eve. "Man I deceav'd" (10.496), says Satan; and later, hurling recriminations at Eve while allowing for their mutual deception, Adam addresses Eve as "thou Serpent" who "Fool'd and beguil'd" him as the serpent also fooled and beguiled her (10.867, 879–80). In her "Forsake me not thus, *Adam*" speech (10.914), Eve adapts Adam's rhetoric to her apology, in which she owns up to having unwittingly "offended," "Unhappilie deceav'd" him (10.916–17), prompting Adam, in his turn, to concede that "the Serpent hath contriv'd / Against *us* this deceit" (10.1034–35; my italics). Woman's deception of man, witnessed to by the Church Fathers of which St. Ambrose is an example ("Adam was beguiled by speech, and Samson was overcome by a word"[67])—such deception registers as proverbial wisdom in *Samson Agonistes*: "wisest Men / Have err'd, and by bad Women been deceiv'd" (210–11). In this instance, Milton's tragedy observes the strategy and emphasis of *Christus Patiens*, the Christian tragedy cited as *Christ Suffering* in the Preface to *Samson Agonistes*, with the Mother of God insisting that woman was deceived first—*never*, but for the serpent, "would the offspring of the rib, / . . . have been deceived / And dared to dare an over-daring deed" (4–6; cf. 943)—even as the verses of the poet-theologian, published as Prologue to *Christ Suffering*, make all of mankind party to "the beast's deceit" (17). If Satan "contrived" by the error of woman "to defeat the human race, God contrived against him," and with woman, to effect mankind's redemption (578–83).[68]

Milton mocks Satan's reading of the Genesis account of Creation according to the sequential principle, as Satan apostrophizes the Earth "as built / With second thoughts, reforming what was old!" (9.100–01) by which logic Man as the center of the new creation surpasses the God who is at the center of the first creation (9.99–113). Similarly, a sequential principle for reading *Paradise Lost* forces us, presumptuously, to credit the narrator's conclusion over God's; indeed, to accept the narrator's conclusion as a corrective to and straightening out of God's crooked theology. Against such a position, it may be argued, first of all, that in *Tetrachordon* Milton privileged the Hebrew Bible over St. Paul's interpretation of it—indeed was chided for doing so by his early critics; and second, that by later commentators, both men and women, Hannah More as well as William Hayley, he was commended for just these swervings from Pauline orthodoxies.[69] The collective force of the statements by God and Satan, Adam and Eve, it would seem, overrules the words of the Pauline narrator: man is "not deceav'd" (9.998; cf. 404 and 1.34–36). In *Paradise Regain'd*, Satan reiterates his own stand on such issues, which is also God's stand: "*Adam* and his facil consort *Eve* / Lost Paradise *deceiv'd* by me" (1.51–52; my italics the second line).

If there is a Miltonic logic to be inferred from these examples, it is that when God and Satan agree the Devil speaks truth; and if there is a larger principle of interpretation, it is that the authentic Milton, an interrogator—and sometimes a transgressor—of orthodox opinion lurks in these sites of contestation from which he often reveals himself as a sect of one, wherein he establishes precise inflections, makes crucial choices, all the while gently nudging us to do the same. Milton's poems may ultimately complete themselves in the experience of the reader; yet a vital part of their experience is of the writer writing. No less important than acknowledging a dialectic between the poet and his audience is determining the ethos of each and, hence, whether Milton's poetry encourages (as some would have it) a dialectic between a pietistic bard and a devout reader or, instead, sets against a text of platitudinous Christianity and submissive orthodoxy one of rebellion and subversion. Herman Melville makes these same points when, underscoring Satan's line in *Paradise Lost* (9.701), "<u>Not just, not God</u>," he remarks that Milton "always teaches under a masque, and makes the Devil himself a Teacher & Messiah," and again, when pondering over *Paradise Regain'd* (4.196–201), annotates: "Put into Satan's mouth, but spoken with John Milton's tongue;—it conveys a strong controversial meaning."[70]

The aforementioned examples reflect correctively on much existing criticism in that, in our search for the author, they push us into often unvisited spaces, those breaches within poems created by inscribed contradictions. At the same time, the examples are not meant to foreclose the possibility of finding Milton in the more usual places: in certain of his characters, including his narrator, especially in the multiple prologues, which, as John S. Diekhoff argued years ago, act as epistles in which Milton can fashion self-defenses and offer self-explanations.[71] On the one hand, the narrator acts as a second self, "whose similarity to the author," says Foucault, "is never fixed and undergoes considerable alteration within the course of a single book":

> It would be as false to seek the author in relation to the actual writer as to the fictional narrator; the "author-function" arises out of their scission—in the division and distance of the two.[72]

On the other hand, the prologues to individual books of *Paradise Lost*, in which the narrator is so conspicuous a presence, have not only a narrative but a rhetorical function: they are centers of ethical proof through which the narrator—and Milton through the narrator—establishes himself as "a composition, and patterne of the best and honourablest things"; in words from *An Apology against a Pamphlet*, as "hav[ing] in himselfe the experience and the practice of all that which is praise-worthy" (YP, 1:890).

Such an understanding is traceable to Jonathan Richardson, Sr., who finds in the accumulation of passages like this one not merely delineations of Milton's mind, or vindications of his character, but the hope of exciting others "to be Enamour'd, as Hee, with the *Beauty of Holiness*."[73] This multifaceted agenda, not restricted to the prologues of *Paradise Lost*, spills over into the narrative proper, which itself functions at times as apologia, particularly in its representations of Satan wherein comparisons involving shimmering likenesses are usually overruled by forced distinctions. If there is a rhetoric to Milton's prologues, there is likewise a rhetorical component to his narratives, Satan's here and Samson's later.

"ALWAYS A KNIT OF IDENTITY . . . ALWAYS DISTINCTION"

Milton was of the Devil's party. If Blake's perception is new, his words are not and, however often misconstrued, serve as a reminder here of occasional blurrings between the thoughts of characters, those of the narrator, and those of the poem's author; and a reminder, too, that Satan, especially in *Paradise Lost*, may be a vehicle for Calvinist doctrines the poem opposes, as well as the entry point for theological positions, eccentric or even heretical, which Milton at times embraces. Criminalizing and demonizing one's enemies was an "art of abuse" practiced by both sides during the civil war years and, in a *Defense of Himself*, described by Milton as "the rhetoric of devils" (YP, 4:765–66; cf. 823).

Alexander More may be miffed that Milton calls him "Satan's monster, the devil's slave, and . . . even the devil himself."[74] Yet Milton seems to get the worst of the deal, bombarded as he was, from the early 1650s right up to the publication of *Paradise Lost*, with persistent abuse. "I will shit and piss all over that man Milton,"[75] John Phillips quotes Salmasius as saying, with Milton himself complaining in the *Defense of Himself* that du Moulin's "*Royal Cry* . . . [has] relegated [him] to the company of devils" (YP, 4:735). "A monster, horrible, deformed, huge and sightless"—these words More quotes from a forthcoming attack on Milton—Milton seeming to du Moulin, more than a man, "a worm," "dragon," or "serpent" and then accused by Adrain Vlacq of "blindness of heart" and by More of "blindness of . . . mind."[76] The appellation sticks so well that in the years from 1666 to 1668 Milton is remembered simply as "*Blinde Milton*" in *Poor Robin . . . An Almanack*, in which he appears on a list with all those who were suspected of making league with the devil and of being one of his limbs. In the shorthand of that appellation, Milton is remembered as a blind guide with his blindness widely accepted as evidence of God's disfavor and of Milton's own dishonor. Would that someone had burned Milton as the hangman had his books, his enemies wished; or as the Elder Brother in *A Mask* would eventually opine of *The First Defense*: "This book is most worthy of burning, the author of the gallows."[77]

If, at the time of the Restoration, Milton was occasionally elided with Samson because of his supposed revenge fantasy of toppling the restored monarchy, he was also—and even more persistently— mythologized as Satan because of his participation in rebellion and sedition. With John Goodwin, he was numbered among the rebellious devils, the "Blinde Guides," of a now stumbling nation: speaking with the devil's mouth and sorted with the devil's party, this "Infamous," "Sacrilegious *Milton*" was called a *"Diabolical Rebel"*—"altogether a Devil" posing as a saint, "a Compendium of all the Villainies and Impieties of the Age"—and presumed already to have gone to "Hell."[78]

Within this context, we can best assess Milton's audacity in beginning *Paradise Lost* in Hell, then in presenting so alluring a portrait of Satan. Milton responds effectively to an horizon of expectation, established by a swarm of adversaries, who are well met by Milton, but with some surprises as he pulls their whiskers before tearing them out. In what must be a carefully calculated gesture, Milton, as if he were blurring into the character of Satan, begins *Paradise Lost* with a descent into the underworld but also, with equal calculation, completes his journey into the underworld with an allusion to the Orpheus story. Returning from Hell, "now with bolder wing," the poet-narrator, as if on Milton's behalf, claims to be singing "With other notes then to th' *Orphean* Lyre," having been "Taught by the heav'nly Muse to venture down / The dark descent, and up to reascend" (3.13, 17, 19–20, 21), and emphasizing, as if in response to Milton's critics, that he is no less differentiated from Satan than are Prometheus, Achilles, Aeneas, and Odysseus. Milton's narrator, moreover, has journeyed into Hell without making of himself a hell or, more important, without (as Orpheus had done) entering into a contract with Pluto—or the devil.

In the very act of shifting the network of classical allusion from Satan to his narrator, or to Milton in his narrator, Milton would seem to invite the further conjecture hazarded earlier in this century by Denis Saurat and implied earlier still by both Mary Wollstonecraft and William Blake: that Milton is his own hero. If heroism in *Paradise Lost* is to be ascertained and measured by a character's resemblance to classical paradigms, then this strategic shift of reference from Satan to Milton makes the poet himself the surest choice and standard for heroism in the poem. In his 1671 poetic volume, Milton shifts the standard of comparison from classical to biblical exemplars of heroism, finding in the life of Jesus, and then in Samson's life, multiplying parallels with his own, yet in the comparison with Samson finally suppressing their likenesses within their still more striking differences. With Samson's story as with Satan's, Milton is telling not an exemplary tale but a cautionary one, which requires him to distance himself from those with whom he had been aligned (often by his adversaries).

Likening Milton to Satan and Samson through creative analogy is the doing of Milton's adversaries, which in *Paradise Lost* and *Samson Agonistes* Milton sets about undoing as part of his apologia. In the process, Milton parodies a venerable tradition of portraiture exemplified quite notably by a portrait of the third-century Roman emperor Commodus as *Commodus-Hercules*—a mode of portraiture in which historical persons are shown possessing the attributes of figures in legend and mythology by way of aggrandizing them through the comparisons. The counter strategy was for Milton's enemies to invoke analogies through which they would ascribe to the poet attributes that would diminish and demean him. In turn, Milton's strategy is to define himself by differentiation and, through differentiation, to fashion and mediate an alternative image of himself.

Milton is joined in this work of mediation through an apologia by Andrew Marvell whose dedicatory poem for the second edition of *Paradise Lost* addresses six charges, most of them deriving from Milton's adversaries: the first that his blindness, coming upon him suddenly, is a mark of divine disfavor; the second that, driven by revenge, Milton, Samson-like in his sedition, is poised to hurl down the pillars of church and state; third, that Milton's projects always seem to involve a twisting and turning of Scripture and a consequent mutilation of God's word; fourth, that this forecaster Milton, lacking authenticity, is a pretender to prophecy; fifth, that in an act of enormous hubris Milton claims to "soar aloft" (37); and sixth that his rhymeless verse is both artless and politically charged.

The Prologue to Book 3, "with the Bard's confession of blindness," is slighted by one critic as an irrelevancy—"no literary necessity"—despite the fact that, as we have seen, it undermines, quite intentionally, earlier attempts to identify Milton within Satan.[79] It also provides Marvell with the arguments he thinks will undermine identification of Milton with Samson. This is the Prologue that, through persistent echo and allusion, is foregrounded by Marvell's poem, which, in defense of the poet, argues, on the one hand, that Milton is no spiteful Samson and, on the other, that apparently unlike Samson but certainly "like *Tiresias*," "Heav'n . . . / Rewards with *Prophesie* . . . [Milton's] loss of Sight" (43–44). As early as *Tetrachordon*, Milton took it for "a generall precept" of all the "Sages, not to instruct the unworthy and the conceited who love tradition more then truth, but to *perplex* and stumble them purposely with contriv'd obscurities" (YP, 2:643; my italics). In *The Second Defense*, Milton confronted his accusers head-on: theirs is a blindness that, "implanted in the inmost faculties, obscures the mind"; his, a blindness that only deprives him of "superficial appearance" but leaves him with "intellectual vision," as well as "the light of divine countenance" (YP, 4:589–90).

At the same time that he is blind, then, Milton is "most keen in vision" and, in language anticipatory of the Prologue to the first book of *Paradise Lost*, prays that by his infirmity he "may . . . be perfected, by this completed," "in this darkness, . . . clothed in light," in "an inner and far more enduring light" of "divine favor" (YP, 4:590). In *Paradise Lost*, therefore, far from perplexing God's word, Milton is, in Marvell's judgment, an inspired interpreter of it: one whose darkness has been illumined by the irradiating power of celestial light and who thus sees and tells of things invisible to mortal sight; one whose rhymeless (unpremeditated) verse is both a token of and testimony to Milton's prophetic office. Even when Samson was admitted to the company of prophets, it was to exemplify the lowest order of prophecy, not the order of prophecy with which Milton aligns both his narrator and himself in comparisons with Moses and John of Patmos.

Milton's own life has been a steady progress toward the truth and, unlike Samson's, stands free of, instead of being shot through with, sometimes suspect conversion experiences. Again unlike Samson, not driven by revenge fantasies and motives, Milton is providentially spared the life that Samson loses. Nor was Marvell alone in defending Milton against charges of vindictiveness. Witness, for example, Edward Phillips whose "Life" of the poet speaks of Milton's own very "generous nature, more inclinable to Reconciliation than to perseverance in Anger and Revenge."[80] More important, witness Milton himself who, while chastising others for the "divine vengeance" they "rashly and absurdly invoke on others," in *The Second Defense* says of himself: "Far be it from me to have so little spirit . . . , or so little charity that I cannot . . . more easily pardon . . . [my enemies]" and thereupon allows that he bears "no grudge whatever . . . against any man" and "endure[s] with the greater equanimity all the curses that are uttered" against him (YP, 4:599, 591, 596). Compare to Milton's posture here that of Samson who sharply rebukes Dalila's pleading for forgiveness and, indeed, mocks those who forgive (759–65). This episode stands in striking contrast with the contextualization for *Samson Agonistes* afforded by its epistolary reference to *Christ Suffering*. There the Mother of God, addressing Peter, assures him that though he "has done great evil," as well as "terrible things," he "can still obtain forgiveness," Peter here "sin[ning] for fear of the mob" (814–19) as Dalila herself sins out of fear that her threatening countrymen will treat her as cruelly as they had Samson's Timnian bride; that Samson's retaliatory spirit will provoke the same spirit in the leaders of her own country.

A pardoner of others, Milton himself, probably owing to Marvell's intervention, won a pardon in 1660 without which we would probably not have any of his last poems to engage in such points of contestation. What Milton says of himself, what his biographers say of him, sets the poet apart from the unforgiving, unpardoning Samson, thus throwing into question the proposition argued most forcefully by Michael Lieb that, because he is Milton's chosen hero, the poet projects himself into Samson, becoming what he beholds, in the process adopting Samson's violence as his own signature as he turns his enemies' "theater of assault" into his own (and Samson's) "theater of destruction." For Lieb, then, "Milton's defense of the regicides is a defense of himself, his support of their cause, a support of his own. In that defense, he himself becomes a strong man."[81] Behind Lieb's argument is a whole tradition of Milton criticism that sees Samson's duplicity and wiliness as of a piece with Rahab's noble lying, Ehud's justifiable deceptions, and Jael's pious fraud; that is, as part of Milton's ongoing "self-justification," which is as evident in *Of Christian Doctrine* as in *Samson Agonistes*.[82]

Milton and Samson shared certain circumstances, to be sure: both seemingly chosen for high exploits, in Milton's words from the *Defense of Himself*, "now to venture into the sun, and dust, and field of battle, now to exert real brawn, brandish real arms, seek a real enemy" (YP, 4: 795). In Milton's case, not before but in the aftermath of blindness, these words themselves were heightened to metaphorical meaning. Engaged in mental fight, both here and in *The Second Defense*, Milton exalts battle by the pen over battle by the sword, extolling "that truth . . . defended by reason—the only defence truly appropriate to man" (YP, 4:553). Likewise, both Samson and Milton, only one of them forgiving, were unfortunate in their marriage choices, each having been stung by women; and both in later life, briefly incarcerated, felt dejected and defeated. For many of Milton's critics, however, it was not just common circumstances that linked Samson and Milton, but shared feelings and opinions that were their outgrowth.

If initially it seemed that Milton made the best of very indifferent subject matter by choosing the Samson story and unleashing its satiric potentiality against bad women and bad wives, before the end of the nineteenth century, the screen of autobiography had been greatly enlarged, with *Samson Agonistes* now being read by David Masson, for example, as "a representation of . . . Milton in his secret antagonism to all the powers and all the fashions of the Restoration" and, still more broadly, as a poem in which Samson's tragedy affords "a metaphor of the tragedy of . . . [Milton's] own life":

> Nothing put forth by Milton in verse in his whole life is so vehement an exhibition of his personality, such a proclamation of his own thoughts about himself and about the world around him, as his *Samson Agonistes.* . . . The Hebrew Samson among the Philistines and the English Milton among the Londoners of the reign of Charles the Second were, to all poetic intents, one and the same person. They were one and the same not only by similarity of their final circumstances, but also by the reminiscences of their previous lives. . . .
>
> There were moments, I believe, in Milton's musings by himself, when it was a fell pleasure to him to imagine some exertion of his strength, like that legendary one of Samson's, by which, clutching two central pillars of the Philistine temple, he might tug and strain till he brought down the whole fabric in a crash upon the heads of the hea-thenish congregation, perishing himself in the act, but leaving England bettered by the carnage.[83]

Yet it is not simply a matter of Milton's gradually emerging from con-cealment in his poetry; for if René de Chateaubriand earlier found "[t]he poet himself is depicted in the person of the Israelite, blind, a prisoner, and unfortunate," even before Chateaubriand, Joseph Ivimey, citing Todd, argued that, whatever the case in his tragedy, "MILTON might be seen in *Paradise Lost*, but not in *Paradise Regained*"—the poem with which *Samson Agonistes* is paired.[84]

In an enormous swing of the pendulum, insisting that "Milton had no thought of creating a personal or political allegory," William Riley Parker stresses (as the first reception of the poem by Marvell had done) differences between Samson and Milton, as if to say that poetry sometimes mimics but seldom replicates autobiography:

> the story of Samson *in its essentials* was not, and could not be, . . . [Milton's] own story. He had not disobeyed God's command, and his eyes had not been put out as a punishment for anything. He had not revealed God's holy secret to a woman, nor had his own wife

betrayed him to his enemies. He had never been glorious like Samson,
and he was not possessed of strength without wisdom. Unlike the
Hebrew champion, he had not dishonored his God; he felt no need for
repentance and regeneration.[85]

Whatever Parker's purpose, Marvell's seem to involve defending
Milton against those detractors who had elided him with Samson and
who eventually would insist upon poet and prototype alike sharing
and expounding a virulent and bruising misogyny that, in *Samson
Agonistes*, it should be noted, manifests itself in rage and eventuates in
massacre. It needs to be remembered that, early on, any reading of
Samson Agonistes that found Milton and his protagonist colluding in a
revenge plot was dismissed as a wild fantasy exhibiting very little "cool
criticism."[86]

In *Killing, No Murder*, Edward Sexby (a.k.a. William Allen) argues
what he thinks is Milton's case that, when the laws are crippled, it is
necessary to turn to the High Court for justice such as is brought
upon the Philistines by Samson. Even if tyranny is one of those
plagues God visits upon the Israelites, Samson is nonetheless justified
in using "private injuries" as "sufficient grounds to make war upon
the Philistins":

> being himself but a private man, and not onely not assisted but opposed
> by his servile Countrymen. He knew what the Law of Nature allowed
> him . . . , to answer for himselfe, that as they did unto him, so had he
> done unto them.

Sexby's Samson incarnates the philosophy of Milton's Satan when, in
Paradise Lost, allowing that he who aspires to "Revenge / . . . must
[soar] down as low / As high," the Fiend comes to realize that, however "sweet" initially, "Revenge . . . / Bitter ere long back on it self
recoils" (9.168–72). What is right for Satan is right for
Samson/Milton especially in the circumstances of 1659, which, Sexby
argues, exhibit the same provocations, the same just fury, the same
opposition and discouragements from Milton's countrymen that
Samson had experienced in his dealings with the Israelites. To those
who contend that "these examples out of Scripture, are of men that
were Inspired by God, and that therefore they had the call and
Authority for their Actions, which we cannot pretend to," Sexby
"answer[s] with the learned *Milton*, that if God committed these
things, 'tis a sign they were lawful and commendable" not despite, but
precisely because, "Neither *Sampson* nor *Samuel* alleged any other

cause or reason for what they did, but retaliation."[87] Revenge and retaliation, bonds shared by Samson and Satan, are bonds that some, like Sexby, would have both figures sharing with God and that for some of Milton's critics ally their poet with both a retaliatory Samson and a vindictive God.

Milton himself, as it happens, is quick to reinforce the distinction between public acts and private enmities, explaining in *The Tenure of Kings and Magistrates* that, "if *David* refus'd to lift his hand against the Lords anointed, the matter between them was not tyranny, but privat enmity, and *David* as a privat person had bin his own revenger, not so much the peoples" (YP, 3:216; cf. 4:402). This is the sort of construction that earlier Hugo Grotius would put on St. Paul's teaching when, discoursing on revenge as a "negative precept," he makes the important observation:

> that the higher powers are constituted Gods Ministers, and the execu-
> tioners of his wrath . . . upon those that do ill; thereby clearly distin-
> guishing between that revenge, which the Magistrate instead of God
> exacts for the publick good, being a part of his prerogative; and that
> which every private man takes upon his enemy with his own hands,
> merely to gratifie his own passion, which the Apostle had a little before
> interdicted.[88]

While Samson may claim ambiguously, "But I a private person . . . / . . . I was no private but a person rais'd / With . . . command from Heav'n" (1208, 1211–12), the unanswered question still posed in the climactic scene of *Samson Agonistes* is whether Samson exacts revenge for the public good or, instead, to gratify his own passions; whether he is, in the words of Grotius, "violently hurried to things unjust."[89] Does he pray, by implication acting as God's emissary, or instead act of his own accord?

The troubled broodings of a scriptural commentator writing just two years before, concerned that Samson doled out revenge for private wrongs, are translated by Sexby from weakness into strength and from fault into virtue as he decries what this commentator had agonizingly concluded, that Samson must have acted as "a publick person, . . . as Gods substitute and vice-gerent."[90] Arguments like these once pinned to Milton, despite the facts that Samson's stumbling rhetoric eventually captures both possibilities and, more, that Milton in his own representation of Samson brackets the scene at the pillars in question marks, may well nudge others into doing as Robert South had done; that is, into invoking the Book of Judges as a mirror upon the civil war

years, "this tragical scene" in England's history, wherein the protagonist Charles I is "a David, a saint, a king" and the rebels are the villains
of the piece, chief among them Milton, "a blind adder" who did "spit
so much poison upon the kings person and cause."[91]

If *Eikon Basilike* cast Charles I as a tragic hero and set history
within a tragic mode, very soon afterward Royalist propaganda shifted
into tragicomedy, with the bellicose Puritans figuring as the comedic
characters until the possibility emerged of history itself being transformed as, in happy conjunction, God and providence effect both the
Restoration of monarchy and the translation of dark tragedy into joyful
comedy. As Nigel Smith reports, "tragi-comedy entered the royalist
frame, as much to ridicule the free state as to indicate hopes of a Stuart
restoration"; it "provided the generic means for Royalists to imagine
the possibility of a happy ending for their plight."[92] In reaction,
Milton mocks the Royalist appropriation of tragedy, in *The Second
Defense* speaking of Vlacq's concern with "the presentation of the
tragedy, as it were, of the King's Cry against us" and then of "Vlacq,
the buffoon" and "More the adulterer and seducer" as "spendid
actors for a tragedy!" (YP, 4:573–74). That is, as Lieb explains, Milton
turns the tables on the Royalists, with their reenactments of tragedy
transformed by Milton into "the lowest and perverse form of
comedy . . . , replete with characters of the most comical sort"; with
their "theater of assault" now "turned against the assaulter."[93] Yet
Milton also attempts a recuperation of tragedy, a purification and
transformation of it, so as to escape the rebuke of those who think, as
does Thomas Hobbes, that, by compounding one's own image with
another man's, by imagining oneself as a Hercules (or a Samson), one
perpetuates deluding fictions of heroism as well as false images of
oneself.[94] Indeed, for the Milton of *Eikonoklastes*, all those kings and
magistrates in the line of Hercules, including Samson presumably, are
subject to and sometimes summoned to judgment, "and somtimes put
to death" (YP, 3:590), even if (to use words from "The Argument" to
Samson Agonistes) "by accident" (CP, 575).

Within such a context, Marvell mediates a Milton differentiated
from Samson; and within this same context, Milton uses *Samson
Agonistes* to reinforce such differentiations and the epistle of that
tragedy to report the "infamy" into which tragedy has fallen "through
the Poets error of intermixing Comic stuff with Tragic sadness and
gravity." During the civil war years, tragicomedy acquired a politics that
Milton obviously abhorred and eventually mocked. At the same time,
even if he equivocates in his *First Defense of the English People* on
whether Samson acts as a public or private man, "whether [he is]

prompted by God or by his own valor" (YP, 4:402), here and in *Eikonoklastes* Milton says explicitly that "*David* as a privat man," knowing that in such circumstances God never dispenses with his laws, "feard to lift his hand against the Lords Anointed" (YP, 3:587). In epistle and in poem, Milton loosens, then breaks the knot by which his adversaries, on account of his supposed lawlessness, alleged instinct for revenge, and seeming support for private vengeance, had bound him to Samson.

Samson as autobiographer sounds very different from Milton as a practitioner in the same genre—as different as Milton's adversaries sound from Milton himself as a polemicist, let us say in *The Second Defense*: "I shall not impute his death as a crime to him, as he imputed my blindness to me" (YP, 4:559). When he felt mighty in strength and was "Full of divine instinct," says Samson, and "after some proof / Of acts indeed heroic . . . / . . . , famous now and blaz'd, / Fearless of danger, like a petty God / I walk'd about admir'd of all and dreaded / On hostile ground, none daring my affront" (526–31). In the self-portraiture of *The Second Defense*, Milton presents himself, confidently yet modestly, as a gentler and wiser man: "I am not tall, but . . . closer to the medium than to the small. Yet what if it were small . . . ? (. . . why is that stature called small which is great enough for virtue?). . . Girded with my sword, as I generally was, I thought myself equal to anyone, though he was far more sturdy, and I was fearless of any injury that one man could inflict on another. Today I possess the same spirit, the same strength, but not the same eyes" (YP, 4:583). Others may have found, if only sarcastically, " 'a great hero . . .[in] a certain John Milton,' " prompting from Milton the humble acknowledgment that, whatever, "I did not realize that I was a hero" (YP, 4:607).

Rarely does it get mentioned (and Lieb is the most notable exception[95]) that Samson's volatile rhetoric finds its parallels not in Milton's attacks upon his opponents but rather in their attacks upon him. When More promises du Moulin's readers that they are about to witness Salmasius "tearing to pieces this disgrace [Milton] to the human race,"[96] he uses with reference to Milton the same language of intimidation Samson deploys against Dalila when she pleads, "Let me approach at least, and touch thy hand": "Not for thy life, lest fierce remembrance wake / My sudden rage to tear thee joint by joint" (951–53). When, in turn, du Moulin imagines Milton being "whirled . . . into the air" and, once felled, "bestrew[ing] the rocks far and wide with his shattered brains,"[97] he attacks Milton with the same language Samson hurls at Harapha: "Go baffl'd coward, lest I run upon thee . . . / . . . swing thee in the Air, then dash thee down / To th' hazard of thy brains and shatter'd sides" (1237, 1240–41).

More telling still are passages from 1 Corinthians 15:32 or 33 cited no less than five times by Milton, very importantly in his *Defense of Himself* (see also YP, 2:507–08; 6:403, 620, 751) and again in the Preface to *Samson Agonistes*—a passage that reinforces the point made in the first of the earlier examples:

> If after the manner of men I have fought with beasts at Ephesus, what advantageth it me, if the dead rise not? let us eat and drink; for tomorrow we die.
> Be not deceived: evil communications corrupt good manners.

In his *Defense of Himself*, Milton says of Alexander More:

> you wickedly attribute to yourself that glorious martyrdom of the Apostle when you say that you fought with beasts, . . . not as a man with a beast, but, yourself a beast, with a human being—that is, with a woman. (YP, 4:751)

That Samson who had earlier torn the lion as the lion tears the kid should address Dalila as a beast, then threaten to destroy her as earlier he had destroyed the lion, speaks volumes.

"Out, out *Hyæna*" (748), Samson rails, as he acknowledges learning from this woman the "Adders wisdom" (936) and as he now fears that, in a fit of "sudden rage," he will "tear . . .[Dalila] joint by joint" (953). When the Chorus (at Samson's prompting) describes Dalila as "a manifest Serpent" (997) and Samson, in his turn, calls her "a viper" (1001), Samson invites from us the very kind of rebuke that Milton delivers to More: you, Samson, are now fighting with beasts "not as a man with a beast, but, yourself a beast, with a human being—that is, with a woman." As if to reinforce this point, there are haunting moments in *Samson Agonistes* when, as Ann Baynes Coiro has brilliantly argued, "Dalila is the voice of Milton the Author."[98]

Both Milton's explicit rebuke of More, and implicit rebuff of Samson, recall an earlier one from *The Doctrine and Discipline of Divorce* aimed at any man who, in his perverse imaginings, turns "this bounty" of God's creation, women, into a stinging "Scorpion, either by weak and shallow constructions, or by proud arrogance and cruelty to them" (YP, 2:595–96). Here, of course, Milton is talking about bad husbands and good wives as opposed to what some think is the reverse situation in *Samson Agonistes*, although the complexity of this poem and the force of its interrogations, together with the stinging rhetoric of both Samson and the Chorus, allow for the questions of just how good a husband is Samson and how bad a wife is Dalila. Is she "the most bird-brained woman ever to have gotten herself involved in major tragedy" or, instead, "a deeply wronged wife"?[99] Milton, the so-called woman-hater, sometimes said to return to the fold by giving women their due in *Samson Agonistes*, by sleight of hand seems instead to be giving Samson his due even as he reminds us, yet again, that the author of a work is always distinguished from the characters he introduces. Well before Mikhail Bakhtin ever formulated the proposition, Milton in his poetry—not just in *Samson Agonistes* but in *Paradise Lost* and, earlier, in *Lycidas*—practiced it: "The author's consciousness is the consciousness of a consciousness . . . , a consciousness that *encompasses* the consciousness and the world of a hero. . . . . The author not only sees and knows everything seen and known by each hero . . . , but he also sees and knows *more* than they do"[100] and, in contrast with them, often thinks—and values—differently.

Milton's practice finds an analogy in Caravaggio's depiction of his own features on the head of Goliath held by David and thrust at the viewer by way of "inviting the spectator to read him."[101] One may read Caravaggio's features in the face of Goliath, Samson's in Harapha, and Milton's in Samson. In each projection, we observe versions of the selves of David, Samson, and Milton respectively—versions of the self sacrificed in each disfiguration, in each self-mutilation. If in Caravaggio's painting, we witness the decapitation of the artist, in *Samson Agonistes* we witness his death or, rather, the death of Milton's violent self, Milton's "repristination" not within, as Lieb argues,[102] but with the extirpation of a culture of violence that is as much the signature of Harapha as of Samson but no longer of Milton. If Lieb presents *Samson Agonistes* as "the expression of Milton's attempt to deal in poetic form with the crisis that faced him during the time the Defenses were produced," in the process turning both Samson and Milton from victim into victimizer and celebrating each in this transformation, my point is otherwise: *Samson Agonistes* mounts a critique of, it does not celebrate a culture of violence; it shows Milton embracing an ethical system to which Samson is a stranger, one trumpeting in poetry the lamentation and declaration of *Christian Doctrine*: "Violence alone prevails; and it is disgraceful and disgusting that the Christian religion should be supported by violence" (YP, 6:123).

The distinctions between Samson and Milton forced by the poem itself are maintained by the pairing of poems in the 1671 poetic volume, reminiscent of the wisdom (perhaps Milton's own?) articulated by

John Phillips: "He is not Christ's, but the devil's, deputy who does not imitate Christ's example."[103] And it is that example, thrust upon *Samson Agonistes* by virtue of the reference to *Christ Suffering* in the poem's epistle, that drives the final wedge between Samson and Milton; that uses differences implied by, or stated within, this epistle to underscore the differences emerging from the poem, with the epistle announcing itself as an apologia, this term explaining one function of the poem itself. In the prefatory epistle to *Samson Agonistes*, with its strong authorial presence, Milton emerges as an interpretive guide, with heroic drama here as in *Paradise Regain'd* affording a continuously relevant literary context for his work. But more important still, in this epistle, Milton invites us to ponder unexpected yokings like Euripides and Seneca, even more than Aeschylus and Sophocles, thus fixing our attention upon the former pair, both of whom have been, for most of the twentieth century, something of a forbidden context for *Samson Agonistes*. Through the examples of Euripides and Seneca, rather as the biblical redactors had done, Milton foregrounds and focuses contradictions instead of eliminating them, and promotes interrogation of scriptural stories instead of easy submission to inherited readings of them. In the end, he advances *Samson Agonistes* as a tragedy of both religious and political thinking, of Christian doctrine, of Royalist as well as Puritan ideology.

CONCLUSIONS, THEN INFERENCES

So what are we to conclude, what can we infer from these observations? *Conclusions first.* Milton emerges from his writings as a "plurality of egos"—in the words of Foucault, as a self that "fragments . . . into a plurality of possible positions and functions."[104] His self-portraits are, in one sense, like those of Pierre Bonnard: they blur. In another sense, they are much more like those paintings, not of himself, in which Bonnard asserts a presence: a knee juts from the frame into the space of the painting. *Only a knee.* Milton's presence in the prose writings, in which he appears as orator/preacher, is more palpable than his appearance, often as an actor, in his poems. In the first instance, Jacques Derrida, following Jean Jacques Rousseau, argues that when the orator/preacher "represents himself, . . . the representer and the represented are one." On the other hand, "the actor is born out of the rift between representer and represented":

> He signifies nothing. He barely lives, he lends his voice. It is a mouthpiece. Of course the difference between the orator or preacher and the

actor presupposes that the former does his duty, says what he has to say.[105]

In his *Defense of Himself*, Milton complicates such a distinction—complicates it enormously—by allowing himself to be placed in "the public theatre"; he then says "we have completed the fourth act of this drama," the "theatre" being a place where orators parry in debate and don different masks (YP, 4:781, 783). Paul Stevens states the case exactly:

> Even in his prose, when he most seems to be speaking in his own voice, and when he is most insistent on his identity and integrity, he says different things in different styles at different times to different people.[106]

Even in his prose writings wherein we witness (again in Stevens's words) "an accelerating plurality of different Miltons," Milton can be a masked presence. In the poetry, more often he is a hidden presence—someone who must be sought out in unexpected places, usually in shadows, fragments, or glimpses, seldom in full-blown portraits. Moreover, as early as *The Reason of Church-Government*, Milton indicates that, even if his more real self is evident in the prose writings, it may be an inferior self. In "this manner of writing," an effort of his "left hand," Milton admits to "knowing my self inferior to my self" (YP, 1:808), to revealing a real self that falls far short of the idealized self-portraits in the poetry.

The self that he is *is* inferior to the self that he aspires to be, except perhaps in *Of Christian Doctrine*, his "dearest and best possession" (YP, 6:121). What the Preface to *Samson Agonistes* establishes conclusively is that, at strategic junctures, the same mind-set producing it is evident in *Of Christian Doctrine* in which within a couple of pages, as we have seen, Milton invokes 1 Corinthians 15, then (as St. Paul had done) slides a passage from Euripides into his text in order to interpret the biblical passage and thereupon explains a biblical idiom with specific reference to the Samson story in Judges. No single citation but this collocation of the same three citations, both in *Christian Doctrine* and in the Preface to *Samson Agonistes*, is sufficiently distinctive of Milton as to indicate that the same hand that wrote the preface to Milton's poem is evident, powerfully so, in *Of Christian Doctrine*, Book 1, Chapter 13. Paradoxically, the work that, because of its superabundance of proof texts and the imitative character of its genre, would seem most to obscure Milton's presence is the work, finally, in which the real Milton most fully, and intriguingly, stands up. For this reason (above all others), the current practice of looting Milton's canon and expelling this work from it is bound to result in the loss of Milton himself, certainly a substantial part of him, and in a new sequestration of this author just as he is in process of being unbound as a poet and reclaimed as a polemicist/politician/theologian. From Milton, as much as from Adam and Eve, flows a "prompt eloquence/ . . . in Prose or numerous Verse" (5.149–50). Milton's left hand is sometimes as adept as his right.

Now for the inferences. We must do more than just ask: where is Milton the author to be found? For, this question typically leads to another: what specifically is *Milton's* function as an author? That is, we need to know what is at stake in authorship, especially when some in Milton studies are now in a phase of denying Milton's authorship of *Christian Doctrine*, thus refashioning not only *the* canon of English literature but Milton's place therein, in the process turning a poet of liberty into one tyrannized by our own craving for certainties and by our own comforting orthodoxies. If we are going to deny Milton authorship of *Christian Doctrine* on the grounds that his radicalism here does not easily conform to the supposed orthodoxies of his last poems, that Milton's so-called "*genuine* ideas are at odds with those" in *De Doctrina*—a work that we are then told makes Milton "the most incoherent thinker in history"[107]—we will necessarily reduce Milton's status from one who, besides authoring books, fashioned a whole tradition of understanding as he altered received readings of the Creation and Fall stories, as well as those of Jesus tempted and Samson triumphant. We will, that is, starch Milton into conformity with the very traditions he resists and, in the act of denying *Of Christian Doctrine* as a context for his last poems, hinder and crop the discovery of the nineteenth century that sheds so much light on the poems of the seventeenth century. Indeed, the very same arguments made in our own time by William B. Hunter were made in the nineteenth century, in the immediate aftermath of the publication of *Christian Doctrine*. Thus Joseph Ivimey, believing that this tract and Milton's poems are "utterly at variance," allowed as how he "certainly" would "be pleased, could any one furnish irrefragable evidence that the manuscript entitled, 'Tractate of Christian Doctrine,' was not written by the eminent man whose '*superscription*' but not whose '*image*,' is stamped upon it."[108] Milton's status as transformational author, creating his own traditions, then using them as provocations for individual expression and as incitements for the formation of whole schools of criticism—this Milton is put at risk when, as an author of many books, he becomes, because some cannot recognize him in *Of Christian Doctrine*, the author of one less book.

After all, it is not as if, once this theological treatise was discovered and published, there were no readers ready to say they found Milton in it; who would not echo the words of Milton's daughter: "I see him! 'tis Him! . . .' tis the very Man!"[109] Discontinuities, inconsistencies, eccentric theories; discrepancies and contradictions; modifications of earlier thinking, regular revision of it, refinements, as well as striking out in new directions—these features are not menacing to authorship, much less denials of it, but evidence of a life in motion and of a mind on the stretch. These features are the badge of an inquiring spirit, the trademarks not of every author but of Milton as an author. Milton at odds with Milton, this text vying with that one, fissures within texts—surely these are not arguments against but signs of Milton's author-ship; of his lifelong project of engendering controversy through which, as he explains in *Of True Religion*, "Senses [are] awakt, . . . Judgement [is] sharpn'd, and the truth . . . more firmly establish't" (YP, 8:437–38).

Milton's aesthetic, in prose works and poetry alike, is derivative from Scripture and, as understood and practiced in the seventeenth century, was founded upon disputation and enquiry. Then, as now, there was a "crisis of meaning" emanating from a fear, not shared by Milton, but very much in the air today, that a "maelstrom" of knowledge—its vying factors and data, its arrayed theories, each ges-turing toward a different and differently nuanced meaning—serves only "to aggravate . . . radical doubt," which, in its turn, leads to "skepticism, indifference or to various forms of nihilism." Milton seems to be saying: when contradiction contradicts itself out of exis-tence, or is displaced by "the principle of noncontradiction," when "dialectical structures" of truth—what the Milton of *Areopagitica* calls "the wars of Truth" (YP, 2:562)—wither into what Pope John Paul II once described as "the unity of truth," then the *truths* of poetry get overrun and overruled by the truth of religion.[110] In such moments, Milton's (as well as our) steady, unstoppable search for truth, if not completely halted, is severely impeded as opposing ways of interpreting the world and human life get lost.

The effect of Milton's authorial maneuverings is to problematize both Scripture and its interpretive traditions, as well as *Paradise Lost*. What we can say—now only provisionally and perhaps never with full certainty—is that Milton means to remind us that his entire poem is the product of a fallen, though not necessarily, false consciousness; that what always seems to falsify consciousness, especially fallen con-sciousness, is its propensity for taking the part for the whole, an improved interpretation (Copernicus's over Ptolemy's, let us say) for the final truth. Indeed, this centering of cosmological theory and dispute in *Paradise Lost* is one of many conspicuous signals that this poem is about what it relates: competing interpretations, the status that should be accorded to each of them, their respective truth-claims and truth-values. *Paradise Lost* is a poem in which a sun-centered cosmology upholds a Christocentric (son-centered) theology—is a poem that out of such interdependency creates what another theologian will call a "science of salvation" wherein Jesus, as both "the true center of the world, and . . . the sun of our souls," subtends a heliocentric astronomy and a theocentric religion.[111] Milton's exceptional education included, as Toni Morrison says of William Dunbar, "the latest thought on theology and science" with a poem like *Paradise Lost* representing Milton's effort, again like Dunbar's, to make theology and science "mutually accountable, to make one support the other."[112]

Milton's foregrounding of contending cosmological theories is, in fact, doubly interesting in as much as this discourse is wedged between two competing Genesis accounts of Creation in what (if now two books) were in the first edition of *Paradise Lost* one book, and in such a way that the lesson drawn from cosmological discourse may be applied to the Creation myth and its interpretive traditions: competing interpretations complicate truth, thereby illustrating the deconstructionist proposition (even as they reject its underlying philosophical skepticism) that "there is a way of thinking about truth which is more adventurous, risky. And at that point, truth, which is without end, abyssal, is the very movement of the drift. There is a way of thinking about truth which is not reassuring, . . . bring[ing] us into a discourse about the truth of truth . . . ; the field is open"[113]—perhaps more in matters of cosmology than in human affairs. In *Paradise Lost*, the one discourse sits in irresolution while the other moves toward resolution.

Books 7 and 8 are a lesson in how "truth" in *Paradise Lost* is processive, in how "resolution" is achieved through gradually unfolding revelation. In Milton's poem no less than in its sourcebook, different accounts of Creation complete but also compete with one another; and the point is reinforced by the further analogy that what comes first in chronological sequence both in the Bible and in Milton's poem, through narrative scrambling, actually appears last. Thus Jonathan Richardson and his son accurately remark, in annotating Book 8.478, that "Here is the First of *Eve*'s History, which is Compleated by what she says to *Adam*" in Book 4.[114] Completed *yes*, but also complicated. And the complications invariably derive from Milton's artistic strategy, so ably described by Richard Corum, of "writing all these narratives simultaneously" and of writing them in such a way that he "leave[s] out not only large segments of each of them but also the temporal, spatial, and generic markers which would allow us to separate them into distinct stories."[115] That is, what may seem separate, discrete panels of narrative continually elide with one another and thus become interdependent elements in interpretation. Still, some narrative panels conciliate, while others collide. The accounts of Creation by Uriel and Raphael exhibit concord whereas those by Raphael and Adam are at odds.

For a poet who can imagine a "bottomless deep" (as Milton does in *Paradise Regain'd*, 1.361, having in *Paradise Lost* already created the "*Vacuum*" of an unfathomable one), where there is "no end of falling,"[116] the very notions of "truth" and "resolution" are likely to be problematical. A poem that everywhere champions moral and political freedom emblematizes both, if we can borrow Stanley Rosen's reasoning, in "the freedom to choose or to reject the Copernican revolution," a main consequence of which, as Milton seems to have understood, was "to transform science into a *fiction* in the literal sense: something not simply arranged but *formed* by human intelligence" whose "truth" therefore is contingent, perspectival. A poem inset with analogies, and in its middle repeatedly testing the divine analogy—whether things on earth correspond with things as they are in heaven—*Paradise Lost* focuses this matter in Books 7 and 8 by running scientific debate between discrepant accounts of Creation, thus analogizing science and religion and thereupon integrating both into fictions, as if to make the point that cosmological theory is, as Rosen remarks of another intellectual revolution, "a radicalized version of the theological problem of the proliferation of sects"; as if to say, as Rosen does, that "whereas there may be one comprehensive truth, there is no single *interpretation* of the truth."[117]

Witness these various formulations of an interpretive problem attendant upon the divine analogy in *Paradise Lost*, each new formulation modifying the other: "what if Earth / Be but the shaddow of Heav'n, and things therein / Each t' other like, more then on earth is thought?" (5.574–76); "who, though with the tongue / Of Angels, can relate, or to what things / Liken on Earth conspicuous, that may lift / Human imagination to such highth / Of Godlike Power?" (6.297–301); "measuring things in Heav'n by things on Earth / . . . that thou maist [know]" the one by the other (6.893–94), if indeed one can know the other at all; "O Earth, how like to Heav'n, if not preferr'd / More justly, Seat worthier of Gods, as built / With second thoughts, reforming what was old! / For what God after better worse would build?" (9.99–102). Questions about whether one can know enough about heaven to make the divine analogy at all meaningful modulate into surmises about whether heaven or earth is the privileged term in the comparison, with Raphael, the narrator, and finally Satan addressing the same issues but reaching decidely different conclusions about them. Not always discoredant though, the voices of Raphael, the narrator, Adam, and Satan sometimes sound strikingly alike and yet decidedly unlike the voices of God and Eve, thus raising the still nagging question: whose is the authoritative voice in this poem? As Walter Clyde Curry says of the voices of Uriel and Raphael: their different accounts of the same episode in *Paradise Lost* are "respectively fragmentary, sometimes hazy, and . . . incomplete," each one lacking "something in the way of completeness, order, and clarity."[118]

Milton's own views, spelled out as early as *Areopagitica*, are deeply engraved in *Paradise Lost:*

> Truth indeed came once into the world with her divine Master, and was a perfect shape most glorious to look on: but when he ascended, and his Apostles after him were laid asleep, then strait arose a wicked race of deceivers, who as that story goes of the *Ægyptian Typhon* with his conspirators, how they dealt with the good *Osiris*, took the Virgin Truth, hewd her lovely form into a thousand peeces, and scatter'd them to the four winds. From that time ever since, the sad friends of Truth, such as durst appear, imitating the carefull search that *Isis* made for the mangl'd body of *Osiris*, went up and down gathering up limb by limb still as they could find them. We have not found them all, . . . nor ever shall doe, till her Masters second comming; he shall bring together every joynt and member, and shall mould them into an immortal feature of lovelinesse and perfection.

"We boast our light," Milton concludes, "but if we look not wisely on the Sun it self, it smites us into darkness" (2:549–50). It may be a union of he/she (author and "Virgin Truth") that allows for the reconstitution of truth here, but the same kind of union—and reconstitution—is sought in *Paradise Lost* by a poet (masculine) who hopes to be joined by "Eternal Wisdom" (feminine) so that his song may be more than an "empty dream" (7.1–39).[119] In the very process, the poet must separate the true from the false feminine, eternal wisdom from empty dream, in books wherein we are forced to look upon the Sun/Son, albeit "wisely."

The radical implications of such a view—that truth is processive, hence always partial—are objectified in cosmological debate but also dramatized within Scripture by the warring hermeneutics encamped around Genesis 1 and 2 and within *Paradise Lost* by the competing versions of Creation proffered by Raphael and Adam. Interestingly, those implications show up only to be suppressed in early commentary on *Paradise Lost*. In a poem that hides so much contemporary history within its master-myth, it is remarkable, only because such instances are so rare, that conspicuous allusions to Galileo (1.287–89, 5.261–63) and Copernicus should balance one another in the two halves of Milton's epic. It is also ironic that two figures experiencing and thus emblematizing censorship should then become occasions for a censorship of sorts within critical commentary. The irony is compounded when we remember that, in the Prologue to Book 7, Milton comes closest to openly addressing his own fears of censorship—"fall'n on evil dayes, / . . . and evil tongues; / . . . with dangers compast round" (25–27), even as he now identifies his muse as *"Urania"* (1) who had given her name to a work by Lady Mary Wroth that had recently been caught up in a scandal of censorship.[120]

Patrick Hume's annotation is curt: *"Copernicus* his Opinion, tho first broach'd by *Pythagoras* and *Aristarchus."*[121] Jonathan Richardson and his son are more expansive, but then their elaboration is all the more curious because it is situated within the context of an open acknowledgment that Milton labors under the "Secret History" of censorship. Indeed, their elaboration is doubly curious inasmuch as it forces the Richardsons to surrender one of their principal critical strategies, that of eradicating contradictions on the surface of Milton's poem by privileging the voice of this or that speaker therein, Raphael's over Adam's let us say. In order to keep *Paradise Lost* remote from its contemporary scene, from any notion of progressive truth or philosophical irresolution, the Richardsons declare flatly that Milton's poem is geocentric even if this theory is voiced by Adam and later Satan while its heliocentric counterpart is formulated by Raphael. The Richardsons are emphatic: Raphael, despite the fact that *he* is the mouthpiece for Copernican theory, is an ancient not a modern and certainly no Sir Isaac Newton. That, they say, "would have been Ridiculous": what is new in cosmology, though not forgotten in Milton's poem, "could not be a part of its System."[122] The argument here is so tendentious that it constitutes a tear in the text of the commentary and is, one supposes, intended to hide something: not just that Milton's system is conflicted, not just its philosophic irresolution, but the very uses to which Milton puts such knowledge by deploying a theory of science to gloss the Creation story of religion, even to subtend the poem's Christocentric theology, and to mediate, at the same time, another problem of the "modern" world, the relationship between the sexes.

It is odd that Milton makes no mention of Tycho Brahe. It is so odd that one wonders if it is not just this mediatorial role, assumed by Brahe in the world of science, that Milton here assumes in matters of religion where he must mediate between two conflicting Genesis accounts, the second probably preceding the first in order of time. One wonders, too, if Brahe does not provide Milton with the hidden logic by which he will eventually privilege Genesis 1 over 2. Brahe had been used to maintain the validity of both Ptolemaic and Copernican theory by arguing that the former pertains to the world before the Fall, the latter to the world afterward. The same sort of logic had been used by biblical commentators to ratify the competing accounts of Creation in Genesis: Genesis 1, coming first in the order of narrative but last in the order of time, depicts the equality of the sexes before the Fall but lost when Paradise is lost; and Genesis 2, the subjection of woman that pertains to fallen existence.

Milton's accommodation of the two texts is altogether more slippery and, with reference to each text, is perspectival: how things were and how they should have been, how things now are and how they will be—or ought to be. Genesis 1, encapsulating an idealism, envisions a mutuality of the sexes under the paternal rule of God; and Genesis 2, displaying the sad reality, explains the relationship of the sexes as owing to Adam's psychology and Satan's pathology. Genesis 2 reflects the unequal relationship of the sexes, woman under man's subjection, that has pertained in fallen history and Genesis 1, the realized equality of the sexes just before Mankind's expulsion from the Garden and the equality to be achieved before the Kingdom of God can commence in history. Milton makes the point adroitly when he speaks of "*Hesperian* Fables true, / If true, here only" (4.250–51), thus insisting upon the contingency of truth.

Milton's compromise solution, that is, can best be understood in analogy with that of Brahe: both change the state of knowledge and alter interpretation by posing problems that, challenging conventional solutions (sometimes only obliquely), effect a break with tradition. Milton's commitment to ongoing revelation makes space for mutating thought and evolving explanations—for the correction of error through the refinement of observation. In his mapping of gender discourses, Milton the theorist seems always to outrun and overrule the traditions, and traditional explanations, he contemplates, in the process appropriating innovations (not always his own) and through them casting such discourses into a distinctly modern form. Milton does not claim to have presented through his concatenated discourses *the* truth but does imply that, because they are more reliable, his observations, along with the interpretations founded upon them, provide readier access to the complete truth.

Competing accounts of Creation (and of much else) in *Paradise Lost* are thus indicators of different states and stages of consciousness—fallen and unfallen, villainous and visionary. It matters that in Book 4 Adam intuits the Genesis 1 account that later, in discursive argument, gets displaced by his own distorting elaboration of Genesis 2. This displacement occurs, a new fiction is created, in just that moment when it behooves Adam to be self-serving. Correspondingly, it matters, again in Book 4, that Satan stumbles into "the truth" of the Genesis 1 account but, more usually, occupies the interpretive space and spouts the interpretive commonplaces of Genesis 2: that Adam is "rais'd / From dust" (9.177–78) and that Eve is the lesser, Adam the "higher" intelligence and "Heroic" figure (9.483, 485). Or to be more delicate still, Milton revises existing explanations, both of cosmology and creation, while holding all such speculation within the realm of hypothesis, thus keeping certain forms of truth tentative. In this poem, with its plentitude of speculation and so replete with theorization, Milton fixes limits on both as he allows for, even urges, concern over conditions and degrees not in other worlds but in this one. The appropriate end of Adam's questioning (and of ours), as he himself perceives, is not a searching of God's "secrets," but acquistion of knowledge: "the more / To magnifie his works, the more we know" (7.95–97). Where there is—or should be—rejoicing on Adam's part is in *this* world, *this* paradise, and in his fair *Eve*.

Some contradictions may achieve resolution in *Paradise Lost*, but not all do, as is befitting a poetic universe that is large, that contains multitudes; that through contradictions subverts all claims to dogmatic certitude both in religion and science; that, as in *Of Christian Doctrine*, values ongoing revelation and multiple possible interpretations over a reading that is certifiably correct. Books 7 and 8 treat contending scientific theories, conflicting religious myths as fictions to contemplate and, if not certifying this rather than that one, nevertheless privilege one over another; and what often gets privileged in this poem are those revelations that come later, if not in order of narrative, certainly in order of time. Contradictions and inconsistencies may effect alarming dislocation in theological but not in poetic systems where the possibilities are completely open, and an utterance may be true or false relatively. The Richardsons understood that "*Milton* is Writing a Poem, not a System of Divinity or Philosophy," but also expected an analogous consistency in Milton's poetical system, the very sort of consistency from which, alas, the poet was now breaking free.[123] What the Richardsons do not understand, as Terry Eagleton informs us in a more generalized context, is that in a poem like *Paradise Lost* "coherence . . .[may be] nothing less than . . . systematic contradiction."[124]

Milton's own rebellious writings, one of which and the dearest of which, is *Of Christian Doctrine*, invite us to read rebelliously: to scrutinize theological no less than scientific and political systems; to sift and winnow and puzzle out beliefs for ourselves; in free discussion, to move against certain conventional opinions, to study sites of conflict and controversy, and, in the process, to wipe away superstition and tyranny both from those systems and from the minds they manacle. If we remember these words as constituting Milton's agenda in *Of Christian Doctrine*, a work that resists both spiritual arrogance and religious dogmatism we may then experience a dawning awareness of what is at stake in denying Milton authorship of the work and, as a consequence thereof, denying Milton's readers this crucial context for his later poems.

Names of authors signify; they are both "description and designation." Hence, as Foucault explains, someone's "disclosure that . . . Shakespeare had not written the sonnets . . . we attribute to him . . . would constitute a significant change and affect the manner in which the author's name functions."[125] Let there be no mistake about it: the same is true, the consequences would be similar, were we now to dislodge *Of Christian Doctrine*—"an identity sign of major importance"[126]—from Milton's canon. Milton as speculative theologian, creating a new system that would deliver us from existing systems—this Milton, a sect of one—would be removed from the landscape of cultural history, its removal modifying that landscape significantly. If the orator's voice gives us a more authentic voice than that of the poet, if an image of Milton emerges from the prose writings in greater clarity and with more certainty, then to deny Milton authorship of *Christian Doctrine* is to rid the world of Milton's heterodoxy, as we exchange the relatively authentic voice of the orator for the fictions and occasional subterfuges of the poet.

If we are going to deny Milton's authorship of *Christian Doctrine* now because the treatise shuns the millenarianism of the early prose works, because its apocalypticism is so much tamer than in *Of Reformation, Areopagitica,* and *Eikonoklastes,* and now because *Of Christian Doctrine* is not easily brought into conformity with the last poems,[127] because its radicalism does not match with their supposed orthodoxy, we should confess immediately that we are privileging what in fact may not exist, an *unchanging* mind, and simultaneously banishing from Milton's canon the work that best evidences the writer's mind in transition. In the same breath, we should acknowledge that a logical extension of the practice of embedding contradictions within a work is to put them at play between works even as we, first, wonder whether Milton's deferral of an apocalypse in history is really a denial of it, whether revisions of apocalyptic thinking should be construed so easily as rejections of millenarianism, and then ask just how conforming to orthodoxies Milton's last poems really are, how much time elapsed before they were so perceived and why *eventually* they were thus understood. What was, what continues to be at stake?

As the eye alters it may find congruence where some see only contradiction; and where there is contradiction, real not feigned, it may be more aptly explained as a staple of the scriptural books, as an aspect of their poetics, hence as a predictable element in any secular Scripture (like Milton's) informed by a poetics that says, in effect, *if you ask no questions you receive no answers.* As Euripides was wont to say: where there are answers, "They manifest themselves in unpredictable ways. / What we most expect / does not happen" as "for the least expected [things] / God finds a way."[128] Or as the poet of *Christ Suffering* will say, echoing Euripides: "God dispenses unexpected things / And often accomplishes what could not be hoped / And things which seemed inevitable do not happen" (1130–32). The answers themselves may be tentative, inconclusive, which is but to say that it is the questions, and our continuing to ask them, that really matter. In these assertions, Euripides and the poet of *Christ Suffering* help to formulate what will likely emerge as the distinctive features of a revitalized Milton criticism, which comes to appreciate *Samson Agonistes*, for example, not as a spiritual triumph but a mental agon; not as a tragedy with a fortunate outcome but one readying mankind for reversals of fortune even as it gestures toward a world of new possibilities—a world, as Alfred Kazin might have said, that finally does away with tragedy; that, running deeper than tragedy, would extirpate it from history.[129]

CHAPTER 2

HORIZONS OF EXPECTATIONS: REPRESSIONS, RECEPTIONS, AND THE POLITICS OF MILTON'S LAST POEMS

Nowhere does a concern for the reception of a work of art or of an artform aver itself fruitful for its understanding. . . . No poem is addressed to a reader, no painting to its beholder, no symphony to its listeners.

—Walter Benjamin

In the triangle of author, work, and public the last is no passive part, no chain of mere reactions, but rather itself an energy formative of history. The historical life of a literary work is unthinkable without the active participation of its addressees. For it is only through the process of its mediation that the work enters into the changing horizon-of-experience of a continuity in which the perpetual inversion occurs from simple reception to critical understanding, from passive to active reception, from recognized aesthetic norms to a new production that surpasses them. The historicity of literature as well as its communicative character presupposes a dialogical and at once processlike relationship between work, audience, and new work that can be conceived in the relations between message and receiver as well as between question and answer, problem and solution.

—Hans Robert Jauss[1]

Invoking an horizon of expectations for a literary text involves determining whether it conforms to—or defies—those expectations, whether it confirms or frustrates them. If there is an ideological bias, it becomes evident when Hans Robert Jauss differentiates between art with a conservative and art with a revolutionary temperament, the former favoring the status quo and the latter seeking emancipation from it—a distinction Jauss himself will use to distinguish literature of the popular culture from that with canonical status. Given Milton's distinctive place in the two cultures, even sometimes the inversion of his expected position, Milton should become a key figure in a study of canonical authors and their sometimes complicated relations with both high- and low- brow culture. Yet behind these qualitative judgments are matters more basic: how to determine an horizon of expectations, in the first place? How to decipher literary norms and values, as well as socio-political-religious attitudes and aspirations within a cultural moment? From these questions emerge still more teasing ones: what is the prevailing image and idea of the author? What is his reputation as person? As artist? How are the writings valued, both by their author and their audiences? Is there overlap or discrepancy between self-representations and representations by others, between an author's valuations of his work and evaluations by others? What are the genres in which those writings are cast, all of which have (as William Empson has taught us) "a rough world-view"[2]—or ideology, and each of which is less a fixed form than an evolving tradition and as valuably examined in a diachronic series as a synchronic cluster? Other works on the same topic, addressing the same questions, even if answering them differently, may prove especially revealing so that, with the example of *Paradise Lost* for instance, if with Jauss we regard it as a poetic commentary on, contradiction of, and supplement to Genesis,[3] then we may wish to read it in relation to other such commentaries belonging to the same cultural moment even as we ask whether Milton is in step with, in advance of, or lagging behind thinking in his own time.

Where there are overlaps, intersections, and transgressions of commonplace interpretations, the crucial question becomes: what is the artistic project—containment or subversion? Is the objective to uphold or resist the dominant culture—its norms and values? Such questions prove inseparable from those that Milton's poems themselves ask—poems that, always brimming over with questions, in the progress from *Paradise Lost* to *Samson Agonistes*, become increasingly interrogative and poems that in their interrogations, however rhetorical and catechetical initially, become progressively more probing—more impudent. What could be more catechetical than the question with which the narrative proper opens in *Paradise Lost*: "what cause / Mov'd our Grand Parents . . . / . . . to fall off / From thir Creator . . ."? and

"Who first seduc'd them to that foul revolt?" (1.28–31, 33) Or what could be less catechetical than this poem's ultimate question: "for on Earth / Who against Faith and Conscience can be heard / Infallible?" (12.528–30) And similarly in *Samson Agonistes*: what more catechetical than "O wherefore was my birth from Heav'n foretold / Twice by an Angel" (23–24)?—and what less so than "what cause / Brought him so soon at variance with himself" (1584–85)? Or, for that matter, what could be less catechetical than the concluding question of *Paradise Regain'd*—"What dost thou in this World" (4.372)?—an old question from which, like all the others in his last poems, Milton coaxes new answers.

WHAT MOVED MILTON?

Start with the title page to the first edition of *Paradise Lost*—its five separate states and two variants—and with what Jerome McGann calls "radial reading," or active reading, which involves deciphering bibliographical codes and which, as "a function of the historicity of texts," investigates their reception history.[4] That history, in turn, as it gathers into focus alternative readings of a text, may also reveal its conflicting commitments, its multiple and sometimes competing contexts, its surface as well as hidden content, its silences, its invisible features. Not just the poem but what surrounds it gives access to its meanings: the ceremonies and protocols of title pages and preliminary material, the use of italics and capitalization, of different type fonts and sizes, of generic and stanzaic forms, of rhyme schemes or the lack thereof. Rhyme schemes sometimes function as generic signals, or markers; and, rhyme, itself dogged by controversy, in Milton's time was irrevocably involved with politics of which the poet's note on his verse is striking evidence.

We need to read both "before" and "after," as well as "between," the lines of a poem, while remembering that protocols of printing, beginning with the title page, can establish unexpected and sometimes peculiar inflections as when, for example, a period is added after "Books" in the last four issues of the first edition of *Paradise Lost*, thus making "**a POEM** IN TEN BOOKS." (with period added, and diminished caps) a separately marked unit that, by virtue of type size and boldfacing, in its prominence overrides the poem's title, "Paradise lost," and even its designated ten-book structure. In short, this poem's formulaic subtitle, "A POEM IN . . . BOOKS," gives to *Paradise Lost* the broadest possible literary categorization. It is *A Poem*, period. But perhaps the most striking feature of all on the title page, once its various elements are put in perspective, is the emphasis accorded "Paradise" by virtue of its (and not "lost") being capitalized. Nor is "lost" capitalized in the running heads for each page of each book of *Paradise Lost*.[5] For a long time, a cliché of Romantic criticism had it that Milton emphasizes the loss of paradise, the Romantics its recovery—a cliché that is effectively challenged when the title pages to the first editions of *Paradise Lost* and *Paradise Regain'd* are set side by side: **Paradise lost / PARADISE REGAIN'D**. While "lost" (without a cap) is diminished, "Regain'd" is enhanced in importance by virtue of its appearance in distinctly larger type than "Paradise." In analogy (and more recently) one is reminded of Toni Morrison fussing over the last word (paradise) of her novel (*Paradise*), the last word, she instructed an unobserving printer, to be printed with a lower case "p." Subsequent printings of her novel, however, observe that injunction.

Milton's subtitle to *Paradise Lost* (did Toni Morrison remember that it initially appeared as *Paradise lost?*) also anticipates an important emphasis and focus. The word "Book" will appear on every page of this poetic text conveniently reminding us of the book's materiality, of the poem fulfilling the poet's idea in *Areopagitica* of "a good Booke" as "the pretious life-blood of a master spirit" (YP, 2:493). The marked endings of each book— "*The End of the First Book*"[6] and so on, as well as the marked conclusion of the poem, "THE END"—are clogs in the narrative, forced stops, which in conjunction impart to *Paradise Lost* a powerful sense of an ending and which, together with other still points in the poem, force its readers into contemplation and reflection. In "The Verse," Milton may promise a poem in which "the sense [is] variously drawn out from one Verse into another" ([a4]),[7] and then from book to book; but with ruptures within and between some books, Milton creates impediments to his announced design, with commentary interrupting the narrative and impeding its flow and with enforced closure at the end of most books imposing unexpected "stops," readers thus bridled before they can press forward, but also stopped in their tracks by the obstructive bulk of the longest books in the poem: the 1290 lines of Book 7 and the 1540 (actually 1541) lines of Book 10.[8] In this way, Milton follows, even outdoes, Spenser in putting brakes on the fast pace of epic narrative; and yet this practice of a forced stop, of emphatic closure, goes back to the 1645 publication of *Lycidas*. Nowhere in Milton's poetry is an ending more boldly marked than here where there are two rows of fifteen stamps, an "E" between them (see figure 2.8), one effect of which is to take two poems, *Lycidas* and *A Mask*, poems seemingly rivaling one another, and then by relegating *A Mask* to an appendix, subordinating

(65)

Thus fang the uncouth Swain to th'Okes and rills,
While the ftill morn went out with Sandals gray,
He touch'd the tender ftops of various Quills,
With eager thought warbling his *Dorick* lay :
And now the Sun had ftretch'd out all the hills,
And now was dropt into the Weftern bay ;
At laft he rofe, and twitch'd his Mantle blew :
To morrow to frefh Woods, and Paftures new,

E

Figure 2.8 The Marked Ending of *Poems of Mr. John Milton* (1675)

it in importance to *Lycidas*. The point is then reinforced years later by the Contents page to the 1673 *Poems*, both by type size and by type facing: **LYCIDAS** versus *A MASK*.

Initially, we learn nothing at all about the generic identity of *Paradise Lost*, its aspirations or castings, only that it will participate in the relative obscurity of poetry, although in "The Verse" we are apprised of Milton's invention, "*English* Heroic Verse without Rime," of its precedents in both "some . . . *Italian* and *Spanish* Poets of prime note" and "our best *English* Tragedies," before we encounter an open declaration of *Paradise Lost* as an "Heroic Poem" ([a3v–a4]). Yet we can also infer from the coupling of title and subtitle that we are about to encounter a religious poem, not a theological tract—a secular Scripture, so to speak—and from attention given to this poem's rhymelessness, suspect, too, that this heroic poem (in its studied disorder and gestures of rebellion) will be cast as a prophecy. Indeed, in its very rhymelessness, *Paradise Lost* resists a chief signature of false prophecy: both the false prophet, that "vast rabble of rhyming, clinching, versing Prophets"; and the badge of false prophecy, that "*tinkling cimbal* . . . sound in the ear," which would, it was said in 1665, "rather inchant the mind then inform it."[9]

Rather, in keeping with the understanding that the words of true prophecy "come without forcing,"[10] thus resembling the natural movements of the mind and the soul, Milton says of his "unpremeditated Verse" (8.24) that its "sense" will be "variously drawn out" from verse paragraph to verse paragraph ([a4]) and, by implication, from book to book of his poem. That is, his verse will burst the boundaries created by rhyme; and books, breaking through arbitrary barriers, will spill into one another. Milton's poetry, deriving from "nightly visitation[s] unimplor'd" (8.22), will resemble nearest those scriptural works of "an exalted Imagination," in the very process putting on display what Milton's same contemporary of 1665, John Spencer, claims was no longer evident in aspiring prophets, the gift of interpreting Scriptures anew, of snatching from them a new revelation. The scriptural revisionism evident in Milton's last poems (*Paradise Lost, Paradise Regain'd*, and *Samson Agonistes*) makes a contrary point, with thunder—and then one: that in the words of Spencer again, prophecy "doth raise in a man a more fine and exquisite power of perception";[11] that it engenders "*more and more perceiving*" ([a2v]) in a poem in which, in Joycean fashion, light increasingly trembles on the horizon of the mind. It is a point that Milton makes here but that he had also made in *Areopagitica* in which "our apprehensions" are said to be "enlarg'd and lifted up . . .[by] degrees" (YP, 2:559) and God is said to enlighten by "steps"—"to dispense and deal out by degrees his beam, so as our earthly eyes may best sustain it" (YP, 2:566).

Milton's titles for his epic-prophecies remind us, moreover, that such captions are words about, and only sometimes words from, a poem until in the examples afforded by *Paradise Lost* and *Paradise Regain'd* both titles are encapsulated within words from the latter poem: "The Son of God . . . / . . . hast *regain'd lost Paradise*" (4.602, 608; my italics). Furthermore, whether the title imparts generic identity or denotes subject matter, it builds expectations, which may be met, surpassed, or broken, as when *Paradise Lost* becomes a poem equally about the recovery of paradise; or as when *Paradise Regain'd* dashes expectations for a poem about the Crucifixion, replacing the expected story of Christ's passion with the wilderness temptations and declaring of them, "A fairer Paradise is founded *now*" (4.613; my italics). It seems as if the space of Milton's titles is continually being invaded by interrogations that challenge rather than meet expectations, which, in *Paradise Lost* the poem surpasses and in *Paradise Regain'd* disappoints, even as the paired titles seem to promise that these poems will always echo one another's songs.

Indeed, Milton's revision of the initial five lines for what is now Book 12, including "the world destroy'd and world restor'd" (12.3), establishes a neat juxtaposition, and thereby reinforces the parallelism with the first five lines of the initial book of the poem: "Of Mans First Disobedience, and . . . / . . . loss of *Eden*, till one greater Man / Restore us, and regain the blissful Seat" (1.1–5). From 1671 onward, when *Paradise Regain'd* was published with *Samson Agonistes*, it is impossible for knowing readers of Milton not to think of his two epics in conjunction, as the twin halves of one vast design. In the Dublin edition of 1724, that linkage is secured as *Paradise Regain'd*, until now paired with *Samson Agonistes*, is on this occasion published as a companion to *Paradise Lost*.[12] This new linkage is ballast for the irony harbored within the initial lines of *Paradise Regain'd*, their echo of Virgil's proclamation (probably written for the *Aeneid* but later excised from it) in which he bids farewell to pastoral poetry as he moves beyond it. Like Virgil, Milton pushes beyond his earlier poetry, including *Paradise Lost*, by establishing radically new norms for heroic deeds and epic heroism as, in *Paradise Regain'd*, he sings of "deeds / *Above* Heroic" (1.14–15; my italics).

In the case of *Paradise Lost*, the first edition holds clues to an original horizon of expectations, and subsequent editions provide evidence of horizonal shifts, some of which are doubtless owing to Milton's recasting of epic and radicalizing of his theology in *Paradise Regain'd*, as well as the inevitable intertwinings of his epic poems with his earlier prose writings. Jonathan Richardson, Sr., makes a crucial point with brutal honesty: " 'tis Remembred *Paradise Lost* was not yet produc'd, and the Writings on which his Vast Reputation Stood were Now Accounted Criminal, Every One of them, and Those Most which were the Main Pillars of his Fame"[13]—that is, *Eikonoklastes* and the two Defenses of the English People. The history of any one of Milton's works, but especially of *Paradise Lost*, harbors this or that "Secret History" (the phrase is Richardson's);[14] and that history, once set forth, makes clear that *Paradise Lost* as a book is "less a product," in the words of Stephen Orgel, "than a process, part of an ongoing dialectic."[15]

Indeed, the history of Milton's diffuse epic includes stories of imitations, adaptations, and appropriations, of translations and of transposings of rhymeless into rhymed verse, of poetry into prose, with early maskings of Milton's poetic content inviting later unmaskings and, with them, the revival of old arguments over whether Milton was a heretic or whether, instead, all those seemingly heterodox moments in Milton's epic are, as Richardson himself conjectured, "very Capable of an Orthodox Construction."[16] It is tempting to quell any controversy over the authority of the editions of *Paradise Lost* in Milton's own lifetime: "So—*Go thy ways, the Flour and Quintessence of all Editors.* [T]he Edition of 1674 is the Finish'd, the Genuine, the Uncorrupted Work of *John Milton*"[17]—or so it seems, until the first two editions of *Paradise Lost* are allowed to interplay, and we witness a poem's symmetrical structure go into concealment even as other parallelisms, together with the poem's thematic core of Christocentric theology and heliocentric cosmology, each subtending the other, gather into steadily sharpening focus. Early editions of *Paradise Lost* interface intriguingly, and complexly, engaging one another in an ongoing dialogue concerning "Things unattempted yet in Prose or Rime" (1.16) or, as Milton had said earlier in his *Areopagitica*, "things not before discourst or writt'n of" (YP, 2:557). It is a discourse of new revelations, not commonplaces, that Milton habitually promises as, for example, in the Prologue to *Paradise Regain'd* in which he says he will "tell of deeds / . . . in secret done, / And unrecorded left through many an Age, / Worthy t' have not remain'd so long unsung" (1.14–17).

Between 1667 and 1674 we move from what Roy Flannagan describes as the relatively "austere aesthetic" of the first edition of *Paradise Lost*, its "economy of page," in which there are no prefatory materials or "accessory ornaments," as if the poem was "designed like a Quaker table, on purpose,"[18] to a second edition with a frontispiece portrait, a significantly altered title page, together with Milton's own note on the verse, preliminary poems by others in advance of Milton's own poem and arguments now appended as headpieces to each book. Peter Lindenbaum puts a telling construction on such observations:

> In a good number of seventeenth-century poetry volumes . . . , the poetry begins with signature B, implicitly leaving the poet space to gather encomia to himself [to be inserted later] while the printer proceeds ahead with his task. [The] 1667 *Paradise Lost* starts with signature A right after [the] title page, suggesting that from the start no prefatory material was intended.[19]

Not from "the start . . . intended" perhaps, but very soon afterward prefatory material was incorporated into the *first* edition. Thus, what is there in the edition of 1674 comes as an afterthought, fragments of which, however, appear in later issues of the first edition, with the full formation not present until "A Poem in Twelve Books" is published in that year of Milton's death. The development of *Paradise Lost* by alteration and accretion, then, is equally the story of its first edition, encapsulated within a movement of page signatures from "*A*" to "a" to "A" (this time in roman caps) as the poem proper commences. It is a poem of false starts as its expanding front matter seems to indicate and as its proliferating proems within the poem proper also seem to testify.

The issue for Flannagan is "inexpensive book design" and subsequently the wish to give a fresh look to a book not selling well, but for others it is an initial thumbing of Milton's nose (immediately evident in his animadversions against rhyme) at "Restoration literary fashions."[20] What Lindenbaum challenges in his shrewd response to Flannagan is the latter's presumptions, first, that there were additional materials available to the printer for inclusion or exclusion, affording Milton the opportunity to economize, and, second, that final decisions were being made by Samuel Simmons rather than (as Lindenbaum argues) by "Milton . . . himself."[21] The task now before us, Joad Raymond chimes in, is to grasp "the cultural significance of the organisation of the page," and then to try "to 'read' typography and the paratext."[22] Moreover, we should also remember, as a printed notice accompanying one first edition of *Paradise Lost* testifies, that Milton retained copyright of his poem during his lifetime and with it kept "control of the text of his poem."[23] Doing so, we should acknowledge immediately that the organization of *Paradise Lost*, from the very beginning, by book and line number, often times with a numerological sophistication, gestures toward (so as to place the poem within) classical and sacred traditions of verse and then within the most refined, and often esoteric, systems of composition. It also provides Milton with a stronger, if often unseen, presence in his poem.

THE EVOLUTION OF *PARADISE LOST*

As McGann acknowledges, to take into account such matters, to observe a poem's operations within a radial field, its interactions with different contexts, affects our readings as well as our interpretations:

> For one thing, it forces us to realize that books involve a "reading" of their audiences which those audiences may or may not realize, and may or may not submit to. [They] . . . interact with . . . audiences by absorbing and regularizing the possible modes of response. [The book may labor] . . . to minimize its own internal conflicts, as well as the possible conflicts its message might generate. In order for us to *read* . . . , then, rather than to be *read by* it, we have to explode the illusion of contextual seamlessness which the work projects. We have to "step outside" that fiction of a homogeneous context and read the work in a framework and point of view which it has not already absorbed and anticipated. This requires reading the work in those contexts which [it] . . . has tried either to forbid, or to declare nonexistent.[24]

In these remarks, McGann provides cues for a preliminary reading of *Paradise Lost*—one commencing with the title pages and continuing with the front matter of the first and second editions, all the while contending with contexts either forbidden or suppressed by Milton, his friends or his editors, as well as his translators, illustrators, imitators, or critics. Here, McGann also gestures toward the recognition that, while books in themselves do not make revolutions, as Adrian Johns remarks, "the way they are made, used, and read just might."[25]

What seizes, then commands, the attention of Milton's first variorum editor is a silence, an omission: *Paradise Lost* has no patron, no dedicatee—an oddity Thomas Newton explains away with the observation that Milton "designed" his poem for no single person but rather "for the wise and learned of all ages,"[26] but also an oddity he then compounds with the acknowledgment that eighteenth-century editors supplied a dedication for the very poem from which Milton deliberately withheld one. Paradoxically, for Newton, the apparent violation of Milton's intention actually accentuates both his aesthetic commitments and his political gesture—"an essentially republican gesture," says Peter Lindenbaum[27]—wherein the dedicatee "*John Lord Sommers, Baron of Evesham*," because of his sponsorship of the famous 1688 edition of *Paradise Lost*, is used to highlight, first, that in the figure of Milton England has finally produced a model "in poetry superior to any or all the nations in Europe" and, second, that, as Newton goes on to say, Milton's life had been dedicated to a "long, and glorious struggle in the cause of liberty"[28] here symbolized by a poet who, commencing his career within an aristocratic patronage system, eventually springs free from it—so free that by 1688 *Paradise Lost*, still without a patron, is published by subscription.

If Milton deliberately omitted a dedication from *Paradise Lost*, he inadvertently left it to his editors and commentators to repair that omission in more or less the spirit of *Paradise Lost*. Thus, it is no small irony that John Dryden, who walked with Milton in Cromwell's funeral procession and is later described by him as a rhymster but no poet, once he gets his hands on Milton's poem and tags it with rhyme, should then supplement it with a dedication, giving "new" meaning to "majesty," an attribute that in a decidedly different sense he will associate with Milton in his epigram for the 1688 edition. In 1677, however, Dryden's title page, inscribed with a dedication, reads: *The State of Innocence, And Fall of Man: An Opera. Written in Heroique Verse, and Dedicated to Her Royal Highness, The Dutchess. By John Dryden, Servant to His Majesty.*

In "The Authors Apology for Heroique Poetry; and Poetique Licence," Dryden makes clear that he was neither long in choosing a topic nor long in writing his poem: "*at a Months warning, in which time 'twas wholly Written, and not since Revis'd*," he says in lines that, effusive with praise for Milton, also, with a nod to Longinus, hint at shortcomings: "*sublime Genius . . . sometimes erres*" yet, in the case of Milton, even if the poet is misguided at times, he should not be "*tax'd . . . for his choice of a supernatural Argument.*"[29] Dryden leaves it to Nathaniel Lee, in a dedicatory poem, to spell out differences between these poets, Dryden, knowing his place as it were, more concerned with reforming poetry than with reforming the world. Yet Dryden is still addressed as "O mightiest of the inspir'd men," who with "new Theams" is employing his pen in order that he may "The troubles of Majestick CHARLES set down." Unlike Milton, Dryden will not "affright" our eyes with heavenly spectacles involving Satan, nor will he cast his poetry as "rudely" or as "roughly" as Milton had done, Dryden thus recreating, according to Lee, the "perfect World" that continually eluded Milton.[30]

If Dryden is here canceling Milton's vision with his own, eleven years later he is responsible for another substitution in which his lamely rhymed and otherwise vacuous epigram, just mentioned, displaces the provocative poems by Samuel Barrow and Andrew Marvell:

> *Three* Poets, *in Three distant Ages born,*
> Greece, Italy, *and* England *did adorn.*
> *The* First *in loftiness of thought Surpass'd,*
> *The* Next *in Majesty; in both the* Last.
> *The force of* Nature *cou'd no farther goe:*
> *To make a* Third *she joynd the former two.*[31]

Dryden's larger project, it seems, is to turn Milton's own poetics and politics on end, thereby anesthetizing the politics that Milton brings out of concealment in his observations on the verse form of *Paradise Lost*: "ancient liberty . . . modern bondage" (a4). While Dryden records the King's "troubles," Milton writes, rather, of a world troubled by kingship and beset with its tyrannies. As Lindenbaum remarks, "the decision to publish *Paradise Lost* on the open market and without benefit of protection or support of some great man represents not simply a religious decision but a political one," especially evident in Milton's "desire to educate a whole nation" through his poem, and to do so from a posture of not just political but also moral independence.[32]

If liberty is the master-theme of Milton's prose works, by virtue of the note entitled "The Verse," it looms equally large at the entrance to *Paradise Lost*, only to be underscored by the generic definition Milton gives his poem (both in the Arguments to Books 1 and 2 and in the Prologues to Books 1, 3 and 4) first as epic, then as prophecy: "the Poem hasts into the midst of things" (*A*2), this epic formula standing out from the environing prose by virtue of its not being printed in italic; then comes Satan's recollection of "*an ancient Prophesie or report in Heaven*" and reference to his wish "*To find out the truth of this Prophesie*" ([*A*2v]). The same point is reiterated in the Argument to Book 2 in which Satan again is said to desire "*to search the truth of that Prophesie or Tradition in Heaven concerning another world and another kind of creation equall or not much less inferiour to themselves*" ([*A*2v]). Lest the idea of prophecy be lost, it is hammered home through allusions to "*Tiresias* and *Phineus* Prophets old" (3.36), as well as Orpheus (3.17) in the Prologue to Book 3 and through the citation of that "warning voice" (4.1) in the abridged Prologue of the subsequent book. Prophecy is then showcased by Marvell in his preliminary poem to the second edition: "Just heaven . . . /Rewards with prophecy thy loss of sight."[33]

As *Paradise Lost* unfolds, however, it becomes increasingly evident that Milton's poem is a critique of the very genres, epic and prophecy, with which it asserts identity. There is no surprise here. As Heather Dubrow astutely observes, Milton's approach to genre, early on, is "complicated" and "ambivalent," in as much as this poet was so aware that "[i]f the hope of creating reformed genres is potentially imperiled by the fallen man who writes them, it is threatened as well by the fallen reader liable to misinterpret them."[34] And the critique itself, an extension into the poem of the one commenced in the note on its verse, is a reminder of the originally subversive thrust of both genres, each of them centered in the human mind and centering on—anatomizing—its operations. With Milton—in what might well be called a principal manifestation of Miltonic Romanticism—epic, prophecy, and tragedy merge into a mental theater in *Paradise Lost* and remain merged in the 1671 poetic volume including *Paradise Regain'd* and *Samson Agonistes*. Genres, once tamed, are now untamed by Milton and, later, his Romantic heirs.

If it is true that illustrations accruing to Milton's poem "complement Milton's arguments,"[35] enabling a better grasp of his complex plot, it is also the case that those Arguments themselves are among the earliest critical commentaries on Milton's poem and that, like many later illustrations, they often exhibit an asymmetrical relationship with the poem they accompany. Like the note on Milton's verse, the Arguments, appended initially as preliminary matter to the poem and only in a second edition fixed to individual books, often exist in tension with the poetry they would elucidate even as they shy away from the controversies lurking within it. Never a polemic, the Arguments are crafted by a wily poet as headpieces to books, which are an active complication of their claims and, on occasion, a subtle subversion of them. The Arguments never announce an interpretation, but they do nudge us toward an ampler understanding of *Paradise Lost*. As improvements to his poem, those Arguments, containing generic markers, also act as generic signals, bringing Milton's poem "more fully in line with the norms for presenting classical epic."[36] Just as importantly, however, as signatures of epic, those Arguments sit in tension (as genre to countergenre) within a poem continually aspiring to the strains of prophecy.

By Milton's time, as Mark Bland allows, "Black-letter, roman, and italic were invested with new associations" and implied "newly assumed functions" with roman and italic often used to discriminate different strands and interwoven material, to layer meanings and even develop tensions among them.[37] If, by the seventeenth century, roman type had become the primary face for poetry, italic, in its developing associations with speech, hence with the orality of a text, was used sometimes for signaling the strong classical and continental influences on a text (*Lycidas* as distinct from the Nativity poem or "The Passion" in the 1645 *Poems*); other times for marking generic differences—to distinguish a play from a poem as on the title page to the 1671 poetic volume; and still other times to create dialectical play between different components of a text, in the example of *Paradise Lost*, between the prose Arguments (in italic) and the poetry (in roman type). By 1673, the huge caps accorded LYCIDAS in the Table of Contents to the volume (see figure 1.2) bring a prophetic character into focus within a poem that is about its formation, and the italicized epigraph, printed not just with the poem, but (in part) here on the Contents page, underscores the oracular character of this poem, a "*Monody*," which "*foretells the ruine of our corrupted Clergie.*"

In *Paradise Lost*, even as rhymeless verse signals prophecy, indeed declares Milton's poem to be a prophecy, the Arguments to Books 1 and 2 promptly call prophecy into question: is it "*ancient Prophesie* or report," "*Prophesie*" or mere "*Tradition*" that Satan hears in heaven ([A2v]); and, if the former, is there any "truth" to garner from searching "this Prophesie" ([A2v])—or is it just crude forecasting? If Milton presses us to question whether the prophecy is true or false, Satan's actions within the poem make us consider both the uses and abuses of prophecy in the modern world. They are also prelude to the poet-narrator's wondering if, "unrein'd," his own song wanders erroneously (7.17–20). If the poem is his invention rather than a gift from the heavenly muse (8.46–47), if it is thus "an empty dreame" (7.39), the poet-narrator wonders if he is not on surer ground when he "Sing[s] with mortal voice" (7.24). By the end of *Paradise Lost*, however, in its final book, prophecy, revived as the poem's principal mode and theme and invoking prophecy as its subtexts, general and local, is again subjected to scrutiny and renewed critique.

The poet knows that one consequence of the Fall, thus delineated in Book 8, is that the mind has been "dark'nd" (8.1054) so that the poet himself, like Adam in the last book of *Paradise Lost*, is limited by fallen (hence sometimes false) consciousness. Thus, even if the poem is a vision emanating from a divine source, it is filtered through, thus subject to the quirks and distortions of, human consciousness. The last book, therefore, presses the questions: what is the efficacy of prophecy in the modern world? What are its limitations in and even perils to fallen existence? How is Book 10, which will later become Books 11 and 12, to be read then: as history (prophecy fulfilled) or as prophecy (history anticipated)? Such questions become self-answering with the emerging awareness that consciousness, awakened in Book 9, sharpens perception in Book 10, in which the gates of understanding are gradually opened in an unending mental progress. It is not so much that Milton searches the past as prophets do the future. Rather, he wrings from the past a revelation of current history and of the possibilities for future history.

Alternatively, when we turn from the Argument for Book 1 to the one for Book 2, we are made to square its claim, that "Satan *debates*" ([*A2v*]), with the poem itself in which Satan does not actually participate in the debate, the outcome of which he nevertheless determines. Probably with Daniel Defoe in mind, Coleridge once remarked that "Readers have learnt from Milton alone, that Satan & Beelzebub were different Persons (in the Scriptures they are different names of the same Evil Being),"[38] thus ignoring the prompt in the Argument to Book 2, *Satan debates*, and so forgetting not only Satan's later declaration, "Both waking we were one" (5.675), but also the emphasis here on the unity of the Devils who, throughout Book 2, "Firm concord" hold (2.497). The debate *is* Satan's in that it consists of alternative plans for action passing through and being weighed within his mind. The participating devils (Moloch, Belial, Mammon, and Beelzebub) can thus be seen as representing different angles of Satan's vision, various layers of his consciousness, diverse aspects of his evil, alternate manifestations of his being, as well as alternative manipulations for achieving his wicked ends. In the end, though, these devils are all interchangeable; they are one with Satan, his different manifestations—all fragments of the same fallen angel.

Long before William Wordsworth, Milton created a poetry in which the mind was his "haunt, and the main region of . . . [his] song";[39] a poetry of consciousness, of process; of a mind-shattering, mind-transforming, mind-expanding drama, which finds its chief expression in Milton's Argument to Book 9 of the first edition with its description of Adam's mind as "*more and more perceiving his fall'n condition*" ([a2v]), the climactic moment of which is registered in Adam's "O miserable of happie!" speech (9.720–850). Moreover, this description of Adam's mental enlargement, not unlike that attributed to Constantine in Milton's *The History of Britain*, a mind "contracted and shrunk up," but then "with a wak'n'd spirit . . . dilating" (YP, 5:124), is an equally apt description for the process Milton's readership now experiences, in parallel with Adam, in the final books of *Paradise Lost*. It is a process capturing the internal movements, the motions of a mind, darkened, as it moves toward enlightenment.

What becomes evident in a juxtaposition of the first and second editions of *Paradise Lost* is a general tendency through revisions in the second edition to highlight, or reinforce, inflections in the first edition. The mental drama, playing itself out in the last half of the first edition and, as we have just observed, inscribed within the Argument to Book 9, is (in the second edition) presented in quick epitome as Milton revises a line in old Book 7, "To whom thus *Adam* gratefully repli'd" (7.641) to read: "Then as *new wak't* thus gratefully repli'd" (8.4; my italics). Recalling a whole parcel of lines, the italicized phrase, *new wak't*, when read fast-forward, anticipates Eve's awakening in the concluding book of *Paradise Lost*: "*Adam* to the bower where *Eve* / Lay sleeping ran . . . but found her wak't" (10.1499). Yet when read by winding backwards through Milton's text, the same phrase recalls "When *Adam* wak't" (5.3), then when Eve "wak'd . . . but with startl'd eye / On *Adam*" (5.26–27), and when she gladly "wak'd" again, in contrast with Keats's Adam, "To find this but a dream!" (5.93). The phrase, new to Milton's second edition, echoes one in the text of *Paradise Lost* from the very beginning: Adam "new wak't" after his creation (7.890) and then awakening to Eve's creation: "I wak'd, and found / Before mine Eyes all real" (7.946–47); "awake I stood" (7.1101), says Adam; "I wak'd / To find her" (7.1115–16).

Ironically, Eve's dream will become more and more the reality into which she and Adam will awaken: both like Samson "wak'd / Shorn of . . . [their] strength" (8.1061–62). Yet if earth signals their fall by trembling, earth also heralds their regeneration—"the Earth now wak'd" (9.94)—and eventually their resurrection. For while metaphorically sleeping, by the end of the poem both Adam and Eve are "found" newly "wak't" as they will finally be "Wak't in the renovation of the just" (10.65). "[B]ut not so wak'd / *Satan*" (5.654–55; my italics). Samson is similarly implicated in a process of awakening—a process in which the spirit returns and lives; but, as Milton explains in *Of Christian Doctrine* with specific reference to the Samson story, this is an awakening into consciousness and a readying for judgment (YP, 6:408). Only Satan is exempt from the process in which first the earth, then Adam and Eve, and eventually the poet-narrator and Milton's readers participate—a process within which comes the promise, threaded through *Paradise Lost*, of a new heaven and a new earth. *New wak't*: an apocalypse of mind is prelude to an apocalypse in history. Already there in *Lycidas*, the idea is now exfoliated in *Paradise Lost*.

The mind, awakening to more and more reality, "*more and more perceiving*," in the words of the Argument to Book 9 ([a2v]), has been the poet's haunt since Book 1—"The mind is its own place, and in it self / Can make a Heav'n of Hell, a Hell of Heav'n" (1.254–55). It remains so in the Argument to Book 4, in its dwelling on "Satan . . . *fall*[ing] *into many doubts with himself*" ([*A*3v]) and in his then entering Eve's mind through dream, the "*troublesome*" ([*A*4]) character of which is accentuated at the beginning of the Argument to Book 5. This episode contrasts with Eve's "*gentle dreames*" ([a3]) noted in the Argument to Book 10, engendering in her a "*quietness of mind*" ([a3]) in anticipation of "A Paradise within thee, happier farr" (10.1478) promised to Adam by Michael in the finale to *Paradise Lost*, and even the "calm of mind" (1758) allegedly achieved by God's servants who, in *Samson Agonistes*, are witnesses to Samson's "horrid spectacle" (1542). As Milton's last poems proceed, their psychological interiority their deepens; and with it, the sense of mental anguish, so movingly rendered, becomes acute in those lines strategically added to the second edition of *Paradise Lost*: "Dæmoniac Phrenzie, moaping Melancholie / And Moon-struck madness, pining Atrophie, / Marasmus, and wide-wasting Pestilence" (11.485–87)—lines that instead of reconceiving, or reenvisioning, the poem underscore the inward turn of the first edition with all of the mental anguish that accompanies physical suffering and the fear of dissolution.

Moreover, the phrase now added to the second edition, *new wak't*, is crucial to thematizing Milton's larger project of showing a world awakening to new possibilities as its inhabitants become better angels of their own humanity. Margaret Fuller put it best when she declared, as previously remarked, that Milton is one of "the Fathers of the Age, of that new Idea which agitates the sleep of Europe, and of . . . America."[40] As Blake and Shelley knew when each of them, independently, called Milton the Awakener, an awakener is in the process both of himself awakening and of awakening others. At its profoundest level, *Paradise Lost* would rouse an entire nation from sleep, even as it renews the earlier ambition of *Areopagitica*, of making "all the Lords people . . . [into] Prophets" (YP, 2:556; cf. 554), of turning England into a nation of visionaries in anticipation yet once more, as the Argument to Book 9 announces, of "the renewing of all things" ([a2v]). Prophecy is restored in the concluding book of *Paradise Lost*, "from . . . [our] eyes the Filme remov'd" (10.412), and in the moment of its restoration we are invited to dream again on the things to come as apocalyptic hope revives, most poignantly near the end of the poem when Adam and Eve wipe tears from their eyes: "Som natural tears they drop'd, but wip'd them soon" (10.1536), Milton thus invoking, as he had done so movingly in *Lycidas*, the apocalyptic promise that a time will come when "God shall wipe away all tears from their eyes; and there shall be no more death, neither sorrow, nor crying" (Revelation 21:4). The postlapsarian books of *Paradise Lost*, in an arc that reaches from the Argument to Book 9 into the last lines of Book 10, are bracketed by apocalypse; and these books themselves are replete with apocalyptic murmurings.

Poets cannot rouse the faculties to act until the eyes have been cleared and the doors of perception opened again, in part by introducing to their poetry a collision of perspectives, sometimes through competing, often contradictory, formulations. The Argument to Book 2 invokes "Tradition" ([*A2v*]) almost as if to alert us that, like prophecy itself, *Paradise Lost* is a poem of traditions, often competing ones, as when the Argument to Book 6 ([*A4v*]-a) reminds us of the apocalyptic tradition of a celestial battle, including the different interpretive schools surrounding it, especially concerning the duration of the battle and the matter of whether the three-day battle is a veiling of the Crucifixon story, as well as of the rival interpretations concerning its triumphant protagonist, whether he be identified as Michael or as Christ. Lines unique to the second edition of the poem reinforce an alignment of Christ's battle at the end of time with his trials in the midst of time: "They eat, they drink, and with refection sweet" of the first edition (5.636) becomes "They eat, they drink, and in communion sweet / Quaff immortalitie and joy" in the second edition (5.637–38)—lines that with their now eucharistic overtones suggest the institution of communion at the Last Supper and thereby reinforce the coding of the Crucifixion story into that of the celestial battle, an idea by no means unique to Milton.

Similarly, the Argument for Book 7 hints at other narrative complexities: Adam's memory, "*what he remember'd since his own Creation*," what *he* remembers especially of "*his placing in Paradise, his talk with God concerning solitude and fit society*" (a), and the veracity of Adam's report when it is juxtaposed with an account of Creation by Raphael that, pointedly, according to the poem, derives not from memory—"I that Day was absent, as befell, / Bound on a voyage uncouth and obscure" (7.866–67)—but from prophetic inspiration, his "words with Grace Divine / Imbu'd" (7.852–53). We may think backwards to the sharp distinction Milton draws, in *The Reason of Church-Government*, between the daughters of memory and those of inspiration (YP, 1:820–21) or look forward in *Paradise Lost* to the moment in Book 9 when God (or God in Christ) mocks Adam's words on solitude in the earlier Book 7: "Where art thou *Adam* . . . / . . . I miss thee here, / Not pleas'd, thus entertaind with solitude" (9.103–05), God (or God in Christ) tells Adam in clear recollection of what Adam tells Raphael concerning his conversation with God: "In solitude / What happiness, who can enjoy alone, / . . . what contentment find?" (7.1001–03). In such moments, the Arguments function as cue cards, alerting the reader to seemingly innocuous detail that eventually becomes fraught with meaning. Furthermore, these Arguments give a supplementary voice to the poet different from the one, both lyrical and autobiographical, that he creates in various prologues to individual books; and different, too, from the voice of the commentator/interpreter sometimes interrupting the narrative, even challenging its drift as in Book 2, when at the conclusion of Belial's speech we hear: "Thus *Belial* with words cloath'd in reasons garb / Counsel'd ignoble ease, and peaceful sloath, / Not peace" (2.226–28).

The Arguments sometimes simplify what the poetry presents complexly and, in their tendency to simplify, especially concerning matters of religion, lead us into theological traps and metaphysical bramblebushes as in the Argument to Book 3, its assertion that "*The Son freely offers himself a Ransome for Man*" ([*A*3]) and then its representation of Satan as not only mankind's deceiver but the deceiver of angels as well ([*A*3v]). In the first instance, the Argument points not only to atonement theory, but to what was made a contentious point within such thinking as early as Gregory Nazianzen and as recently as Hugo Grotius. In the second example, Satan's deception of Uriel alerts us to what God himself will say, that "Man falls deceiv'd" (3.130), a position Satan shares in *Paradise Regain'd*— "*Adam* and . . . *Eve* / Lost Paradise deceiv'd by me" (1.51–52) but that, again in *Paradise Lost*, Milton's (unreliable?) narrator will challenge: that Adam falls, "not deceav'd, / But fondly overcome with Femal charm" (8.998–99). Or as other examples, take Book 9 in which the prose Argument relates what Adam teaches Eve in contrast to the poetry of that book, which, arguably, tells the story of what Eve teaches Adam. Or take, again, the Argument to Book 10, which signals the arrival of a "denounc[ing]" angel ([a2v]) who, if stern in his edict, is nonetheless "milde" in his address and also "benigne" in his demeanor (10.286, 334) and the platitudes of which emphasize Eve's "submission" ([a3]) in contradistinction to the poetry in which Eve eventually rivals Adam in her heroism. If Adam supposed Eve sleeping, he "found her wak't" (10.1499).

The poetry, then, is not only an active complication of the prose Arguments but, occasionally, challenges positions or platitudes the

Arguments inscribe. Sometimes, as in Book 9, when not the Father but the Son journeys to the Garden for the judgment of Adam and Eve, an Argument may revise Scripture by contradicting it (Genesis 3:8–24) and then complicate the contradiction by shifting in 1669 from "Son" to "Angels,"[41] perhaps flirting with Socinian heresy that denies the Son membership in the trinity by sometimes according him the status of a mere angel.[42] In the absence of certainties, two possibilities present themselves. The shift from "Son" to "Angels" (a2) may be no more than a compositor's error, a trick of the eye or slip of the hand, which transfers "Angels" from line 1 of the Argument to line 4. Or just possibly the shift may be more a sleight of hand, an example of heresy flickering in *Paradise Lost*, its author or printer (for just a moment) teasing the reader with Socinianism by demoting the Son to a position, in the world of *Paradise Lost*, even inferior to Satan, who is described as "of the first, / If not the first Arch-Angel" (5.656–57).

Throughout, but especially here, Milton's poem has been altogether slippery in establishing a knit of identity between the Father and Son only then to force distinction (or vice versa). In the Argument to Book 9, as we have seen, a distinction is drawn ("*He sends his Son*"). In the poem proper, the Father addresses "Assembl'd Angels" (9.34), then sends his Son in judgment (9.55–56), "both Judge and Saviour sent" (9.209). At the same time, though, the Father and the Son blur into one:

> unfoulding bright
> Toward the right had his Glorie, on the Son
> Blaz'd forth unclouded Deitie; he full
> Resplendent all his Father manifest
> Express'd. (9.63–67)

The Son is thereupon perceived as God: "the voice of God they heard / Now walking in the Garden" (9.97–98), and is so represented by the poem's narrator: "God / Approaching, thus to *Adam* call'd aloud" (9.101–02); and again: "the Lord God heard" (9.163). Does the Argument, then, hint at a heresy the poem erases? Or are we rather left with the question of whether the Son is one with the Father or, alternatively, exalted from among the angels and still holding on to his identity as one of those fragments of deity, which are as much emanations and revelations of the Son as He is of the Father?

What these features, including the few (seemingly inconsequential) revisions of the first edition, highlight, the preliminary poems to the second edition underscore, first, through the perplexing contradictions each poem inscribes and, second, through each poem's contrarious relationship with its counterpart. Each poem seems to subvert its own chief claim: Samuel Barrow seeing a secret history folded into Milton's epic narrative and attributing a poetics of discovery to a poem whose epic character promises what E. M. W. Tillyard calls "communal or choric quality";[43] Andrew Marvell hollowing the radical ideology and revisionary thrust from a poem that he thereupon declares to be a prophecy. In contradicting themselves and one another, these poems imply that *Paradise Lost* is itself a poem imbued with and inspired by contradiction and, even more, that it submits to the very kinds of readings against which especially Marvell protests. The contexts forbidden, or seemingly declared nonexistent, are finally the ones that really matter. Herman Melville is just one historical reader who, in his annotations to *Paradise Lost*, made precisely this point as he comprehended, immediately it seems, that Marvell's Milton is a poet with "a twist," whose doubts are expressed equally in *Paradise Lost* and *Samson Agonistes* and whose intentions are quite rightly "still 'misdoubted' by some," with Melville then quipping: "First impressions are generally true, . . . Andrew."[44]

The contradiction at the heart of each poem opens upon various contradictions between the two poems: the countergenres they invoke, together with their contending traditions (now classical and epic, and now scriptural and prophetic); the different aesthetic experiences the poems forecast, the one promising a disclosure of hidden truths and the other an unperplexing conveyance of received interpretation of the Genesis story. And not just their contestatory relationship with one another but the mediatorial functions these poems perform for *Paradise Lost* require attention: their flirtations with the political implications and disclosures of Milton's poem, their eyes fixed on *Paradise Lost* to be sure (in the case of Barrow, that poem's sixth book) but with (in the instance of Marvell) a darting glance at *Samson Agonistes*, indeed, their apparent cognizance of the politics of *both* these poems, the militarism of the one and vengeful violence of the other; their respective imaginings—and negotiations—of different horizons of expectations involving both national and sexual politics; and especially in the example of Marvell, the fashioning of an apologia for Milton, from Milton's own defenses of himself in both prose writings and poetic Prologues to *Paradise Lost*, in the face of virulent attacks upon Milton, earlier by Roger L'Estrange and more recently by Samuel Parker and probably Samuel Butler. Those attacks reveal just the kind of threat Milton was thought to be: as Sharon Achinstein explains, "he represented . . . literary enthusiasm, a powerful force that embodied the most dangerous aspects of revolutionary energy: the conviction that one's ideas were divinely inspired and the belief that individual choice and experience could guide moral actions."[45] No wonder that Dryden's own project should involve obscuring the contexts, as well as the problems, that Barrow and Marvell had identified, that a chief item on his agenda should involve contradicting Milton out of his contradictions.[46]

Within the context of these poems and their conflicting generic signals, and within the context of *Paradise Lost* itself, whose dialectical framework emerges from a system of genres and countergenres—epic and prophecy, pastoral and satire, tragedy and comedy—we can best understand what it is that Dryden would neutralize in his rhyming version of *Paradise Lost*, which, now dedicated to and courting favor with royalty, by changing Milton's poem into scenes, "would show it in a Play" (22), and by tagging the verse would align Milton's poem, both generically and prosodically, with the newly emergent heroic drama. The very transgressions and energies Barrow and Marvell would tolerate are the ones Dryden would curb. He knew that Marvell's defense of Milton's rhymeless poem could be read as a justification of both Milton's religious enthusiasm and political aims, not to mention his unnerving sexual politics; that in his poem's rhymelessness Milton encoded his revolutionary message, inscribing his poem through this very gesture of defiance with the signature of prophecy. Thus, Dryden had to tag Milton's lines, conventionalizing his verse, and, simultaneously, alter the generic identity of *Paradise Lost*. He also had to restore Milton's poem to the safe politics of patronage, bringing it nearer the thrones of church and state. The art of criticism may very well depend upon our perceiving the hidden roads that go from poem to poem, the revisions by one poet of another poet's revisions. But in the case of Dryden, it is not revisions so much as restorations and excisions that beg for attention, that account for Dryden's "hostility" to Milton and, correspondingly, explain "the banked fury and contempt" directed toward Dryden in Milton's headnote to *Paradise Lost*,[47] and punctuated by the concluding verse paragraph of Marvell's dedicatory poem.

Indeed, what Dryden neutralizes in *The State of Innocence*, he effectively empties from *Paradise Lost* when, in 1688, his epigram (see figure 2.9) substitutes for the mediatorial poems of Barrow and Marvell even as it intersects with both of them, the beginning of Barrow's poem and end of Marvell's, but in a way that cancels out their middles—their substantive cores. It needs to be said at the outset that

Three Poets, *in three distant* Ages *born*,
Greece, Italy, *and* England *did adorn*.
The First *in loftiness of thought Surpass'd*,
The Next *in Majesty; in both the* Last.
The force of Nature *coud no farther goe:*
To make a Third *she joynd the former two.*

R. White *sculp*

Figure 2.9 The Frontispiece to *Paradise Lost*, 4th ed. (1688)

Barrow and Marvell, on the one hand, and Dryden, on the other, "were each, from opposite points of view, aware of what Milton was up to in *Paradise Lost*, and that while Marvell assumed a role of political disingenuity, Dryden who admired Milton and had even helped to shield him from . . . punishment . . . , tried to appropriate and tame the poem whose subversive force he intuited."[48] At the same time, by investing Milton with a national identity and installing him as England's epic bard, Dryden paves the way for Milton's soon becoming a national icon.

Dryden's "loftiness of thought" catches the spirit of Barrow's "sublime poem of Mighty Milton" and, similarly, Dryden's "The Next in Majesty" recalls from the dedicatory poem Marvell's "That majesty which through thy work doth reign" (31), as if to suggest that Dryden, like Milton, but now on a cherry stone, will overgo the precursor poets, in this instance Barrow and Marvell, by joining together in his own compact encomium their claims for Milton's sublimity and majesty. If the substance of Dryden's poem is derivative, so too is its conception: "Let Greece boast . . . , let Rome boast . . . ! England boasts of Milton," writes Selvaggi, "in his one self full match for the other two combined" (CM, 1:156, 157). At the same time, the cost of Dryden's remembering a Milton who surpasses Homer and Virgil in both sublimity and majesty involves excising from the poems by Barrow and Marvell everything that really matters. As he represses Book 6 as a site of revelation and thereupon the prophetic character of Milton's poem, its thrust and parry, he also obliterates its politics, cultural and sexual, the latter also evident in the poem's rhymelessness, as well as its transgressive maneuvers and subversive gestures, even if hinted at only by the blurrings and denials of Barrow and Marvell.

It has been said that "it was John Milton who made [Tonson] . . . . And Tonson, in his turn," let us add, with some help from Dryden, who "unmade John Milton"; who, in the very act of taming *Paradise Lost* into a classic, helped "to kill off the work and its author"[49] by denying both their chosen status as cultural outlaws. It is these tamers of Milton, these self-proclaimed improvers, turning *Paradise Lost* into a correct poem, whom the young Thoreau accused of sacrilege and profanity. Invested with a politics of which Dryden would divest it, in 1688 *Paradise Lost* is simply reinvested with another (for some, more palatable) politics, Milton's poem now appearing, some would argue, as a "piece of Whig propaganda."[50] If, in imitation of the wit of Warren Chernaik, Peter Lindenbaum can say "that in the 1645 *Poems*, [Humphrey] Moseley kidnapped Milton and made a royalist out of him," it should now be allowed that in 1688 Jacob Tonson and

Figure 2.10 John Baptist Medina's Illustration to Book I of *Paradise Lost* ("Satan Calling up His Legions")

company hijacked Milton and made a Whig of him—again, probably in ways that would have been "much against his will."[51] At the same time that Dryden's poem steers clear of Milton's theological and political radicalism, dulling the poem's subversive edge, newly added illustrations subdue many of the poet's transgressions, nowhere more evident than in their conventional and vulgarizing representations of a Satan who, in Milton's poem, has not yet lost his "Original brightness" (I.592) but whose glory, in these illustrations, is completely obscured (see figure 2.10).

If Dryden's lines hide Milton's politics, even as they obliterate his religious enthusiasm, if the illustrations by John Baptist Medina and others bury Milton's transgressions of scriptural traditions (see, e.g., figure 2.10) much as Dryden had done in *The State of Innocence*, the exhaustively annotated edition of *Paradise Lost* (1695) by Hume follows suit, further removing Milton's poem from fields of contestation in the way that, as Anne Middleton explains, annotations, at once "strangely evasive" and interpretively reticent, typically repress relations between the text and the world.[52] Even if these annotations, contextualizing *Paradise Lost* with the classics, with the Bible, together with the elaborate tables of descriptions, similes, and speeches, help to lay a foundation for criticism, that foundation was laid, as Newton complained, in "heaps of rubbish."[53] What gets lost at the end of his own century, in part through Dryden's repressions, is not fully recovered until the end of the next century, largely through the intervention of Blake, who understands above all else that Milton's mind thrived on opposing traditions; that his genius, formed out of their collisions, expressed itself through creative contradictions, as well as unique inflections, within the disparate discourses and dialogic narratives of his last poems. Supposed lapses, slips, inadvertencies—the very features earlier commentators would remove from Milton's poetry—are the places where Blake would search for its secrets.

ADDITIONS CHIEFLY, BUT . . .

The book like the text of *Paradise Lost* develops by accretion: with the addition of illustrations, as well as a subscription list (1688); a commentary of 321 pages, plus tables of descriptions, similes, and speeches (1695), those tables then greatly expanded in early eighteenth-century editions until *Paradise Lost* is published with a full index in 1724; a dedicatory page (1705), along with catalogues of emendations (1725); eventually essays in criticism like Addison's cited in an Advertisement (1724) and the next year published with Milton's poem (1725); plus lives of the poet, the first of them appearing with a postscript in 1725; and, finally, annotations by various hands eventually achieving the clout of a variorum edition (1749) at which time a book published as one is bloated into two volumes.

Emendations early and later in *Paradise Lost* are especially telling as, in an initial example, they show Milton, through repeated alterations of the lines concerning "the Sons of *Belial*" (1.500–05),[54] opening space for a more radical discourse on sexuality, including homosexuality, and, then, through the Samson simile (9.1059–61), reveal him lassoing the heroes (Adam and Eve) of the one poem to the protagonist (Samson) in another. When Patrick Hume annotates *Paradise Lost*, and then appends probably someone else's "Table Of . . . *Similies*," the only simile there included for Adam alone is the comparison of "*Adam* sinful to the shorn *Sampson*,"[55] this "Table" thus drawing attention to what Milton's emendation obviously means to highlight. This in an edition that presents *Paradise Lost, Paradise Regain'd*, and *Samson Agonistes* for the first time between the same covers, as if they were the component parts of a trilogy, the first two parts of which afford interpretive perspectives on the last. Indeed, Milton's simile in *Paradise Lost*, in its reference to "*Herculean Samson*" (9.1060), establishes a point of contact between all three of these poems; for not only are Adam and Eve enmeshed within the simile here, but later the Son will be as well through the Hercules simile folded into the triumph song of *Paradise Regain'd* ("As when Earths Son *Antæus* . . . / With *Joves Alcides*" [4.563–65]). By tradition, of course, Hercules is Samson's counterpart in Greek mythology, hence in *Samson Agonistes*. In Milton's poetry, Hercules is typically glimpsed in moments of triumph—from the Nativity ode onward. Yet it is not so much a triumphant as a tragic Samson whom we glimpse in Milton's last poems—a point reinforced by the Samson simile in *Paradise Lost*, introduced at precisely the moment that, shifting into another key, the poem's narrator surrenders the heroism of epic poetry to tragedy. The shift is decisive: tragicomedy gives way to tragedy in *Paradise Lost* with that accent then deepening in *Samson Agonistes* in which, in the front matter to this poem, the word *tragedy* is repeated nearly a dozen times. In the 1671 poetic volume, it is Jesus, not Samson, who establishes the new standard and exhibits the new norms of a heroism emanating from "deeds / Above Heroic" (1.14–15).

One effect of tabulating additions and emendations is to represent the poet as his own editor as if, before the fact, to counteract whatever damage might be done by a Richard Bentley who, inventing an editor for Milton's poetry, holds that editor responsible for everything that seems erroneous in Milton's text. No less important than additions and emendations, or the aforementioned absences and evasions in *Paradise Lost*, or even its hidden links with other poems, are these early presences:

(1) the title page to the first edition of *Paradise Lost*, its five states and two variants, in which twice in 1668 (but not always) the poem's author, nearly anonymous, is identified only by his initials "J. M." (cf. figures 2.11 and 2.12);

(2) the alteration of that title page in the second edition of *Paradise Lost* for the sole purpose of marking the structural revision from "TEN" to "TWELVE BOOKS";

(3) the frontispiece portraits sometimes tipped into copies of the first edition (for example, The Folger Library copy[56]), remarkable chiefly because a frontispiece portrait becomes a regular feature of the second edition of *Paradise Lost* just as it had been of the 1645 *Poems of Mr. John Milton*, and of the more recent publications of both Milton's *Art of Logic* and *The History of Britain*;

(4) the note from "The Printer to the Reader," indicating the author's concern for his readership—a concern that (if anything) is accentuated in the final issue of the first edition, and in all copies of the second edition of *Paradise Lost*, where, with the deletion of the Printer's note, the author's addresses to the Reader (now unmediated) are all the more prominent;

(5) those addresses themselves that take the form, first, of an explanation as to "why the Poem Rimes not" and, second, of prose "Arguments" initially printed as front matter to the poem but, in the second edition, printed as headpieces to its individual books;

(6) the poems by "S. B., M. D." and "A. M." (presumably Dr. Samuel Barrow and Andrew Marvell) that in the second edition of *Paradise Lost* displace some of the original front matter with such displacements, in their turn, becoming a regular feature in subsequent editions of the poem.

And, finally, along with these ceremonial gestures, there are the protocols of printing like capitalization, punctuation, type size, italics, and boldfacing, which establish unexpected and sometimes peculiar inflections as when, as previously noted, a period is added after "Books" in the last four issues of the first edition, thus making "A **POEM** IN TEN BOOKS." a separately marked unit that, by virtue of type size

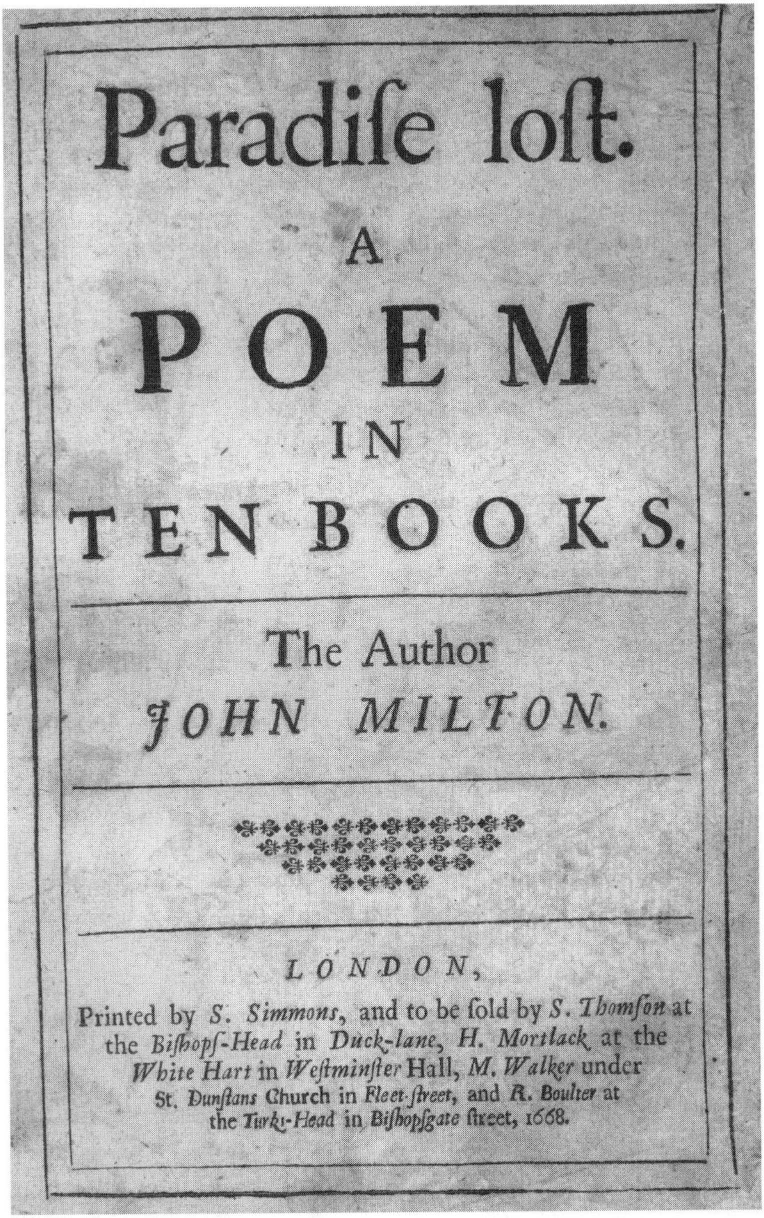

Paradise lost.

A

POEM

IN

TEN BOOKS.

The Author

JOHN MILTON.

❊❊ ❊❊ ❊❊ ❊❊ ❊❊
❊❊ ❊❊ ❊❊ ❊❊
❊❊ ❊❊

LONDON,

Printed by *S. Simmons*, and to be fold by *S. Thomfon* at
the *Bifhopf-Head* in *Duck-lane*, *H. Mortlack* at the
White Hart in *Weftminfter* Hall, *M. Walker* under
St. *Dunftans* Church in *Fleet-ftreet*, and *R. Boulter* at
the *Turks-Head* in *Bifhopfgate* ftreet, 1668.

Figure 2.11   Title Page No. 2 to *Paradise Lost* (1668)

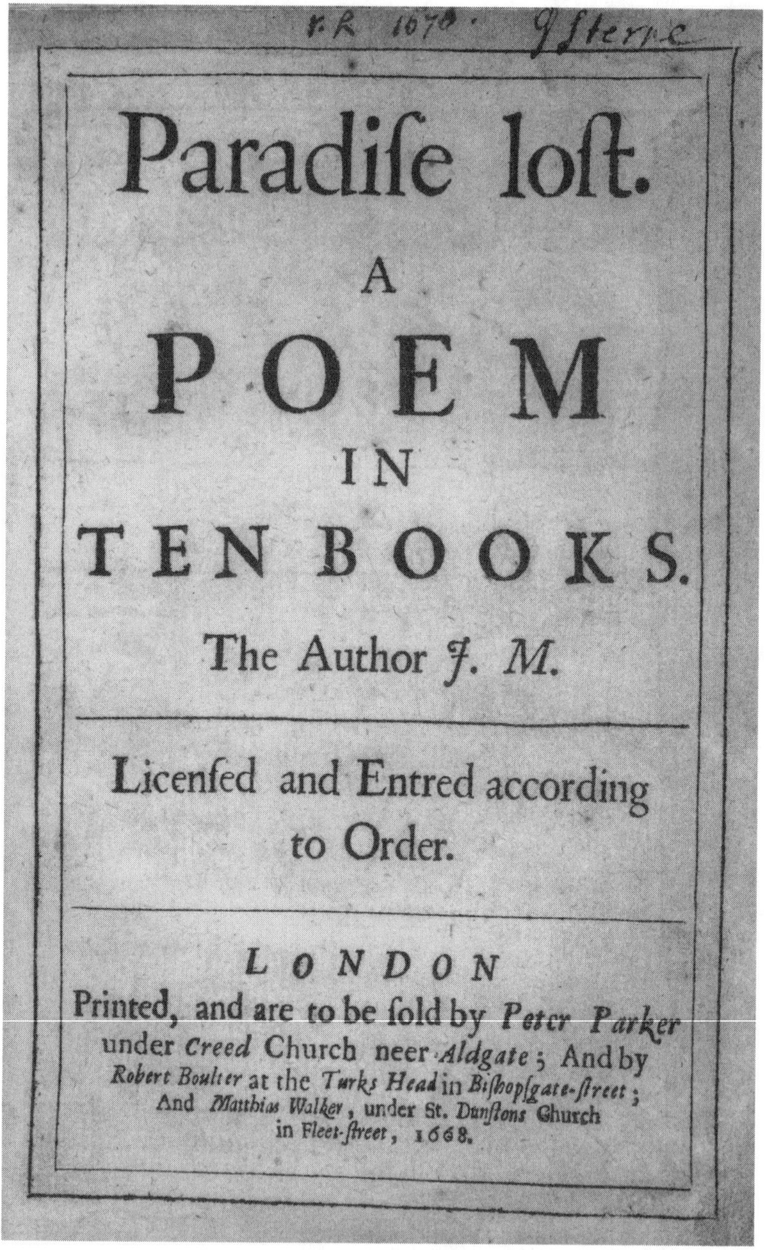

Paradiſe loſt.

A

POEM

IN

TEN BOOKS.

The Author *J. M.*

Licenſed and Entred according to Order.

LONDON

Printed, and are to be ſold by *Peter Parker* under *Creed* Church neer *Aldgate*; And by *Robert Boulter* at the *Turks Head* in *Biſhopſgate-ſtreet*; And *Matthias Walker*, under St. *Dunſtons* Church in *Fleet-ſtreet*, 1668.

Figure 2.12 Title Page No. 2 (Variant) to *Paradise Lost* (1668)

and boldfacing, in its prominence overrides the poem's title, "Paradise lost."

Such typographical devices, before 1695, throw accent marks, in descending order of importance, upon the broad generic character of *Paradise Lost* (it is "A POEM") and then upon its structure, which, if "TEN BOOKS" in 1667, is "TWELVE BOOKS" in 1674. Moreover, on the poem's title pages, all belonging to the year 1668, the author's name, once spelled out and twice abbreviated as "J. M.," is always capitalized, thus giving the poet nearly as heavy an accent as the poem's politically charged title, which, under the cover of ancient history, seemed for some to reflect upon the loss of paradise now—with the failure of the Puritan Revolution. Yet what is still more remarkable about Milton's title page, together with the original front matter, is that poet and poem, poem and reader are all bound inextricably in single compact as if to insist upon the poet's presence in a poem that completes itself in the mind of the reader. Moreover, as we proceed from title pages where Milton's name (in initials only) is nearly anonymous to later ones (still belonging to the first edition) where the poet's name, even if muted by comparison with other elements of the title page, is nevertheless spelled out, and then onward to the second edition of *Paradise Lost*, where the poet's image is, as it were, flashed across the title page by virtue of its frontispiece status—when we take all this into account, the conclusion seems obvious. *Paradise Lost* is a poem that, in its front matter, becomes increasingly self-referential, paving the way for our regular sightings of Milton in the multiple Prologues to his epic-prophecy, in virtually all its characters, as well as within certain of the narrator's disruptive intrusions within the poem proper.

Milton's titles, for poems and prose works alike, provide a virtual map of seventeenth-century titling practices; and the eventual fate of some of his titles in the hands of eighteenth-century editors ("Sonnet XIX" becomes "On His Blindness," and more famously *A Mask* becomes *Comus*) is ample enough evidence of how generic authority, as well as thematic focus and positioning of characters, once established, can be muted, or lost, by unauthorized emendation. Most often, such emendations result in misconstrued inflections—or misconstruals of interpretation. Milton had already proved himself a master at naming poems in *Lycidas*, a title thick with allusion, and again in *A Mask*, a title notable for its generic specificity.[57] On the other hand, as both these poems and his sonnets testify, Milton was no less adept at using generic wrappings to hide the sometimes subversive content of his poetry. He knew, that is, how to use titles to withhold signals instead of telegraphing them; how to shut windows on—and deny access to—areas titles might otherwise open. An example is afforded by *Poems of Mr. John Milton* (1645), where the poet probably learned from his publisher, Humphrey Moseley, how to make his poems look (at least initially) as if they are part of a series including his contemporaries Thomas Carew, William Cartwright, John Suckling, and Edmund Waller even as he was probably reminded, through the portraits by William Marshall, that, by making some poets look alike, they could all blend together,[58] producing (on first tasting) the same vanilla flavor.

In the instance of *Paradise Lost*, the title alludes explicitly to the Creation/Fall story in Genesis; and once *Paradise Regain'd* is published in 1671, these now parallel titles, with a single change of detail, will always echo one another's songs, thereby suggesting that Milton's interest here stretches from the loss of paradise in the Hebrew Bible to its recovery in the New Testament. Nevertheless, on the title pages of all seventeenth-century editions, the poem's title of *Paradise Lost* is overruled by a subtitle, hugely prominent, that offers the broadest possible literary categorization: "A POEM," period. Initially, we learn nothing at all about the generic identity of this poem, its aspirations or castings, only that *Paradise Lost* will participate in the relative obscurity of poetry. The subtitle is neutrally declarative, not interpretive—or just plain secretive, at least until the second edition when the newly added reference to "TWELVE BOOKS" may mean to hint at generic affiliation, even continuity, with *The Aeneid*, at least from the perspective of modern readers, or even may be intended to distance Milton from Camoens's ten-book epic.[59] In any case, the force of the first part of the subtitle is to free *Paradise Lost* of any specific generic identity even while sequestering it within the broad category of *poetry.*

Rather than conferring knowledge, then, Milton's title page seems to withhold it, now hiding secrets, now hinting at them, with the overly prominent subtitle of the poem, while never denying, seeming to offer escape from—or at least an evasion of—the main title, and, in its very lack of generic specificity, denying *Paradise Lost* the interpretive authority, bias, and focus inhering within individual genres. If Milton's title locks the poem into Christian tradition (the subtitle makes clear that the accompanying work is a religious *poem*, not a theological tract), and if a part of the subtitle hints at its moorings in epic tradition, the newly added dedicatory poems by Barrow and Marvell, aligning *Paradise Lost* with epic and prophetic traditions respectively, simply anticipate the conflicting generic signals implanted within a poem, which, instead of declaring, emplots within its revelation the realization that *Paradise Lost* is a prophecy.

Milton's art of titling, in all the late poems, is the art of adapting the most traditional, the safest of titles to masked interests, with Milton thus writing about the loss of paradise not in time-past but now; about the recovery of paradise not on the cross but in the wilderness; and about Samson, not in a comedic mode, but in his tragic dimension, in a poem that instead of merely purveying traditions prosecutes them. But perhaps more surprising, the modern supposition that Milton's structural revision is intended to align *Paradise Lost*, now "A POEM IN TWELVE BOOKS," with the classic line of Virgilian epic is just that—a *modern* supposition. When the issue was addressed at all by Milton's early editors, the twelve-book structure was explained not as "part of a wider Virgilianizing," "not . . . with respect to the *Aeneis* (for . . .[Milton] was, in both senses of the phrase, above Imitation)" but, instead, with reference to the poem's internal logic according to which, "because the length of the Seventh and Tenth [books] requir'd a Pause in the Narration, He [Milton] divided them, each into Two."[60] Indeed, the fact that this "new Edition, carefully corrected," bears on its title page (in this 1725 edition, for the first time) an epigraph from Homer's *Odyssey* (see figure 2.13) hints that, for his invention, Milton's classic line is better traced to the Homeric tradition of moral and philosophical—not militaristic—epic. For the sake of his reputation, apparently, Milton is best segregated from what we know as the tradition of "secondary" or written epic fraught with politics and emanating from Virgil, and aligned instead with the original of all the blind bardic poets, Demodicus: "[he whom] the Muse had loved greatly, and gave him both good and evil. / She reft him of his eyes, but gave him the sweet singing / art" (6.63–65).[61]

By the turn into the eighteenth century, in any event, Milton's politics had been sufficiently stripped from *Paradise Lost* that the typography of the title page, as is already evident in the 1695 edition, can now give secondary emphasis, unabashedly so, to the poem's author, not its structure; and by 1749 *Paradise Lost* has been so completely aestheticized, and its politics anesthetized, that the poem's title can finally receive the primary accent mark. Indeed, over time *Paradise Lost* was shown to be, "more than a classic, a scripture," and, once achieving " 'scriptural status,' " was used by Richard Bentley and later Thomas Newton as a defense for "orthodox Christianity." Furthermore, often "amended . . . by Scripture's standards," this or that passage was revised or rejected as "inconsistent" with the

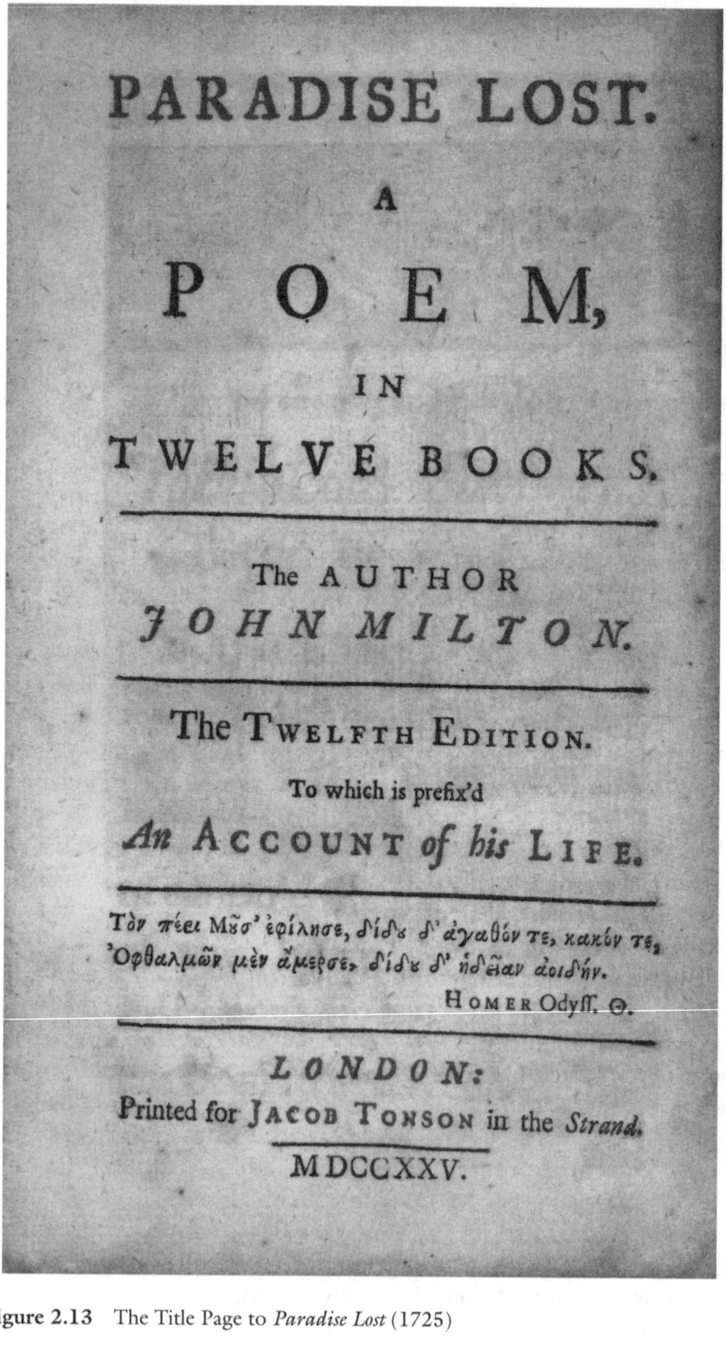

PARADISE LOST.

A

POEM,

IN

TWELVE BOOKS.

The AUTHOR
JOHN MILTON.

The TWELFTH EDITION.

To which is prefix'd

An ACCOUNT *of his* LIFE.

Τὸν πέει Μᾶσ᾽ ἐφίλησε, δίδε δ᾽ ἀγαθόν τε, κακόν τε,
Ὀφθαλμῶν μὲν ἄμερσε, δίδε δ᾽ ἡδεῖαν ἀοιδήν.

HOMER Odyſſ. Θ.

LONDON:
Printed for JACOB TONSON in the *Strand.*

MDCCXXV.

Figure 2.13 The Title Page to *Paradise Lost* (1725)

supposed truths of the Bible.[62] The wish of some to purge *Of Christian Doctrine* from Milton's canon is founded upon these mid-eighteenth-century presumptions concerning the conforming spirit of *Paradise Lost*, not earlier ones emphasizing the poet's republicanism or liberalism and sometimes religious heresies.

Within *Paradise Lost*, however, there are turbulent waters everywhere, pointing to hermeneutic trouble, interpretive quagmires. Narrative flow is further disrupted, still points occur, every time an allusion opens upon and deepens into a context; when explicit analogies are discredited, or flatly denied, by implicit comparisons as, for example, when Satan, seeming superior in strength and fortitude to Prometheus, hence infinitely greater in his heroism, is shown to be, once the context of the Prometheus story is invoked, not only ethically inferior to Prometheus but downright villainous. If the allusion harbors a knit of identity, its context insists upon distinction. As Julia M. Walker has argued,[63] allusions sometimes afford not a subtext but an antitext and often imply a politics, too, as when, in the Prologue to Book 3, the poet-narrator, through the Orpheus analogy, is now caught up in the same system of classical allusion and valuation that previously enveloped Satan, Milton's point being that the poet goes into Hell but makes a pact with no one, unlike Orpheus who enters into a compact with Pluto for the return of Eurydice. That is, Milton anticipates and repudiates those who identify him with Satan. Here and elsewhere action is disrupted by forced contemplation in *Paradise Lost*, commentary on the story impedes its narrative flow, theology gets in the way of poetry. Contradictions abound. And as a consequence thereof, a genre that had been an arena of pleasure becomes a theater for contemplation with the poet himself emerging as an increasingly prominent—and controlling—presence in his poems.

Still further evidence of the poet's presence in *Paradise Lost*, as we have seen in chapter 1, is afforded by the printer's note to the reader of the first edition, which, implicating the poet as a party interested in his readership, announces the dialogic function of this poetic text—a function highlighted by the poet's own animadversions against rhyme as a "troublesome and modern bondage" threatening the "ancient liberty" heralded by heroic song, as well as by "Arguments" with a sometimes asymmetrical, even contestatory, relationship with the books they introduce. Not only does Milton's blank verse announce a politics to the poem's readership; by the third decade of the eighteenth century, blank verse is established as "the idiom of opposition"[64] in English poetry, indeed becomes so conventionally the idiom of opposition that poets like Blake, wishing to surpass

Milton in their formation of an oppositional poetics, will move beyond blank to free verse.

If the *The Marriage of Heaven and Hell* represents a moment of breakthrough in the history of Milton criticism, the creation of a new horizon of expectations deriving from a radically new understanding of Milton and revisionary interpetation of his poetry, it also marks a moment of recovery. *The Marriage* recaptures the earliest horizon of expectations for *Paradise Lost*, all that is lost, first, in Dryden's curbing of Milton's prophetic imagination and rooting out of his transgressive maneuvers in *The State of Innocence* and, later, in his displacement of the poems by Barrow and Marvell, then repressed by many eighteenth-century commentators, even as *The Marriage* turns on end, in its acknowledgment that Milton is of the devil's party, Dryden's devaluation of Milton and eventual denial of him a place among the triumvirate of epic poets (by 1697, Homer, Virgil, and Tasso) for having made "the devil . . . his hero, instead of Adam."[65]

In the eighteenth century, the same rhetoric of abuse that initially enveloped Milton the Republican now ensnares Milton the alleged Whig, with this poet once more being named a member of the "diabolical party," again with the express intention of "invalidat[ing] the authority of Milton," yet this time with a chastisement of such maligning critics: do they "not perceive . . . the indecency, the inhumanity, of likening . . .[their] adversaries to devils?"[66] In the topsy-turveydom of *The Marriage*, Blake converts a rhetoric of abuse into one of praise, an indecency into an insight, a slight into a celebration. Itself a prophecy about the formation of the prophetic character, who is delineated in his true and false aspects by the opposing examples of Milton and Swedenborg, *The Marriage* presents the former as a poet of principle who, changing his mind and altering his opinions, avoids breeding reptiles of the mind. The very fact that Milton altered his opinions, the aforementioned critic argues and Blake implies, should prevent criticism from altering its high opinion of this poet.

Blake recovers the Milton tradition, which is a tradition of revolution, understanding of Milton what has recently been said of Blake himself, that it is his "very relationship to the Bible which makes him the revolutionary artist . . .[and] pits him . . . against all complacent religious and literary stances."[67] Blake restores Milton to the tradition of radical prophecy; he tears down the partition between prose works and poetry, in the process reviving, as well as refining, Milton's philosophy of contraries, together with its attendant dialectics, in which Milton's polemics and poems alike have their deepest moorings. With the creation of *Milton a Poem*, Blake presents the poet as England's

"Awakener," advancing him as a positive example of the negative adage, "He whose face gives no light, shall never become a star,"[68] even as his poem becomes a monument to Milton, the likes of which no poet had ever before, or has since, created for another and then asks monumentally the underlying question of most Milton criticism: "what mov'd Milton?"[69]

THE POLITICS OF POETRY

"Milton's reputation has . . . no great shrine," complains Peter Levi, "no house or tomb to focus it."[70] Such a concern is traceable to the eighteenth century at which time, however, it receives a decidedly different spin. In a "Postscript" to his "Life of Mr. John Milton," Elijah Fenton tells of a friend visiting St. Gile's Church and of his being shown "a small Monument" to Milton, its inscription illegible, a defacement that "cou'd never have happen'd in so short a space of time, unless the Epitaph had been industriously eras'd: and that supposition carries with it so much inhumanity, that I think we ought to believe it was not erected to his Memory."[71] Milton's early reputation is not a matter of missing monuments but of erasure apparently; and yet, despite erasures, as well as silencings, the 1688 edition of *Paradise Lost* is nevertheless credited, as early as 1705 and repeatedly thereafter, with marking a turning point in Milton's reputation: from 1688 onward, *Paradise Lost* is said to be so well received "that notwithstanding the Price of it was Four times greater than before, the Sale encreas'd double the Number every Year. The Work is now generally known and esteem'd."[72]

Statistics by themselves are revelatory: the first edition of *Paradise Lost*, which numbered 1300 copies, its stock depleted by 1670, was followed by a second edition of 1500 copies, with some 10,000–12,000 copies in circulation by 1712. An inventory of these early editions teaches again the lesson Milton inscribes within his poem "*On Shakespear*" (1630): poets have no need for monuments, for they create their own in the very poems they write. At first glance, it would seem that the reception history of *Paradise Lost* begins not just with a pause but a twenty-one year silence. What the historical record shows is a reception history, modest yet important, and certainly continuous in the very years when, allegedly, the poem has no reportable reception. It is a history scripted by men and women alike—and subsequently hidden.

So much conflicting comment would appear concerning the commencement of Milton's reputation and its then current status, which came to be increasingly involved with the fortunes of *Paradise Lost*, that, in 1734, Jonathan Richardson felt obliged to set the record straight:

> It has been a Current Opinion that the late Lord *Sommers* first gave this Poem a Reputation. . . . *Paradise Lost* was known and Esteem'd Long before there was Such a Man as Lord *Sommers*. The Pompous Folio Edition of it with Cuts by Subscription in the Revolution-Year, is a Proof of what I Assert.[73]

John, Lord Somers is usually credited as the guiding force behind the 1688 edition illustrated by Medina, along with Bernard Lens and Henry Aldrich. Then "Current Opinion," apparently, was represented by those like John Dennis who lamented: "How long did *Milton* remain in Obscurity, while twenty paltry Authors, little and vile if compared to him, were talk'd of and admir'd?" And subsequently Dennis complained: "the generality of the Readers of Poetry, for twenty Years after it was published, knew no more of that exalted Poem, than if it had been writ in *Arabick*."[74]

Yet, when speaking within his correspondence "*Of all the Commentators on the Paradise Lost*," Dennis also allows for the existence of some critical attention of which his twentieth-century editor is dismissive:

> *Of all the Commentators on the Paradise Lost.* Strictly speaking, there had been only two up to the time when Dennis wrote this letter: Addison, and the slightly mysterious "P. H." . . . Only one edition had been printed to which the name of an editor had been attached: . . . Tickel . . . 1720. . . . The brief, and usually incidental, remarks of such men as Marvell, Dryden, Roscommon, Bysshe, and Coward scarcely entitle them to be called "commentators."[75]

Dennis's editor makes no mention of the fact that Tickel's edition of 1720 is the *eleventh* edition of *Paradise Lost*, and none of the fact that Milton's first editor is John Hughes, whose volume appeared (without crediting Hughes) the year before, in 1719.[76] Neither does Dennis's editor acknowledge female commentators or readers, nor does he seem to recognize that both translation and imitation are imaginative, and often subtle, forms of commentary; that illustration itself is interpretation; that, in the words of Jonathan Dollimore, at this point in history "appropriations were not a perversion of true literary reception, *they were its reception*."[77] All of these comments are crucial to charting the unfolding of an understanding of *Paradise*

Lost—a poem that, as it moves through history, evokes "the readers's horizon of expectations . . . only in order to destroy it step by step," as well as a poem that reveals "a process of directed perception."[78] That is, *Paradise Lost* reflects an early horizon of expectation that, over time, it alters. As contemporary report modulates into critical response, a finer understanding of the poem emerges, gradually, belatedly.

But back to Richardson, whose initial point is that sumptuous editions, illustrated books, attest to an *achieved* reputation, although this observation also contains (nearly in parentheses) the acknowledgment that *Paradise Lost* is republished in 1688, this "the Revolution-Year"—the ackowledgment, it would seem, that whatever its own political content this poem is being made to serve others' political interests.[79] Moreover, this observation follows an earlier admission that Milton has no monument in Westminster Abbey: "[I]t was not permitted upon Account of his Political Principles," which, according to William Winstanley writing in 1687, have caused Milton's poetic fame to go out "like a Candle in a Snuff," ensuring that "his Memory will always stink."[80] These are the same political principles prompting Addison's lament of 1694 wherein the critic detects, and is deeply troubled by, a political subtext in an epic poem "whose clean Current, tho' serene and bright / Betrays a bottom odious to the sight."[81] Within Milton's lifetime, by the best of his critics, this poet is associated with political intrigue and motives, which doubtless occasion some of Andrew Marvell's brooding in his 1674 dedicatory poem to *Paradise Lost*, but which also prompted the occasional admission that Milton's failure to effect reform in the world of politics does not mean that the reforms he sought should not be effected.[82]

But back yet once more to Richardson, who continues with his corrective to "Current Opinion" by way of explaining his query: "[I]s it not sufficient Reproach to our Country that *Paradise Lost* lay Neglected for Two or Three Years?":

> Sir *George Hungerford*, an Ancient Member of Parliament, told me, many Years ago, that Sir *John Denham* came into the House one Morning with a Sheet, Wet from the Press, in his Hand. What have you there, Sir *John*? Part of the Noblest Poem that ever was Wrote in Any Language, or in Any Age. This was *Paradise Lost*.

Denham died in 1669, a fact which, if this story is not apocryphal, helps to situate it in time, as does Richardson's further report: " '[T]is Certain the Book was Unknown till about two Years after, when the

Earl of *Dorset* produc't it."[83] Suffering from a mental disorder in 1666, Denham is known to have addressed Parliament "sanely" in 1667,[84] the probable date for Denham's reported reception and somewhat later than another reported response, this one from the Quaker Thomas Ellwood who allows that, once having read *Paradise Lost* in manuscript, he said to its author: "Thou hast said much here of *Paradise Lost*; but what hast thou to say of *Paradise Found*?"[85] It is well to remember that Ellwood had recently been incarcerated as a political prisoner just as Milton had been (however briefly) during the first year of the Restoration. It is also well to note the curious deflection from a poem Milton has written to one that, by Ellwood's account, he had yet to write.

Denham and Ellwood, then, represent two decidedly different receptions of *Paradise Lost*: one of expectations surpassed and the other, apparently, of expectations dashed. Within the history of Milton criticism, these two receptions might be accorded paradigmatic status. Yet Richardson has still other receptions and valuations to report (implicitly and explicitly) through a coffee-house story told to him by Dr. Tancred Robinson but actually deriving from Fleet Sheppard (Sir Fleetwood Sheppard), according to whom Milton's poem was available as "*Wast Paper*" at one booksellers: after a happy retrieval of the poem, "My Lord took it Home, Read it, and sent it to *Dryden*, who in a short time return'd it: *This Man* (says *Dryden*) *Cuts us All Out, and the Ancients too*."[86] At least this is the version of the story available in most published accounts. Yet, as William Riley Parker has documented, this version is also corrected by Richardson: "Lord Dorset (not Sheppard . . .) 'told . . .[the story] to Dr. Robinson . . . at the Grecian Coffee House.' "[87] The manuscript life also helps make sense of Richardson's report already cited: " '[T]is Certain that Book was Unknown till about two years later, when the Earl of *Dorset* produc't it." The supposed misprint (*two* for *twenty*) is probably not a misprint at all so long as we understand that, in this context, "produc't" refers not to the publication of the 1688 edition in which Dorset played a role, along with Lord Somers, Francis Atterbury, and Dryden, but to the act of producing *Paradise Lost* for Dryden; that is, of giving Dryden his own copy of the quarto edition of Milton's poem. The Earl of Dorset, we know, bought *Paradise Lost* "for a trifle" (probably in 1667) and "read it many times over" and, when giving his copy to Dryden, learned that Dryden "had never seen it before."[88]

Among poets, Milton's contemporary reputation commences with Denham and Dryden,[89] not with Barrow or Marvell, each of whom, though, figures importantly in such a history and neither of whom was ever subject, as Dryden was, to Milton's scorn: a rhymester perhaps, but no poet, Milton allegedly said of his contemporary. That scorn, moreover, squares with Annabel Patterson's contention (and I would add, Milton's own perception) that, while Marvell would protect the poet, Dryden would violate his vision, so much so that Gerard Langbaine would complain that *The State of Innocence* is "guilty of many absurdities, which are not in *Milton.*"[90] Moreover, Dryden's opinion of *Paradise Lost* had currency in Milton's own time in ways that earlier, private, often unpublished observation did not, though the existence of such opinion obliges us to examine commentary even before Dryden if we are ever going to set straight the historical record. It also requires us to observe that, whatever Dryden says early on, and later in lines published under the frontispiece portrait to the 1688 edition (see figure 2.9), elsewhere when Dryden comments on Milton, his approval is far more guarded. Other published comment curbs the seeming hyperbole registered in Dryden's lines, so much so that in 1685, unwilling to defend Milton's "antiquated words, and the perpetual harshness of their sound," Dryden will ask: "am I . . . bound to maintain, that there are no Flats amongst his Elevations, when 'tis evident he creeps along sometimes, for above an Hundred Lines together," especially in those areas of the poem where he is following Scripture?[91] And he creeps along often enough that by 1697, as we have already observed, Dryden does not even give Milton fourth place among the epic poets, chiefly because he made the devil rather than Adam his hero. Apparently, Dryden's dethroning of Milton is a countermove against a tendency then taking hold in Milton criticism, but it may also be explained in terms of the critique of Milton that, having already taken shape in *The State of Innocence*, is implied by the different accents of that work's shifting title: *The Fall of Angels and Man in Innocence* in 1674, and in 1677 *The State of Innocence, and Fall of Man.*

Unlike Milton's, Dryden's fallen angels have no luster, deliberately. And if in Milton's poem the fallen Adam becomes blasphemous, his blasphemy is by Dryden shifted to Eve. Dennis once remarked that, in Book 2 of *Paradise Lost*, "Milton . . . makes the Devils . . . blaspheme in a most outragious Manner; and yet, as they speak agreeably to their Characters and the Occasion, no Man has ever been so weak or so unjust, as to accuse *Milton* for that Blasphemy."[92] Apparently, not even Blake, who, as we have seen, warns against quoting Satan's blasphemies from Milton and then giving them as Milton's opinions. None may accuse Milton, but Dryden thus accuses Eve, and that accusation speaks volumes about each poet's supposed commitment to a feminist agenda.[93]

From such negativism, even from the seemingly positive gesture of Dryden's translating Milton's poem into a play, in the process changing its title from *Paradise Lost* and then dropping its already announced title, *The Fall of Angels and Man in Innocence*, in favor of *The State of Innocence, and Fall of Man*, we can infer that Milton's topic, the loss of paradise, was not for Dryden an altogether congenial choice, hence by some contemporaries judged unworthy of attention— whether for aesthetic or other reasons we are not always told. However if Nathaniel Lee's comments are relevant, both aesthetics and ideology come into play—or, more exactly, supposed aesthetic faults are used to mask objections to ideology (Milton "rudely cast what you cou'd well dispose" and thus by him "no perfect World was found").[94] From positive report, on the other hand, we can gather that *Paradise Lost* sufficiently fired the enthusiasm of one reader that he passed it on to Dryden and, more, that *Paradise Lost* in the judgment of both Denham and Dryden, at least initially, surpassed any poem yet written—in any country or any age. Whether its *nobility* is a feature of its matter or manner (or both) we are left to speculate—and then this evidence is only hearsay.

If we do thus speculate, we are bound to wonder: what were the expectations of a contemporary readership concerning *this poet* (John Milton) and *this poem* (*Paradise Lost*)? How are expectations created, and by whom? Presumably by how any poet has come to be "known"—through representations by others and through self-representations. The dominant ideology, together with the ideologies competing with it, help to define an horizon of expectations for any poet, especially one who deploys the master-myths of his culture. The method of deployment matters too: how is the material coded, both interpretively and generically, and how is it gendered? Does the poet stay within the margins of conventional discourse, the boundaries of received form, or transgress them; and what is the nature, the extent of his transgressions? That is, once expectations are formed, are they furthered or frustrated—and by whom: the poet or his readers? Or are expectations modified and, if so, again by whom and to what end?

Jonathan Richardson may declare, but William Riley Parker and John Shawcross have provided documentary evidence that we have dated the commencement of Milton's reputation as a poet rather too late. This has been so, in part perhaps, because we have failed to perceive (or possibly have chosen to ignore) the extent to which the reputations of poet and polemicist were nearly always intertwined, hence interdependent and reciprocally illuminating, with Milton's political tracts contributing majorly to the formation of an horizon of expectations for his last poems. In any event, the historical record is unmistakable: Milton did not exist in splendid isolation, nor did *Paradise Lost* meet with embarrassing neglect in the period between its first publication and Milton's death. Moreover, it was supposed not during his lifetime, but afterward, that Milton's poetry was inoculated against politics; that, in *Paradise Lost*, a dejected Milton renounced his previous political commitments.

More forcefully than Parker, Shawcross annihilates the argument that "Real criticism of *Paradise Lost* begins only with the last decade of the century"[95]—an argument that carries no more historical authority than the similar one concerning *Lycidas*: "this great poem seems to have passed unnoticed during Milton's lifetime. . . . No contemporary printed allusion to the poem has been so far discovered."[96] Such comments never see the trees. It is often said that *Lycidas* is a coda to the Edward King memorial volume in which it was published last, deliberately so, as a response to the poems that precede it. Yet that claim begs the question of whether *Lycidas* is part of a dialogue among poets and, if so, the further question of what sort of comment those poems make on Milton's, especially in its abandonment of a regular rhyme scheme, in its questioning of providence and inveighing against a corrupt clergy. Is the imagined dialogue among these poems an important part of the early reception of *Lycidas*? Does not this dialogue commence with many of the poems wrapping themselves as meditations around the initial poem by Henry King? Correspondingly, Humphrey Moseley, in an epistle "To the Reader" included as front matter to the 1645 *Poems of Mr. John Milton*, clearly alludes to the opening lines of *Lycidas* in his metaphoric representation of Milton's poems: "*these ever-green, and not to be blasted Laurels.*"[97] Insofar as the frontispiece to this volume is less portraiture than illustration, in depicting the piper and the bard, the illustration comprehends the progress of the entire volume figured most conspicuously not only in *L'Allegro* and *Il Penseroso* but just as strikingly in *Lycidas*. And whether by Milton's choosing, or someone else's, *Lycidas* is the poem that, by virtue of boldfacing, stands out among all the others in "The Table Of the *English* Poems" for the 1673 edition of the *Poems*: **LYCIDAS** (see figure 1.2). It is the poem that eventually will be printed first, hence given privilege of place, when Milton's *Poems* are republished in 1695.

THE POEM NEARLY ANONYMOUS

References to *Lycidas* in correspondence between John Beale and John Evelyn, describing Milton as a superb "Pindariste" and praising *Lycidas* for exhibiting "the Pindarique way," varying his numbers and distancing his rhymes, help to document a seventeenth-century reputation for *Lycidas*.[98] For this reason, perhaps, Peter Levi assumes that *Lycidas* is "an inescapable influence" on Thomas Creech's translation of Theocritus, although specific instances of Milton's influence, once Creech's translations are scrutinized, are not easily ascertained or documented.[99] More revelatory, perhaps, is the *supposed* reception of *Lycidas* by M. De St. Evremond and Edmund Waller, fabricated in the eighteenth century by John Langhorne (1773–79), which may, in fact, reflect accurately on the late seventeenth-century reception of *Lycidas*. In this imaginary exchange of letters, Waller writes:

> There is one *John Milton*, an old Commonwealth's Man, who hath, in the latter Part of his Life, written a Poem intituled *Paradise Lost*; and to say the Truth, it is not without some Fancy and bold Invention. But I am much better pleased with some smaller Productions of his in the Scenical and Pastoral Way, one of which [is] called *Lycidas*.[100]

To these words, St. Evremond responds:

> The Poem called *Lycidas*, which you say is written by Mr. *Milton*, has given me much Pleasure. It has in it what I conceive to be the true Spirit of Pastoral Poetry, the old *Arcadian* Enthusiasm.[101]

But one need not rely on mere conjecture, for in the seventeenth century, there are these lines (or just phrases) in Marvell's poems: the "gadding Vines" (610) and "heavy sedge" (642) in *Upon Appleton House*, "the last . . . brain" (28) in *Flecknoe*, the "beaked promontories" (358) in *The First Anniversary*, and "purple locks" (67) and "thou art gone . . . thou art gone" (299, 303) in *A Poem upon the Death of his Late Highness*. All are plausibly reminiscences, or echoes, of *Lycidas*.[102] Then, too, there is the accumulation of phrases like "Flame in the forehead of the azure skie," or "Pansie streakt with shining Jet, / The tufted Crowtoe, glowing Violet, / . . . the Faire Primrose (that forsaken dyes) / The Daffadillies with cups fill'd with teares, / All *Amaranth's* brood that Embroidery weares, / To strew her Lawreat Hearse" in the poetry of Robert Baron published in 1647.[103] Perhaps more telling, though, is the judgment of *Lycidas* implied by different placements: its appearing last, as both epitome and coda, in

Justa Edovardo King Naufrago (1637) and *The Poems of Mr. John Milton* (1645), but (as we earlier noticed) it is also being printed for the first time as headpiece to the volume in the 1695 *Poems upon Several Occasions.* By the end of the century, apparently, *Lycidas* has achieved preeminence among Milton's lyric poems—a point reinforced by the fact that, as early as 1729, Moses Brown, after citing Theocritus, Virgil, and Spenser, concludes that Milton is among several still more recent poets who "deserve perhaps as much Praise for what they have given us of this Kind as any of the Former."[104]

In a "Pastoral" poem specifically addressed to Milton, we may expect quiet invocation and subtle interplay with *Lycidas*, which is precisely what we find in Charles Goodall's poem, "A Propitiatory Sacrifice."[105] With its anguished "no more," the poem with two poets, one bringing the ivy, the other the myrtle, depicts a pastoral world shattered, a paradise destroyed: "*Flowers* . . . droop their sickly head" and "*Death* has stopt the *Springs* of *Paradise.*" Still, the poets sing, now thou art "dead . . . dead / . . . consecrated *Head,*" "now *thou* art gone," irrevocably so. The poet, in his "*Apostate Rhimes,*" claims that his muse is "On surer *Wings*, with an immortal flight"; and the poem itself concludes with a guardian angel looking down "with *indignation*" only to find the deceased poet, "mounted up on high," rising like a phoenix into paradise as his poem becomes an everlasting monument to his fame.[106]

Uncertain, erratic rhyme in *Lycidas* is, by the end of Milton's century, taken as a gesture of rebellion on the part of a poet who is the "first to *sence* converted *Doggerel-Rhimes*" and who, one surmises, is the modern-day Orphic poet, as well as Promethean poet, now renewing the "old prophetick strain."[107] Whatever may threaten him in this world, be that Death or the Furies, the poet's dreams will not be surrendered, nor will his visions be suppressed.[108] Milton has come to embody the true spirit of pastoral poetry, that Arcadian enthusiasm, both of which are at one with the spirit of prophecy.

Otherwise, in the seventeenth century, there are likely echoes of Milton, both in phrase and repetition, in poems by William Walsh: "*Sicilian* Muse, my humble Voice inspire"; "*Begin, my Muse, begin th'* Arcadian *Strains*"; "While Rocks and Caves thy tuneful Notes resound, . . . / The hungry Wolves devours [*sic*] thy fatten'd Lambs"; and the possibility of influence here is strengthened by the more insistent echoes of Milton, if not in *Eclogue IV*—"Sicilian *Muse begin a loftier Flight*"—then certainly in *Delia. A Pastoral Eclogue* (both these poems dated 1703): "*now no more* . . . Begin, my Muse! Begin your mournful Strains! . . . *now no more* . . . now Thou art gone . . . *now no* more . . . this sudden Change"; and finally "Delia *is* Dead . . . The Glory of our blasted Isle is Dead."[109]

More intriguing still is the striking parallelism between the opening lines of *Lycidas* and the first lines of "To the Excellent *Orinda*." The year of the latter publication is 1667; the occasion, the publication of *Poems by the Most Deservedly Admired Mrs Katherine Philips the Matchless Orinda*, one offshoot of which is the appearance of this Orinda poem, presumably by an Irishwoman who signs herself "Philo-philippa." Written at least four years earlier by a woman whose identity Philips claims she was unable to determine, the poem in its initial verse paragraph, if it does not invoke, surely invites comparison with another poem composed some thirty years before, twice since published and soon to be published again, and, as we have seen, already several times echoed. That poem, namely *Lycidas*, in its initial movement, accords privilege of place to Phoebus Apollo: "But not the praise, / *Phœbus* repli'd, and touch't my trembling ears; / Fame is no plant that grows on mortal soil" (76–78). And the same poem, in its very first lines, represents the poet as writing under "Bitter constraint" and so, "with forc't fingers rude," disturbing the "season," shattering the leaves of laurel, myrtles, and ivy in order to fashion a garland (this poem of praise) for "Young *Lycidas*," "dead, dead" *Lycidas* (1–9).

These are the harsh words leveled by "Philo-philippa" against, if not Milton specifically, then poets like him, who write in *his* tradition of pastoral:

> Let the male Poets their male *Phoebus* chuse,
> Thee I invoke, *Orinda*, for my Muse;
> He could but force a Branch, *Daphne* her Tree
> More freely offers to her Sex and thee,
> And says to Verse, so unconstrain'd as yours,
> Her Laurel freely comes, your fame secures:
> And men no longer shall with ravish'd Bays
> Crown their forc'd Poems by as forc'd a praise.[110]

Even if not so intended (although, in this instance, I suspect that what cannot be proved is in fact the likelihood), the perspective opened upon *Lycidas* (as well as Milton) by these verses—and by verses of other women poets of the seventeenth century—is striking. No sooner has Milton asked the "Sisters of the sacred well" to commence their playing—"Begin then, . . . / Begin, and somewhat loudly sweep the string"(15–17)—than he imagines "som gentle muse" (gendered male) favoring "my destin'd urn, / And as *he* passes," turning, then bidding "fair peace" (19–22; my italics). Read through the lens afforded by the poetry of "Philo-philippa" and others, Milton's lines may allow women to be accomplices of the poet (they provide the music), but simultaneously subordinate them to the role of accompanist in a poem whose inaugural vision culminates in the utterance of Phoebus Apollo only after Calliope, here speechless, is also rendered helpless: "What could the Muse *her* self that *Orpheus* bore, / The muse *her* self for *her* inchanting son" (58–59; my italics except for *Orpheus*).

Whether direct or oblique, what else could woman's response be to a poem, we might ask, wherein she and her music are a poetic fiction and the poetry of the shepherd-poet and his male muses all we hear—all that matters; wherein, repeatedly, his words yield an exalted "strain," "a higher mood" (87); wherein, if not silent or powerless like Calliope, woman is a mindless reveler within a scene of tragedy ("Sleek *Panope* with all her sisters plaid" as "that fatall and perfidious bark / Built in th' eclipse . . . / . . . sunk so low that sacred head of thine" [99–102])—or willfully inattentive ("Where were ye nymphs when the remorseless deep / Clos'd o're the head of your lov'd *Lycidas*?" [50–51]); wherein she is a seductive distraction ("To sport with *Amaryllis* in the shade" [68])—or a fatal attraction with shepherd boys like Lycidas caught in "the tangles of *Neæra*'s hair" ([69]); or, worse, wherein she is the destructive element itself ("the blind *Fury*" [75]) through whose agency Lycidas, like Orpheus, meets his fate and under whose aegis the poem, in a "dred voice" (132), represents the world destroyed only to be followed by a vision (now produced under the aegis of the gentler male muse Alpheus) of the world restored. That vision is framed by warblings of consolation within a poem that is otherwise remarkable for its rugged verse: jagged meters, contorted syntax, and irregular (often distant) rhymes. All this occurs, moreover, within a poem described as "a melodious tear" that, while inscribing the clichés of pastoral verse—"rurall ditties . . . / Temper'd to th' oaten flute," "soft layes," is finally about the disruption of its own pastoral world by "lean and flashy songs / Grat[ing] on . . . scrannel pipes of wretched straw" and eventual abandonment of that world as the poet looks beyond pastoral: "To morrow to fresh woods and pastures new" (14, 32–33, 44, 123–24, 193).

The Prologue and Epilogue to *Lycidas* would allow women to strike decidedly different postures in relation to Milton. The Prologue may engender an antithetical stance, like that of "Philo-Philippa," who, in those lines already cited, represents male poets like Milton as usurpers, if not rapists, and women as the rightful poets, in a poem that proceeds to regender the poetic faculties, as well as the elements of poetry and the virtues it would inculcate, as feminine. The Epilogue to *Lycidas*, on the other hand, especially when it is construed as Milton's farewell to pastoral poetry, allows for a response rather like the one of Aphra Behn who, in "To Mrs. W. on her Excellent verses," represents herself in the moment of inspiration when a "Mighty Spirit" appears, her soul is "Rais'd," and cast about her is "a Dazling Light." The record she provides of taking possession of the vision and thereupon moving into its realm, whether or not it relies upon Milton, nevertheless replicates the experience of *Lycidas* and, for that matter, the movement of the 1645 *Poems of Mr. John Milton*:

> So the All-Ravisht Swain that hears
> The wondrous Musick of the Sphears,
> For ever does the grateful Sound retain,
>   Whilst all his Oaten Pipes and Reeds.
> The Rural Musick of the Groves and Meads,
> Strive to divert him from the Heavenly Song in vain.
>   He hates their harsh and Untun'd Lays,
> Which now no more his Soul and Fancy raise.[111]

As Jane Lead will later do, Behn here joins her own poetic voice with Milton's.

The recovery of seventeenth-century women's poetry allows for an imaginative reconstruction of what their response to poets like Milton and poems like *Lycidas* might have been. If, in *Lycidas*, Calliope is voiceless and powerless, as well as denied the consolation that is ours, in the poetry of Elizabeth Thomas she rises up to sing "Of mighty Poets" and, herself consoled, becomes the voice of consolation: she remembers her "dearest *Orpheus*, [who] *Pluto*'s Favour won" and who, "for too much Kindness to his Wife, / . . . was by *Bacchannals* depriv'd of Life; / Who tore his Limbs, in *Hebrus* cast his Head." That is, Thomas remembers the same grim details that Milton reports, right down to nature's plaintive elegy, and lets us hear from Calliope the same words that by Milton are addressed to his woeful shepherds: "weep no more." In Thomas's poem, consolation comes to Calliope through the realization that she mothers a long line of poets, includ-ing Virgil, who "With *Eagles* Wings, . . . soar'd above the Rest," "doubly" possessing "*Orpheus* spirit." Even with this consolation, though, Calliope still has cause for grief; for what was once the fate of poets is now the fate of their poems, which are "maul'd and torn" and, once dismembered, "Burlcsqu'd, obscur'd, and in Travesty shown," their "sacred Lines profane[d]" by translators and interpreters who ought instead, by polishing the verse, its "soul express."[112]

In this same poem, "mighty" Dryden is addressed just as Marvell had addressed Milton, with Thomas, at the same time, representing Virgil's debt to Dryden as Dryden (and some of his followers) represent how Milton's debt should be calculated by Dryden: Dryden turned the brick of his precursors' poetry into marble, thus eclipsing them much as Dryden claimed Milton had excelled Homer and Virgil. Moreover, by establishing numbers and setting rules, Dryden is said to have both curbed the excesses of earlier poets and, in the process, diminished their poetic heat.[113] The same sort of praise comes to Dryden in an elegy by Lady Sarah Piers, wherein Dryden's death is represented in language reminiscent of Adam's fall in *Paradise Lost*: "All Nature trembled" and "Earth did under strong Convulsions groan." Dryden, who was "no more / No more," is yet once more said to surmount Homer and Virgil ("To him proud *Greece* and *Italy* must bow") where Piers's muse is Dryden's muse and the muse of these poets' also Milton's muse, Urania.[114]

Within this context, we may begin to wonder about the extent to which Milton and his admirers, including Dryden, should be credited with formulating an idiom for encomiastic poetry, especially when one remembers the terms by which, in yet another poem, Piers exonerates still another friend rather as Marvell had already exonerated Milton: "Your fable's clear, no rule you have transgrest, / Chaste all your thoughts, yet Nature still exprest."[115] If there is indebtedness here, if Milton is comprehended within their range of reference, many of these poems suggest that, what was initially at issue for Milton's female readership and what later criticism then chose to hide, was the sexual politics—or the politics generally—of Milton's poetry. In either case, the politics is complicated, enormously so; and if the "Orinda" poem by "Philo-philippa" does harbor an allusion to *Lycidas*, it allows us to say rather more precisely how Milton's sexual politics was construed and represented in 1667 and thus to calculate what the horizon of expectation would have been for *Paradise Lost* published in the same year.

These verses—and especially the Orinda poem—hold multiple interests: first, for their subtle critique of gender markings in *Lycidas*, which, for the most part, are in accord with those in the early prose works, including the divorce tracts; second, for the signally important, and timely, reception they afford for Milton the poet as we consider what Milton is on record as having said concerning women and what he has yet to say in the still unpublished last poems; third, for the questions that are bound to emerge from such reflections, especially when lines written before and published in the wake of the first appearance of *Paradise Lost* are read in the aftermath of this poem's publication. Whatever conclusions we may reach concerning the figuration of woman in *Lycidas*, as well as the early prose works, does the Milton of *Paradise Lost*, not to mention *Paradise Regain'd* and *Samson Agonistes*, stand in the same place he once did—and hold tenaciously to the same attitudes?

If Milton is comprehended within the system of allusion in the Orinda poem, it becomes a poem that forges a paradigmatic response to him—a response that is regarded (even today) as *the* characteristically female response to this supposedly bruisingly misogynistic poet. If the correspondence between the first lines of the Orinda poem and those for *Lycidas* is more than mere coincidence, that coincidence rolls over into heavy irony when it is remembered, initially, that the verses by "Philo-philippa" revise a male myth of poetic creation and thereupon the patriarchal myth of human creation just prior to the publication of *Paradise Lost* in which Milton's muse is now gendered female (and not just his muse but also Wisdom) and his Eve (also a poet) is by the end of that poem a poet who, speaking prophecy, stands at the head of a line of female prophets as both their progenitor and their authorizing voice.

What is equally remarkable: this poem sets forth the terms by which *Paradise Lost*, once published, will eventually be censured by women for portraying them as soul-less—a paradigmatic response that, running from Sarah Fyge Egerton to Mary Astell, eventually is codified by Dr. Johnson. At the same time, though, the Orinda poem also tilts in another direction, thus pointing to the terms by which Milton, after another turn of the critical lens forced by the shock accompanying the recognition of his many transgressive maneuvers in *Paradise Lost*, will be embraced by women as their ally and sponsor. If in its opening lines the Orinda poem figures Milton as a prototypically masculinist and patriarchal poet, it also anticipates the swerve from a masculinist and patriarchal tradition of poetry through which Milton signals his interrogation of attitudes his poem is often thought (usually by men) to promulgate.

Almost prophetically, the Orinda poem defines the features that, once detected in *Paradise Lost*, will allow for the appropriation of Milton's poem as a woman's text and that will account for a shift into (or sometimes just toward) a paradigmatically positive and sometimes downright feminist response to *Paradise Lost*. The revisionary attitudes toward women, and toward poetry, that the Orinda poem would instill in its readers are the very ones that the Milton of *Paradise Lost* embraces: the feminization of the poet's muse, the admittance of women to the pantheon of poets, together with the admission that "The Soul's the same" and in men and women "alike in both doth dwell," and the correlative admission that woman no less than man has "heart" and, like *Him*, can participate in the so-called "manly Vertue":

> If Souls no Sexes have, as 'tis confest,
> 'Tis not the he or she makes Poems best:
> Nor can men call these Verses Feminine,
> Be the sense vigorous and Masculine.[116]

Men may celebrate their heroes without interruption; but women, while portraying the lives of such heroes, in their poetry never forget to report their blemishes, nor the hero's fall. (Their representations of Samson are a striking example.)

Women thus temper masculinist idealisms with hard realities and, simultaneously, explode masculinist fictions and pretentions concerning unpremediated verse and unfettered muses. At least, women ask about the efficacy of such freedom, even as they measure masculinist poetic achievement by the consonance between soul and sense and by the subjects their supposedly "vast World affords."[117] Some of these pretentions are there in *Paradise Lost*: in its adventurous song and unpremediated verse, in its singing of things unattempted and hitherto invisible to mortal sight; in its taking for its province all of history (past, present, and future), together with an entire cosmos (hell, heaven, and earth, both before and after the Fall). Yet such pretentions might also be forgiven a poet of equally apparent humility who converts his unfettered poetics into the master-themes of his poem: ancient liberty, modern bondage, future deliverance.

We may not know what first impelled Milton's poetry toward politics; but *Lycidas*, with its sharp political edge, shows Milton, between the first and second printings of this pastoral elegy, not making a new poem but, instead, gathering into focus the one he already had made, centering the poem's political content through the foregrounding device of its epigraph: "to foretell," *to prophesy*, "the ruin of our corrupted Clergy then in their height" (see figures 1.1 and 1.2). Whether the example is *Lycidas* or *Paradise Lost*, the more conventional genres of pastoral and epic are here overruled by the subversive form of prophecy, one of whose teachings, as Paul West observes, is that "Poets are supposed to be masters of intuition, each a prophet to himself."[118] The question lurking within recent fictionalized accounts of Milton by Paul West and Peter Ackroyd, is the one to which William Blake gives sharpest focus: is Milton a prophet delivered by, or enchained within, his own prophecy?[119]

In the twentieth century, two positions separated by an interval of fifty years confront one another. First, according to Parker, "Milton had tried to put politics out of his mind": by the time he turned to *Paradise Lost*, Milton the artist "emerged from the chrysalis of controversy."[120] For James Grantham Turner, who urges "the integration of poetry and prose, the literary and the political" in commentary on Milton, the situation is otherwise: "Political *engagement* may then have generated rather than aborted Milton's epic vision; in the words that Dryden applied to Charles II, 'crisis' may have '*authorized*' his skill."[121] Demotion of the prose writings, disconnecting them from the poetry, then depoliticizing the poetry—these impulses, as Turner perceives, have run through Milton criticism from the very beginning. Such impulses translate into an agenda for the 1688 edition of *Paradise Lost* and for much criticism of Milton during the first half of the eighteenth century. But criticism should not be allowed to conceal the interfacing of religion and politics in Milton's poetry from the very beginning, nor the fact that the suppression of its political resonances has been the critic's way of undoing an early, supposed alliance between Milton's prose and poetry. These suppositions become all the more plausible if, in response to Jauss's urging, we follow the footprints of the immediate receptions of Milton's writings, especially of *Paradise Lost*.[122]

The moment Milton's prose writings are brought in contact with, and allowed to afford an interpretive context for Milton's last poems, different forms of the same questions arise concerning each of them. What are the points of intersection, of divergence? Are the poems replications of earlier postures, redactions; or revisions of previous positions? How are scriptural sources and citations used in polemics and in poems? And with reference to the poems, what are their scriptural sources (acknowledged and hidden), and how do those sources relate to Milton's *poems*—as shadow texts or subtexts or cotexts? Indeed, how do Milton's *poems* relate to one another? Are the poems elaborations or exfoliations, simple mirrorings, or significant modifications of one another's visions? Is their relationship one of concord or contention?

And what of their relationship to their scriptural counterparts: are the poems safe or risky elaborations of them? Are the biblical stories, along with the master-myths they enshrine, a way of evading or encountering, of screening or searching, the history of Milton's own times? Do Milton's last poems authorize one hermeneutic—or accommodate several—that over time have become attached to each of their stories? How easy are the accommodations, if that is in fact Milton's tactic? Do these poems promulgate or prosecute received interpretation(s); and to what extent do their religious/theological wrappings conceal a political agenda? How hidden are Milton's politics? Do these poems have a submerged, barely decipherable, political content—or rather a sheathed yet still sharp political edge? The irony tucked away in the inaugural phase of Milton criticism (to which we will momentarily return) is that expectations created for the poet by his prose writings—for a poet no less rebellious in his religion than in his politics (however compatible those expectations may be with the poems Milton wrote)—were resisted by different readers for various reasons: in order to protect the poems themselves from the threat of censorship and Milton from the consequences thereof; or, sometimes, in order to allow for appropriations by those with contrary ideological commitments and a competing political agenda. As George Sensabaugh reports in this connection, Nathaniel Lee imagined Milton rising from the dead, filing off the rust, and another—"the right Party" choosing.[123] So successful were early commentators in presenting a Milton eventually recovering from "his early bout of radicalism"[124] that, by the early eighteenth century, it was a cliché of Milton criticism that "His Judgement, when dis-engag'd from Religious and Political Speculations, was just and penetrating."[125]

Whatever the motive, the results were usually the same: Milton's poems, especially *Paradise Lost*, were rescued from the clutch of the prose works and represented as swerving from Milton's earlier subversions, religious as well as political—as swerving so completely that we are now only beginning to retrieve as a vital presence in criticism issues too long absent (but in the beginning never completely missing) from Milton commentary. If it was once fashionable to date the emergence of Milton's reputation as a major poet from 1688, the fashion constituted a convenient evasion of the conflicting signals, the ideological dis-ease, of early Milton criticism. The 1688 edition of *Paradise Lost* allowed for the mainstreaming of Milton as *the* reigning poet in the venerable tradition of epic (witness Dryden's now famous epigram), as a poet *in* step with the newly founded political liberalism and well *in*side the confines of religious orthodoxy. Witness the conforming spirit of the illustrations by Medina and others (see, e.g., figure 2.19).

This *appropriation* of Milton heralds others, but it also has its harbinger in an earlier stage of Milton criticism. Then critics valued Milton's poetry for the traditions, literary rather than intellectual, which it accommodated. Somewhat later, they would displace Milton's politics with a theology emptied of its subversions, thus privileging *Paradise Lost* over *Paradise Regain'd*, or would displace Milton's politics to a poem like *Samson Agonistes*, which those politics, in their most extreme version, could marginalize and trivialize. This history in its abstract, philosophical form is inscribed in *Paradise Lost*. The same history, now concretized, is written during the first century of Milton criticism and bears retelling only because it keeps reproducing itself, with variations to be sure, right up to the present time and, so doing, becomes paradigmatic for repeated evasions and concealments. Shawcross is right: one of the byproducts of this history, of these critical attitudes—of conventionalizing *Paradise Lost* and radicalizing *Paradise Regain'd* and *Samson Agonistes*, of theologizing the former poem and politicizing the later ones—is the "misreading" of all these poems.[126]

OTHER EARLY RECEPTIONS

If it can be said that Parker summarizes and Shawcross supplements the history of Milton criticism up to and through the time when *Paradise Lost* was published, it must also be acknowledged that Shawcross's supplementations have the effect of subverting Parker's conclusions concerning Milton's withdrawal from politics in the last poems. That is, the evidence assembled by Shawcross shows that, however submerged, politics is well within the horizon of expectation for this poet and his *Paradise Lost*—a poet whose reputation, during most of his century, was founded chiefly upon the divorce tracts, in which Milton was said to have scored his points at the expense of Scripture, twisting and turning, mutilating, then murdering, God's word; and upon the political pamphlets in which, having murdered God's word, he now defends killing the king, God's vicar on earth.[127]

For his "sins," both religious and political, Milton was targeted for abuse: "wilde, mad, and frantick," he was to be "hiss'd at rather then confuted"—hooted from the stage of history as a forecaster and false prophet and as one whose opinions were "Anabaptisticall, Antinomian, Hereticall, Atheisticall."[128] Descibed as "A monster horrible, deformed, huge and sightless," whose only relationship to laws is that he broke them, and denounced for "criminal madness," Milton, "whether a man, or a worm," in the words of Peter

Du Moulin, should himself be burned, not just his books (YP, 4:1045, 1076, 1050). At the Restoration, his books finally were burned (along with those of John Goodwin), a point Milton's early biographers and, for other reasons, some detractors never tired of making.[129] This divorcer and king-hater, sectarian and heretic, regicide and blasphemer, was like Sampson in his spiteful revenge, in his desire to pull down the pillars of both church and state; and was like Satan in his rebellion and subversion. With Goodwin, as we observed in the previous chapter, Milton was numbered among those devilish rebels and "Blinde Guides" of a now stumbling nation—"a blind adder," Robert South called him, in contrast with Charles I who, according to Roger L'Estrange, in the end took "almost certain *Inspirations* [from] *the Holy Spirit.*" Speaking with the devil's mouth and sorted with the devil's party, this "Infamous," "Sacrilegious *Milton*" was called a "*Diabolical Rebel*"—"altogether a Devil" posing as a saint, a compendium of the most hated villains and their various villainies—and presumed already to have gone to "Hell."[130]

It should come as no surprise that Milton would be accused of heaping upon others the rhetoric of abuse now being heaped upon him, what in his *Defense of Himself* he himself calls "the devil's rhetoric" (YP, 4:823; cf. 765–66). Alexander More had complained, for example, about Milton referring to him as "Satan's minister, the devil's slave, and . . . even the devil himself" (YP, 4:1104) even as Milton would protest in his *Defense of Himself* against those who "relegated [him] to the company of devils" (YP, 4:735). In 1667, just days after *Paradise Lost* is registered for publication, John Beale, fretting over Milton's politics, worries that the poet is "too full of the Devill" and thus will be "doeing mischeefe" in whatever poetry he may write.[131] Once *Paradise Lost* is published, thinking it a "pity he ever wrote in prose," immediately troubled by open assertions of politics in the poem's concluding books and the "persecutory imagination" behind the offensive orthodoxies in earlier ones, Beale eventually lights on Milton's Satan, as well as "the long *blasphemies* of the Devils," which he finds "too execrable to be adorn'd with the powre of elegant verse," although he also allows that, of those fanatics who speak sacrilege, "Only Milton had a good smack ['of true Poesy']." There are evidently some "Pollutions of Scriptures" in *Paradise Lost*, together with aberrations in its theology, that make Beale wish for more strenuous censorship of—and in—a poem, the "propheticall note" of which is struck in Beale's recollection of the biblical promise "*that young men shall see visions, & old men shall dreame dreames*" and then silenced in Beale's accompanying reserve

concerning Milton's claims to divine inspiration.[132] Continually
needled by Milton's theology, its scandals and blasphemies, especially evident in Book 10 of *Paradise Lost* and its exaltation of Eve,
citing 10:918, 927, 954, 972, Beale, eventually comparing Milton
to Abraham Cowley, labels the former a "fanatic" for having "put
such long & horrible Blasphemies in the Mouth of Satan" whereas
"Cowley in his Davideis allowed Satan but one Verse for his
Blasphemy—And Satan, said he, spake the rest in Lookes."[133]

From the very beginning, there were those like Beale and Bishop
Hacket of Lichfield whose suspicions of Milton, once they read
Paradise Lost, turned into downright distrust: a "Phanatic," Beale had
called him, "a Socinian" in his theology, Abraham Hill had thought;
"that serpent Milton, a dead dog," Hacket calls him, "a canker worm,
a petty schoolboy scribbler."[134] What was submerged or hidden, an
often unseen presence in *Paradise Lost*, sat boldly on the surface of
Christian Doctrine, leading its earliest readers to find therein "*the
strongest Arianism . . . throughout*" (Phillippus van Limborch) in "a
pernicious Booke, of that late Villain Milton's" (Sir Joseph
Williamson), "seditious Treasonable writing," "venemous" and full of
"impudent assertions" (Sir Leoline Jenkins)—a book "fitter to be suppressed than published" (Daniel Elsevier) unless, of course, the reader
were an admirer in which case Milton could be lauded, as he was by
Daniel Skinner, for evincing an "unbyassed . . . search after Truth"
and for displaying himself as "a constant Champion for the liberty of
Opining."[135]

However, it is the negative impressions of Milton that predomi-
nate, at least initially. Those impressions, fostered chiefly by Milton's
prose writings, are the shapers and purveyors of Milton's reputation,
even as a poet; and they are foregrounded, starkly so, in the years from
1666 to 1668 by a single entry—"*Blinde Milton*"—in *Poor
Robin . . . An Almanack*, an entry that reveals how profoundly early
representations of Milton taint the reception of *Paradise Lost*. The
entry always appears in relation to the month of November, that
month of plotting (even by poets). Drawing upon Adrian Vlacq's
description of Milton's "blindness of heart" and Alexander More's
pique over Milton's "blindness of . . . mind" (YP, 4:1089, 1103), as
well as Roger L'Estrange's portrayal of Milton as a practitioner and
promoter of sedition in *No Blinde Guides* (1660), this entry also gathers its point from the logic of the various representations in what the
subtitle to many of these volumes calls this "Almanack After a New
Fashion." For every month there are two calendars, one white and the
other black (so to speak) and two different chronologies, one of

loyalists and another of fanatics; one cataloguing heroes and saints, some mythological, some historical; the other computing, in analogy, the names of notorious villains and sinners—or "mock-Saints"— with Milton's name, in 1666, paired with Saturn's, the mythological type of whom Milton, apparently, is the historical representative and perversion.[136] The implication is that Milton as well as "*Saturn* signifies . . . the devil and all"; the implied castigation is clearly directed against Milton's politics in this series of mock-calendars tabulating "the Round-heads, or Fanaticks: with their several Saints days" and with the names of "their chief Ring-leaders most eminent for Villany [*sic*]."[137]

Not just Milton, but John Bradshaw, Henry Ireton, James Nayler, and *St. Oliver*—all famous (now infamous) for their participation in the Revolutionary government—appear together in a sequence of mock-calendars; and all of these figures are aligned *as plotters* with "Guido Faux"; *as political leaders* with Nero; *as would-be prophets* with Tom-of-Bedlam, Merlin, Mother Shipton, and Jane Shore; and *as artists* with Lucian and Rabelais. In subsequent editions of this almanac, moreover, Milton's name is moved to the head of the list for November, appearing opposite now All Souls' (1667, 1668) and now All Saints' Day (1669), with the suggestion that as an apostate Milton is a lost soul, as well as a limb of Antichrist, the prototypical figure for these plotters and mock-saints who, sometimes poets, are part of "that Rebellious force" that brought death to "Good *pious* Charles."[138] Blake may have thought that Milton was of the Devil's party without knowing it, but certain of Milton's contemporaries (allowing for this affiliation) thought Milton knew full well whose side he was on and were not inclined ever to let him forget. Before the publication of *Paradise Lost*, the time would come when "the Writings on which his Vast Reputation Stood were . . . Accounted Criminal, Every One of them, and Those Most which were the Main Pillars of his Fame."[139]

The indictment against Milton falls hard—is rendered without equivocation. The entry encoding it speaks through a shorthand, an epitome, referring to the reputation won by Milton the polemicist in which some would now try to wrap Milton the poet.[140] The notion of a seditious Milton is a reputation that sticks, for even after Milton's name disappears from *Poor Robin*, he continues to be dubbed "apostate bard" and, in images that recall the poet's not always pejorative association with Samson and Satan, is referred to as "a blind adder," "a Shimsi" or, as already noticed, "that serpent Milton."[141] These tendencies to mythologize Milton as Samson and Satan retain currency (even today) as evinced in Peter Ackroyd's novel, in which Milton, escaping to New England, is analogized with Samson and, by echoing his language, elided with Satan: "better to be great here . . . then to serve evil men in London. . . . All hail, you happy fields."[142]

The prologues to *Paradise Lost*, in their defensiveness, admit as much: Milton has fallen on evil days *and evil tongues* but, even in changed circumstances, remains steady in his principles; his blindness, no sign of dishonor, is the badge of his prophetic office and divine favor. *Blind* Milton may be, but he can nevertheless *see* and *tell* of things invisible to mortal sight. His song may be of loss but glimpses a recovered paradise at the end of time as well as the promise—an historical possibility still—of a paradise in history ("then the Earth / Shall all be Paradise, far happier place / Then this of *Eden*, and far happier daies" [12.463–65]), with Milton figuring himself as a New Moses who will lead a New Chosen People into the still Promised Land. Representation is fronted by self-representation, Milton here challenging his detractors from the high ground, the expansive spaces, of *Paradise Lost*.

For a long time, it has been acknowledged that the multiple prologues to *Paradise Lost* are apologiae: sites and centers of ethical proof from which Milton counters *ad hominem* arguments. In view of his reputation, what too often gets lost is Milton's audacity in beginning his epic in hell—with what has been for many an appealing portrait of Satan. If we are to believe John Toland, that portrait, with its political resonances, caused Milton problems immediately. The licenser Thomas Tomkins, his suspicions roused by the image of the rising sun perplexing monarchs (I.594–99), "would . . . suppress the whole poem for imaginary Treason."[143] Yet the very fact that *Paradise Lost* was not suppressed suggests, as Nicholas von Maltzahn proposes, that whatever suspicions the poet of *Paradise Lost* might have aroused, they were allayed both by "the apparent orthodoxy of much of the poem" and also by the poem's "engrossing elaboration of its themes," which, even if veering toward heterodoxy, was wrapped in a complexity sufficient enough to elude the grasp of the readership Tomkins was charged with protecting.[144]

That Milton could nevertheless win a favorable judgment from some of his readers, early ones, is attested to by the first documentable receptions of *Paradise Lost*, once the poem was published. Besides the reception by Beale scattered over time (1667, 1668, 1669, 1670, 1679, 1681), there are two letters by John Hobart, dating from early 1668, that first assert, then reaffirm an extraordinarily high evaluation of Milton's poem. These letters between cousins, one of whom, having presented a copy of *Paradise Lost* to the other, eagerly awaits a response, are interesting chiefly as evidence of Milton's power *as a poet* to refashion his reputation, to control through the power of his word (and the word of others) the early reception of his poem.[145]

In each of Hobart's letters, there is some indication that the verse form, "not very com[m]on," was initially unsettling and, in its rhymelessness, may have seemed a disturbing, even disruptive, presence in the poem—a coded gesture of rebellion in a poem judged "more extraordinary for . . . matter, then verse." These letters also indicate that Hobart is aware of other writings by Milton, "severall pieces, good & bad," which "some moderne creticks will condemne," he says, regarding this author as "guilty" (because of his politics presumably). But if so, such suspicions are allayed by, or perhaps just easily evaded in, a poem that, not only rivaling, surpasses the achievements of Milton's eminent precursors, ancient and modern. Not wishing to "injure" Milton with too extravagant, "too advantagious" praise—or perhaps not wishing to "injure" the poet by getting too near the "matter" of his poem—with a practiced restraint and in studied generalities Hobart claims that Milton occupies "soe high a place amounge our eminent Poets" because, like Homer and Virgil, he redeems language "from obscurity" and exercises it with an astonishing "liberty."[146]

So effective was Milton in embedding generic signatures that this poem, called simply "A Poem," is instantly recognized as an epic outdoing all others, those by Homer and Spenser especially:

> The subject [is] great, & it has this advantage, That ye Theme it treats off, is as much above Hyberbolyes; or Tropes, as others are usually below them: Some resemblance it has to Spencers way, but in ye opinion of ye impartiall learned, not only above all moderne attempts in verse, but equall to any of ye Ancie[nt] Poets. And his blinde fate dose not barely resemble Homers fate: but his raptures & fancy brings him uppon a nearer paralele: I must confess I have been strangely pleased in a deleberate & repeated reading of him, & more ye last tyme then ye first. . . . [M]y owne delight . . . has been soe excessive, That I can say truly I never read any thing more august, & withall more gratefull to my (too much limited) understanding.[147]

Given Hobart's praise of Milton's matter over his manner, his remarks are curiously elusive. We learn only that Milton's subject is great; that his theme (never stipulated) in manner surpasses all other such attempts; that Milton's prophetic raptures exceed Homer's and even Spenser's with which, in any event, they find a nearer and neater parallel. On the face of things, subject, content and theme—each is addressed without ever being identified or explored; each, if not voided, gets swallowed up in Hobart's aesthetic approval. But there is also a subtext to these observations, a commentary decipherable by inference.

In correspondence that is chiefly political, the author of these letters, Sir John, who once supported the Commonwealth and later, supporting the Restoration of Charles II, took a pardon in June, 1660, can himself be expected to speak guardedly of Milton. Hobart is sensitive to the unconventionality of Milton's verse and language, aligning *Paradise Lost* with a native literary tradition and crediting Milton with outdoing Spenser, his chief competition in that tradition. (Dryden's later proposition, that Spenser is Milton's original, is already in place.) In his mention of the prose writings, which constitutes a veiled reference to Milton's politics, Hobart at least hints at the possibility, so astutely formulated by Terry Eagleton, that Milton's transgressive gestures in this poem suggest that *Paradise Lost* is "a radically political act"—an "assertive appropriation" of classical modes and models "for historically progressive ends."[148] Yet because of Hobart's curious deflections, his backing away from what he most admires in the poem, *its matter*, this kind of interpretive possibility remains submerged, though not completely silent, in a criticism with an aesthetic turn and focus. It would be hard to find a better illustration of the proposition that "reception mechanisms [for *Paradise Lost*] . . . at an early stage succeeded in aestheticizing potentially subversive material."[149]

Paradise Lost is obviously implanted with various interpretive codes; but in the early receptions, even where the prevailing concerns suggest otherwise, it is the aesthetic code that predominates, and predominates so completely, that the political code, when not fully silenced, is sealed within insinuations. Hobart's reception, in this sense, achieves paradigmatic status. It hardly matters whether those receptions reported by Richardson are apocryphal or not[150] because their forms and terms, in a more restrained and pedestrian key, are authorized, if not authenticated, by Hobart's documentable reception: *Paradise Lost*—a poem for all times, epic in ambition and achievement, the noblest ever written—is authored by a poet who overgoes all his competition, both ancient and modern. "The conservative Hobart," according to von Maltzahn, thus "welcomes Milton's Christian epic," with its "reassuringly holy purpose," as "a counterweight to the irreligious court culture" and its blasphemous burlesque of the Lord's passion by what Hobart calls "some persons of quality, but more infam[y]," who "Inverted the Sacred & Solemne Tragedy [of the Passion] into ridicule." As von Maltzahn goes on to say, "Hobart clearly distinguished *Paradise Lost* from the earlier controversial writings for which Milton was infamous. Milton's politics he abhorred. The poet was 'a criminall & obsolete person,' Hobart's association elsewhere of the word 'obsolete' with the cause of Buckingham shows he meant it to signify rebellious independency, or any alliance with the sects."[151]

Yet if we conclude with von Maltzahn that *Paradise Lost* "relieved the anxieties" created by Milton's polemics,[152] we must also wonder, in the face of Hobart's comments on those who burlesque, ridicule, and invert the *tragedy* of the Crucifixion, if he slides by Book 6 of Milton's epic unaware of the way in which it hides this story in the basement of a book that, mocking the heroics of violence, parodies conventional atonement theories as much as it ridicules the heroics of classical epic poetry. Then come *Paradise Regain'd* and *Samson Agonistes* in which the Crucifixion story acts as a shadow text for both poems, each of which, as it happens, implying a critique of the atonement theories it invokes, with the Milton of *Paradise Regain'd* "err[ing] very widely"[153] in his religion by substituting redemption in the desert for salvation on the cross and with Samson himself mocking the philosophy of forgiveness worn so conspicuously on the sleeve of the Crucifixion episode that his own story invokes.

That Milton is evasive when it comes to the Crucifixion story, hiding it in the allegory of his celestial battle and altogether eschewing it in *Paradise Regain'd*, then merely alluding to it in his Preface to *Samson Agonistes*, in his reference to *Christ Suffering* and in the poem proper barely hinting at it through cryptic typological reference, may have led John Norris, by way of conventionalizing Milton, to Miltonize his own "The Passion of our B. Saviour represented in a Pindarique Ode" through echoes of *Paradise Lost*. Those echoes, in turn, implicate Milton in a story that, always skirting, never really telling, he repeatedly evades as, at best, he uses what will be Norris's "*Tragic Scene*'s" and "*Map* of Woe" as inlays in *Samson Agonistes*.[154] Book 6 of *Paradise Lost* first, and later Milton's brief epic and tragedy, all seem to burlesque, parody, and invert the tragedy of the Crucifixion even as they suppress and hide the atonement theories founded upon it. Indeed, by the nineteenth century, Milton was thought to have torn Christ from the firmament in *Paradise Regain'd* and, in that poem, to have redefined the moment and nature of Christian redemption.[155] If Milton exercises language with an astonishing liberty (as Hobart contends), it may be just one more way of encoding liberty as his master-theme.

If there is a latent anxiety in Hobart's letters, it may replicate, in less extreme form, the more obvious discomfort of Ellwood, who eschews comment on the one poem (*Paradise Lost*) by wishing for another (*Paradise Regain'd*), and may be replicated, in turn, but now with a poetic rather than ideological emphasis, by Denham and Dryden in the awe they express at Milton's outdistancing all his eminent rivals. A predictable anxiety is registered at the margins of one poet's discourse concerning the unexampled and perhaps unmatchable successes of another—the sheer awe at Milton's achievement harboring the frustration of fellow poets who, in the face of another claiming so much imaginative ground for himself, are forced to clear new, perhaps less desirable and desired, poetic space for themselves.

The probable cause for fellow poets' frustrations is that Milton has brought the highest form of poetry, the venerable epic, to perfection and has won for himself "The title of Most Excellent."[156] In the words of Edward Phillips, Milton has "lately published *Paradise Lost*, a poem which, whether we regard the sublimity of the subject, or the combined pleasantness and majesty of the style, or the sublimity of the invention, or the beauty of its images and descriptions of nature, will, if I mistake not, receive the name of truly Heroic, inasmuch as by the suffrages of many not unqualified to judge it is reputed to have reached the perfection of this kind of poetry."[157] Subsequent to Milton's death, when Ellwood need no longer mince words, he celebrates Milton's triumph in poetry and prose equally, and equally the examples of epic as represented by *Paradise Lost* and *Paradise Regain'd* in which "The common Road foresaking" Milton is "a new track making."[158] What Ellwood gives with one hand, Edmund Waller takes away with another: "The old blind schoolmaster hath published a tedious poem on the Fall of Man. If its length be not considered as merit, it hath no other."[159] And what merit there may be in its length is eventually qualified by Dr. Johnson's "None ever wished it longer than it is."[160]

In different ways, for different reasons, the aesthetic code so governs the early reception of *Paradise Lost* that one must ask at the outset whether Milton himself is not partly responsible for the state of affairs of which nowadays some critics complain:

> Criticism has tended to contrast the aesthetic and the political. We think of genius and partisanship as at odds. . . . We evaluate the greatest writers as those least fettered by their age. Such appraisals have too often announced Shakespeare's detachment from Tudor politics; and they have too often presented Milton's poetry as a retreat from political

concerns. The intention of Milton and Shakespeare to engage political arguments will remain a matter of interpretation. What is incontestable is that their languages were perforce political and necessarily conveyed political meanings. There is an important sense in which no seventeenth-century literature is not also political.[161]

How is it possible for such a poem as *Paradise Lost*, in part at least on the affairs of state, on the state of the nation, initially to go unde-tected? Milton, one supposes, never meant to announce political attachments, only to deflect attention from them by their artful con-cealment within the deep structure of his poem, deferring them until better (because both less dangerous and more receptive) times. Ellwood's forthright representations of Milton excelling (indeed tri-umphing) as both polemicist and poet, of Milton as a trailblazer—such representations coming only after Milton's death opens the possibility that Ellwood's earlier reported response, perhaps politically motivated, amounts to a deliberate jamming of Milton's message. Even if apocryphal, the story told by Thomas Warton, who attributes it to T. Tyers, makes an important point concerning Milton's predica-ment: "when Milton was on the run, he had a mock funeral that made Charles II laugh when he heard about it."[162]

MEDIATING MILTON'S VISION

It is important to remember that if censorship forced Milton to cam-ouflage his politics, it also forced politically sensitive and sympathetic readers of his poetry (Ellwood perhaps and Marvell almost certainly) to camouflage their political readings, which, more often than not, instead of making Milton into a champion of this or that cause, pro-vided an occasion for examining the problematical moral and ethical issues that his politics raised: the relation of religion and politics, first of all, and the role of violence as a means to an end—apocalypse now or apocalypse deferred. As Milton learned to circumvent the bans of censorship by devising an art of crypsis through which he forces us to read between the lines, to wrest significance from silence, and wherein mere flickerings of unorthodoxy really matter, it becomes increasingly clear that the issue is not whether Milton withdraws from republican-ism in the face of its betrayal but rather what sort of critique he can mount as he tries to account for political disappointments and revolu-tionary failures. The revolutionaries were in some ways wrong. Hence, they (and not the Revolution) were Milton's target. Not his ideals but their implementation created a problem when, as Newlyn explains, "the leaders of the Revolution who initially had right on their side. . . . allowed evil to become their good";[163] they became what they beheld. Milton embedded a critique easily ignored by his contemporaries yet readily accessible to future generations for whom Milton was no less seditious in his intentions but who simply came to value sedition differently.

In other instances, as with the initial pages of the third chapter of *The History of Britain*, possible erasures of, and apparent emendations of judgment on, contemporary history, plus a heightened pretense of discussing remote history, make it difficult to know "to what extent . . .[Milton] means to blame his own party" or even to what extent contemporary history is really at issue. For this reason, as Peter Levi goes on to say, "There is no English poet about whom there are so many major mysteries."[164] Nor is there any other poet of the seventeenth-century who so carefully selected for the master-myths of his poetry those biblical stories through which current history was so regularly glimpsed and so often being read. The stories of mankind's fall, Jesus's temptations, and Samson's demise—all are stretches of biblical history that in Milton's day were commonly correlated with the history of Britain.[165] Milton bends biblical history toward contemporary history, applying old to new history, in the understanding that history, where it does not repeat itself, may nonetheless rhyme.

The initial receptions of *Paradise Lost* reveal Milton's success in fashioning poems that speak obliquely, in whispers, but also, in their statements as much as in their silences, anticipate expectations inscribed, receptions instated, during the 1670s, most notably by Barrow and Marvell, whose dedicatory poems form a headpiece to the second edition of *Paradise Lost* (1674). Their poems deserve more attention than today they typically receive principally because, for a long time read as prologues to *Paradise Lost*, they had an astonishing impact, for better or worse, on the early reputation of both poet and poem, furnishing the commonplaces for Milton criticism in its formative stages: "Consummate Poet," "sublime poem," "mighty Milton" to whom all poets, whether ancient or modern, must now yield; "Poet blind, yet bold," "strong," "Mighty Poet" whom "Heav'n . . . / Rewards with Prophesie" and whose verse contains "a vast expence of mind" and in its "vast Design" and "Theme sublime" so fully compensates for artistic irregularities that it need "not Rhyme."[166]

Barrow and Marvell thus generate the clichés of Milton criticism such as are still—some will say *still too much*—with us even as their poems are generated by the complaints that were then being leveled against Milton as man, thinker, and polemicist particularly with regard to his religious enthusiasm and political radicalism. Indeed, the attacks upon Milton from the pens of Roger L'Estrange, Samuel Parker, and Richard Leigh (or more probably Samuel Butler[167]) present in epitome the criticisms of Milton that, addressing, Barrow and Marvell, through their respective poems, would answer. The old charges, for twenty-five years or more leveled against Milton, are, by these Miltonoclasts, revived: (1) that Milton is a heretic in both religious matters and politics as is evident in his manglings of Holy Scripture, his twistings and turnings of it to his own ends (the creation of an inventive theology) and evident, too, in his blindness, a mark of God's disfavor and punishment; (2) that Milton's fanaticism puts him in league with the devil whose agent Milton is in history, a fanaticism most conspicuously evident in those poisonous and libelous tracts where Milton defends regicide; (3) indeed, that Milton's heterodoxy and nonconformism, even to his own principles, spill over into his poetry which, supposedly full of light, is encrusted with dark meanings and which, despite its rejection of rhyme, nevertheless uses rhyme internally—and artlessly, even as that poetry, pretending to prophecy, makes extravagant (and extravagantly repeated) claims of inspiration.

Before returning to the dedicatory poems by Barrow and Marvell, we should remember from earlier discussion that they are simply the last features, during Milton's lifetime, added to a poem that, since its publication, had been adding new material by accretion. As we have seen, bibliographical features shared by the first and second editions of *Paradise Lost*, as well as differences between them, tell one part of the story of this poem's early reception (an author nearly anonymous, "J. M.," eventually is identified on the title page as John Milton, a printer's note to the reader is appended to explain the poet's newly added apologia for rhymeless verse, as are arguments newly devised to accompany each book). The poems by Barrow and Marvell, distinctive of the second edition, tell another crucial part of the same story. Insofar as Milton's last poems (all of them) are tracts for their time ("intensely political poems," in the words of Christopher Hill[168]), they enter history in a moment of turmoil, both in religion and politics, and reflect that history, exhibiting its conflicts. Indeed, contending traditions in religion and science, competing hermeneutics and cosmologies, are the epicenter of *Paradise Lost* whose poet, if not narrator, is like Jesus and Samson, a nonconformist hero at a time when all pressures conspire to compel conformity.

But more, the poems by Barrow and Marvell, as previously noted, each align Milton with a different poetic tradition (the one classical and epic, the other scriptural and prophetic), thus pointing to the competing generic signals of *Paradise Lost*, the inward strife that is its hallmark. These dedicatory poems forge contrary perspectives on Milton's epic-prophecy, asking that it be read in very different ways: as a poem of new and perhaps unexpected revelations (Barrow), or, in the case of Marvell, as a poem not finally unsettling because it holds fast to the time-honored truths of Christianity, not ruining the scriptural tales, and holds fast also to the commonplaces of culture, received interpretation, thus not at all perplexing the usual explanations. If read as companion poems affording contending perspectives on *Paradise Lost*, these pieces may be seen as establishing the different lines of critical inquiry, the conflicting attitudes toward Milton, that ever since have been at the heart of Milton criticism. Is *Paradise Lost* a poem of disclosure, revealing (in the words of Barrow) "whate'er lies hidden in all the world" (5–8)? Or is it a poem written to allay all doubts—to put to rest a hermeneutic of suspicion—by promoting rather than prosecuting the old verities? The immediate effect of reading these poems together is to throw us into a quandary—is to bracket *Paradise Lost*, as well as our interpretive efforts, in question marks.

But let us remember, too, that what we are here bringing under review are *poems*. If poetry, according to Milton, is more simple, sensuous, and passionate than rhetoric, in this comparison it is also more given to ambiguity, even mystification and obscurity, and more rife with tension. Poetry hides more: it can be more elliptical and evasive, less direct than oblique, and is more apt to have troubled waters beneath its calm surface. In the examples afforded by Barrow and Marvell, each poem seems to have the same subtext, as it were; each seems to be responding to the same horizon of expectations for *Paradise Lost*, but responding differently—Barrow's through a curious focalization and Marvell's by a calculated contradiction. H. L. Benthem reminds us that Milton's closest friends, when they learned of the imminent publication of *Paradise Lost*, were filled with suspicions concerning the poet's intentions: would his poem be about the loss of paradise then—*or now*? From everything Theodore Haak confided to him and from his own reading of the poem, Benthem reports, " 'this very wily politician . . . concealed . . . exactly the sort of lament' " his friends feared he would write and did so in a poem that would use scriptural myth to mask political commentary.[169] Within such a context, these dedicatory poems reveal their own complicity in Milton's disguised intentions as they may be inferred from a poem of "dark paths," with a "labyrinth perplex'd of heaven's decrees."[170]

The oddity of Barrow's poem—as Christopher Hill might say, written in "the decent obscurity of a Latin poem"[171]—resides in the sharpness, the expansiveness of its focalization of the celestial battle in Book 6, which always seems to have had readers who believed, as did this 1764 commentator, that the English civil wars were imagined therein:

> The Michaels and Gabriels, &c. would have lengthened out the battles endless; nor would any solution have been found, had not Cromwell, putting on celestial armour (for this was Milton's opinion) like the Messiah all armed in heavenly panoply, and ascending his fiery chariot, driven over the malignant heads of those who maintain tyrannic sway.[172]

If *Paradise Lost* is a poem of disclosure, inscribing a secret history as Barrow implies and Milton's early editors speculate—if *Paradise Lost* is a poem that speaks through contradictions, tears on its surface and whispers from its wings—is Barrow then, through this unexpected yet extensive focalization, pointing to where the secret history is hidden? It is at the end of this narrative, we should remember, that Raphael confides: "I have reveal'd / What might have else to human Race bin hid" (6.895–96). Similarly gathered into focus by Wentworth Dillon, Earl of Roscommon, the celestial battle in *Paradise Lost* is also a civil war, as Milton himself emphasized (6.667), as well as one of those places in the poem where subsequent commentators have seen pointed political observation peeking out from under its mythic coverings.[173] The surface analogy between the rebellious Puritans and Satan, the King and God hides the more immediately relevant analogy between the King and his men, who resemble the Satanic rebels, though they attribute rebellion to others, and God whose allies are the Puritan saints, the quellers of such rebellion. However, this surface analogy is not simply a subterfuge; for Milton's critique, here as in *Samson Agonistes*, cuts both ways—against the Royalists primarily, but also against the excesses and enthusiasms of Cromwell and his army. It is seldom noted that *Paradise Lost* begins and ends in prophecy with the intention, apparently, of putting prophecy itself under review.

This same sort of reading between the lines helps to unpack the significance of Marvell's still more curious poem, which has both a private and a public dimension, the former containing a gesture through which Marvell carves out poetic space for himself, staking claim to the middle ground of poetry as it were, and the latter containing a gesture on Milton's behalf through which Marvell would secure for this poet of paradise the ground he has claimed for himself. This latter project requires no small amount of subterfuge on Marvell's part, one signal of which is the apparent contradiction that is allowed to sit on the surface of his poem. Only after Marvell has emptied *Paradise Lost* of its potentially subversive content—that is, only after he has modified existing expectations—does he ally the poem with the most subversive of poetic traditions: "Just Heav'n . . . / Rewards with *Prophesie* thy loss of sight" (44; my italics). This claim has the effect of undermining the principal assertion of the poem so far; for prophecy, by the most restrained definition then common, refers to a new revelation, a new interpretation, that will displace the old (not preserve and confirm it) and that will advance understanding toward a higher truth than that already proclaimed. (This is why there were edicts against prophecy, especially political prophecy, during the early modern period.)

The remainder of the poem, in its invocation of the rhyme controversy, in its endorsement of Milton's own asseverations on rhyme, moves in concert with, while also providing further testimony for, the subversion, which now belongs to both poets, Marvell as well as Milton, Marvell encoding within his poem, through its organization into verse paragraphs of unequal length, one of the subversive signatures of Milton's own poem. Rhyme was a matter not just of aesthetics but of politics, as Milton's early readers were quick to notice in their references to Milton's rhymelessness allowing his poetry to tower in the sublime, to Milton's freeing poetry of this monkish, iron chain, rhyme being as much the emblem for stultifying theology as for repression in politics. Rhymeless verse, perhaps because it came to be associated with "verse unfallen, uncurst,"[174] was the expected flag of prophecy, an outward sign of its inward defiance, and, because of its studiously unpremeditated appearance, a sign, too, of its inspiration. An aspect of "Masculine Rhetorick," blank verse is opposed to the "*tinkling cimbal*" of rhyme, or feminized poetry, that, making "a pretty sound . . . for a time," would "rather inchant the mind then inform it."[175] This gesture of rebellion aligns Milton's poem with the revolutionary impulses of scriptural prophecy while encoding what has always been Milton's master-theme: the recovery of ancient liberty from modern bondage.

This is but one of the many splicings that cause Marvell's poem to lock arms with Milton's. Moreover, it is such splicings that point to the "serious truth"[176] of his no less than Barrow's verses: that they are a representation of the very strategies of subversion, of the multiple subterfuges, embedded in *Paradise Lost* and a representation, especially in the instance of Marvell's poem, of Milton's own self-representations. No blind guide, Milton was rather a poet who, if blind, could truly see. What must ultimately be said about both of these dedicatory poems is that they are entry codes into the very kind of readings that Marvell only *seems* to protest against; they are a reminder of the fact to which Stephen Greenblatt has alerted us: that literature, which is subject to censorship and that has passed through it, can be "relentlessly subversive," although the very form in which it is cast may have effected its evasion of censorship by seeming to provide containment for the kind of questioning that the poem, instead of restraining, actually provokes.[177]

If *Paradise Lost*'s identity as epic signals the containment of subversion, its alternative identity as prophecy suggests that it is such containment that is being subverted. *Paradise Lost* is a still more exaggerated example than Greenblatt's *King Lear* of a text that strains "the process of containment . . . to the breaking point"; that, in the words of Newlyn, releases "the prophetic potential of *Paradise Lost* from the epic mode in which it is confined."[178] Each of Milton's poems is, as Peter Conrad observes, "an iconoclasm, shattering the models which have given it form, rebutting its own history," both aesthetically and intellectually.[179] Milton's poetry thus creates a poetics and spawns a whole tradition of revisionism; and there is no better illustration of this fact than that, from Boileau to Harold Bloom, the best critics have credited Milton (not always approvingly) with doing precisely what Marvell says the poet will not do: *ruin the sacred truths.* Thus Boileau speaks of those poets who in the representations of Satan and of Hell, "mingling falsehoods with those Mysteries, / Would make our Sacred Truths appear like Lyes," thus filling their supposedly "Christian Poems" with "Fictions of Idolatry."[180] And apparently Boileau has Milton in mind.

But *Paradise Lost* is also a poem that turns the critique upon itself, upon its own generic identity, in such a way as to suggest the uses and abuses, the hopes for and hazards of prophecy in a fallen world. *Paradise Lost* begins with Satan's remembering, then responding, to a prophecy concerning a new world. The attainment of a new world is always the objective of prophecy even when the new world is not envisioned therein; yet as Satan's response makes clear, the idealisms of prophecy are often subject to perversion. Even as Milton privileges prophecy he registers a certain distrust of it because, in a fallen world, this instrument for creation can become an agent in destruction, thus turning God's device for deliverance *from* into Satan's means of deliverance *into* thralldom and servitide. To be privy to God's prophecy (as Satan is) may result in man's freedom becoming his bondage. By deforming prophecy, Satan, ironically, devises just the sort of world that makes prophecy necessary, even if in that world prophecy remains a peril because, as Adam shows in Books 11 and 12, prophecy is always subject to the misconstruals and confusions of fallen consciousness. This same critique of prophecy increasingly came to be wrapped around the Samson story once the Puritan Revolution had failed.

Of the two dedicatory poems, moreover, Marvell's has the unique feature of aligning *Paradise Lost*, through implied allusion, with *Samson Agonistes*; and the Samson allusion, in turn, has caused some to think that Marvell means to represent Milton as "a latter-day Samson braced to bring down the pillars of his society upon the heads of its leaders" in "an act . . . of revenge." Yet Annabel Patterson's identification of Milton with his "heroic avenger in *Samson Agonistes*,"[181] though accepted by many critics both before and since, runs across the grain of a poem where the Samson story becomes an anti-text through which Marvell disengages Milton from the Samson analogy:

> the Argument
> Held me a while misdoubting his Intent,
> That he would ruine (for I saw him strong)
> The sacred Truths to Fable and old Song
> (So *Sampson* groap'd the Temples Posts in spight)
> The World o'rewhelming to revenge his sight. (5–10)

Edward Le Comte similarly misses this point as he makes another (certainly crucial) one: "In 1674 Andrew Marvell associated Milton with Samson pulling down the temple. . . . . This is the sort of reader [with Marvell, Le Comte would include Edward Phillips] best qualified to know what was under the surface of *Samson Agonistes*."[182] It is notation of difference here, not similitude, that enables readers to penetrate the surface of Milton's poem.

The Milton who does not go gentle into that good night—who goes out of the ring swinging, out of life raging with one last revenge fantasy—does not sort well with the Milton of the early biographers who report that if, in old age, he exhibited any religious identity it was with the Quakers; nor does such a Milton sort well with what Marvell here says as he forces a contrast between Sampson who, spirited by the revenge motive, loses his life and Milton who, having relinquished such a motive, is providentially spared his through the intervention (we are probably meant to remember) of Marvell himself. Such an alignment between *Paradise Lost* and *Samson Agonistes*, an alignment implicating

Adam and Samson in the same arc of tragedy, is encouraged in the sixth edition of *Paradise Lost* (1695) where, in "A Table of the most remarkable Parts" of Milton's poem, under "Similes," the only one listed compares "*Adam* sinful to shorn *Sampson*."[183] The abutment of these two poems, with the Adam/Sampson simile as a hinge, we mentioned earlier and will return to later in this chapter.

Meanwhile, what merits emphasis here is the fact that Marvell's poem is one of two defenses of Milton that Marvell composes: "[his] dignified defence of Milton in *The Rehearsal Transpros'd*, and his poem before the second edition of *Paradise Lost*, are the culmination of over twenty years of discipleship and friendship."[184] This poem especially focuses the contradictions that are at the heart of Milton's poetic vision and, in concert with the poem by Barrow, the two poems relating to one another dialectically, pulling (at least on the surface) in opposite interpretive directions, emblematizes the dialectical nature of Milton's own poem. As Jonathan Richardson was later to observe, *Paradise Lost* is a poem of *contradictions* that does "More than Whisper."[185] Those contradictions, sometimes implanted within the fissures of the text, announce conflicts and confusions that, instead of being evaded, should be emphasized, although it is just this aspect of the poem that commentators as early as Theodore Haak,[186] even if unintentionally, obliterate through their imitations, translations, critiques, and illustrations in the very process of sanitizing the poem of those conflicts and contradictions that, once erased, enable the conventionalization of Milton's politics and theology. From Dryden onward, the critic's strategy is to contradict Milton out of his contradictions.

HORIZONAL CHANGES

Let us now return to Jonathan Richardson with whom an earlier section of this chapter began, this time attending to the annotations for *Paradise Lost* credited to both father and son, keeping in mind that both apparently were acutely sensitive to what had been the damaging consequences of Milton's own political principles and to the extent to which Milton's poem, itself occasioned by political circumstances, and secretly representing them, had also been aligned with political occasions, perhaps other than those Milton would have wished to sponsor or serve. Without in any way forcing the politics of *Paradise Lost* into the open, the Richardsons nevertheless acknowledge that there is a hidden politics to this poem; that it arises out of a political situation awkward, even dangerous, for Milton; that in the Prologue to Book 7, in its reference to "fall'n on evil dayes" (25), Milton hints at the "Secret History" inscribed by his poem.[187] The Richardsons, that is, hint at what Christopher Hill, Annabel Patterson, Nancy Armstrong and Leonard Tennenhouse have been telling us: that we "must deal with the fact that censorship returned with a new vigor in 1662. That is what killed off the political Milton, leaving us with the poet—or so a tradition of criticism," now under challenge, "has claimed."[188] Nor should it be forgotten that Milton's adversary Roger L'Estrange, obsessed with the political Milton, was the presiding official during this new phase of censorship and was still deriding "blind M[ilton]" as one of the *"Super-Reformists"* who speak "the *Language of the Beast.*"[189]

Not just the Richardsons but also Francis Peck, in the eighteenth century, thought there was something curiously amiss in the current representation of Milton with reference not just to *Paradise Lost* but also to *Paradise Regain'd*: "I have often wondred in my self how the PARADISE REGAIN'D, under all this load of prejudice, hath nevertheless passed so many editions as I feel it hath."[190] Daniel Defoe had already remarked that Milton's two epics, "tho' form'd in the same Mould, . . . have met with a most differing Reception in the World." If "the first passes . . . for the greatest, best, and most sublime Work . . . The other is call'd a Dull Thing, infinitely short of the former," even if Milton regarded it as "the better Poem of the two, . . . without Comparison the best Performance."[191]

The prejudices against *Paradise Regain'd*, whether they stem (as Milton and Defoe report) from a preference for the subject of losing paradise rather than regaining it or, instead, are owing to the more conspicuous transgressions of religious orthodoxy in *Paradise Regain'd*, reflect upon another kind of prejudice that was keeping *Paradise Lost* trapped within the interpretive codes of theology and aesthetics. By now it was a cliché of criticism that the *Aeneid* was the great political, *Paradise Lost* the great religious epic, and the function of that cliché was to hold these poems hostage to very different contextualizations. What had become a divorce between politics and theology in the eighteenth century was in Milton's time still very much a marriage both sanctified and celebrated by *Paradise Lost*, yet also now violated by an interpretive tradition, then in its formative stages, that would neutralize, by way of silencing, the politics in Milton's poetry, in *Paradise Lost* no less than in *Samson Agonistes*; that would then snare both poems within the nets of orthodoxy. If, contrary to what Newton has said, *Paradise Lost*, through its twelve-book structure, *does* gesture toward Virgil's *Aeneid*, the allusion may have less to do with identifying a poem of which *Paradise Lost* is an imitation and everything to do with locating *Paradise Lost* within a tradition of political poetry of which Milton's poem is a continuation.

Translation and adaptation, imitation and illustration, editorial emendation and excision, all of them the rage during the eighteenth century, though we may see each of them as an aspect of Milton's burgeoning reputation, were also conspiratorial; each was a tactic, or could be so used, for suppressing the subversion. Witness, first, what happens to the last books of *Paradise Lost*, usually excluded from the translation mania of the eighteenth century. The most overtly political books in the whole of Milton's epic, they are censored by aesthetic condemnation. If these were the books in which politics was seen breaking through the surface of Milton's poem, they could be detoured, evaded on other grounds: as failures of poetic imagination in a poem already overlong; as mere excrescences in a poem that, by the end of its tenth book, had already accomplished its improvement of the epic tradition; as floundering the very moment they abandon mythology for history and, worse, politics.

Even Book 10 was thought to have shown signs of flagging genius as when the epic vision now becomes personalized and privatized in autobiographical encroachments such as would envelop the whole of *Samson Agonistes*, where a bickering Adam and Eve, Samson and Dalila are none other than the squabbling John Milton and Mary Powell. If there was a politics in either poem, it was (in its positive aspect) a sexual politics, altogether conventional, in which Milton upheld the authority of the husband, even sanctioned despotic rule by him, and (in its negative aspect) a politics petty and churlish, surly and acrimonious, with Milton hiding in Book 5, for example, when Satan goes off into the northern reaches of heaven, a fulmination over Royalist Scotland and then hiding in Book 11, in the account of the world destroyed by a flood, "To teach . . . that God attributes to place / No sanctitie" (836–37), a jibe at Archbishop Laud over his manner of consecrating churches.[192] There were but these few traces of politics—of Milton the polemicist—in *Paradise Lost*; and if they were not easily detectable in the last books, those books could be avoided as artistic disappointments or, as such, could even be salvaged by thematizations which, theologizing these books, could integrate them into a poem essentially religious, surely not political, in design and thrust.

For *Paradise Lost* to be political in the eighteenth century, if that meant an inscription of Milton's politics, was to risk trivialization and marginalization such as *Samson Agonistes* experienced at the very time that *Paradise Lost* was being institutionalized and canonized. It was hard for anyone, really, to deny Milton his politics, or to write politics out of his poetry generally: the tactic, pure and simple, was to evacuate politics from *Paradise Lost* and empty it into *Samson Agonistes*—was to save the one poem by sabatoging the other or, in the case of Milton's tragedy, by adapting what could not be adopted, converting this poem into operatic spectacle, translating it into typological, theological drama and substituting apocalyptic clamor for eschatological despair.

The eighteenth century recognized in *Samson Agonistes*, perhaps mistakenly, the revenge tragedy (or fantasy) of Christopher Hill:

> Let us consider his tragedy in this allegorical view. Samson imprisoned and blind, and the captive state of Israel, lively represents our blind poet, with the republican party after the Restoration, afflicted and persecuted. But these revelling idolators will soon pull an old house on their heads; and GOD will send his people a deliverer. How would it have rejoiced the heart of the blind seer, had he lived to have seen with his mind's eye the accomplishment of his prophetic predictions! when a deliverer came and rescued us from the Philistine oppressors.

Samson Agonistes, apparently, is being read in this way, especially by those overcome with "the wildness of fanaticism and enthusiasm." Yet the commentator here summarizing this fashion of reading the poem is calling for a criticism less "mystical and allegorical," and more "sceptical than dogmatical,"[193] in the very century when, through adaptation and translation, *Samson Agonistes* is being transformed into a drama of regeneration, a divine comedy, the very terms by which this poem is often read today.

The theologizing of *Paradise Lost*, the politicizing of *Samson Agonistes*—the institutionalizing of both poems within these disparate categories—can be dated from Thomas Newton's variorum edition of 1749. By this time, when Newton's commentary on *Paradise Lost* was first published, earlier expectations concerning *Paradise Lost*, if not Milton himself, had become dislodged and, under the weight of Newton's commentary, were all but silenced, at least for a time. Newton is a particularly interesting interpreter because, for all his maneuverings in behalf of securing *Paradise Lost* as a purely theological poem, integrity prevents him from altogether scrapping the poem's political content, although from Newton's perspective that content seems to be confined to, contained by the last, the inferior, books of the poem—the Nimrod passage in Book 12, "which has always been supposed to allude to . . .[Milton's] own times,"[194] affording the notable example: "And from Rebellion shall derive his name, / Though of Rebellion others he accuse" (36–37). "This [passage] was added," Newton conjectures, "probably not without a view to his own time, when himself and those of his own party were stigmatiz'd as the worst of rebels."[195] Newton's integrity obliges him to acknowledge a strain in Milton that he himself, at least with reference to *Paradise Lost*, does not wish to credit. In one way or another, each of his major predecessors had made such a gesture without usually acknowledging the extent to which Milton rewrites the Nimrod and other stories with a political valence in order to denounce not only the Royalists but just as often the treacherous Parliamentarians. Milton's political critiques, like his gender discourses, are double-voiced and display a dual consciousness. They reflect on history usually obliquely and always complexly.

By 1698, John Toland, as previously noted, discerns a similar encoding of British history in the very first book of *Paradise Lost*:

> I must not forget that we had like to be eternally depriv'd of this Treasure by the Ignorance or Malice of the Licenser; who, among other frivolous Exceptions, would needs suppress the Whole Poem for imaginary Treason in the following lines.

> As, when the Sun new risen
> Looks thro the Horizontal misty Air
> Shorn of his Beams, or from behind the Moon
> In dim Eclipse disastrous Twilight sheds
> On half the Nations, and with fear of change
> Perplexes Monarchs. (1.594–99)

But Toland is also quick to turn from the public and the political to the personal and autobiographical in a poem that "perpetuats the History of [Milton's] own Blindness";[196] and quick, also, to place the political under the aspect of personal history, as the Richardsons will do in their exfoliation of the secret inscribed in the Prologue to Book 7 and as Newton will later do in his annotation for the Nimrod passage in Book 12. Eventually, the politics implicit in Book 6—"how plain are the civil wars imagined in the sixth book"—conceivably part of a critique of the Revolution, is reconceived by conservative apologists as Milton's recantation of the Revolution. Thus in 1764, the commentator just quoted will cite an earlier one, also writing in *The London Chronicle*, who, in mock defense, will ask of Milton, usually supposed to be of the devil's party: "[H]ow could he better refute the *good old cause* he was such an advocate for, than by making the rebellion in the poem resemble it, and giving the same characters to the apostate angels as were applicable to his rebel-brethren"?[197]

This strategy of letting politics undergird autobiography in a poem that was thought to transcend both is particularly evident in the memoir by Francis Peck in which we are not allowed to forget Toland's comment about the censor with reference to the perplexed monarchs of Book 1, but also where the political is said to be submerged within the autobiographical mode as early as *Lycidas* and its reflections on the corruption of the contemporary church and as late as *Samson Agonistes* in which "the severe satyr on woman, in SAMSON'S discourse with DALILA," is taken as conclusive evidence that Milton "still resented . . . MARY POWELL," as likewise is Adam's misogyny in *Paradise Lost* (10.947ff.). Both *Paradise Lost* (7.24–38) and *Samson Agonistes* (695) are thought to register Milton's fears of being tried for his life by Charles II and his judges or of "being torn in pieces by the mob, just as ORPHEUS was." But it is again Books 11 and 12 in which traces of the political, however scant, are strongest: in the Nimrod passage reminiscent of *Lycidas* where yet once more the poet registers his aversion to the clergy in any guise.[198]

What is evident from the foregoing comments is that a political interpretation had already been affixed to *Paradise Lost* and *Samson Agonistes*, even if submerged within the autobiographical content of each poem. Newton's project of claiming *Paradise Lost* as a theological poem by marginalizing, even silencing, its politics had already been undertaken, this time with *Samson Agonistes* as the target, in Handel's *Samson: An Oratorio*. What is curious in light of these parallel efforts is that Newton should simply shift what was once thought to be the political content of *Paradise Lost* to *Samson Agonistes*, taking his initial lead from John Jortin's annotation for line 241, "That fault I take not on me":

> Milton certainly intended to reproach his countrymen indirectly, and as plainly as he dared, with the Restoration of Charles II, which he accounted the restoration of slavery, and with the execution of the Regicides. He pursues the same subject again [lines] 678–700. I wonder how the Licensers of those days let it pass.

Then Newton himself chimes in, saying of line 268, "But what more oft in nations grown corrupt," that here too Milton "very probably intended . . . a secret satir upon the English nation, which according to his republican politics had by restoring the King chosen *bondage with ease* rather than *strenuous liberty*." When Samson declares later, "So much I feel my genial spirits droop, / My hopes all flat" (594–95), Newton speculates that "Milton in the person of Samson describes exactly his own case, what he felt and what he thought in some of his melancholy hours." Alternatively, when the Chorus contemplates "th' unjust tribunals, under change of times" (695), doubtless Milton himself, in their voice, reflects upon "the trials and sufferings of his party after the Restoration" and probably has "in mind particularly the case of Sir Harry Vane"; and of course, Newton continues, "this was his own case; he escaped with life, but lived in poverty, and tho' he was always sober and temperate, yet he was much afflicted in the *gout* and other *painful diseases*."[199]

The excesses of Samson and the Israelites are not Milton's own, Newton seems to be saying, with both being merely counters through whom the poet can vent his own, and his party's frustrations, even in "bold expostulation," both "with Providence for the ill success of the *good old cause*" and with its leaders who managed to overthrow monarchy "without being able to raise their projected republic." They fell lower than they did rise because of "trespass" and "omission" by which Milton means, according to Newton, that the "Independent Republicans," quarrelling among themselves, made no viable constitution, no "new modelling" of either the law or the national religion. By the end of *Samson Agonistes*, however, Milton's otherwise controlled critique gives way to "that inveterate spleen," focused on "*Dagon* and his Priests" (1463), which Milton always unleashed against "public and establish'd religion."[200] If there was a politics to Milton's poetry, a poetry to his politics, both were emptied into *Samson Agonistes*, a poem that, harboring such content more easily than *Paradise Lost*, could be marginalized and trivialized by it. Very simply, *Samson Agonistes* was an autobiographical poem tethered to Milton's own times, a poem written in analogy with classical tragedy but unworthy of comparison with it—the poem by Milton that ignorance has admired and bigotry applauded, therefore a poem that the world could easily let die.

The abuttment of *Paradise Lost* and *Samson Agonistes* is encouraged by Marvell's poem and, later, by the 1695 table of similes, but also by the Samson simile in Book 9 of *Paradise Lost* (1059–62), as well as by the last books of *Paradise Lost*, their allusion to deliverance "By Judges first, then under Kings" (12.320) where, as Hume observes, Samson is obviously comprehended under the title of Judge.[201] The relationship between these poems is further secured, now as if by an iron link, with the proclamation in *Samson*, "Just are the ways of God, / And justifiable to Men" (293–94), echoing the prologue to the earlier poem where Milton promises to "justifie the wayes of God to men" (1.26). Additional echoes shore up this intertexuality, first by establishing a link between Samson's "many evils have enclos'd me round" (194) and the poet-narrator of *Paradise Lost* "with dangers compast round" (7.27), then hitching Manoa (in his suggestion that "perhaps / God will relent, and quit thee all his debt" [508–09]) to Belial (in his proposal that God "in time may much remit / His anger" [2. 210–11]). In the progress of *Samson*, though, his "The way to know were not to see but taste" (1091) recalls the contention of both Satan and Eve that to "freely taste" is "to know" and "to be wise" (9.732, 758, 759) and, more, Adam's ironic address to Eve: "I see thou art exact of taste" (9.1017). Eventually, the two poems are riveted: the "universal groan / . . . [in which] the whole inhabitation perish'd" (1511–12) to Nature's "groan" (9.1001), marking the falls of Eve and Adam. The fall of individuals is irrevocably involved with the fall of nations.

This alignment of poems, the intertexuality between them, makes a telling point: the tragedy enfolded in the one poem is exfoliated by the other with the paradise lost by Adam being but a metaphor for John Milton and his Englishmen who are unparadised by the failure of the Puritan Revolution, the Samson story mirroring that failure. Yet Samson's tragedy defeats, Milton's liberates—or should. The problem is that we are still in the vise of the tragedy from which Milton won release, at least for himself. "[W]e . . . no longer know what is tragic and what is not," writes Stanley Cavell, "so it is not surprising that tragedies are not written."[202] To which we might add: nor is it surprising that when they are written we do not understand them and in our misunderstandings, or refusals to understand, let tragedy repeat itself until it collapses into farce. It is odd that our first critical inquiries about tragedy, the great tragedies, seem always to involve source-study, which leads to other literary texts usually, to other artificial formations, and away from human life, actual *lived* history, political and religious history, which are the blood and guts, the body and bones of tragedy. As Jonathan Dollimore reminds us, tragedy is "resolutely political" in the early modern period,[203] powerfully so in Milton's usage, where it is at once recreation of and resistance to tyranny. Not in literary tradition but in the history of Milton's own times, we find the earthly foundations for a new Jerusalem of the spirit that is, after all, the desire and soul of all great tragedy and the very heart of Milton's last poems.

Milton's idealisms were tempered, not defeated, by the failure of the Puritan Revolution. After his death, in the very twilight of his own century, Milton would be used to illustrate the proposition that poets oppose all systems of enslavement, "that there is no where a greater Spirit of Liberty to be found, than in those who are Poets."[204] In poetry no less than in prose, Milton committed himself to rescuing his people from bondage, to reviving their liberty and restoring their freedom. No poem is a better exemplar of these commitments than *Samson Agonistes*, nor a finer illustration of how complexly Milton's poetry enfolds a nuanced political vision, together with a refined critique of it. That understanding subtends the recovery of *Samson Agonistes* today, and then discovery within this tragedy of a way, through analogy, of anatomizing our own historical moment.

CHAPTER 3

QUESTIONING AND CRITIQUE:
THE FORMATION OF A NEW MILTON
CRITICISM

Here, among broken statues and pillars,
I ask how did Samson bring down the temple . . .

Did he embrace the pillars as in a last love
Or did he push them away with his arms,
To be alone in his death.

—Yehuda Amichai

Samson Agonistes is a troubling work at any time, for it is a
timeless study of the self-righteous instinct urging all defeated men
to vengeance and violence. As such, it is a work which remains curi-
ously open, for who can without confounding ambivalence be sure
who this English Samson is meant to stand for, or who next might
feel justified in invoking his example.

—Robert Scanlan[1]

If they did not invent the question, *why Milton*, the Romantics lent
fashion to it, empowering Milton by making him whole again and,
simultaneously, giving force to his poetry by reading it as if it were a
true history. They also read it in the future tense, so that poems
emerging from one moment of crisis could reflect upon, and explain,
another crisis in history when, once again, tyranny and terror ruled.
In the early years of the twenty-first century, the sense of crisis is

undiminished. The question, *why Milton*, is no less urgent; and the worry that Milton may have written poetry as propaganda for warfare remains intense. Witness the web-magazine essay, "*Samson Agonistes* (Confession of a Terrorist/Martyr)," and *The Boston Globe* piece, "Was [Milton's] Samson a Terrorist?" together with *The New York Times* articles: "Is Reading Milton Unsafe at Any Speed?" and " 'Paradise Lost' for the Modern Day."[2] Two of Milton's last poems have come to figure centrally in our national discourse, *Samson Agonistes* especially so. In view of this clamor, it is remarkable, yet no wonder, that Milton's tragedy had seven announced performance readings in 2003–04, all but one of them in New York City. With various voices from the academy, the journalistic press, as well as the popular culture conspiring as one, it is as if Milton's tragedy were now being rescued by history *for* history—in this time, for this place—as another nation's poem unfurling *our* national drama.

READING HISTORY, THEN AND NOW

So start with what most of us agree on, *Milton matters*—but by way of acknowledging that disagreements emerge (and sometimes become disagreeable disputes) the moment we ask *why* Milton matters, and then entwine with this question another, "Who Reads What How?"[3] We are caught by surprise, often dizzyingly so, when, still mired in the culture wars of the last century, we discover that the *who* on one side of the debate achieves consensus with the *who* on the other side in the claim that, even if (in our time) a monument to dead ideas, Milton is a reliable index to the starched theology and bruising politics, including sexual politics, of his own era. If, in *Paradise Lost*, the Son acts as God's emissary during the celestial battle, in his later-published tragedy, masked as Samson, Milton (it is sometimes said) performs the same role within a revenge fantasy. Thus tearing down the pillars of church and state, he leaves in ruins a government whose restoration he had opposed and by which he had been incarcerated. The gist of such an argument is obvious: Milton's excellence is his relevance to the seventeenth century and irrelevance to our own—with Milton, then, seeming to embrace the very values that, having outgrown, we now oppose. Whatever enlightened values may be today, Milton's, apparently, are the values of yesterday. But no news here: *Samson Agonistes* was, has been, and still is part of a culture war with Milton's tragedy, as Sharon Achinstein remarks, "bear[ing] the mark of that contest in its very name."[4]

Some one hundred and twenty five years ago, in the grip of what he calls "the Puritan Samson Agonistes," Peter Bayne concluded that "[t]he spiritual depths of Christianity, the Divine power of kindness and self-sacrifice, were fully fathomed" in *none* of Milton's last poems, wherein dwells instead "the inspiration of Puritan battle."[5] And in the aftermath of 9/11 comes this bitter complaint from Michael Mendle:

> I write in the wake of the terrorist attacks, which confirm in their way the full hideousness of Milton's fantasy of exterminatory hatred upon "all who sat beneath."[6]

John Carey, aware of the same harrowing ironies and analogies, asks, in his anniversary reflections on 9/11: "Is . . . [this] what *Samson Agonistes* teaches?"[7] Or, alternatively, are the lessons the poem supposedly teaches the same ones we learn from it?

Is Milton's poem a manual for killing? Is it a polemic on behalf of war? Is the history it reports a record of servitude or freedom, of history repeated—or renewed and transfigured? And does Samson's life distill into the resume of a terrorist? What are the consequences, we might go on to ask, of reverting to earlier readings of *Samson Agonistes* as a poem in which the protagonist, not morally compromised, takes, in "a death so noble" (1724), "magnanimous revenge upon his enemies";[8] readings that find in the tragic "action of *Samson Agonistes*, a *moral* greatness;—namely, the sacrifice is of one's own self for the sake of others. . . . In the case of Samson," this critic continues, "the sacrifice is that of life itself, for the sake of God and country,—religion and patriotism."[9] What are the risks both here, and later, in ratcheting up our claims and applauding Samson as "a great guerilla leader"?[10] Is the Samson story—should it be allowed to become—a fuse for a much larger war of civilizations?

Margaret Thatcher seems to think so, as she invokes "the strong man" of *Areopagitica*, awakening from sleep and shaking his invincible locks. Most readers of Milton are quick to identify this strong man as Samson; and Thatcher, as if in response to the Miltonic injunction, "Let not England forget her precedence of teaching nations how to live," is just as ready to invoke this image of Samson as a model for what America should be today: a nation acting "vigorously," "deploy[ing] its energies militarily" and moving against "aggressive ideology," while leaving such matters as the promotion of "civil society" and "democratic institutions . . . to others."[11] The good news (for Thatcher) is that America is a modern-day Samson, a superpower, eager to practice the politics of retaliation. The bad news (for us) is that

America is still naive about the avenging hatred such power arouses. America has yet to learn from Milton's tragedy that redemption comes not through repetition of the Samson story but from resistance to it, or refiguration of it such as we find in both *Samson Agonistes* and Robert Medley's illustrations to Milton's tragedy.

Samson Agonistes is described repeatedly as Milton's "drama of denunciation and personal invective," as his left hand writing poetry, as his "scourge [on] a backsliding nation" and prophecy of "the vengeance to come," as his "jeremiad on current affairs," and as his Puritan attachment to "the potency of a fanatical idea" in which, nourished by faith, true heroes surrender themselves to "an overruling Providence" as they claim "a *favoured* communion with the Divine Being."[12] As if it were a propaganda piece in behalf of a discredited regime and a failed ideology, Milton's tragedy is often read as a polemic against the Philistines and Dagon rather than (in parallel with the Book of Judges) as a critique of the English people, Milton's allies rather than his enemies—and as a scrutiny of their God. Moreover, through his own revisions and transgressions of the Judges narrative, Milton urges, as poets since have done, that his own poetry, not "univocal in a theological sense," is "pluralist" and "open"—an insistent questioning, the exact "opposite of the sealed . . . text of religion."[13] Milton's aim in *Samson Agonistes*, no less than *Paradise Regain'd*, is to stretch biblical stories beyond their existing parameters, in the process authorizing no single interpretation of a scriptural tale but, instead, privileging hermeneutical suspicion over complacent exegesis. As Margaret Kean so wisely observes, Milton puts "all authorities past and present under scrutiny, making them the subject of debate," as he then "strives to re-invest his telling of events with the full impact of a revolutionary moment."[14] Through reconfigurations of biblical stories, history, once reinterpreted by them, can then be made anew.

Poems of a piece, especially in terms of their interplay with their scriptural counterparts, *Paradise Regain'd* and *Samson Agonistes* display the same assimilative tendencies. Each poem embraces competing hermeneutic traditions neither reconciled nor harmonized but in tension, and in such a way as to foreground difficulties and conflicts, thus besieging us with critical dilemmas and often interpretive quagmires, but in ways, too, that transform physical into mental spaces and horizontal into vertical journeys, literal yielding to figurative readings. If *Samson Agonistes* is a precursor of Byron's mental theater, the Son in *Paradise Regain'd* is the prototype of Blake's mental traveler. If Milton becomes Blake's great modern-day exemplar of such, he does so in a poem to which Milton gives his name and the subtitle for which, as Northrop Frye once quipped, should be "Paradise Regained by John Milton" (without a comma).

So far as *Paradise Regain'd* is concerned, during the early modern period, interpretive fault lines emerge early, with John Calvin remarking that, while "[i]t is sayd that Christ was set vpon a pinacle of the temple," we are nonetheless left to wonder "whether he was caried vp on high in deed, or whether it was done by a vision": are the temptations of Jesus "reall," or do they "rather belong to vision."[15] If Calvin prefers that we are left wondering as a better alternative to "quareling," another commentator of the early modern period would halt such inquiry altogether: "whether he were carried through the aire, or whether it were done by a vision, it is not for the godly to searche."[16] This debate is worth foregrounding only because Milton reignites it, allowing the narrator of *Paradise Regain'd* to represent the story as real and the narrator of *Paradise Lost* to push the story oppositely, here reporting Adam as saying, "Ascend, I follow thee, safe Guide," whereupon both Adam and Michael "ascend / In the Visions of God" (11:371, 376–77):

> It was a Hill
> Of Paradise the highest, from whose top
> The Hemisphere of Earth in cleerest Ken
> Stretcht out to amplest reach of prospect lay.
> Not higher that Hill nor wider looking round,
> Whereon for different cause the Tempter set
> Our second *Adam* in the Wilderness,
> To shew him all Earths Kingdoms and thir Glory.
> His Eye might there command wherever stood
> City of old or modern Fame.
>   . . . and where *Rome* was to sway
> The World: in Spirit perhaps he also saw . . .
>   . . . but to nobler sights
> *Michael* from *Adams* eyes the Film remov'd
>   . . . then purg'd with Euphrasie and Rue
> The visual Nerve, for he had much to see. (11.376–415)

In *spirit perhaps* Jesus later sees what Adam here sees *in vision*: "*Adam*, now ope thine eyes . . . His eyes he op'n'd, and beheld a field" (11.423, 429).

Precisely here, Milton is thought to tilt the whole wilderness hermeneutic toward metaphoric reading: "Milton has ingeniously introduced Michael foretelling the blindness of the human mind," and so confirms the whole idea of Jesus experiencing the wilderness temptations "with his visionary faculties"—indeed, the very notion that "the gospel account . . . was only an *history of a vision*."[17] If Milton has an interpretive precursor, it is Joachim of Fiore for whom we must all "Clear the eyes of the mind . . . ; follow the angel in spirit," "going from illumination to illumination, from the first heaven to the second, and from the second to the third, from the place of darkness into the light of the moon, that at last we may come out of the moonlight into the glory of the full Sun."[18] The Son sees amidst the blaze of noon, whereas Samson remains eyeless. He mounts the pinnacle of vision, whereas Samson walks a darkened plain. As he does with the wilderness story, so Milton does with the Samson story: he conjoins (without reconciling) different interpretive traditions, then circulates them within his tragedy,[19] and in such a way as to let the Samson story, reconfigured, emerge as a critique of violence, with all that such a critique entails: laws and justice, means and ends, morality and terrorism, and that "bottomless casuistry"[20] into which cultures of violence can lead.

Accordingly, never forgetting Samson's swagger and bluster, Milton raises the issue of Samson's culpability and accomplishes an unveiling of it as he forces the questions: does God dispense with his laws, and to what extent has Samson's own aggression provoked aggression against his people? In *The First Defence of the English People*, Milton is insistent: "the law allows no exceptions," nor are "any exemptions" found in Scriptures, where "the law of God does most closely agree with the law of nature" (YP, 4:365, 373, 422). Milton is unequivocal: "a law which overthrows all laws cannot itself be a law" (YP, 4:401). In epitome, the law makes of Samson an outlaw, within which context it needs to be remembered that the first recorded act of Samson is one which involved a violation of the law, with his life, then, becoming a whole series of such violations.

Yoking together *The Doctrine and Discipline of Divorce* and *Samson Agonistes* through the sexual metaphor of grinding at the mill, Milton presents Samson, first, as going awhoring in order to throw into contention Samson's own flouting of laws he is expected to uphold and, then, as married for a second time in order to interrogate the lawfulness of those marriages. By simultaneously questioning whether Samson has a divine warrant either for his marriages or for going to the temple/theater, Milton brings into dispute the proposition justifying all that Samson does, namely that the most troubling of his actions are divinely motioned and approved; that his is a tragedy wherein Samson's mind is repeatedly subdued to the dispensations of providence. Rather, in keeping with one of Terry Eagleton's characterizations of modernist tragedy, in *Samson Agonistes*, "the pact . . . between fate and freedom begins to break up, as a self-determining subject," acting of his own accord, "squares up to an external compulsion,"[21] as when Samson feels some rousing motions within.

THE USES AND ABUSES OF PROPHECY

It was still being said at the end of the nineteenth century (and it continues to be said today) that "Samson was a hero raised up by Heaven" and that, correspondingly, "Milton viewed himself . . . as raised up by Heaven."[22] Yet few who say so acknowledge, much less document, Milton's emerging suspicion of an idea which, for a while, had caught him within its embrace. Would that Milton "had considered . . . the wildness of fanaticism and enthusiasm," writes one of his eighteenth-century critics.[23] In that very complaint, however, this commentator crafts the bold outlines of a critique, which Milton begins in *The Tenure of Kings and Magistrates*, suppresses in *The First Defence*, and, eventually retrieving in *A Treatise of Civil Power* and then in his epics, threads through his entire tragedy.

During the heyday of the Revolution, Milton had been quick to align Oliver Cromwell's successes with divine favor, indeed to see himself no less than Cromwell's army, as God's ally in these victories. Thus, in his *Second Defence*, in possession of "an inward and far surpassing light," Milton writes (as he had similarly done in the peroration to his *First Defence*):

> if God wished those men to achieve such noble deeds, He also wished that there be other men by whom those deeds, once done, might be worthily praised and extolled, and that the truth defended by arms be also defended by reason—the only defence truly appropriate to man. (YP, 4:553; cf. 4:536)

Earlier, in *Elegy V*, Milton imagines himself in a state of "holy frenzy" (CM, 1, 1:197) and then, in *To My Father*, invokes those exemplary bards of former times, those apparently Samson-like bards with "unshorn locks" (CM, 1, 1:273). Poetry and prose, at least initially, do not possess equal claims to inspiration. In *The Reason of Church-Government*, "an inward prompting which now grew daily upon me" (YP, 1:810) comes upon Milton the poet, whereas in *An Apology for a Pamphlet*, with "the example of *Luther*," Milton the polemicist is quick to challenge those who "think inspiration only the warrant thereof" when "judgement" itself may better explain polemical vehemence (YP, 1:901).

Subsequently, yet before Milton celebrates Cromwell as an agent of providence, in *Eikonoklastes* he mocks Charles I for laying claim to it: "Most men are too apt . . . to interpret and expound the judgements of God, and all other events of providence or chance, as makes most to the justifying of thir own cause . . . ; and attribute all to the particular favour of God towards them" (YP, 3:428–29). A man of violence, Charles exhibits "an excessive eagerness to be aveng'd" (YP, 3:379). An agent in "horrid massacher" (YP, 3:470), himself "caus[ing] the slaughter of so many thousands" (YP, 3:481), Charles, as here represented by Milton, may evoke the Miltonic adage that "judgement rashly giv'n ofttimes involves the Judge himself" (YP, 3:481). Indeed, Milton himself acts as judge when he contends that Charles was put under the power of the Army by God "out of his Providence," as Milton says in *The Tenure of Kings and Magistrates* (YP, 3:193), and subsequently is executed, in words from *Eikonoklastes*, by "the powerfull and miraculous might of Gods manifest arme" (YP, 3:555). In yet another transference of such rhetoric, in *The First Defence*, it is William Laud, along with Salmasius, who is now upbraided for "proclaim[ing] that he was archbishop 'by the providence of God' " (YP, 4:481).

If *The Tenure of Kings and Magistrates* and *Eikonoklastes* are companion pieces of sorts, the first tract theorizing Revolution and the second affording an apologia for the revolutionaries, the latter tract, in crucial moments, also counters the claims of the former one. Yet *The Tenure of Kings and Magistrates* is the more telling text; for even as it removes the taint of enthusiasm and zealotry from the Army that exhibited both, even as it taunts the ministers for whom "Providence . . . must be the drum, . . . the word of command, that calls them from above" and who, in "thir postures and thir motions," lay claim to both, it also cites among its authorities in the second edition the likes of Peter Martyr and Martin Luther (YP, 3:243–58). For them, claims to inspiration are meaningless without the certification of divine commission and permissible only when acts proceed from a public, never a private, person—a distinction Milton had blurred in the first edition of *The Tenure of Kings and Magistrates* only to sharpen it here.

Still more telling is the fact that in this prose work the following remark, without naming Samson, seems to comprehend him:

> For if all human power to execute, not accidentally but intendedly, the wrathe of God upon evil doers without exception, be of God; then that

power, whether ordinary, or . . . *extraordinary* so executing that intent of God, is lawfull and not to be resisted. (YP, 3:197–98; my italics)

Eikonoklastes, as well as *The First Defence*, will then credit the Army with the divine instigation that *The Tenure of Kings and Magistrates* denies it. In a parallel maneuver, in *Samson Agonistes* Milton will have its protagonist exclaim,

> I begin to feel
> Some rouzing motions in me which dispose
> To something *extraordinary* my thoughts. (1381–83; my italics)

But Milton, already suspicious of inspiration, will also compound uncertainty in his tragedy by pressing the questions of whether the poem's climactic action is divinely commissioned or of Samson's "own accord" (1643).

In *The First Defence*, Milton avers that, "chang[ing] circumstances . . . through the agency of men," God opens a path for the revolutionaries to follow:

> We followed him . . . with reverence for the traces of the divine presence at every step we entered on a path surrounded by no shadows, but rather illumined . . . by his guidance. (YP, 4:394–95, 305)

Accordingly, victories were accomplished "not . . . without divine inspiration" (YP, 4:536). Moreover, if such feats were guided by "divine inspiration," so too were Milton's defenses of their efforts, which with "the same assistance and guidance" were themselves divinely wrought (YP, 4:537, 536). Yet, Milton, the exemplar of a changing mind, if he thought, in the late 1640s and early 1650s, that events could not have happened but by the will of God, later in the same decade, as Cromwell would come to do, cast suspicion on such claims, arguing in *A Treatise of Civil Power* that "no man can know at all times" if "divine illumination . . . be in himself" (YP, 7:242). Initially, Milton never questions God's ministers, nor queries divine directions; but eventually he begins to worry over those avengers who execute God's wrath on those who do evil and to worry, too, over how we know just who those people are whose evil makes them worthy of extermination.

In *A Treatise of Civil Power*, Milton admits that some who have had recourse to divine inspiration (like the magistrates and kings of old) have used it as a justification for force. But he also avers that what was done under the law may no longer be appropriate under the Gospel. In Milton's words, "We read not that Christ ever exercis'd force but once; and that was to drive profane ones out of his temple, not to force them in" (YP, 7:322). Indeed, Milton says this after conceding that all too often men, once inspired, act again after inspiration has been withdrawn, such people furnishing, as Hugo Grotius claims, a dangerous example of being in the spirit only to end in the flesh. Milton's thinking on inspiration becomes irrevocably involved with his rejection of force, his insistence upon its unlawfulness in religious matters where outward force is a disparagement and degradation of Christ and his spiritual kingdom, with Milton now distinguishing between carnal and spiritual warfare, the one the way of Satan and the other, the way of the Lord. Inspiration and force, both indices to Milton's changing mind, also come into play in complicated, even confounding ways, both in the dedicatory poems to *Paradise Lost* and in the epic itself.

When Andrew Marvell declares of Milton that "Just Heaven . . . / Rewards with prophecie thy loss of sight,"[24] he credits *Paradise Lost* with what that poem slowly, yet surely, brings under scrutiny. Milton's poem may begin and end in prophecy even as questions quickly tumble forth: is it "report" or "prophecy" to which first Satan and subsequently Milton's audience respond? What if the poem's claims to inspiration are a mere fiction, and all be false? And even if it is a vision, what are the limitations on prophecy in a fallen world? The final books of *Paradise Lost* explore the impairments of vision once the mind has been darkened, while Milton's final poems—*Paradise Regain'd* and *Samson Agonistes*—are haunted with questions of how their respective heroes know, and of how *we* know, whether the spirit of the Lord is upon them. In their odd inversion of scriptural chronology, they may even dramatize Milton's remarks (as reported by Moses Wall) concerning that "retrograde Motion of late, in Liberty and Spiritual Truths" (YP, 7:511). Indeed, Milton's final trilogy of poems should not be segregated from the letter, dating from mid-December, 1659, where Milton quips in response to Henry Oldenberg's inquiry concerning whether he plans to compose a history of England's commotions:

> I am far from compiling a history of our political troubles . . . ; for they are worthier of silence than of publication. What we need is not one who can compile a history of our troubles but one who can happily end them. For I fear . . . lest to the lately united enemies of religion and liberty we shall, in the midst of civil dissensions or rather insanities, seem too vul-

nerable, though actually they will not have inflicted a greater wound on religion than we have long been doing by our crimes. (YP, 7:515)

Milton's last poems (and especially *Samson Agonistes*) recast such observations as prophetic utterances.

Within Milton's own writings, the trajectory of the Samson image moves from the resurrected Samson of *Areopagitica* to the fallen Samson of *Paradise Lost*; from Charles I as Samson in *The Reason of Church-Government*, where his locks are likened to the law, to Milton as no Samson in *Samson Agonistes*, where the flash point of the Samson story is its hero's repeated and increasingly audacious claims to divine inspiration in contrast with Milton's growing reticence about making such assertions, let alone acting upon them. Just as in Milton's day Europe was asking what went wrong in England, in *Samson Agonistes* Milton asks the same question as now, through Milton and especially his tragedy, America is compelled to address similar questions about itself, as well as its religious assumptions, which have fostered self-righteousness and threatened mass violence. As darkness becomes visible, as we see where such assumptions lead, we may wish that earlier we had abandoned them. Indeed, as M. G. Lord says, our own wrestling with such questions understandably "recalls Milton in its effort to put a human face on the perpetrators of evil"[25] and, even more, in its eventual need to cast off error by annihilating the propositions by which cultures of violence are perpetuated.

While Milton may have believed that his *Of Christian Doctrine* is inspired by God, he also insists on sparing use of his own words, "even when they arise from the context of revelation."[26] The Son's silences, very notably, contrast with Samson's garrulity. In *Paradise Lost*, in the line "By Judges first, then under Kings" (12.320), Milton remembers that the failure of the judges made kingship necessary and thereupon frets over those people "feigning . . . to act / By spiritual [power], to themselves appropriating / The Spirit of God" (12.517–19). In the same poem, moreover, for all its bravura when it comes to claiming inspiration, Milton must ask, *what if this all be a fiction*: "[what] if all be mine, / Not Hers who brings it nightly to my Ear" (9.46–47)? Those *what ifs* concerning divine promptings and motions from above form the very core of the uncertain world of *Samson Agonistes*, indeed are the signatures of uncertainty in a poem that asks whether Samson's "part" in this tragedy is really "from Heav'n assign'd" (1217) and whether his actions here are truly a "command from Heav'n" (1212).

As with prophetic illumination, so with prayer. Milton's early poetic career climaxed in the crisis lyric, *Lycidas*, a poem that completes the poetic volume, *Justa Edovardo King Naufrago*, itself commencing with the heroic image of Edward King kneeling in prayer as his ship goes down. The Revolution itself began with invocations of Samson at prayer—with Samson as an icon for the New Model Army and as an example of force with force triumphing: "force with force / Is well ejected" (1206–07). Yet the Revolution continues with the infamous portrait of Charles at prayer, published as the frontispiece to *Eikon Basilike*, then ridiculed by Milton in *Eikonoklastes* as "a Masking Scene" (YP, 3:342–43). Not only does the Revolution end with Samson having lost much of his power to inspire by force of example, hence with Milton's finally leaving open the question of whether Samson is (or is not) at prayer in the moments just before the temple/theater comes down. Milton, apparently, became increasingly suspicious of public worship and pietistic prayer, in *Samson Agonistes* moving back and forth from God's causing "a fountain at thy prayer / From the dry ground to spring" (581–82); to "one prayer yet remains," a prayer for "speedy death" (649–50); to a world seemingly "deaf / To prayers" (960–61); to the question, why do our prayers "draw a Scorpions tail behind" (360); and ultimately to the equivocation in which Samson is described "as one who pray'd, / *Or* some great matter in his mind revolv'd" (1637–38; my italics).

Perhaps Milton sensed, as Heymann Steinthal would later state, that the prayer when Samson worries he may die of thirst is but "a fiction," humanizing a character, eventually all too human, when in the Book of Judges he "prays to be endowed with strength to avenge the loss of one of his eyes." When Samson dies, he "remains dead," his story then inviting the inference that not Samson but Israel and its God are this story's "hero."[27] In an illustration to *Samson Agonistes* by Richard Westall, the Messenger, no figure of piety but an image of horror, "is represented as imitating the attitude of Samson performing what he relates" (figure 3.14).[28] The illustration does not let us forget Milton's injunction in *Eikonoklastes*: "Privat praiers in publick, ask something of whom they ask not, and that shall be thir reward" (YP, 3:456). In *Samson Agonistes*, the Chorus appeals to a contrarious god that he "turn / . . . [Samson's] labours, for thou canst, to peaceful end" (708–09), yet despite its appeal cannot avert the temple catastrophe, whether or not it occurs with Samson himself in an attitude of prayer. Whether in its theorizing of tragedy, or in its reinterpretation of the Samson story, Milton's poem, perhaps more so than John Penn ever thought, "anticipated . . . latest opinion,"[29] at once reconstituting the genre of tragedy and revising interpretation of the story Milton casts into it.

SAMSON AGONISTES.

PAGE 67.

Publish'd March 25ᵗʰ 1797. by J. & J. Boydell, & G. Nicol, Shakspeare Gallery, Pall Mall, & Nᵒ 90, Cheapside.

Figure 3.14 Richard Westall's Illustration for *Samson Agonistes* (The Messenger Reporting the Catastrophe)

In *The Tenure of Kings and Magistrates* and *A Treatise of Civil Power* and then in both *Paradise Lost* and *Samson Agonistes*, the rhetoric of inspiration is eyeballed with suspicion. It is language coded into the preliminary matter—the "persuaded inwardly" of the Argument to *Samson Agonistes*—and thereupon woven through the entire poem: "inward light" (162), "motioned . . . of God" (222), "intimate impulse" (223), "divine impulsion" and "prompting" (422), "divine instinct" (526), "work from Heav'n impos'd" (565), "command from Heav'n" (1212), "part from Heav'n assign'd" (1217), "Some rouzing motions" (1382), "presage in the mind" (1387), "Spirit . . . rush'd on thee" (1435), "With inward eyes illuminated" (1689). Samson's entire life, its every episode (as he would have it) is a fulfillment of "Divine Prediction" (44). It is as if Milton is here moving toward the more mocking posture, in another century and in another country, assumed by the American president John Adams: "[i]t will never be pretended that any person employed . . . [in national leadership] had interviews with the gods, or was in any degree under the inspiration of Heaven."[30] It can only be deplored, moreover, that, as Adams thinks, the tales, legends, and sagas often assimilated to Jewish and Christian revelation have had the effect of bloodying those religions. Indeed, what Adams implies is that it is no act of heroism but one of presumption to declare that God is on one's side, but an act of heroic humility to ask, or simply to hope, that a nation's actions put it on the side of God and not at odds with Him. The prayer is not that He be on our side but that we be on His.

The Samson story, it now seems, is the tragedy of a nation mapped in the migratory journey of the tribe of Dan from the extreme southwest of Palestine to the extreme north—from Gaza (in Samson's day, an opulent city, "the outpost of Africa, the door of Asia,"[31] an intellectual and commercial center superior to any city in Palestine, a place Samson leaves in ruins), to Dan, which becomes a ruined city, with justice itself in ruins, as the Danites destroy this city, in the process turning their newly founded habitation into a place of idol worship. Moreover, in Samson's tragedy, in this national tragedy, is writ the tragedy of the world: "the breakdown of the public body," "the death knell of the world," "[t]he whole world structure . . . brought down," "the overthrow of the world."[32] Such is the dire warning of the Samson story, especially as it is unfurled in Milton's poem, where the demise of an individual is prelude to the defeat of a nation. If *Samson Agonistes* commences with its protagonist imaging himself as a "Sepulcher, a moving Grave" (102), it concludes in the recognition, to adopt the words of Paulus Cassel, that the temple/theater itself, in "a terrific crash," becomes "a vast sepulchre."[33] As the Israelites go in search of Samson's body, "Soak't in his enemies blood" (1725), we are witnesses less to "A life Heroic" (1711) than to "Blood, death, and deathful deeds" as nearly a "whole inhabitation perish[es]" (1513, 1512). The fate of Samson is thus written into the eventual fate of the Danites, which then is written into the fate of the Philistines. It may well be that Johann Gottfried Herder's own grasp of the intricacies of the Samson narrative caused him to conclude that "the life of man may be considered as a miniature of the fate of nations."[34] In the Samson story, biography and history converge—apocalyptically.

GREGORY NAZIANZEN, THE THEOLOGIAN

Long ago, one reader put it this way: by the time Milton presents the 1671 poetic volume, "his sentiments are altered, his passions had subsided . . . , and he had learned wisdom from experience; or had been disgusted by the conduct of his political associates."[35] Milton may not repudiate the Revolution, but he has come to wonder about the ways of some of the revolutionaries, with *Paradise Regain'd* mounting such a critique in the face of *Samson Agonistes*.

Like other of his contemporaries, Milton emphasizes that, contrary to Mark 1:12, the Spirit "*led* . . . , it did not drive"; the Spirit offered "sweet invitation," not "compulsion" or "violence."[36] Jesus, that is, was led by the Spirit into the wilderness, "not by an unnatural violence, but by a supernatural inspiration and inclination"; he was led by "the Good Spirit to be tempted of the devil,"[37] with the very language of *led*, defining the uniqueness of the wilderness temptation, its interiority, as well as its visionary status (cf. *Paradise Lost*, 11.376–84). The key line in *Paradise Regain'd* describes Jesus "Into himself descended" (2.111); a horizontal journey within time and space becomes a vertical and an interior journey into the wilderness of the self, into the very center of one's being. To be *led* into the wilderness, according to Hugh Farmer, means that "he was now conveyed thither in a spiritual manner, in vision or mental representation, under a divine inspiration."[38] Indeed, by the nineteenth century, Milton is credited with transforming the Wilderness temptations into a visionary drama.[39] Moreover, this idiom of inspiration is ubiquitous in *Paradise Regain'd*: "Thou Spirit who ledst this glorious Eremite / Into the Desert" (1.8–9); "led on, / He enter'd now the bordering Desert wild" (1.192–93); "by some strong motion I am led" (1.290) "he still on was led" (1.299). Does the same spirit who leads Jesus rush upon and then lead Samson: "He led me on to mightiest deeds" (638), declares Samson who later acknowledges to Dalila, "I led the way" (823), even as later he will be "led" (and also lead another) into catastrophe (1629, 1635)?

Within its scaffolding, *Samson Agonistes* may contain assumptions previously credited by Milton; but the failure of the Revolution seems to have left Milton with an urgent need to reexamine those assumptions—where they lead and how to modify them, especially those that breed contempt, foster cruelty, and foment violence. Kindled not by the energy of the historical moment but by its frustrations and fanaticism, *Samson Agonistes* is a protest poem in its every aspect: in its epistle, even in its generic and prosodic forms, directing "a counterblast"[40] at the Restoration, its aesthetics and politics, as well as the theological tenets and religious values subtending both. Thus, E. K. Chambers wonders, "How should . . . not . . . [Milton's] heart swell with indignation? How should he not think the vials of the Almighty wrath were preparing for so faithless a generation?" But Chambers also frets: "nay, more, the expression [here is] so outspoken that one hardly understands how the Restoration censorship can have let it pass."[41] In a poem long suspected of terrifying the censors (more so than anything in *Paradise Lost*), Milton is imagined as crafting his prefatory epistle to *Samson Agonistes* as a subterfuge. Thus, aware of the precarious ground on which he was treading, Milton, according to A. J. Grieve, may have "deliberately put the censor off the track by his Preface, which deals with everything but the autobiographical design."[42]

Deserving "close study" of what is "stated or implied in it,"[43] precisely because it is an aspect, as Elizabeth Sauer remarks, of "the poet's effort at locking the text in particular interpretive traditions,"[44] Milton's prefatory epistle is freighted with significance, especially in its invocation of Gregory Nazianzen (330?–390?), Bishop of Constantinople, who, like Milton, was an orator/poet/theologian, all in one. Like Milton, Gregory was also briefly incarcerated and left to posterity the memory of three daughters often represented as nuisances.[45] Indeed, the very mention of Gregory Nazianzen, named "not at all coincidentally,"[46] tags Milton's poem as, in some sense, autobiographical, with Gregory himself affording a precedent for thinking that the poet should himself be a true poem; that autobiography and tragedy are inextricably involved with one another in a poetry of meditation, full of calamities and misfortunes, where internal struggle culminates in self-definition and discovery.[47] The poem maps that struggle—and mythologizes it even when (to adapt Gregory's words) the poet's "lips are fettered."[48]

Gregory is prone to thinking of himself and others in terms of biblical analogies: of his father as "a second Aaron or Moses," "a second" or "new Abraham," or "the great Noah"; of his mother as an Eve/Miriam; and of himself as a second Samuel, or as a Job in his afflictions, or as an Elias or John in the desert, or even as Elijah or Jesus in self-communion.[49] The very mention of Gregory in Milton's prefatory epistle thus invokes both the autobiographical character of Gregory's poetry and, in the allusion to *Christ Suffering*, suggests the scriptural typology in which Gregory regularly wraps himself. Through the allusion to what he supposes to be Gregory's tragedy, Milton forces the questions of how apt the Samson/Christ typology is to his own poem, of whether he is himself caught within the embrace of that typology, and of the extent to which (again to adapt Gregory's words) we here witness "Christ, arming His athlete with his own sufferings."[50] However unwittingly, the questions that are said to structure Gregory's theological poetry inform—and organize—Milton's own poems of 1671 (see figures 3.15 and 3.16): What am I to believe? Who was, who am I, and who am I to be? And not just the questions but also the tactic of metrical experimentation in tragedy where "Gregory sometimes violated the established rules."[51] Gregory and Milton are equally prone to placing gestures of artistic rebellion at the forefront of their poetry and of inscribing within it "a tragic description of the evils of the time," of "the testing and refining . . . [people] endured."[52]

Over a century ago, A. Wilson Verity, describing Milton's situation, detected his strategies:

> He could not, without offending his friends and doing violence to his own professions, write anything which should have any affinity with the acted drama of the moment. But there would be no occasion of offence in a work which, free from the associations of the contemporary playhouses, frankly took shelter under the authority of classical tragedy.[53]

Indeed, as Kenneth Burke once said in a sly cross-referencing of *Samson Agonistes*: "whenever you find a doctrine of 'nonpolitical' esthetics affirmed with fervor, look for its politics";[54] and as he might have gone on to say, in the case of Milton, expect an enmeshment of politics and theology. Know that when Milton is ostensibly seeking aesthetic perfection he is not fleeing politics but, instead, grasping for political wisdom and ethical insight. Writing in different centuries, Verity and Burke intuit the operative strategies, in which aesthetic matters become a political subterfuge, in a poetry of agonized, unfolding perception with

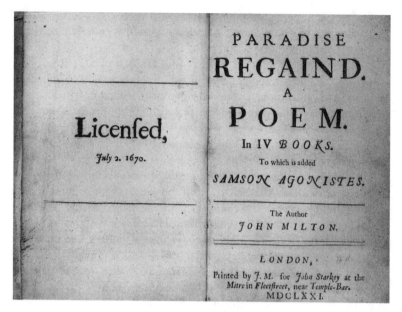

Figure 3.15 The Title Page for the 1671 Poetic Volume

a penchant not only for speculative thinking but for (what is for the most part anathema to Gregory) both dialectical thinking and theological dispute.

Yet neither Verity nor Burke (in fact no one to my knowledge) has seen the shelter, or the precedent, Milton was creating for himself in the citation of Gregory Nazianzen who, also writing under censorship, was a master of subtlety and nuance and hence a model for tactics of evasion and strategies of subversion. Nevertheless, and relevantly, Verity knows that, often cited by Elizabethan apologists for the stage as evidence of church approval for drama, Gregory could become a sanction for some of what Milton protests against.[55] Correspondingly, because *Christ Suffering* (as Milton calls this poem in his prefatory epistle to *Samson Agonistes*) was valued as establishing a text for those manuscript pages lost from Euripides's *The Bacchae*, it could similarly act, along with St. Paul's epistle, as another sponsor for the Euripidean tradition of tragedy, here in Milton's epistle inflected as a crucial context for this dramatic poem.

It is a tradition of closet drama—of play-writing, not theatergoing—that Gregory initiates and that, in his turn, Milton, through

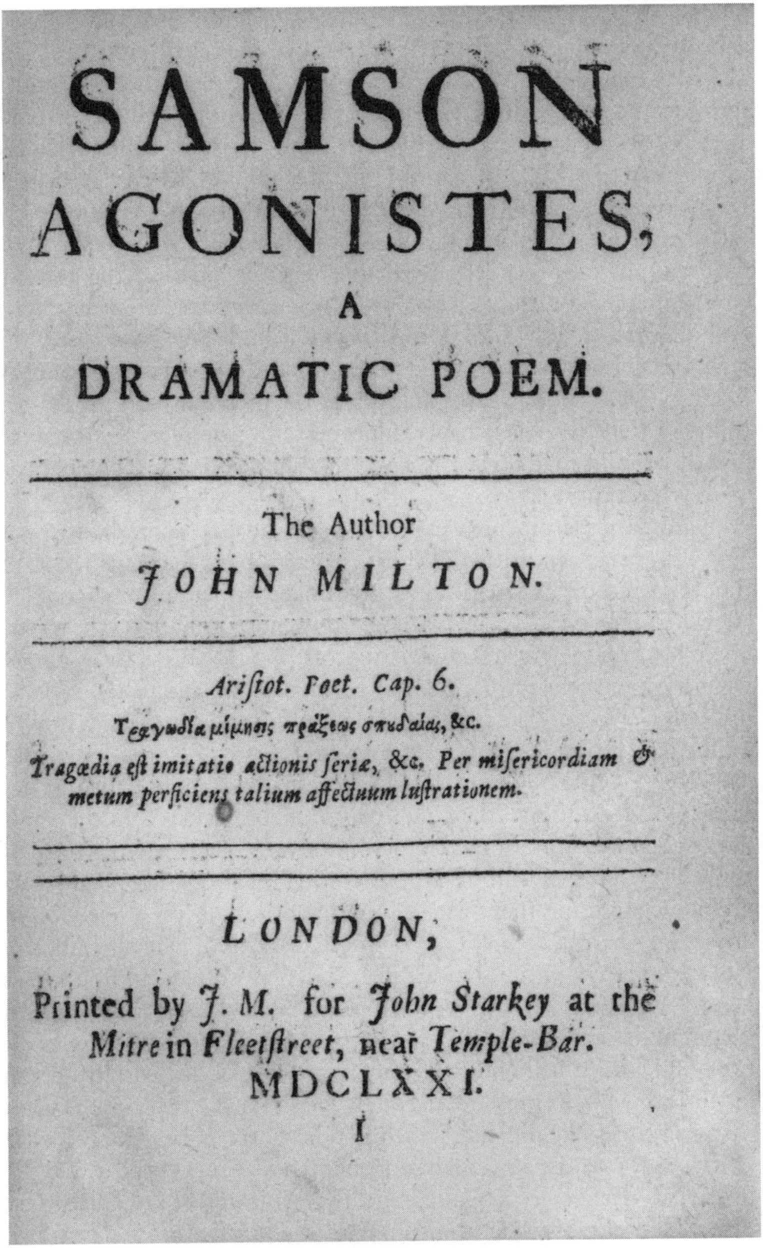

SAMSON AGONISTES,

A

DRAMATIC POEM.

The Author
J̃OHN MILTON.

Ariſtot. Poet. Cap. 6.

Τεχνωδία μίμησις πραξεως σπυδαίας, &c.

Tragædia eſt imitatio actionis ſeriæ, &c. Per miſericordiam &
metum perſiciens talium affectuum luſtrationem.

L ONDON,

Printed by *J. M.* for *John Starkey* at the
Mitre in *Fleetſtreet,* near *Temple-Bar.*
MDCLXXI.

I

Figure 3.16 The Separate Title Page for *Samson Agonistes* in the 1671 Poetic Volume

Samson Agonistes, perpetuates. If pressed, Milton might even have appropriated Gregory's words for describing the relationship between *Samson Agonistes* and *Christ Suffering*: "a second theatre, and a second tragedy."[56] Moreover, when the allusion to Gregory is read as harbouring a reminder of that "long-standing controversy as to whether the 'Playe of Christ'. . . , as Stephen Gosson called it in his *Schoole of Abuse*, was intended for acting or was composed 'dialogue-wise . . . to be reade, not to be played,' "[57] the allusion itself may tease us into wondering whether *Samson Agonistes*, supposedly never intended for the stage, is, in such protestations, an invitation to eventual production. After all, *Samson Agonistes* was "produced" in imitative snippets by John Dryden and lured commentators as early as Francis Peck (1740) into imagining or preparing play-texts for Milton's tragedy, which has an unexpectedly complex performance history commencing no later than 1900, but perhaps reaching back as early as a century before.[58]

Milton's prefatory epistle, then, chafes against some of its own claims, yet also acts as one of those "reception mechanisms" that, in the very act of "aestheticizing potentially subversive material,"[59] anesthetizes politics, but without diverting attention from the poem's "ethical effect" and "spin-off."[60] In this way, *Samson Agonistes* seems to embrace the Gregorian proposition that, capable of "a higher sense," the crudest of Hebrew legends proffers lessons in ethics and espouses a moral vision of the world, even as it asks "whether all this be truth, or fable foreshadowing the truth in fictions," yielding at last "their *undisguised* theologians."[61] In the Son's famous renunciation of the classics in *Paradise Regain'd* is a trace of both Gregory and Milton, whose emptying of classical forms as a prelude to infusing them with Christian content is less a rejection of classicism than a complex accommodation of it, which embraces Isocrates as an oratorical model, Plato as a philosopher, and Euripides as a poet and sage. In this assimilation of two cultures, Milton's own accommodation, achieved by splicing classical and Christian traditions and culling from both exemplary models, occurs within a poem in which the poet's presence, strongly felt, is itself not without "security measures."[62] Still, the principal point here is that the classical sanctions for Christian thinking, forbidden in Gregory's day, are the ones that Gregory recuperated and that Milton will later reify—no place more notably than in his Preface to *Samson Agonistes* in which he speaks of St. Paul quoting Euripides, one of two blunders for which this Preface has been faulted. The point is as pertinent to Samson's as to Milton's time—and equally so to our own.

Gregory Nazianzen was one of the Church Fathers whom Protestant reformers were comfortable citing, especially so because of the mediatorial role he had played in theological dispute, as well as his cautionary approach to Scriptures.[63] Even in fleeting moments, Gregory may have as much to teach us about the theology and politics of *Paradise Lost* as he does about those same topics in the poetic volume of 1671, which finally forces the question: what are we to make of the fact that the theologian invoked in the Preface to *Samson Agonistes* blunts what has been supposed to be that poem's ideological thrust?: "I will not strike with fury." Or as Gregory says of Christ: "He reproves . . . but smites not."[64] Is not *Samson Agonistes* a closet drama precisely because its action should not be imitated—should not be enacted on the stage of history and, if it is, promises not the sense of an ending, in which history is transformed, but endless cycles of history repeating themselves in a drama produced way beyond its fifth act?

As Gregory explains in his "First Invective against Julian," force by force is the way of tyrants and force by gentleness, the way of the Lord—a point that undergirds *Christ Suffering* as well, in which Gregory, supposed by Milton for the purposes of his Preface to have written the play, is again bent upon eliminating a culture of violence.[65] "[L]et us not do the same things that we have blamed in others . . . , let us detest all thoughts of retaliation," Gregory proclaims in his two invectives against Julian where, referring to "the just dispensations (balances) of God," he figures a deity "Who knows how to temper calamity with mercy and to chastise arrogance with disgrace"; Who, through acts of divine correction, is "ever inclining towards mercy." "[L]et mercy temper justice," Gregory declares, recalling his insistence that "nothing so serves God as mercy because no other thing is proper to God, whose *mercy and truth* go before" all else.[66]

Gregory thus anticipates the God of *Paradise Lost* who makes "Mercie collegue with Justice" (10.59) and in whom "Mercy first and last shall brightest shine," in whom "Divine compassion visibly appeer[s]" (3.134, 141), as well as the God of *Samson Agonistes* who spares some from the wholesale slaughter reported in Scripture. While the spirit of the Lord may have departed from Samson, evidently it has not yet left history, with those spared in the justice unique to Milton's poem recalling the great miracle wrought at the first Pentecost "when 3000 were converted . . . and . . . filled with the spirit of God" (Acts 11.41).[67] At this point in *Samson Agonistes*, it may be worth remembering Gregory as he lashes out against those who, "under the dominion of their anger, thrust away or strike at whatever comes in their way, even though it might well be spared."[68] In *Samson Agonistes* what is spared is owing not to Milton's Samson but to Milton's God. In this poem, Milton restores providence to retaliation as he removes blind chance from it. Justice belongs to the Lord.

In the emphasis he gives to patience in the face of anger and to forgiveness fronting revenge, in his insistence with Isaiah that always "a remnant shall be saved" (10:22), no less than in his advancement of a new Atonement theory, in his contention that the measure of Christ's (and of man's) superiority is in the things "He *refrained* from doing, though He had the power,"[69] Gregory reveals that his overriding purpose is to instil hope in a nation divided and among a people despairing. In parallel moves, Gregory shifts the inflection from the Crucifixion to the Resurrection just as Milton moves it from the Cross to "the Desert" as the place where, in *Paradise Regain'd*, "*Eden* [is] rais'd in the wast Wilderness" (1.9, 7) and "A fairer Paradise is founded *now*" (4.613; my italics). In his brief epic, Milton affirms with Gregory that "the goal of all my hopes is here"[70]—in this world, and not in one to come. In his 1671 poetic volume, he emblematizes through Gregory a newly humanized Christianity founded upon a resurrection of the spirit within and upon the recovery of a paradise within.

The proposition, *beyond revenge, hope*—the mantra of *Christ Suffering* as much as it is of Milton's 1671 poetic volume—may therefore be less an anathema to poets than to politicians and may simultaneously be a mark of the authenticity of poetry: of what one poet calls its "dialectic between what . . . [man] is and what he is becoming,"[71] paralleling a culture's own drive toward creation and change. The same point is implicit in Milton's description of the Restoration as a "long . . . Lent of Servitude" (*The Readie and Easie Way*, YP, 7:408) to be followed, presumably, by a resurrected spirit and a renovated world. As in *Paradise Lost*, so in *Samson Agonistes*: "pessimism and anger are expressed in the context of an ideal optimism" and, as Matthew Jordan explains, with "a sense of how people and things ought to be."[72] Milton's is a world in which light flickers, then fails; a world that turns dark before its lights come on again.

Rather than agitating for revenge and advocating acts of destruction, *Samson Agonistes* looks askance at both the ethic and enterprise of revenge, at those who arrogate to themselves a Christ-like spirituality and purpose and at those whose private faith diminishes, then defeats, the public causes of truth and justice. That Dalila makes the point in no way vitiates its validity: "to the public good / Private respects must yield," "Virtue, as I thought, truth, duty so enjoining"

(867–68, 870). *Samson Agonistes* is a poem that faces down just the kind of criticism lodged against Milton and his tragedy, first of all in the eighteenth century and more recently in the aftermath of the September 11ᵗʰ terrorist attack, with the biblical dictum, "God will not do wickedly, . . . [he] will not pervert justice" (Job 34:12)—even as simultaneously it worries over Manoa's proposition, "Sad, but thou knowst to Israelites not saddest / The desolation of a Hostile City" (1560–61). One may thus imagine Milton, along with Euripides, locking arms against those who would destroy a city, or reduce a nation to ruins. *Samson Agonistes* is less an exaltation of a hero than a problematizing of a then received notion of heroism, hence a poem meant to worry our humanity as if Milton were here saying of Samson what Gregory once said of another: "I saw the man *before* his actions exactly what I afterwards found him *in* his actions . . . [and] exclaimed . . . , what an evil the world . . . is breeding."[73] In the end, Samson may be no example of "redemption through immolation" but, as Norman Mailer might say, yet another "shard in the spiritual wreckage of the world."[74]

If, in driving the infidels from Nazianzum, Gregory's father was thought to illustrate the assertion that "good Men did not always preach up *Passive Obedience*," Gregory himself usually casts a dubious eye on self-fashioned miracle-workers and destroyers—on the use of un-Christian practices to advance the Christian religion. Indeed, Gregory comes to think that by demolishing a pagan temple, "according to the Power he had received from the Emperor," Mark of Arethusa drew upon himself "the Hatred of the People, as a Heathen would have been detested by the Christians, if he had pull'd down one of their Churches." Gregory comes to wonder whether such actions spring from providential retaliation or from an evil mind and, thereupon, suggests that it is "[a]s if . . . nothing to pull down their temples," such people on either side never displaying the patience Jesus shows his enemies, with Christians themselves (as Gibbon reports) exhibiting so much "vehement zeal" in the toppling of the temples of the Emperor Julian and his deities that, in their own lawless conduct against sacred edifices, they themselves provoked their enemy into violation of "the laws of prudence, and even of justice."[75] In the temple catastrophe, the same kind of criticism, in Milton's poem, is read back on to Samson.

Confronting what we are likely to perceive as an inversion of the circumstances on display in Milton's retelling of the Samson story, Gregory, as Jean Le Clerc reports, argues that "the greatest Satisfaction of the Christians, after *Julian's* Death," is "that those who had persecuted the Christians, were ridiculed upon the Stage, and Public Places and Assemblies." Yet such violence was also short-lived inasmuch as "*Gregory*, who had begged of God that *Julian* should be punished; as soon as he died, look'd upon the Pagans with Pity, and exhorted the Christians to treat 'em with Mildness."[76] It is the foundation stone in Gregory's theology that God gives "a sword, not to punish, but to threaten; not to destroy, but to appall"—and to awe; that "man is likest God," not when acting as a minister of His wrath, but "when he is dispencing [God's] mercy";[77] when, as in *Paradise Lost*, Book 6, he checks "His Thunder in mid Volie, for he meant / Not to destroy" (6.854–55). As Gregory puts it: "we show that our warfare is in behalf of Christ by fighting as Christ."[78] *Man is likest God when he is dispencing God's mercy*. That is Gregory's language from his "Oration to the People of Nazianzum," which sounds very much like the language Milton will use in *Eikonoklastes* when, having invoked Gregory as an intellectual ally, he insists that "God judges not by human fansy"; that God asserts "his Justice . . . [only] to the magnifying of his own mercy" (YP, 3:430, 432). In *Paradise Lost*, the Son attests: "I shall temper so / Justice with Mercie" (10.77–78), having already driven home the point that "to create / Is greater then created to destroy" (7.606–07).

As poet, orator, and especially theologian, Gregory Nazianzen, in name, bears a reputation invoked by Milton's prefatory epistle to *Samson Agonistes* and affording him precedent for much of what is distinctive to his tragedy, including its infusion of spiritual autobiography and disposition as drama. In one of his many wise remarks, Balachandra Rajan reports that "Milton could be contemptuous of 'Ancient Fathers' except when they were intelligent enough to agree with him."[79] Gregory was writing at a time when, in parallel with Milton's, "What belonged to the theatre was brought into the Church and what belonged to the Church into the theatre";[80] when churches thus turning into theaters found their representatives, in another metamorphosis, becoming actors in a play, as if Gregory were here explaining the conversion of the Judges temple into the "spacious Theatre" (1605) of *Samson Agonistes*. Moreover, Gregory was as committed to reviving expired tragedy, to achieving "a higher strain of tragedy,"[81] as he was to ridding its hybrid form of those comedic moments in which Christianity was often invoked merely to be mocked.

Tragicomedy was, for Gregory, an invention of the evil one now desolating the world, Gregory here reminding us of Milton's own rejection of the intermingling of tragedy and comedy but also of

Paradise Regain'd in which the Son diminishes tragedy as a fallen form in the face of Satan's Aristotelian exaltation of tragedy to the apex of the genres. Gregory and Milton alike, infusing classical forms with Christian content, would use their respective distillations of tragedy to authorize classical poets, especially Euripides, as sanctions for Christian thinking, in this way bridging cultures more often pitted against one another. The orations of Gregory, the prose writings of Milton—both are shot through with citations of and allusions to classical tragedy as if to remind us yet again, in the words of Henry Peacham, that "the Apostles themselues haue not disdained to alledge the authoritie of the heathen Poets. . . . As also the fathers of the Church, Nazianzen."[82] What Gregory understood is that tragedy is the form through which to envision the desolation of the world, a condition he reached beyond when he wrote, "before him is the Garden of Eden, behind him a desolate wilderness,"[83] words which might serve as an apt epigraph for Milton's 1671 poetic volume.

Finally, it is Gregory's reputation as *the theologian* that affords an important perspective from which to interpret *Samson Agonistes*. In his trinitarianism, a queller of controversy and in his Atonement theory, an instigator of it, particularly in his objection to the ransom theory as a vestige of an all-too-primitive Christianity, Gregory is notable for his freewill theology, as well as his proto-Arminian leanings, evident in his insistence that good is cultivated by our own choice, and by the motions of the will. That is, says Gregory, God placed man in paradise, "having honoured him with the gift of free will, in order that good might belong to him as the result of his choice."[84] But even more noteworthy are his objections to temple trashing and demolition (by the faithful and infidels alike), his embrace of a theology of charity and forgiveness, his opposition to a culture of violence and pressing for a humanized Christianity, which features, reemerging in Milton, have led one of Christianity's harshest critics to conclude of this poet that he is "a broader and more adroit kind of man than is usually thought, less pedantic and self-enclosed, more humane, more capable of entering into other people's motives and sentiments."[85] If it is so, "that all characters are on trial in a civilized narrative," if "the word *civilized* distinguishes between ancient myth and its modern retellings,"[86] then Milton himself is brought into the dock for judgment, and what we confront there is a humane Milton indeed. It is a Milton who would usurp for himself the title of theologian and for whom (as with Gregory) humanity becomes inhumane when perseverance becomes compulsion and apparent goodness, a means of savagery; for whom the hopes of *Paradise Regain'd* are shipwrecked in the turn backward to the world of *Samson Agonistes*.

If, as has been suggested, the Resurrection story was, early on, evacuated from the Samson legend,[87] it is returned to the margins of the Samson story, is restored as a possibility, in the very moment that *Christ Suffering* is written into the prefatory epistle to Milton's tragedy, this very citation supplying the segue from *Paradise Regain'd* to *Samson Agonistes* (CP, 574). It is the modifying context afforded by *Paradise Regain'd* and reinforced by citation of Gregory Nazianzen that best explains what Thomas De Quincey describes as "a tragedy of most tumultuous catastrophe," which, in "its most exquisite form," exhibits the "fine transfiguration of moral purpose that belongs to a higher, purer, and far holier religion."[88]

In more recent reflections on tragedy, Tony Kushner, rather than reinventing, vindicates tragedy, much as Milton would do, by extrapolating from its history tragedy's enduring mission of making available "the possibility of a new understanding." For Kushner, one prong in the paradox of tragedy is its "creative aspect: new meaning flows to fill the emptiness hollowed out by devastation" as we determine which path to take: that of fiery anger and unremitting spite or, again in Kushner's words, that of "imagination, compassion, and courageous intelligence."[89] In choosing among such options, all of us are engaged in shaping interpretation of *Samson Agonistes* and of history (the civil war in England or 9/11 and its aftermath); and in the ensuing actions of history, as well as in our interpretations of them, we all become implicated as we decide, and then promulgate our decision, concerning whether *Samson Agonistes* is an appeal to hurl down a city or, in conjunction with *Paradise Regain'd*, an announcement about dwelling in possibility, about recovering paradise by building up a new Jerusalem of the spirit. In its continual hankering after a better self and better time, Milton's 1671 poetic volume is a provocation to mental fight and a perpetual prompting to spiritual adventure.

Samson Agonistes AND THE TRAGEDY OF HISTORY

Milton criticism, initially drawing its leads from contexts narrowly defined and restrictive in application, is progressively taking direction from contexts compounding, steadily shifting, multiplying in number and often eliding with one another. In Milton's poetry, "context keeps expanding,"[90] not infinitely so, but so much so, that it is almost as if Milton's last poems prophesy the postmodern proposition that "a multiplicity of contexts determines how influential . . . [a poem] will be."[91] The "surprise," as opposed to the "enterprise" of contextualization,[92] so far as Milton's writings are concerned, comes from watching Milton's poetry of contexts modulating into a poetry affording a proliferation of contexts for subsequent literature, sacred and secular, in so many of which instances, in active interplay, the texts and contexts, in their interdependencies, are also mutually illuminating.

Yet regardless of the context, whether it is afforded by Milton's tragedy or its source in the Book of Judges, each context eventually rivets attention to the moment of terror at the temple/theater when, having already slaughtered thirty, then a thousand, now in taking down "a Hostile City" (1561), Samson slaughters thousands more than in all his life he had slain before. It is one of the coincidences of history that the rhetoric of biblical commentary just before 9/11 will match with the rhetoric of some Milton criticism in its aftermath. Thus one commentator on the Book of Judges will proclaim that Samson is "like a modern suicide bomber" and, simultaneously, will advance Samson's story as "a warning, not an example."[93] Just as England could find its tragedy in the figure of Samson, America can now find its in *Samson Agonistes*—a poem that without salesmanship, as Arthur E. Barker once expected, has become "a relevant tract for the times."[94]

The Bible itself is mute on the details of this final "desolation" (1561); although for two centuries now, through its annotations, it sometimes invokes Milton's account as scriptural supplement:

> those two massive Pillars
> With horrible convulsion to and fro,
> He tugged, he shook, till down they came and drew
> The whole roof after them, with burst of thunder
> Upon the heads of all who sate beneath.[95]

That said, we can focus on questions underscored by Milton's tragedy: Is *Samson Agonistes* an embrace—or simply a representation—of violence; an incitement to—or indictment of—terror? Is revenge a divine instinct or a human impulse; and is it to be condoned or condemned? And what of anger in *Samson Agonistes*? Where is this poem's supposed politics of retaliation driving us? Is the poem itself caught in the paradox of asserting continuity with institutionalized religion as it contemplates, in the image of Dagon's temple destroyed, institutionalized religion in collapse? What image of deity here prevails, the God of the Apocalypse or the God of the Gospels: the figure of a wrathful, avenging God, "cultivated by the . . . self-righteous," or "the reverse . . . image of God as a broken body, as an executed political criminal?"[96]

What Philip Fisher seems to construe as a "vehement, spirited anger," working itself through progressive states until it reaches "finality" in the epitomizing line in Milton's tragedy, "calm of mind all passion spent" (1758), at times seems more like "uncompassionate anger" (818), "anger, unappeaseable," raging like a "tempest never to be calm'd" (963–64).[97] This trait of character may be better comprehended in terms of a question: Is Samson's anger "an excess" or "a defect" or, rather, a mark of Aristotle's honorable man, "angry at the right things and with the right people, . . . as he ought, when he ought, and as long as he ought"?[98] If judges signal the invention of a legal system, as well as society's intervention with punishments meant to eliminate retaliation, it is of some moment that Samson in the Book of Judges, from whom Milton withholds the very appellation of judge, is engaged throughout his life in acts of revenge. With those acts escalating, the question becomes, to adapt one of Fisher's finest formulations,

> Should . . . [they] be forgiven? Should . . . [they] be ignored? Must retaliation happen? If it happens, will it lead to a response and a spiral of violence that has no easy exit?[99]

Is Samson ultimately a person whose only exit, whose "dire necessity" (1666), is that he "inevitably" must pull down "destruction" on himself (1657–58)? Is this the bind in which Samson, supposedly "a person rais'd / With . . . command from Heav'n / To free my Countrey" (1211–12), is finally caught? Are we, in turn, the ongoing victims of that anger?

And what *of* violence in Milton's tragedy? In the character of Samson, does Milton underwrite or undermine its practitioners, together with those cultural authorities and institutions that would validate them? Legitimating them, is he complicit in such practices; or interrogating them, does he reject the cultural barbarism subtended by the Samson story and coded into the poem in the famous line, "A thousand fore-skins fell, the flower of *Palestin*" (144)—into the very indignity of counting dead bodies? To what extent are Milton's critics, as opposed to Milton himself, responsible for those harsh rebukes, over the centuries, from which John Carey and others have tried to shield the poet, with Carey, for one, reminding us that "Milton's drama is . . . a drastic rewriting of the Samson story":

> [*Samson Agonistes*] calls into question Samson's motivation, and
> whether he has any divine sanction for his suicide attack . . . . Crucially,
> Milton omits Samson's prayer. . . . In this final stage of the drama we
> cannot know what is going on in Samson's mind. . . . All through this
> last phase Milton hides Samson's thoughts and, for that matter, God's.
> When he destroys the theatre Samson may think he is carrying out
> God's will, or he may be following his purely human impulse to
> revenge.[100]

"There is insufficient evidence to eliminate any of these possibilities"
from a poem, concludes Carey,[101] that treats the Samson story less as
a record than as an echo of history. In *Samson Agonistes*, Milton
creates a tragedy that in its aftermath resonates with history—a poem
in which there seems to be a causal relationship between personal
tragedy and national disaster, between Samson defeated and a nation
in ruins, and in which Milton not only stages the crises of his culture
but structures a critique of them. Even by those who find in *Samson
Agonistes* "the noblest conception of . . . [Samson] in modern
poetry," we are reminded that "no . . . national renovation" is
achieved by him.[102] That is not part of his story.

Carey seems to get it just right when he concludes that, seeing
9/11 under the lights of *Samson Agonistes* makes it all the more evident that the premises underlying each tragedy belong to a world that
Milton has outgrown and would have us do the same. *Samson
Agonistes* is not trivialized by politics, nor does it trivialize 9/11, so
long as we remember that the lesson, here, is not that history repeats
itself but that history rhymes and that within the vast complexities of
their worlds, in the words of Salman Rushdie, "one man's hero is
another's villain."[103] One nation's freedom fighters are another's
terrorists. In fact, deriving its potency from the imprecision and
incompleteness of such parallels, from "a principle of inexact analogy,"[104] *Samson Agonistes* helps explain not only what happened on
9/11, but why it happened and then how, in practicing a politics of
resentment and retaliation, a nation compromises its own moral
authority. Moreover, as Annabel Patterson would probably go on to
say, *Samson Agonistes* does so by "offering . . . readers a *choice* of interpretations, arising out of a welter of conflicting textual directions,"
with Milton thus "creat[ing] the readerly equivalent of Arminianism,
hermeneutical free will," in a poem of extraordinary "density" that then
becomes a swirling "vortex of possible or alternative meanings."[105]

In *Samson Agonistes*, meaning is lodged within proliferating contradictions, including a writer's simultaneous toleration of violence
and revulsion in the face of it such as we find in *Of Christian Doctrine*
as its author argues, on the one hand, that "some hatred . . . is a
religious duty, as when we hate the enemies of God" (YP, 6:743); that
"we are not forbidden to take or to wish to take vengeance upon the
enemies of the church" (YP, 6:755); having already argued that we
should not "*bear a grudge against . . .* [our] *fellow-countrymen*," or
"*pay back evil*" or "*take revenge . . . repaying evil with evil*," for "it is
disgraceful and disgusting that the Christian religion should be supported by violence" (YP, 6:755, 123). Very simply, *Samson Agonistes*
is a reminder that we must refuse easy answers even as we resist
uncomplicated allegiances; that poetry repeals traditions and voids
conventions; and that the truths of poetry are plural not singular and,
in Milton's tragedy, so resistant to easy ideological unravelings, that
they are not encapsulated by Samson, or Manoa, or the Chorus. If
answers in their inconsistency are inadequate, questions in the poem,
if insistent, are interconnected and, while usually unanswered, not
always unanswerable. This is a poem that mirrors cultural violence
without summoning us to mimic it. Thus, in a turn of the critical lens,
Milton's tragedy may seem to unleash its subversive forces against the
very system of beliefs others have thought it is meant to support. Not
so much a rehearsal of existing interpretation but, instead, part of a
contestatory tradition, *Samson Agonistes* tries the reader's aptitude for
*re*interpretation.

Especially in *Samson Agonistes*, we gather in an enormous grief as
we respond to all-too-recent tragedy with Milton's gift of tragic
poetry and, simultaneously, marvel not at this poem's didactic clarity
but at its moral quandaries; at what William Empson might call their
"awful warning."[106] That is, *Samson Agonistes* is a poem, unconfined
by the problems of its own day, which confronts the perils of ours—
and at a time when catastrophe humbles us by its enormities, by the
smallness of our understanding of them, and, instead of ensnaring us
within, would liberate us from what has been called that "dangerous
dance of hate and revenge in which we are engaged."[107] Milton's
hard-won insight is that violence is a way of killing the future by
destroying its possibilities, with the actions of his great poems, as
G. Wilson Knight comprehends, shaping themselves prophetically
"into one remarkable prefiguration of our own gigantic, and itself
archetypal, world-conflict," and with Milton's Samson, it would
seem, himself a weapon of mass destruction, figuring all those
people in history who, in Knight's words, "ruthlessly override ethical

objections in obedience to an all-demanding intuition, considering themselves . . . the 'scourge of God.' "[108] Milton's last poems, in different ways perhaps, yet none more powerfully than *Samson Agonistes*, are apt companions as, confronting global hatreds and anger, we are haunted by images of hubris flaunted only to be followed by stunning defeat. Milton's tragedy, especially, is meant to worry our humanity.

Milton's last poems, interdependent and mutually illuminating, are integrated into a trilogy, each affording a modifying context through which the others may be interpreted. Terrorism is an issue in each poem. Satan is Milton's proto-terrorist whose strategy when the celestial battle commences, as Abdiel perceives, is to terrify heaven (6.134) even if, as *Paradise Lost* then makes clear, Satan's forces are the first to experience terror: "Amaze, / Be sure, and terrour seis'd the rebel Host" (6.646–47). This moment stands in striking contrast to the climax of the celestial battle when the Son, an accomplished practitioner of shock and awe tactics, "into terrour chang'd / His count'nance" (6.824–25) and, now leaving the rebellious angels "Thunderstruck . . . / With terrors" (6.858–59), checks "His Thunder in mid Volie, . . . mean[ing] / Not to destroy, but root them out of Heav'n" (6.854–55). Subsequent to their fall, terror becomes the preserve of the fallen angels, described by Satan as the "Terror of Heav'n" (2.457), with Satan himself just routed by terror reportedly facing "grieslie terrour . . . Unterrifi'd" (2.704–08). Terrorizing thunder will become a feature of the world after the fall (10.666–67), and terror itself an aspect of death, yet a feature, too, that God bids Michael to hide (11.111) and in opposition to which God ordains his laws so that "terror [may] cease" (12.238).

In *Paradise Regain'd*, it is the Son who, terrorized by ugly dreams, remains unterrified (4.421–25) and who, eventually "with awe / . . . all unarm'd / Shall chase . . . [Satan] with the terror of his voice" (4.625–27). Initially, Milton may have allowed for divine intervention, for what in *The Reason of Church-Government* he called God's "engines of terror" (YP, 1:847), until he came to associate tactics of terror with Charles I and the church evangelicals and, thereupon, became increasingly less certain of the justice, or the virtue, in wantonly exercised power, better checked than fully unleashed. Finally, though, Milton does not confuse the Messiah of *Paradise Lost* with the Samson of his tragedy, seeing in them (as does G. Wilson Knight) a single "strength thunder[ing] down on wrongdoers," though he does couple *Paradise Regain'd* and *Samson Agonistes* in the same poetic volume "to elucidate the relation of New Testament ethics to international affairs"[109] and, simultaneously, in looping back to *Paradise Lost* in the final lines of *Samson Agonistes*, contrasts the Son, checking his thunder in mid-volley in order to avoid destruction, with Samson who, as "cloudless thunder bolted" on the heads of the Philistines (1696), produces "Blood, Death, and deathful deeds . . . / Ruin, destruction at the utmost point" (1513–14). Samson's life and hence his death are tales of terrorism proliferating. If Milton's tragedy climaxes in a spectacle of "terror," the poet's intention, if it can be inferred from the prefatory epistle to this poem, is not to raise but "to purge the mind of those and such like passions" (CP, 573).

Criticism may commence in the study of contexts for Milton's poetry yet, in a turn of the lens, climaxes in a glimpse at Milton's last poems as a context for history not just in Milton's but in our time. The centrality of the past and the present to *Samson Agonistes*, it appears, has a reach beyond the poem itself. More than of their own age, Milton's last poems, as Peter Bayne suggests, are the morning of its future.[110] It is no wonder, then, that in the second decade of the last century, as he moved to assess Milton's modernity, Martin Larson got so many essential matters right: most important, that "an emancipated student of the past," Milton was "the herald of an age" that would eventually dawn; and that increasingly apprehensive of "orthodox Christianity" as exemplified in "The Passion" and worrying over his "utter inability to think himself into that state of mind which is the essence of Christianity," Milton transgressed and transfigured both the Bible and Christian orthodoxy founded upon it, in the process modifying Christian mythology and humanizing Christianity itself. *Paradise Lost*, though, has more "discordant or contradictory" elements than Larson thinks,[111] which, in their turn, pave the way for *Paradise Regain'd* and *Samson Agonistes*—poems which, published together, mark new directions in Milton's thinking as well as evidence its persisting uncertainties.

Milton *matters*, in part, because with *Samson Agonistes* we see America, along with England, "responding to its tragedy," as Derek Walcott urges it to do, "with tragic poetry" that makes a nation's eyes "clear with grief."[112] Milton *matters* because, in facing tragedy, he forces us to reach beyond an axis of good and evil in the world—beyond mere dismissal of our enemies as an evil empire—to a more ambiguous reality. Milton's tragedy *matters* especially because it is a challenge to the past—an invitation to restore, even to establish, its relevance to the present time not by reinventing Milton but by recuperating his tragedy through reversion to earlier readings of *Samson Agonistes*.

By way of acknowledging that Milton wrote his last poems in the future tense, the defining poets of British Romanticism, Blake and Wordsworth, summon *him* to spiritual adventure. Uniting with Blake,

Milton lends a hand to building "Jerusalem / In England's green & pleasant Land"; and in an apostrophe, Wordsworth declares:

> Milton! thou shouldst be living at this hour:
> England hath need of thee: . . .
> Oh! Raise us up, return to us again.[113]

The Romantics mince no words: Milton *matters* as a poet who, in *Paradise Lost* and *Paradise Regain'd*, is represented (most notably by Blake and Shelley) as the prophetic soul of the wide world, dreaming on things to come, and who, in *Samson Agonistes*, is seen as a prophetic tragedian, warning future generations of catastrophes that, if not awake to their missions, they will fail to avert. Wordsworth may have written *The Prelude* as an exfoliation of the last books of *Paradise Lost*, and if that is so, it needs reporting that Percy Bysshe Shelley's *Prometheus Unbound*, while it recapitulates the dethronement of the Satanic selfhood and attendant apocalypse of mind in *Paradise Regain'd*, while it reiterates the often supposed regeneration of Samson, is impelled, in its fourth act, by the realization that Milton withholds from his last poems not the promise but the vision of the world restored, of history renovated. That is, the first three acts of Shelley's lyrical drama are reiterations of the individual regeneration figured in Milton's 1671 poetic volume, even as, once the pit is barred and the serpent bound (not by God but by Promethean man), Shelley's fourth act supplements personal redemption with a vision of historical renovation, of the world's renewal.

Initially, one may think of Shelley's unheroic Prometheus, "eyeless in hate," evoking Milton's Samson, "Eyeless in *Gaza*" (41); or of Count Cenci rejoicing in the catastrophe where "most favoring Providence was shown / Even in the manner of . . . [his young sons'] deaths":

> For Rocco
> Was kneeling at the mass, with sixteen others,
> When the Church fell and crushed him to a mummy,
> The rest escaped unhurt.[114]

The last of those lines contains a hauntingly ironic echo of the verse from *Samson Agonistes*, "The vulgar only scap'd" (1659). In *Prometheus Unbound*, however, through allusion, Shelley will pointedly reverse the regressive ordering of poems in Milton's 1671 poetic volume so as to suggest that Samson emblematizes the world from which Shelley's Prometheus springs free, in a poem that swings on its axis from Prometheus imprisoned, to Prometheus liberated, to the world's wilderness becoming a paradise. Turning Milton's regression of history into an historical progress, Shelley insinuates that *Samson Agonistes* (and *The Cenci*), both worlds without eyes, eventually give way to *Paradise Regain'd* (and *Prometheus Unbound*), worlds replete with vision, where people see again.

Old world fronts the new in *Prometheus Unbound*, which boldly scores the ironies of judges misjudging, of leaders misleading, and of both then being summoned to judgment by their enemies. It is no longer Samson threatening Dalila and Harapha but now the Furies, Shelley's new "ministers of pain and fear / . . . and hate" (1.452–53), who threaten to rend Prometheus "bone from bone, / And nerve from nerve" (1.475–76). It is Prometheus, not Samson, who now images *Christus patiens* (1.584–85), Christ as "suffering man" (1.817), and who, descending into the grace of life (3.3.113–14), "shall rise / Henceforth the sun of this rejoicing world" (2.4.126–27). Samson's world of "Blood, death, and deathful deeds . . . / Ruin, destruction at the utmost point" (1513–14), rendered by Shelley as a world of "dead Destruction, ruin within ruin," as the wreckage of "a city vast" (4.295–96), becomes "a new earth and sea / And a Heaven where yet Heaven could never be" (4.164–65). It is a world not that pairs strength with wisdom, coming up short on the latter, but one in which "wisdom . . . is strength" (2.4.44). It is the same world imagined by (but beyond the grasp of) the Creature at the epicenter of the twenty-four book version of Mary Shelley's *Frankenstein*.

In her novel subtitled "The Modern Prometheus," the Samson story, probably impressed upon Mary Shelley's consciousness by a recent reading of *Samson Agonistes*, is similarly invoked by the Creature who, "torn" by "supernatural force . . . from . . . [Felix's] father," is then "dashed . . . to the ground and struck . . . violently," but who also initially resists such retaliatory gestures, even if he "could have torn . . . [Felix] limb for limb, as the lion rends the antelope." In contrast, Victor Frankenstein, "trembling with passion, tore to pieces" the female monster he was in process of creating, causing the Creature to withdraw, "with a howl of devilish despair and revenge."[115] Mary Shelley's novel forces the question not only of who is the modern Prometheus but of who is the modern-day Samson. Is it the Creature who is thrown to the ground by Felix as Samson would do to Harapha, running upon him, "And with one buffet lay thy structure low," and "then dash thee down" (1239–40). Or is the modern-day Samson Frankenstein who, first wanting "to trample" the Creature "to dust," later tears apart his female counterpart as Samson threatens to do to Dalila, "lest fierce remembrance wake / My sudden rage to tear thee joint by joint" (952–53) and as formerly Samson had torn "the Lion, as the Lion tears the Kid" (128). Samson is as desirous of "mortal fight" with Harapha (1175) as Frankenstein is of "mortal combat" or "mortal conflict" with the Creature.[116]

In imitation of Samson, it seems, Victor Frankenstein, under the guidance of providence, "the spirits that I had invoked to aid me" and acting in accordance with a "purpose . . . assigned to me by heaven," performs as avenger and destroyer, as one of God's "ministers of vengeance,"[117] in contrast to the moment in *Paradise Lost* when "the angry Victor" recalls "His Ministers of vengeance" (1.169–70). Victor is adamant: he is "the mechanical impulse of some power," performing "a task enjoined by heaven" and, eventually appropriating the power of God, would then enlist Captain Walton as one of his own "ministers of vengeance."[118] This vengeful god, with ministers of his wrath, is not Milton's god but, rather, as Milton's poem testifies, god as he is perceived and portrayed by Satan—and later by Mary Shelley's Frankenstein/Prometheus and her poet husband's Prometheus/Satan/Samson. They are collectively what, in *Prometheus Unbound*, Shelley calls "the ministers of pain . . . / . . . and hate / And clinging crime" (1.452–53), those who transfix and destroy with their bolts of thunder and lightning.

Lest the point be lost, Mary Shelley drives it home again in *The Last Man*, in which not unmanned by a woman as Samson is, Lionel Verney, like Milton, is inspired by woman, Urania, and her wisdom. If initially Lionel devises schemes of vengeance, he quickly comes to the realization that there is no glory in massacre, no honor in spilling human blood. Eventually, it is the political fanatics, the would-be prophets, who, in "the delirium of fanaticism," imagine themselves as God's "satellites."[119] This is a novel in which, in language both biblical and Miltonic (tugging and straining are Milton's additives to the Judges description), Samson figures as a great natural force first: "Suddenly the wind veered from south-west to west, and then again to north-west. As Sampson with tug and strain stirred from their bases the columns that supported the Philistine temple, so did the gale shake the dense vapours propped on the horizon"; but later Samson figures as a force of both cultural terrorism and self-destruction as Adrian, unrelenting, witnesses "his wretched enemy," the political fanatic, the false prophet, "pull[ing] destruction on his head, destroying with his own hands the dominion he had erected."[120]

What the Shelleys aver, as if in collaboration with Lord Byron, is that much "heterodox opinion,"[121] much audacity, is inscribed in both *Paradise Lost* and *Samson Agonistes*, the latter of which poems "Milton keeps tragic to the last."[122] Byron's Manfred, his "own soul's sepulcher,"[123] finds his counterpart in Milton's Samson, "My self, my Sepulcher, a moving Grave" (102), just as in *Childe Harold's Pilgrimage* and *Don Juan* Byron finds his counterpart in the ostensibly autobiographical poet of *Samson Agonistes*, a poet who teases us into seeing similarities only to force altogether more important distinctions upon us. As poet-historian, Milton comprehended the efficacy of analogies for the understanding of history; and thus, as much as the Bible provided him, he provides us, especially through his last poems, not just with apt analogies for but with mythic paradigms of our history, past and present: of paradise lost and eventually recovered and, in *Samson Agonistes*, of history as both a tale of tyranny and terrorism. If the point of the argument is moral condemnation or approbation, the analogies predictably gather around Milton's Satan or Messiah. Alternatively, if the objective is moral analysis, the analogies are more likely afforded by Milton's Samson. Milton's last poems are less about heroes than about the problematics of heroism. Biography and history are inextricably entwined, the character of the individual and the state of the nation. Whom do we encounter in Milton's tragedy, "Shemshûm el Jebbâr, 'Samson the Hero' "—or a character like the Israeli, Levi Eshkol, remarkable for his own magnanimity, once called "Shimshon der Nebechdikker—Samson the nerd"?[124] In Samson do we discover a nation in its invincibility or vulnerability, in its strength or helplessness—or a nation that, neither/nor, is rather a split image, a divided entity?

Samson Agonistes, at its every juncture, seems ready to give us the slip. In *Paradise Regain'd*, an Aristotelian Satan advances tragedy to the forefront of the genres, while the Son, unpersuaded, remembers tragedy as a fallen form and, in this sense, the invention and an insignia of Satan. With deepening ironies, readers exit Milton's brief epic only to encounter, at the portal of his tragedy, an epistle, which, echoing Satan's earlier words concerning "the lofty grave Tragœdians," "teachers best / Of moral prudence," "High actions, and high passions best describing" (4.261, 262–63, 266), instructs us that tragedy, just as Satan says, "hath been ever held the gravest, moralest, and most profitable of all other Poems," with Aeschylus, Sophocles, and Euripides eventually named as "the three Tragic Poets unequall'd yet by any" (CP, 573, 574). But the Son had protested: "Alas what can they teach, and not mislead"; "Much of the soul they talk, but all awrie" (4.309, 313). "*Greece* from us these Arts deriv'd; / Ill imitated," scolds the Son, who concedes to Satan only that "where moral vertue is express't / By light of Nature not in all quite lost," even if "such [come] from thee," there may still exist some ethical import and value (4.338–39, 351–52, 350). Not only is the priority of tragedy as a generic category under challenge here, but so too is the matter of models, classical or scriptural: which of them to privilege? And which is the better repository for true heroism? Milton criticism, from John Dryden onward, has been locked in combat over a similar question: who are Milton's heroes? And, when critics divide over the issue, often hopelessly, the question morphs into another: how does Milton direct our perception of heroism, especially in *Samson Agonistes*, in which a narrative scaffolding is missing?

At the beginning of the twentieth century, urging its "sublime dialogue" and their tragic ironies upon the reader, the biblical exegete G. H. S. Walpole identifies *Samson Agonistes* as a fit guide to, and ample meditation upon, Judges 16:23–31 as he argues that "[t]here is no prayer for the vindication of God's glory such as Milton fondly imagines," but here in Judges, "only the natural wish for personal vengeance." In this story, by repeatedly laying claim to divine inspiration, Samson attributes all he does to God; hence is certain "that God will avenge Himself" but within a "history," as Walpole concludes, which "gives us no reason to believe that Samson's chief desire was to glorify God by his death."[125] Eventually, inevitably, the contrast between Samson and Christ, owing to their respective death scenes, comes into focus. The prayer Walpole thinks is in Milton's poem is *not*, thus underscoring the contrast between Samson asking his God for vengeance against the Philistines and Christ asking forgiveness for his tormentors. In their respective death scenes, Samson reveals "no . . . penitence, only a thirst for vengeance," in contrast with the "patience and meekness" of Christ who never, as Samson does, cries out for revenge "but only for the salvation of His enemies."[126] In his death, Samson hopes to destroy the world that Christ would save. "Samson died as he lived," Walpole concludes, and thus a "life that might have been great was one of destruction for selfish purposes, . . . summed up in the words, 'He slew more in his death than he did in his life.' "[127]

These are contrasts, though Walpole never quite says so, that Milton's own poem forces into consciousness and that emerge from the uncertainty in *Samson Agonistes* concerning whether the protagonist's final action, his destruction of the temple/theater, is God's doing—or Samson's own. In view of seventeenth-century representations of Samson as a hero of prayer, especially in the opening pages of the prayer book for the New Model Army, the uncertainty concerning Samson's prayer in Milton's poem—"he stood, as one who pray'd, / *Or* some great matter in his mind revolv'd" (1637–38; my italics), the obvious excision of the supposed words of Samson's prayer from the text of Milton's poem—these details make it likely that, here in *Samson Agonistes*, Milton prosecutes a tradition of representation that earlier the Puritan revolutionaries had promulgated.

Eventually, and in greater detail than is possible here, we need to take stock of what Hans Robert Jauss would describe as the huge "hermeneutic difference between the former and the current understanding of a work," in this instance of *Samson Agonistes*, by way of "rais[ing] to consciousness the history of its reception."[128] Perhaps surprisingly, in the instance of *Samson Agonistes*, hermeneutic distance broadens rather than narrows over time. The literary past of Milton's tragedy is thus retrieved by recent criticism (seldom knowingly) as it draws past interpretations into the present and develops as well as deepens them with new contextualizations, thereby situating *Samson Agonistes* within a new conversation in which, more elusive than the usual context or subtext, Milton's tragedy functions as a shadow text. Its reception begins with the title page for Milton's 1671 poetic volume. It is given initial articulation by John Beale as he declares that "Milton is abroad againe, in Prose, & in Verse, Epic, & Dramatic" in obvious and early reference to *Paradise Regain'd* and *Samson Agonistes* and in continuing consternation over the "*blasphemies*" of *Paradise Lost*,[129] which, a century and more later, Lord Byron will extend to *Samson Agonistes*.

If Andrew Marvell is the chief early fretter over the ideological leanings of Milton's tragedy, Lord Byron eventually overgoes Marvell by arguing that Milton's "epics . . . prove nothing"; hence Byron would like "to know what . . .[Milton's] real belief was. The 'Paradise Lost' and 'Regained' do not satisfy me on this point,"[130] whereas *Samson Agonistes*, in its more humane Christianity (in what Leigh Hunt calls its "more *Christian* Christianity"[131]) apparently does. Though Byron always fixes his inflection on the essentially undogmatic character of Milton's writings, it is especially from Milton's tragedy that Byron learned his poetics of the persona as Milton's sway over his writings shifted over time from *Lycidas*, to *Paradise Lost*, to Milton's tragedy. If Milton may have once contradicted himself into contradiction, in *Samson Agonistes* he contradicts himself out of it, knowing that the curse of forgiveness involves remaining hopelessly bound to retaliation and forever menaced by it, hence in the face of forgiveness never able to practice it. The last infirmity of the noble mind, shed by Milton but not Milton's Samson, is, as Jerome McGann remarks, the "impulse to revenge wrongs and to triumph over enemies."[132] The creative mind, opened not closed, exemplified by a cadre of Promethean poets like Dante, Tasso, Milton, and Byron himself, breaks free of its manacles and, with its prophetic eye, moves toward enlightenment.

Lest anyone should think that the interpretation here embraced is a distinctly postmodernist phenomenon, let us remember that, if the typological/regenerationist reading of *Samson Agonistes* is fixed by George Frederick Handel's *Samson: An Oratorio* (composed in 1742 and performed in the Lenten season of 1743), "the reading" of Milton's tragedy we now associate first with John Carey and Irene Samuel was already in place embryonically before Milton's death, in Andrew Marvell's dedicatory poem to *Paradise Lost* and its depiction of Samson, "grop[ing] the temple's posts in spite." The trajectory of one interpretive line moves from Marvell, on to Dr. Johnson, who ascribes the plaudits often bestowed on *Samson Agonistes* to "ignorance" and "bigotry," then on to Shelley's Samson-like Prometheus ("eyeless in hate"), to Mary Shelley's avengers (both Frankenstein and his Creature), to James Montgomery's Samson in his fallenness and transgression linked to Satan within a poem "uninviting both in its theme and the treatment of it," and, finally, on to George Gilfillan's Samson whose hand, as he stands at the pillars, "has few flowers in it. . . . His spirit is that of Abimelech," and whose actions within the poem itself bare "the wrath of Heaven" and threaten "to crush wonder . . . rather than to awaken . . . admiration."[133]

What began as a commendation of Milton's ethic over that of Samson, in time, deepens into a condemnation of Milton and Samson as representatives of the same ethical system, with Peter Bayne, in the grip of what he calls "the Puritan Samson Agonistes," concluding that "[t]he spiritual depths of Christianity, the Divine power of kindness and self-sacrifice, were fully fathomed" in *none* of Milton's last poems, wherein dwells instead "the inspiration of Puritan battle."[134] Yet as if in response to Bayne, and in a gesture that returns to Marvell's condemnation of Samson, but commendation of Milton, J. Howard B. Masterman, in 1897, sought to free *Samson Agonistes* from a politics of violence and religion of retaliation. Here in Milton's poem is *the tragedy of Puritanism*, which, he says, "appears as the blind and discredited champion of Divine Vengeance," now hostage to a "brute secular force" and to "religious seductions" that "might hope to strike one more blow for freedom," only to "perish in the overthrow of its enemies." The whole point of Milton's 1671 poetic volume, Masterman supposes, is to present as "a great alternative . . . the victory of patience and self-repression—the Divine overcoming of evil with good"; to choose as "the better part . . . to be patient" and, despite the penalty of disappointment, "to hope."[135] Or put differently, the question lurking between the covers of this poetic volume is whether Milton's head was filled with the hardest and most dismal tenets of Calvinism, or whether, instead, those tenets, embedded in *Samson Agonistes* to be sure, are signatures of the atrophying world of Milton's tragedy, not of the new paradise he envisions.

It simply will not do to argue that "Heterodox views put forward in nine pages of a book [by John Carey] intended for students would probably have received little scholarly attention had Carey not also edited *Samson* in Longman's Annotated English Poets series";[136] for those "heterodox" views were already inscribed within the critical tradition evolving from *Samson Agonistes*, as early as Andrew Marvell. Moreover, because they are also a part of the Samson hermeneutic, the next question is whether, through the influence of Milton's tragedy, those same elements by the end of the nineteenth century are secured within biblical commentary pertaining to the Samson story. If influence once reached from the Bible to Milton, does it now redound from Milton's poem on to scriptural exegesis?

MILTON'S INFLUENCE ON THE BIBLE

An alternative tradition of *Samson* criticism is enabling just because it presses old questions upon us, but allows for new solutions to them, in this way drawing *Samson Agonistes* out of relative seclusion, even as it releases meanings over time embedded in Milton's poem, through new and opportune contextualizations. One such context begins to assert itself when, instead of asking about the Bible's influence on Milton, we consider, alternatively, Milton's influence on the Bible; that is, the extent to which, like *Paradise Lost* and *Paradise Regain'd*, Milton's biblical tragedy is eventually involved in shaping a new hermeneutic, in this instance for the Samson story. What kind of presence does *Samson Agonistes* have in biblical commentary written subsequent to it, and what do we learn about Milton's poem from a biblical hermeneutic subtly shaped by it? The crucial century is the nineteenth, and the important years the later ones in that century, by which time it is conceded that "[t]he noblest conception of . . .[Samson] in modern poetry, is that of Milton's *Samson Agonistes*." Yet this concession is also accompanied by uneasiness over Milton's "treat[ing] only the end of Samson's life, and notwithstanding its lofty thought and Christian fervor disfigures the beautiful simplicity of Scripture by operatic additions."[137] If it sounds like Milton's Samson is fast becoming Handel's Samson that should not obscure the fact that Milton's additions signal hermeneutic trouble, as it were, even as they herald new interpretive possibilities.

Nevertheless, Milton continues to be invoked on both sides of a divided Samson hermeneutic, now as a proponent of a more dignified representation of Samson and now as an author who would deepen the tragedy of *Samson Agonistes* by revising the Judges narrative so that Manoa, by Milton's account "still alive at the time of Samson's catastrophe," is no longer spared the sorrow of Samson's final days.[138] W. A. Scott is yet another commentator of the latter half of the nineteenth century who, if critical of Milton's ambivalence toward his protagonist, nonetheless illustrates the impact of Milton's poem on an evolving Samson hermeneutic, one feature of which is that the scriptural story of Samson, and Milton's version of it, blur indistinguishably into one another. Milton is therefore a signally important authority when redactions and supplements of Scripture become both tests of the truth of the Judges history and radical complications of it.

Scott's title-page epigraph—"there will I build him / A monument"—is from *Samson Agonistes* (1733–42), as are many of the epigraphs appended to individual chapters of this commentary, where Milton's tragedy is a regular point of reference, as well as a valuable guide through interpretive cruxes as when Samson is "persuaded *inwardly*" to go to the temple/theater or when, on the evidence of "Samson's prayer," he is redeemed for heroism. Scott lets interpretive tensions sit on the surface of his commentary, for example conceding that, taken whole, the scriptural history of Samson may discourage the invocation of him as an exemplary model: "Samson's acts are more for wonder than for our imitation."[139] Martin Luther thought so too.

Yet that said, if Milton is chided for his failure to appreciate fully (and admire) Samson's character, putting into his mouth as he hurls down the temple a "dying speech . . . not true to the text, nor worthy of the occasion," Scott rebukes Milton for producing a Samson insufficiently heroic, hence inadequately revealing "zeal for the divine glory" and unready to fulfill in his death the promised deliverance, "the mission for which he had been raised up."[140] Redeeming his divine commission, Samson should have redeemed both himself and his people. If not Milton's Samson, the Samson Scott envisions resembles one who, in the twentieth century, will come to be associated with William Riley Parker, F. Michael Krouse and the whole regenerationist tradition of *Samson* criticism that, with a powerful reach into scriptural commentary, produces the regenerate Samson of James L. Crenshaw: a Samson defeated in life, triumphant in death, his tragedy metamorphosing into a divine comedy. And Crenshaw's Samson is, from his vantage point, Milton's Samson, depicted "as one who correctly perceived divine purpose behind his stirrings of passion." Yet the generic casting Crenshaw gives to the Samson story "as a tragic-comedy" is precisely the one Milton would tear from it,[141] and in such a way that commentators on his tragedy will be forced to countenance in Samson both "savagery and recklessness."[142]

This Samson, whose history is one of "moral declension," "one of the most sad and most awful, histories in the whole Bible," is, as Christopher Wordsworth portrays him, an example of the abuse of scriptural gifts, "the miserable consequences of such misuse, and thus . . . a solemn warning." Known for his acts "of cruelty . . . , and of wanton destruction . . . , and of vindictive spite," Samson—his history "a *warning*"—"sends us to Christ" as a countermodel. As if in response to Scott's heroized Samson, including Scott's complaint about Milton's seeming ambivalence concerning Samson's heroism, Wordsworth remembers that "*Milton* . . . in his Samson Agonistes, near the end, introduces Manoah as burying . . .[Samson] and building him a monument," but in such a way as to blame Samson's miseries on his nuptial choices rather than, more broadly, on "his misuse of God's gifts, his vain-glorious self-confidence, forgetfulness of God, and disobedience to His will and word." As if in a postscript to Milton's tragedy and as an elucidation of it, Wordsworth complains that Milton is not critical enough of a "Samson . . .[who] did not leave God to work out His own vindication by lawful means, but endeavored to obtain his ends by means which involved self-destruction, for which indeed he prayed. *An unhappy end.*"[143]

If another hermeneutic is achieving dominance, it is a dominance partially secured by the interrogations and probings of *Samson Agonistes*. A case in point is an 1882 commentary that invokes lines from Milton's tragedy to describe Samson's death. Having already cited Milton as the representer and interpreter of Samson par excellence, J. J. Lias depicts a far more complicated Samson, often taken as a type of his country, whose story emerges as a profound critique of its culture. The Samson story *in context* is both an index to the morals of the Israelites, a mirror on the connection between apostasy and national ruin, and a protest against base ideas of God then in currency, with Samson himself revealing "a picture of human nature . . . unsubdued by the Gospel of Christ." In a commentary that resists any alignment between Samson and Christ, Lias emphasizes that Samson, who "cannot be said to have in any sense delivered Israel," is driven from beginning to end by revenge. Vengeance, according to Lias, is "the matured intention of Samson's mind": "[He] had not learned the deeper lesson: 'Vengeance is Mine . . .' The whole picture of Samson is admirably consistent with what we elsewhere learn of the man and his age."[144] One thing is certain: by the 1880s, it is commonplace to urge that students of the Bible "would do well to refer to Milton's 'Samson Agonistes,' "[145] not merely for elaborations of the Judges account and for glimpses of an heroic Samson but for the revelation of a Samson ambiguous, even defective, in his heroism.

In 1885, *Samson Agonistes* is cited again, this time by A. R. Fausset, within a commentary which, finding that the Judges themselves imperfectly realized the divine ideal, that their degeneracy ushers in earthly monarchy (a point Milton himself emphasizes in *Paradise Lost*, 12.320), also represents Samson as "a strange compound—an embodied paradox," indeed a "strange combination of paradoxes": one who is a judge but who leaves justice in seeming ruins; one who, mocking others, is himself mocked; who, though he never delivers his people, manifests the eventual possibility of doing so; and who, even if as "the embodied type, *the type of Messiah, especially in his death*," falls way short of him:

> The Antitype infinitely exceeds the type: Samson prayed for vengeance, Christ prayed for the forgiveness of his murderers. Samson died to crush his foes with him; Christ died for His enemies. . . . Samson fell to rise no more; Jesus died to rise again.[146]

By the second decade of the twentieth century, Abram Smythe Palmer, threading into his commentary references to *Samson Agonistes*, presents some intriguing variations on the usual rendering of the Samson story, the new landscape of which, if I may draw upon one of Palmer's sources, resembles "the panorama of the places" from which Samson came and to which he goes, this topography "serv[ing] as text, so to speak, to . . . the artless but interesting commentaries, which checked, completed, and sometimes even contradicted one another, according to the turns of the conversation or the personal character of the speakers."[147] In the background of Palmer's commentary are these accounts.

This one first:

> At 'Ain Shemĕs there is the sanctuary of Abu Meîzar. Abu Meîzar is a
> nickname, meaning "the father of the woolen mantle or head-dress."
> One Christian feast day Abu Meîzar penetrated into the church,
> disguised as a monk. He seized hold of the central column sustaining
> the building, crying: *Ya Kudret Allah,* "O power of God," and over-
> threw the church, which fell in ruins and crushed the congregation.[148]

A place of ruins nearby, we are told, was similarly an arena for slaughter and massacre, where soldiers lopped off heads and left brothers
slain.

Later, it is explained that at " 'Ain Shemĕs, well-established as the
counterpart of the Beth-Shemesh of the Bible," was discovered yet
another "version of the legend of Abu Meîzar, who was also
called . . . *Abu'l 'Âzem* and Shemshûm el Jebbâr, 'Samson the hero' ":

> There was once at R'meileh, which is the ancient name of 'Ain Shemĕs,
> a church of infidels. Abu Meîzar said to the inhabitants of Sar'a . . . ,
> his native place: "What will you give me, if I kill the Christians and
> destroy their church?" "We will give you a quarter of the country,"
> they answered him. Then Abu Meîzar entered into the church, where
> he found the Christians assembled for prayer, and pulled it down on
> top of them and him, by giving a mighty kick of the column, crying,
> "*Ya Rabb!*" "O Lord!" He had said previously to his compatriots at
> Sar'a, "Search in R'meileh, you will find me lying on my back, and the
> Christians on their bellies. . . ." The old people say: "*beîn Sar'a ú Beît
> el Jemâl enkatal Shemshûm el Jebbâr,*" between Sar'a and Beît el Jemâl
> the hero Samson was killed.[149]

Palmer then uses these accounts to explain his own Samson, who,
characterized by "grotesque and uncouth methods," "savagery and
recklessness," is no enthusiast for political independence and delivery;
and whose "tragedy" at the temple is one in which, glimpsing now
Hercules and now Samson, we should also notice that "the place
which the story selects for the mighty sun-hero to finish his chequered
career in blood and darkness is the most western city of Palestine."[150]
Palmer continues by putting this construction on the tales just
related:

> A fanatic in modern times has striven to emulate the exploits of
> Samson. There was a Christian church at 'Ain Shemĕs . . . , the ancient
> Beth Shemesh . . . One Abu Meîzar (otherwise known as Shemshûm el

Jebbâr, "Samson the Hero,". . . forced his way into the building, seized hold of the central sustaining column, and, invoking the power of God, pulled it down, overthrowing the church, which fell in ruins and crushed the congregation of fellahin.

From his own version of this newly discovered material, Palmer will conclude that, for some, the Samson story, "this equivocal section of the Book of Judges," once lifted from Scriptures, might be relegated to "folk-tale [literature] and other Apocryphal writings" and, quoting Milton on Samson quitting himself like Samson, contends that "nothing in [Samson's] life became him more than leaving it."[151]

Palmer writes in the wake of commentators like Heinrich Graetz, who think that both "Jephthah and Samson, . . . disregarding order and discipline, brought their powers to bear, as much for evil as for good," with Samson himself faulted, indeed "censured," in Jacob's prophecy of Dan (Genesis 49:16–18) for his deployment of sneaky "stratagems and unexpected attacks," never "improving the state of affairs."[152] For just these reasons, yet another commentator concludes that "the moralizing improvement of the history in the Book of Judges is not carried beyond the story of Jephthah."[153] Samson, according to this same commentator, "while he makes havoc among the Philistines, . . . in no way appears as the champion or deliverer of Israel."[154]

The question becomes again, as it had been for Milton: does this Judges narrative picture a Samson animated by the spirit of God? If so, only as an afterthought, as C. F. Burney argues, as he speculates that Judges 13 is added to the story of Judges 14–16 where Samson seems "to have no commission at all, and . . . no higher guide than his own wayward passions." The story may evolve toward "full acceptance of Samson as a member of a series of divinely commissioned *Judges*"; yet it is also redacted by an editor who seems to have "laboured under a sense of the moral unsuitability" of a hero "too firmly enshrined in the popular imagination" to be excluded and too troubling to be fully embraced. Hence, says Burney, Judges 16 and the story of Abimelech are evidently "restored" by the same hand, which is also responsible for imaging the odd, "unfitting" fate of a "hero" who ends his life as a prisoner, enslaved by unbelievers and going to death with them.[155] Indeed, as Graetz claims, the so-called "hero-judges . . . , especially Jephthah and Samson . . . evince so few of the national characteristics that they might equally well pass for Canaanites, Philistines, or Moabites. Of Samson it has been asserted that he is cast in the mould of the Syrian Hercules."[156]

His own legend a fusion of eastern and western mythology, his own person in our time emblematizing now Israelis, now Muslims, and now Christians, Samson is a mirror on every side of a conflict—and part of each side's rhetoric. In this context, what is so remarkable about *Samson Agonistes* is not Milton's giving shape to this or that reading of the Samson story but, instead, his capturing so ably the contradictions within the scriptural versions and subsequent interpretations of the tale, along with the fissures existing between the known and later to be discovered versions of the story. That is, Milton's poem embraces a spectrum of Samsons rather as does Wiseman's nineteenth-century commentary, among them the "malignant savage, ever relentlessly rushing into broils and mortal combat, from the almost fiendish revengefulness of his nature." Yet like Wiseman, Milton refuses to restrict himself to any single delineation, allowing his poem to become, instead, a gallery of portraits, including without singly endorsing the Samson of Bishop Wordsworth, who, as we have seen above and as Wiseman is quick to acknowledge, "speaks of Samson as a man who courted self-destruction, whose last act involved a refusal to leave God to work out His own vindication by lawful means, whose dying prayer stands in sad contrast to the dying prayer of our blessed Saviour, and who can only be spoken of as having come to 'an unhappy end.' "[157] The Samson story, owing in part to Milton's intervention, is finally restored to its tragic dimensions.

MILTON'S (POST)MODERNITY

In the twentieth century, the regenerationist Samson is founded upon the notion that the Milton of *Samson Agonistes* has finally emerged from the chrysalis of political controversy—a very different Milton from the liberationist poet, the subversive cultural presence, in an African-American literary tradition. In his autobiography, Malcolm X numbers Milton among the eye-openers, the awakeners of the people, in part because he is introduced to Milton through the Charles W. Eliot edition, which insists upon the intimate—and mutually illuminating—relation between Milton's poetry and the history of its time. Milton's is a poetry that derives its significance from its own time even as it sheds important light upon it. Milton's is a poetry that, struggling against the outworn creeds of an atrophying religion, obliterates the pastness of the past and that, written emphatically in the present tense, strives to wrest from the present a new future. Unlike King James who, according to Malcolm X, "poetically 'fixed' the Bible . . . and . . . enslaved the world," if in the process the Bible became a "locked door" of deliberately "frustrated understanding," it was Milton who, resisting those who had twisted Christianity into an instrument of oppression, opened the locked doors of Scriptures, in the very process affording "new evidence . . . to document the Muslim teachings":

> In . . . The Harvard Classics, I read . . . *Paradise Lost*. The devil, kicked out of paradise, was trying to regain possession. He was using the forces of Europe . . . I interpreted this to show that the Europeans were motivated and led by the devil, or the personification of the devil. So Milton and Mr. Elijah Muhammad were actually saying the same thing.[158]

Indeed, in the very act of unmanacling the mind, Milton, as much as Muhammad, may be said to have revealed "the interrelated meanings, and uses, of the Bible and the Quran,"[159] neither of which, as Malcolm X avows, should be used to justify cruelty and slaughter, to promote a religion of crucifixes and guns, or, as the poet William Blake objected, to hide religion in war. Still, as Michael Lieb has shown, at many points Elijah Muhammad would be at one with Keats in saying that life to Milton is death to me, especially in the emphasis that even Milton's enlightened Christianity gives to the divinity of Jesus and in its supposed privileging of high culture over the culture of the streets.[160]

Malcolm X, on the other hand, like Milton, casts himself in the role of a prophet, but also demythologizes Christianity into the here and now and, in any comparison of Jesus and Samson, would probably emphasize that Jesus works for the betterment of mankind, not its undoing; indeed, that he sacrificed himself for the good of the human race, planting good where others had sown evil. In his own demythologizing of Scriptures, under the cover of paradise lost at the beginning of time, Milton writes of paradise lost now—*now* with the failure of the Puritan Revolution. As we have already noted, he writes of paradise recovered not on the Cross but *here* in the wilderness, even as he sees in the Samson story another of those false apocalypses that occur when history reverses course, turning back again into its former self, when history has become a dead end, seemingly with no exits. Milton's last poems, in their very juxtaposition, offer an escape, though; hence are part of the resolution. In fact, Malcolm X sees himself standing in very much the same relationship with Martin Luther King as that struck by *Samson Agonistes* in relation to *Paradise Regain'd*. Malcolm X's writings, like *Samson Agonistes*, are less an embrace of wanton violence than a representation of it, without which alternative, without which representation, it is all the more difficult to embrace, or yield to, the more pacifist idealisms of Martin Luther King or of Milton in *Paradise Regain'd*. Strength is never enough; for "[e]ven Samson, the world's strongest man, was destroyed" and thus is eventually numbered with those who, "mak[ing] heroes of themselves" by killing, do so on the grounds that this is what God or "Allah wanted him to do."[161]

Violence in self-defense, anger, and hatred as aspects of a just war— each subtends a theology of violence and religion of sacrifice, each complicates the world by compromising an ideology of war and peace as it authorizes retaliation and sanctions aggression in a world where "wanton violence," as Malcolm X explains, often overwhelms all claims to "justice"; where fighting precludes uniting in common cause and community; where terrorists terrorize but then are themselves terrorized; and where all hopes for paradise are "*twisted* . . .[into] pie in the sky and heaven in the hereafter" instead of heaven "right *here* . . . on *this earth* . . . in *this life*."[162] If near the end, his home bombed by Muslims, Malcom X came to understand that certain Muslims would kill so long as they thought God willed them to do so; if he came to ask, what is the Muslim religion doing to us, where is this thirst for retaliation driving us, Milton asks similarly, through the joint publication of *Samson Agonistes* and *Paradise Regain'd*: what has Judaism done to us through the violence so often sanctioned by the story of Samson? What has Christianity done to us through the violence harbored in—and culturally promulgated—by the Crucifixion story? If Malcolm X could not pinpoint his own philosophy, Milton may have had a similarly difficult time defining his own, managing no more finally than the jostling perspectives of *Paradise Regain'd* and *Samson Agonistes* and the theological quagmires and ethical bramble bushes into which those poems lead us. It is, nevertheless, the politics of violence, coupled with the promise of a paradise regained, that neither Ralph Ellison nor Toni Morrison addresses in isolation from Milton, even if Ellison does so directly and Morrison only obliquely, each coming to understand with Malcolm X (and presumably Milton) that violence, chartering terror, compromises and often contravenes justice. As Malcolm X might say, Milton was providing black culture with an infusion of "intellectual vitamins."[163]

If there is (and not everyone thinks there is) *an acquist of wisdom* from Milton's tragedy, it is strongly focused by the Judges biographies, newly inflected by Milton's distinctive recasting of the Samson story, and given striking reinforcement by three different novelists (two of them African-American) writing on the cusp of the new millennium—Ralph Ellison, Toni Morrison, and Philip Pullman. Each writer couples the politics of violence and prospects for recovering a lost paradise with the arduous wisdom that "those who reject the lessons of history, or who," in Ellison's words, "allow themselves to be intimidated by its rigors, are doomed to repeat its disasters."[164] In *Juneteenth*, Ellison addresses such a politics and such a promise with explicit reference to the Samson story and, it would seem, in a continuing response to Kenneth Burke's initial labeling of *Samson Agonistes*, if not as "propaganda," then as "moralistic prophecy, . . . a kind of 'literature for use,' " full of "righteous ferocity," by which violence, incorporating with suicide, effects more violence as Samson's wrathful God, authorizing his acts of destruction, also allows for their reenactment. In this reading, *Samson Agonistes*, with its "modalities of holy war" and "theocratic rage," is a "celebration," in "sullen warlike verse," by "a cantankerous old fighter-priest," of a hero who, in the course of translating political controversy into high theology, "talks of patience" but "mouths threats of revenge in the name of God."[165]

The Phrase "*On its face*"[166] is a complicating gesture in Burke's reading, allowing Ellison to worry, as Morrison will also do, that the actions of such people, instead of issuing from God, are a massive force of godless nature and of cultural terrorism in both of which guises, as we have seen, Mary Shelley represents Samson in *The Last Man*. Milton forces us to consider the same issue, first, by juxtaposing Satan and the Son of *Paradise Lost* and then by letting the Son and Samson face one another as agents of a terror, which, checked by the Son, is unchecked by Samson. Or as Burke would have it, in the depths of Milton's poem, surface identification becomes disidentification as Milton repudiates the philosophy of retaliation, the politics of terror, by annihilating his former self, what he now construes as his Satanic self, in the character of Samson. In the end, Milton may have initially allowed for divine intervention until he became increasingly less certain of the justice, or the virtue, in wantonly exercised power better checked than fully unleashed so as not to produce "Ruin, destruction at the utmost point" (1514). From such scenes of devastation comes the tragic realization, as Ellison would have it, that a nation must be "conditioned to riding out the chaos of history as the eagle rides out the whirlwind."[167]

Milton is one of the figures from whom Ellison acquired his literary education concerning both the politics of literature and its interlocking aesthetics; from whom he derived the lesson that some literature perpetrates the very violence it was shored up against and propagates a theology that could prove the world's undoing. Thus, after the *Hudson Review* printed Burke's essay on *Samson Agonistes* called "The

Imagery of Killing" (1948), instead of eliding suicide and the temple disaster, the Ellison of *Invisible Man* has his narrator shudder: "Whoever else I was, I was no Samson. I had no desire to destroy myself . . . ; I wanted freedom, not destruction."[168] Elsewhere, Ellison responds to Burke with the hope "that his own work, involved in sacrifice and ritualistic killing, would offer more complexity," as Milton hoped of his own, " 'the kind that giveth life and light.' "[169]

Ellison's sense of that complexity emerges in the 1999 publication of *Juneteenth* in which, at the novel's intellectual center, there is this exchange between Body and Bliss:

> Say . . . , Body said, can't you hear? I said do you remember in the Bible where it tells about Samson and it says he had him a boy to lead him up to the wall, so he could shake the building down?
>
> That's right, . . .[Bliss] said.
>
> Well answer me this, you think that little boy got killed?
>
> *Killed*, I said; who killed him?
>
> What I mean is, do you think old Samson forgot to tell that boy what he was fixing to do.
>
> I cut my eyes over at Body. I didn't like the idea. Once Daddy Hickman had said: *Bliss, you must be a hero like that little lad who led blind Samson to the wall, because a great many grown folks are blind and have to be led toward the light.* The question worried me and I pushed it away.

Bliss will then tell Body, "Forget about Samson, man," apparently remembering the rest of what he had been told when, earlier, he speculates to the Reverend Hickman, "We were eyeless like Samson in Gaza?" With razor sharp irony, Hickman retorts:

> Amen, Rev. Bliss, like baldheaded Samson before that nameless little lad like you came as the Good Book tells us and led him to the pillars whereupon the big house stood—Oh, you little black boys, and oh, you little brown girls, you're going to shake the building down! And then, oh, how you will build in the name of the Lord!
>
> Yes, Reverend Bliss, we were eyeless like unhappy Samson among the Philistines—and worse . . .
>
> And WORSE?
>
> Worse, Rev. Bliss, because they chopped us up into little bitty pieces . . .
>
> We were eyeless . . .
>
> . . . No eyes to see.
>
> We were truly in the dark.[170]

Bliss is here asked a question he does not want to address (what did "that little lad" know, and when did he know it?), and hidden within this question—the truth that keeps eluding Bliss—is an issue that Stanley Fish, almost alone among Milton's critics, comprehends as an integral part of the Samson literary tradition wherein the boy guide "always escapes, and in one version is converted on the spot."[171] The questions Bliss (and others) have shied away from are ones that Milton addresses and answers without evasion as the Messenger, in *Samson Agonistes*, reports: "they led him / Between the pillars; he his guide requested . . . / . . . He *unsuspitious* led him" (1629-30, 1635; my italics). In this usually unnoticed, but telling, emendation of the Judges story, not to mention earlier play versions of the Samson saga, Milton, as he deepens the horror of the final catastrophe, acknowledges as Ellison seems to comprehend, that Samson is a fixture within a culture of supposed heroes who, "killing multitudes," are themselves in need of the deliverer they sought to be. Milton's point, driven home by Ellison, is that all of us, including Samson presumably, should "be interrogated not by our allies or enemies but by our conduct and by our lives"; that it is our "ideals, which interrogate us, judging us, pursuing us, in terms of that which we do or do *not* do."[172] If there is a Samson in Ellison's novel, it is a Samson (by the name of Hickman) who, betrayed by the women in his life and at times by his own people, ready to meet a lion in his path, undergoes a conversion experience founded upon what we have here described as the tragic insight of *Samson Agonistes*. If Bliss is the apostate Samson, Hickman is the true Samson compounded of "strength . . . *and the breadth of spirit.*"[173]

What, apparently, the Samson story taught Milton (and later Ellison) is that blood spilled in violence begets more violence, that "bloody retaliation" breeds "foolishness," and that those who see nothing and hear nothing but revenge, who "dull their senses to the killing of one group" of people, even if it be the Philistines, "dull themselves to the preciousness of all human life."[174] In the character of Samson, with his ache for vengeance, in his eye-for-an-eye philosophy, we see what to pray, and not to pray for; we observe the cruelty of religious sects generally, hence what Hugo Grotius once called "the Justice of the Unjust."[175] In Milton's title character, no less than in the Samson of Judges, we behold "a portraiture . . . of the moral condition [not just of Samson but] of his people,"[176] past and present, and, simultaneously, learn that, instead of crying out against others, we must sometimes cry for our people in what Ellison would call their "feasting on revenge and sacrifice." In his words, "God never fixed the dice against anybody. . . . His way may be mysterious but he's got no grudge."[177]

As much as Ellison, Toni Morrison understood that Milton was an experimental theologian and, like Philip Pullman as well, instead of targeting Milton's poetry for critique, evokes it as a model for mounting her own critiques of God and religion, theology and politics—a critique that, like Milton's, frets over a god whose mission (at least in a poem like *Samson Agonistes*) seems to be grinding people into dust and over a religion that, no longer a compendium of questions, was fast becoming a catechism of answers. In Ellison's *Juneteenth*, a true "drama of redemption," tragic insight comes in "the blaze of sun," in Ellison's reflections "on the moral significance of the history we've been through."[178] In Morrison's *Paradise*, as in *Samson Agonistes* ("O dark, dark, dark, amid the blaze of noon" [80]), violence occurs, an imagined massacre ensues but in what Morrison describes as "sunlight . . . yearning for brilliance."[179] In the words of Morrison's prophetic novel, when are we going to learn that God does not "thunder instructions or whisper messages into ears. Oh, no. He is a liberating God"; how are we "going to be His instrument if . . .[we] don't know what He says?" When, finally, will we comprehend that our theologians must stop crediting those who claim "God at their side" in murder, and rather "take aim" at such; at those who act as God's instruments, "His voice, His retribution," and think themselves executors of his justice, forgetting that "God's justice is His alone." We need to govern the seemingly "ungovernable" and "ravenous appetite for vengeance, an appetite . . .[that we need] to understand in order to subdue."[180]

Samson, with what Pullman might call his "blood-soaked consciousness,"[181] may be ruled by what he thinks is the justice of his anger; but, in contradistinction, anger at injustice impels Milton to compose *Samson Agonistes* (to appropriate language from one of Milton's letters) as an instrument for "the sharpening rather than the blunting of . . . [our] mental edge" as he expresses, first in prose, then in poetry, that "wisdom exceeds strength, as much as arts of peace surpass the stratagems of war": "But what is strength without a double share / Of wisdom" (53–54).[182] Or what is strength that does not know its own limitations as Ellison asks, while reflecting upon both the narrator's weakness and that of his grandfather in *Invisible Man*— a weakness through which each comprehends the oppressor's weakness. "There is a good deal of spite in the old man, as there comes to be in his grandson," so that, says Ellison, "the strategy he advises is kind of jiu jitsu of the spirit, a denial and rejection through agreement":

> Samson, eyeless in Gaza, pulls the building down when his strength returns; politically weak, the grandfather has learned that conformity leads to a similar end, and so advises his children. Thus his mask of meekness conceals the wisdom of one who has learned the secret of saying the "yes" which accomplishes the expressive "no."[183]

By Ellison's logic, Samson is revengeful without being resourceful, with Ellison here pointing the way toward what Stanley Edgar Hyman describes as a supremely "ironic and sophisticated consciousness."[184] If Milton—or rather his Samson—here falls short it is so that, as Thomas Jefferson said of John Locke, "where he stopped short, we may go on"[185]—partly by never forgetting that poetry is not hemmed in by mere representations of paradises lost and regained. In the words of one recent poet, "poetry is certainly not a 'paradise lost' nor is it a 'golden age.' On the contrary it is a question that begets another question."[186] It is a knot of questions engendering other questions, most of them marked by recalcitrance, and very few accompanied by unequivocal answers; and partly, too, by hypothesizing that, moving forward without practicing revenge, we may at last break through the gridlock of history.

Only then, when we have toppled the zealots, will heaven become a place for the living and not the dead; and then we will know, both as Morrison tells us in the last words of her novel and as Philip Pullman insists in his, that we will find our paradise in this world or not at all. In the words of Pullman, who affords an important new reception of Milton at the turn into this new millennium, "we have to build the Republic of Heaven where we are, because for [many of] us there is no elsewhere";[187] we have to regain the lost paradise not by another's but by our own initiative, not beyond but within history. And Pullman's words, just this side of the new millennium, are but an echo of Morrison's words on its other side: "How exquisitely human was the wish for permanent happiness, and how thin human imagination became trying to achieve it," people not always "shouldering the endless work they were created to do down here in [p]aradise."[188]

Did Samson shoulder his burden? That question should remain at the heart of our criticism of *Samson Agonistes* in order to ensure that it always has a heart. If not self-answering within Milton's tragedy, this and other such questions may nevertheless show Milton partially

answering himself out of himself; out of those writings, their "religion . . . full of intellectual daring," especially *Paradise Regain'd*, with
which *Samson Agonistes* is in engaging and steadily enlightening dialogue.[189] It was once fashionable to deny the typological connection
between these poems—a connection that works great mischief within
the interpretive framework of these poems. Just how becomes evident
when we remember, as Peter Martyr does, the argument that Samson's
Naziriteship is a temporary, not permanent, condition—a period of
retirement and contemplation before a return to action. Martyr thus
insinuates an analogy between the Samson story and the tale of Jesus
tempted, each protagonist retreating to the mountain at nighttime and,
in daytime, returning to his people.[190] This is precisely the analogy
thwarted, the typology frustrated, by *Samson Agonistes* and the ultimate
index to its tragedy, which questions rather than confirms the idea,
promulgated in its aftermath, that Samson "stopt the mouth of vindictive Justice."[191] Through their coupling, through this dialectic of
world-views and opposition of ethical systems, Milton's poems of 1671
propose that, where there is an enlarging instead of a cinching of human
consciousness, the attendant apocalypse of mind effects a transition in
history that, stymied by one ideology, is accelerated by another. The
tragic insight of the one poem effects what Ellison would probably call
"the mind-jolting revolution" of the other, through which our dreams,
instead of founded upon rubble, become "the blueprints and mockups
of emerging realities."[192] Then, as well as now, in the searing words of
the Polish poet Leon Staff, "Even more than bread we . . . need poetry,
in a time when it seems that it is not needed at all."[193]

NOTES

PREFACE

1. The epigraphs accompanying this Preface are from Philip Pullman, "Introduction," *"Paradise Lost": An Illustrated Edition* (Oxford and New York: Oxford University Press, 2005), 9; and from Daniel Johnson, "London Letter: Mixed Feelings Over 'Paradise Lost' Film." For Johnson's remarks, see both the op-ed page of *The New York Sun* (October 13, 2005), and <http://www.Christianitytoday.com/ct/2005/142/31.0.html>.
2. Harold Bloom, *Genius: A Mosaic of One Hundred Exemplary Creative Minds* (New York: Warner Books, 2002), 56.
3. Add to these examples such titles as Eva Figes's *The Tree of Knowledge* (New York: Pantheon, 1990), Phillip Pullman's trilogy *His Dark Materials* (New York: Alfred A. Knopf, 1996, 1997, 2000), Peter Ackroyd's *Milton in America* (New York and London: Doubleday, 1997), and James Patterson's *The Big Bad Wolf* (Boston, New York and London: Little, Brown and Company, 2003), where the culprits or champions are Milton's characters, or Milton himself, or (in the last instance) Miltonists.
4. See John A. Howard, "The Family: America's Hope," *The Family in America*, Online Edition, 16, 11 (November 2002): This piece begins with "a lesson from John Milton."
5. Aldous Huxley's title, appropriated from Milton, is here appropriated from Huxley by Roland Salazar Rose, "Eyeless in Gaza," *Salazar Gallery* (2001) at <www.salazargallery.com/About/Eyeless/html>.
6. Nigel Smith, *Literature and Revolution in England 1640–1660* (New Haven and London: Yale University Press, 1994), 1.
7. See the powerful Introduction by Laura Lunger Knoppers and Gregory M. Colón Semenza, in *Milton and Popular Culture*, ed. Knoppers and Semenza (New York: Palgrave Macmillan, 2006), 1–19.
8. Michael Bérubé, "Public Image Limited: Political Correctness and the Media's Big Lie," in *Debating P. C.: The Controversy over Political Correctness on College Campuses*, ed. Paul Berman (New York: Dell, 1992), 161.
9. Pullman, "Introduction," *"Paradise Lost,"* 10.

10. Victoria Kahn, *Wayward Contracts: The Crisis of Political Obligation in England, 1640–1674* (Princeton and Oxford: Princeton University Press, 2004), 263–64.

11. See Anne Davidson Ferry, *Milton's Epic Voice: The Narrator in "Paradise Lost"* (Cambridge, MA: Harvard University Press, 1963), 17, 44–65.

12. C. S. Lewis, *A Preface to "Paradise Lost"* (London and New York: Oxford University Press, 1942), 78–79.

13. Mary Ann Radzinowicz, "The Politics of *Paradise Lost*," in *Politics of Discourse: The Literature of Seventeenth-Century England*, ed. Kevin Sharpe and Stephen N. Zwicker (Berkeley, Los Angeles, and London: University of California Press, 1987), 208, 214; and see in the same volume, Earl Miner, "Milton and the Histories," 199.

14. Ruth Kelso, *Doctrine for the Lady of the Renaissance* (1956; rpt. Urbana, Chicago, and London: University of Illinois Press, 1978), 5.

15. See Herbert N. Schneidau, "Biblical Narrative and Modern Consciousness," in *The Bible and the Narrative Tradition*, ed. Frank McConnell (New York and Oxford: Oxford University Press, 1986), 148–49.

16. Christopher Hill, *The English Bible and the Seventeenth-Century Revolution* (London: Allen Lane, and New York: Penguin, 1993), 373.

17. See Smith, *Literature and Revolution in England*, 1–19.

18. Nancy Armstrong and Leonard Tennenhouse, *The Imaginary Puritan: Literature, Intellectual Labor, and the Origins of Personal Life* (Berkeley, Los Angeles, and London: University of California Press, 1992), 47.

19. Gerald Graff, *Beyond the Culture Wars: How Teaching the Conflicts Can Revitalize American Education* (New York and London: W. W. Norton, 1992), 159. A few of the ideas presented in this preface are treated more expansively in my essay, "Milton's Transgressive Maneuvers: Receptions (Then and Now) and the Sexual Politics of *Paradise Lost*," in *Milton and Heresy*, ed. Stephen B. Dobranski and John P. Rumrich (Cambridge and New York: Cambridge University Press, 1998), 244–66.

20. The front of this medal carries the Russian text "John Milton (1608–1674)"; and its reverse side the Pushkin quote cited in the text under note 21. The medal was designed by the Russian sculptor M. Romanovskaya and then struck in the year 1984 by the Leningrad (St. Petersburg) Mint.

21. I am grateful to Vladimir Lenskiy, New York City, for this translation.

22. S. Margaret Fuller, "The Prose Works of Milton," *Papers on Literature and Art*, 2 vols. (London: Wiley and Putnam, 1846), 1:39.

23. James Joyce, *Dubliners*, ed. Jeri Johnson (Oxford and New York: Oxford University Press, 2000), 160.

24. Arthur M. Schlesinger, Jr., quoting Jack Lang, the French Minister of Culture, in *The Cycles of American History* (Boston: Houghton Mifflin, 1986), 156.

25. Schlesinger, *The Cycles of American History*, 165.

26. Ibid., 373.

27. See Schlesinger's reflections on Ralph Waldo Emerson's "The Conservative," in ibid., 23.

28. Dinesh D'Souza, *Illiberal Education: The Politics of Race and Sex on Campus* (1991; rpt. New York: Vintage, 1992), 238.

29. C. S. Lewis, *A Preface to "Paradise Lost*," v.

30. William Blake, "The Marriage of Heaven and Hell," in *The Complete Poetry and Prose of William Blake*, rev. ed., ed. David V. Erdman (Garden City, NY: Doubleday, 1982), 35. See also Richard Strier, "Milton's Fetters, Or, Why Eden Is Better Than Heaven," *Milton Studies* (a special issue entitled *John Milton: The Writer in His Works*) 38 (2000): 169–97.

31. John Peter, *A Critique of "Paradise Lost"* (1960; rpt. New York: Columbia University Press and London: Longmans, 1962), 164.

32. J. B. Broadbent, *Some Graver Subject: An Essay on "Paradise Lost"* (London: Chatto and Windus, 1960), 288.

33. See ibid., 291. and Cf. Alicia Ostriker, *Stealing the Language: The Emergence of Women's Poetry in America* (Boston: Beacon Press, 1986), 41.

34. A. J. A. Waldock, *"Paradise Lost" and Its Critics* (London: Cambridge University Press, 1947), but also Broadbent, *Some Graver Subject* 287.

35. See John T. Shawcross, *Rethinking Milton Studies: Time Present and Time Past* (Newark: University of Delaware Press, 2005); Peter C. Herman, *Destabilizing Milton: "Paradise Lost" and the Poetics of Incertitude* (New York and Basingstoke: Palgrave Macmillan, 2005), and Michael Bryson, *The Tyranny of Heaven: Milton's Rejection of God as King* (Newark: University of Delaware Press and London: Associated University Presses, 2004).

36. Stanley Fish, *How Milton Works* (Cambridge, MA and London: Belknap Press of Harvard University, 2001), 14, 113.

37. Ibid., 238, 128.

38. In this annotation to John Toland's *Life of Milton*, Herman Melville continues: "I doubt not that darker doubts crossed Milton's soul, than ever disturbed Voltair. And he was more of what is called an Infidel"; see *Melville and Milton: An Edition and Analysis of Melville's Annotations on Milton*, ed. Robin Grey (Pittsburgh, PA: Duquesne University Press, 2004), 121.

39. Bill Readings, *The University in Ruins* (1996; reprint Cambridge, MA and London: Harvard University Press, 1999), 85.

40. See Melville's annotations in *Melville and Milton*, ed. Grey, 121, 158, 173, 187.

41. See Mario M. Cuomo, *Why Lincoln Matters: Today More Than Ever* (New York, Toronto, and London: Harcourt, 2004), 11–12. My own book was in progress and titled before Cuomo's appeared.

42. Gordon Teskey, *Delirious Milton: The Fate of the Poet in Modernity* (Cambridge, MA and London: Harvard University Press, 2006), 62.

CHAPTER 1   "READING" MILTON: THE DEATH (AND SURVIVAL) OF THE AUTHOR

1. The epigraphs for this chapter derive from Samuel Taylor Coleridge, *The Romantics on Milton: Formal Essays and Critical Asides*, ed. Joseph Wittreich (Cleveland: Press of Case Western Reserve University, 1970), 270, 277; and Mikhail M. Bakhtin, *Art and Answerability: Early Philosophical Essays*, ed. Michael Holquist and Vadim Liapunov (1990; rpt. Austin: University of Texas Press, 1995), 12. I have read, too late to assimilate to this chapter, the fine book on the same topic by Stephen M. Fallon, *Peculiar Grace: Self-Representation, Intention, and Authority in Milton* (Ithaca: Cornell University Press, 2006). Fallon's book was still in preparation when my own went to press.

2. In conjunction with Milton's own observations, see the revealing remarks by Anne Ferry, *The Title to the Poem* (Stanford, CA: Stanford University Press, 1996), 129.

3. Leah S. Marcus, *Unediting the Renaissance: Shakespeare, Marlowe, Milton* (New York and London: Routledge, 1996), 226.

4. See John Knowles, *The Life and Writings of Henry Fuseli, Esq. M. A. R. A.*, 3 vols. (London: Henry Colburn and Richard Bentley, 1831), 3:124.

5. See Mary Wollstonecraft, "Advertisement," in *"Mary" and "Maria,"* ed. Janet Todd (London and New York: Penguin, 1992), [3], as well as Todd's "Introduction," ibid., [vii].

6. Michel Foucault, "What is an Author?" in *Language, Counter Memory, Practice: Selected Essays and Interviews*, tr. Donald F. Bouchard and Sherry Simon (Ithaca, NY: Cornell University Press, 1977), 115.

7. I have here adapted Milton's words from another context to articulate what will become the chief concern of this chapter.

8. J. Martin Evans, "The Birth of the Author: Milton's Poetic Self-Construction," *Milton Studies* (a special issue entitled *John Milton: The Writer in His Works*) 38 (2000): 47, 55, 57, 58.

9. William B. Hunter, *The Descent of Urania: Studies in Milton, 1946–1988* (Lewisburg, PA: Bucknell University Press and London and Toronto: Associated University Presses, 1989), 101.

10. See John S. Diekhoff, ed., *Milton on Himself: Milton's Utterances upon Himself and His Works* (1939; rpt. New York: Humanities Press, 1965).

11. Louis A. Renza, "A Veto of the Imagination: A Theory of Autobiography," in *Autobiography: Essays Theoretical and Critical*, ed. James Olney (Princeton, NJ: Princeton University Press, 1990), 292.

12. William Wordsworth, *The Prelude*, in *The Poetical Works of Wordsworth*, ed. Paul D. Sheats (Boston: Houghton Mifflin, 1982), 133.

13. John T. Shawcross, *Intentionality and the New Traditionalism: Some Liminal Means to Literary Revisionism* (University Park, PA: Pennsylvania State University Press, 1991), 170. Similarly useful

distinctions are formulated by Bakhtin, *Art and Answerability*, ed. Holquist and Liapunov, 12–14; but see too Russell Fraser, "Milton's Two Poets," *Studies in English Literature 1500–1900*, 34, 1 (Winter 1994): 109–18. On different versions of the 1645 frontispiece, see Elizabeth Skerpan-Wheeler, "Authorship and Authority: John Milton, William Marshall, and the Two Frontispieces of Poems 1645," *Milton Quarterly* 33, 4 (December 1999): 105–114; and for an intriguing discussion of the usual frontispiece, its Janus-faced character, see Gary Spear, "Reading Before the Lines: Typography, Iconography, and the Author in Milton's 1645 Frontispiece," *New Ways of Looking at Old Texts: Papers of the Renaissance English Text Society, 1985–1991*, ed. W. Speed Hill (Binghamton, NY: Medieval and Renaissance Texts and Studies, 1993), 187–94.

14. Marshall Grossman, *The Story of All Things: Writing the Self in English Renaissance Narrative Poetry* (Durham, NC and London: Duke University Press, 1998), xiv.

15. Shawcross, *Intentionality and the New Traditionalism*, 170, 179.

16. John Guillory, *Poetic Authority: Spenser, Milton, and Literary History* (New York: Columbia University Press, 1983), 161, and Adrian Johns, *The Nature of the Book: Print and Knowledge in the Making* (Chicago and London: University of Chicago Press, 1998), 264.

17. Robert M. Durling, *The Figure of the Poet in Renaissance Epic* (Cambridge, MA: Harvard University Press, 1965), 2, 4.

18. See Robert McMahon, *The Two Poets of "Paradise Lost"* (Baton Rouge and London: Louisiana State University Press, 1998), esp. 1–22; and Balachandra Rajan, "The Imperial Temptation," in *Milton and the Imperial Vision*, ed. Balachandra Rajan and Elizabeth Sauer (Pittsburgh, PA: Duquesne University Press, 1999), 312. Jane Melbourne propounds an interesting thesis easily inferred from her title, "The Narrator as Chorus in *Paradise Lost*," *Studies in English Literature 1500–1900* 33, 1 (Winter 1993): 149–65.

19. Barbara Lewalski, *"Paradise Lost" and the Rhetoric of Literary Forms* (Princeton, NJ: Princeton University Press, 1985), 186, 214, cf. 218.

20. Thomas Newton, ed., *"Paradise Regain'd" . . . to Which Is Added "Samson Agonistes"* (London: W. Strahan, J. F. and C. Rivington, 1785), 249.

21. David Masson, ed. *The Poetical Works of John Milton*, 3 vols. (London: Macmillan, 1874), 2:91.

22. See C. S. Jerram, ed., *"Samson Agonistes"* (London: English School Classics, 1890), x, and Edmund K. Chambers, ed., *"Samson Agonistes"* (London: Blackie and Son, 1897), 17.

23. See Anon., ed., *"Samson Agonistes": A Dramatic Poem* (London and Glasgow: Collins's School Classics, 1879), 3; and cf. A. Wilson Verity, ed., *Milton's "Samson Agonistes"* (Cambridge: Cambridge University Press, 1892), 164; ibid., 165; A. J. Wyatt, ed. *Milton's "Samson*

Agonistes" (London: W. B. Clive, n. d.), 27 (Wyatt is here quoting Richard Garnett). See also A. J. Wyatt and A. J. F. Collins, ed. *Milton: "Samson Agonistes"* (London: W. B. Clive, 1911), 13–14, and H. M. Percival, ed., *Milton's "Samson Agonistes"* (London: Macmillan, 1890), xxv, xxxi.

24. See Henry Redman, Jr., on Gaspard Ernest Stroehlin, Augustin Filon, and Louis Raymond de Véricour, respectively, in *Major French Milton Critics of the Nineteenth Century* (Pittsburgh, PA: Duquesne University Press, 1994), 315, 331, 120, 121; see also Francois René de Chateaubriand (65–66) and Philaréte Chasles (93), the latter of whom yokes *Comus* and *Samson Agonistes* together and gives to *Samson Agonistes* the same generic label that Percy Bysshe Shelley gives to *Prometheus Unbound*: "drama lyrique" (or "a lyrical drama").

25. See Andrew Marvell to John Milton (June 2, 1654), "Milton's Private Correspondence," YP, 4:864; and Ann Manning, *The Maiden and Married Life of Mary Powell . . . and the Sequel Thereto Deborah's Diary* (London: J. C. Nimmo and New York: Scribner, 1898), 351.

26. John Aubrey, "Minutes of the Life of Mr John Milton," in *The Early Lives of Milton*, ed. Helen Darbishire (1932; rpt. London: Constable, 1965), 3.

27. Jonathan Richardson, "The Life of the Author," in ibid., 231, 254.

28. See Skerpan-Wheeler, "Authorship and Authority," 107.

29. See Hugo Grotius, *His Sophompaneas, or Joseph. A Tragedy. With Annotations by Francis Goldsmith* (London: William Hunt, 1652), and also the legend accompanying the frontispiece portrait for Grotius's *Of the Law of Warre and Peace. With Annotations*, tr. Clement Barksdale (London: T. Warren, 1655): "See you not Learning in his Lookes. / See it more lively in his Bookes."

30. Georges Gusdorf, "Conditions and Limits of Autobiography," in *Autobiography*, ed. Olney, 35, 36.

31. See William Riley Parker, *Milton: A Biography*, 2 vols. (Oxford: Clarendon Press, 1968), 1: 289. But Milton may also turn this play upon himself as John Shawcross suggests and Skerpan-Wheeler reports; see the latter's "Authorship and Authority," 106, but see also 107, for "the possibility of a Milton joke," both self-referential and infinitely more delicate in its play.

32. Barbara Lewalski, "How Radical Was the Young Milton?" in *Milton and Heresy*, ed. Stephen B. Dobranski and John P. Rumrich (Cambridge and New York: Cambridge University Press, 1998), 66. See also Lewalski, *The Life of John Milton: A Critical Biography* (Oxford and Malden, MA: Blackwell, 2000), esp. 87–197.

33. John K. Hale, "*Paradise Lost: A Poem in Twelve Books*, or is it Ten?" *Philological Quarterly* 74, 2 (Spring 1995): 137. See also John K. Hales, *Milton as Multilingual: Selected Essays, 1982–2004*, ed. Lisa Marr and Chris Ackerley (Dunedin: Otago Studies in English 8, 2005), 193–208.

34. As quoted by Richard Brilliant, *Portraiture* (Cambridge, MA: Harvard University Press, 1991), 13.

35. Ibid., 10.

36. See John Milton, *Poems, &c. Upon Several Occasions* (London: Thomas Dring, 1673). See inside of front cover, Huntington Library Call No. D-X / M 2161 / 106455. The comment is signed: "J. D. Lewis."

37. Brilliant, *Portraiture*, 132.

38. Roland Barthes, "The Death of the Author" and "From Work to Text," in *The Rustle of Language*, tr. Richard Howard (New York: Hill and Wang, 1986), 51, 61–62.

39. McMahon, *The Two Poets*, 3.

40. William Blake, "Annotations to Swedenborg's *Heaven and Hell*," in *The Complete Poetry and Prose of William Blake*, rev. ed., ed. David V. Erdman (Garden City, NY: Anchor, 1982), 601.

41. Barthes, "The Death of the Author," in *The Rustle of Language*, tr. Howard, 49.

42. Humphrey Moseley, "The Stationer to the Reader," in *Poems of Mr. John Milton* (London: Ruth Raworth for Humphrey Moseley, 1645), a4v.

43. Margaret Bottrall, *Every Man a Phoenix: Studies in Seventeenth-Century Autobiography* (London: John Murray, 1958), 3.

44. Northrop Frye, *Fearful Symmetry: A Study of William Blake* (Princeton, NJ: Princeton University Press, 1947), 325–26.

45. Stephen B. Dobranski, "Licensing Milton's Heresy," in *Milton and Heresy*, ed. Dobranski and Rumrich, 150, 140; cf. 146, 154.

46. See the superb exploration of many of these issues in relation to one frontispiece by Stephen B. Dobranski, "Burghley's Emblem and the Heart of Milton's *Pro Populo Anglicano Defensio*," *Milton Quarterly* 44, 2 (May 2000): 33–48.

47. Johns, *The Nature of the Book*, 117; see also 127–28. For interesting speculations on Milton and his printers, see again Sabrina A. Baron, "Licensing Readers, Licensing Authorities in Seventeenth-Century England," in *Books and Readers in Early Modern England: Material Studies*, ed. Jennifer Andersen and Elizabeth Sauer (Philadelphia: University of Pennsylvania Press, 2002), 217–42.

48. Yet as Evans notices, if not reduced to initials until the third issue of the first edition, Milton's signature, as one moves from the first to the second issue, "shrinks visibly"; see Evans, "The Birth of the Author," 47.

49. Mark Bland, "The Appearance of the Text in Early Modern England," in *Text: An Interdisciplinary Annual of Textual Studies*, ed. W. Speed Hill and Edward M. Burns, 11 (1998): 100; and Roy Flannagan, ed., *The Riverside Milton* (Boston and New York: Houghton Mifflin, 1998), 1135.

50. Orgel, "Afterword: Records of Culture," in *Books and Readers in Early Modern England*, ed. Andersen and Sauer, 286.

51. John Leonard, " 'Thus They Relate, Erring': Milton's Inaccurate Allusions," *Milton Studies* (a special issue entitled *John Milton: The Writer in His Works*), 38 (2000): 96–121.

52. Peter Levi, *Eden Renewed: The Public and Private Life of John Milton* (New York: St. Martin's Press, 1997), 95; cf. 45.

53. Noting that "Milton . . . was not a popular man," R. G. Moyles seconds David Masson's earlier suggestion, arguing that "many people, seeing the name JOHN MILTON on the title-page, would throw down the book with an exclamation of disgust"; see Moyles, *The Text of "Paradise Lost": A Study in Editorial Procedure* (Toronto, Buffalo, and London: University of Toronto Press, 1985), 14. While Moyles thinks this view "is most likely correct" and accounts for slow sales, he also conjectures that "maybe it was not Milton's name at all but the absence of any guide to what the poem contained which had slowed sales" (ibid.). See also Masson, *The Life of John Milton: Narrated in Connexion with the Political, Ecclesiastical, and Literary History of His Time,* 7 vols. (London: Macmillan, 1880), 6:623. Valuable perspectives on the conditions of writing in the Age of Milton are afforded by Christopher Hill, "Censorship and English Literature," in *The Collected Essays of Christopher Hill: Volume One, Writing and Revolution in Seventeenth Century England* (Amherst: University of Massachusetts Press, 1985), 32–71, and also 133–87; and Annabel Patterson, *Censorship and Interpretation: The Conditions of Writing and Reading in Early Modern England* (Madison and London: University of Wisconsin Press, 1984), esp. 111–17, 176–80; and also by Patterson, *Reading between the Lines* (Madison: University of Wisconsin Press, 1993), esp. 36–56, 244–75, 276–97.

54. Johns, *The Nature of the Book*, 147.

55. Nicholas von Maltzhan, "Milton's Readers," in *The Cambridge Companion to Milton,* 2nd ed., ed. Dennis Danielson (Cambridge and New York: Cambridge University Press, 1999), 240.

56. See Sharon Achinstein, "Milton's Spectre in the Restoration: Marvell, Dryden, and Literary Enthusiasm," *Huntington Library Quarterly* 59, 1 (1997): 3. See also Achinstein, *Literature and Dissent in Milton's England* (Cambridge and New York: Cambridge University Press, 2003), esp. 172–81. In "Milton," in *The Cambridge History of the Book in Britain,* ed. John Barnard and D. F. McKenzie, with the assistance of Maureen Bell, 4 (Cambridge and New York: Cambridge University Press, 2002), Joad Raymond reports that "*Paradise Lost* was the first book Samuel Simmons entered into the Stationers' Register under his own name" (4:383).

57. Johns, *The Nature of the Book*, 134–35.

58. Ibid., 100.

59. Robert J. Griffin, "Anonymity and Authorship," *New Literary History* 30, 4 (Autumn 1999): 888, 885. See also Anne Ferry, "*Anonymity:* The Literary History of a Word," *New Literary History* 33, 2 (Spring 2002): 193–214.

60. See John T. Shawcross, both "The Balanced Structure of *Paradise Lost*," *Studies in Philology* 62, 1 (January 1965): 696–718, and "The

Son in His Ascendance: A Reading of *Paradise Lost*," *Modern Language Quarterly* 27, 4 (December 1966): 388–401. See also by Shawcross, *With Mortal Voice: The Creation of "Paradise Lost"* (Lexington: University Press of Kentucky, 1982), esp. 42–55.

61. Anne Middleton, "Life in the Margins, or What's An Annotator to Do?" in *New Directions in Textual Studies*, ed. Oliphant and Bradford, 180. See also Stephen B. Dobranski, "Samson and the Omissa," *Studies in English Literature 1500–1900* 36, 1 (Winter 1996): 162–63, as well as Dobranski, "Text and Context for *Paradise Regain'd* and *Samson Agonistes*," in *Altering Eyes: New Perspectives on "Samson Agonistes*," ed. Mark R. Kelley and Joseph Wittreich (Newark: University of Delaware Press and London: Associated University Presses, 2002), 30–53.

62. See Gordon Teskey, ed., "On the Text of *Paradise Lost*," in *"Paradise Lost": A Norton Critical Edition*, ed. Gordon Teskey (New York and London: W. W. Norton, 2005), xxviii.

63. John Spencer, *A Discourse Concerning Prodigies . . . The Second Edition . . . To which is added . . . Vulgar Prophecies* (London: J. Field, 1665), 2nd pagination: [A3v], 132, 134.

64. See the intriguing reflections of Angelica Duran, " 'Milton and His Condemnation of Rhyme' by Jorge Luis Borges," *PMLA: Publications of the Modern Language Association* 120, 5 (2006), forthcoming. In the same volume, see "Criticism in Translation," and see also "Milton Among Hispanics: Jorge Luis Borges and Milton's 'Condemnation of Rhyme,' " *Prose Studies* 28, 2 (August 2006): 1–11.

65. See both John Leonard, " 'Thus They Relate, Erring,' " 96–121, and John K. Hale, "The 1668 Argument to *Paradise Lost*," *Milton Quarterly* 35, 2 (May 2001): 87–97.

66. McMahon, *The Two Poets*, 24; see also 155.

67. St. Ambrose, "The Prayer of Job and David," in *Seven Exegetical Works*, tr. Michael P. McHugh (Washington, DC: Catholic University of America Press, 1972), 357.

68. *Christus Patiens*, referred to in the Preface to *Samson Agonistes* as *Christ Suffering*, is here translated by Alan Fishbone from *Christus Patiens, Tragoedia Christiana*, ed. J. G. Brambs (Lipsiae: B. G. Teubneri, 1885). This Fishbone translation is printed in *Milton Quarterly* 36, 3 (October 2002): 130–92.

69. See Joseph Wittreich, *Feminist Milton* (Ithaca, NY and London: Cornell University Press, 1987), 20, 164; see also 67, 76.

70. Herman Melville, in *Melville and Milton: An Edition and Analysis of Melville's Annotations on Milton*, ed. Robin Grey (Pittsburgh, PA: Duquesne University Press, 2004), 157, 158, 173.

71. See John S. Diekhoff, "The Function of the Prologues in *Paradise Lost*," *PMLA* 57, 3 (September 1942): 697–704, and *Milton's "Paradise Lost": A Commentary on the Argument* (1946; rpt. New York: Columbia University Press, 1963), 13–27.

72. Foucault, "What Is an Author?" in *Language*, tr. Bouchard and Simon, 129.

73. Richardson, "The Life of the Author," in *The Early Lives of Milton*, ed. Darbishire, 247.

74. More, *Ecclesiastae & Sacrarum Litterarum Professoris Fides Publica*, YP, 4:1104.

75. "The Response of John Phillips," YP, 4:911.

76. See More's dedication to du Moulin's book, "To Charles II," and then du Moulin's, *The Cry of Royal Blood to Heaven against the English Parricides*, as well as Adrian Vlacq, "The Printer in His Own Behalf," and More, *The Public Faith*—all in YP, 4:1045, 1050–51, 1089, 1103.

77. See Parker, *Milton*, 2:975.

78. See Roger L'Estrange, *No Blinde Guides in Answer to a Seditious Pamphlet of J. Milton's* (London: H. Broom, 1660), A2; Thomas Long, *Dr. Walker's True, Modest, and Faithful Account of the Author of Eikōn basilikē* (London: R. Taylor, 1693), 2; Joseph Jane (1660), in William Riley Parker, *Milton's Contemporary Reputation* (Columbus: Ohio State University Press, 1940), 105; anon., *A Third Conference between O. Cromwell and Hugh Peters in Saint James's Park* (London: Thomas Mobb, 1660), 8; and again Long, *Dr. Walker's True, Modest, and Faithful Account*, 2–3; G. S., *Britains Triumph, For Her Imparallel'd Deliverance* (London: n.p., 1660), 15.

79. For McMahon's contrary arguments, see *The Two Poets*, 39, 41.

80. See Edward Phillips, "Life of Mr. John Milton," in *The Early Lives of Milton*, ed. Darbishire, 67.

81. See Michael Lieb, *Milton and the Culture of Violence* (Ithaca, NY and London: Cornell University Press, 1994), 236, 260, 263; see also 235, 240.

82. See *Of Christian Doctrine*, YP, 6:758–72, as well as the note here on later portions of Milton's theological treatise as *apologia*.

83. See *The Complete Poetical Works of John Milton*, 5th ed., ed. Henry John Todd, 4 vols. (London: Rivingtons, Longman, 1852), 3:323. David Masson, *The Life of John Milton: Narrated in Connexion with the Political, Ecclesiastical, and Literary History of His Time*, 7 vols. (1881; rpt. Gloucester, MA: Peter Smith, 1965), 6:676, 664, 670, 677.

84. See René de Chateaubrand, *Sketches of English Literature: With Considerations on the Spirit of the Times, Men, and Revolutions*, 2nd ed., 2 vols. (London: Henry Colburn, 1837), 2:106; and Joseph Ivimey, *John Milton: His Life and Times, Religious and Political Opinions* (New York: E. Wilson, 1833), 234.

85. Parker, *Milton*, 1:314.

86. John Upton, "An Answer to Some Criticisms on Milton's Paradise Lost," in *The Memoirs of Thomas Hollis*, comp. Francis Blackburne, 2 vols. (London: n.p., 1780), 2:624.

87. Edward Sexby, *Killing, No Murder* (London: n.p., 1659), 9, 16.

88. Hugo Grotius, *His Three Books Treating of the Rights of War and Peace*, tr. William Evats (London: Margaret White, 1682), 24.

89. Ibid., 25.

90. J. Ley, W. Gouge, M. Vasaubon, F. Taylor, E. Reynolds-Swalwood, and John Downame, *Annotations upon All the Books of the Old and New Testaments*, 2 vols. (London: Evan Tyler, 1657), 1: annotations to Judges 16:28, and 14:4 and 15:7.

91. Robert South, "A Sermon Preached before King Charles the Second . . . On the Thirtieth Day of January, 1662–3," *Sermons Preached upon Several Occasions*, rev. ed., 7 vols. (Oxford: n.p., 1823), 3:416 (see also 431), 421, 439.

92. Nigel Smith, *Literature and Revolution in England, 1640–1660* (1994; rpt. New Haven and London: Yale University Press, 1997), 10, 77.

93. Lieb, *Milton and the Culture of Violence*, 201, 205.

94. Smith, *Literature and Revolution*, 160.

95. Lieb, *Milton and the Culture of Violence*, 159–263.

96. See More's dedication ("To Charles II") to du Moulin, *The Cry of Royal Blood*, YP, 4:1045. As Lieb explains, the implicit allusion here is to Achaemenide's description of the Cyclops smashing bodies and bloodying them against the rocks (*Milton and the Culture of Violence*, 167).

97. Du Moulin, *The Cry of Royal Blood*, YP, 4:1078.

98. Ann Baynes Coiro, "Fable and Old Song: *Samson Agonistes* and the Idea of a Poetic Career," *Milton Studies* 36 (1998): 143.

99. See Irene Samuel, "*Samson Agonistes* as Tragedy," in *Calm of Mind: Tercentenary Essays on "Paradsie Regained" and "Samson Agonistes"* (Cleveland and London: Press of Case Western Reserve University, 1971), 248; and William Empson, *Milton's God*, rev. ed. (London: Chatto and Windus, 1965), 211.

100. See Mikhail Bakhtin, *Art and Answerability: Early Philosophical Essays*, ed. Michael Holquist and Vadim Liapunov, tr. Vadim Liapunov (1990; rpt. Austin: University of Texas, 1995), 12.

101. See Leo Bersani and Uysse Dutoit, *Caravaggio's Secret* (Cambridge, MA and London: MIT Press, 1998), 2.

102. See Lieb, *Milton and the Culture of Violence*, 227; see also 181–200.

103. Phillips, "The Response of John Phillips," YP, 4:943.

104. Foucault, "What Is an Author," in *Language*, tr. Bouchard and Simon, 130.

105. Jacques Derrida, *Of Grammatology*, tr. Gayatri Chakravorty Spivak (Baltimore and London: Johns Hopkins University Press, 1976), 305.

106. Paul Stevens, "Milton, Drama, and the Nation State," *Elizabethan Theatre XV*, ed. C. E. McGee and A. C. Magnusson (Toronto: P. D. Meany, 2002), 304.

107. William B. Hunter, *Visitation Unimplor'd: Milton and the Authorship of "De Doctrina Christiana"* (Pittsburgh, PA: Duquesne University Press, 1998), 153 (my italics).

108. Ivimey, *John Milton*, 262, 265.

109. See Jonathan Richardson, Sr. "Life of the Author," in *The Early Lives of Milton*, ed. Darbishire, 229.

110. I have used Milton and the late Pope to contrast the poet's with the theologian's truth, drawing phrases from "John Paul's Words: '2 Modes of Knowledge Lead to Truth in All Its Fullness,' " *The New York Times*, October 16, 1998, A10.

111. Cardinal Pierre de Bérulle as quoted by Colleen McDannell and Bernhard Lang, *Heaven: A History* (New Haven and London: Yale University Press, 1988), 157. Walter Clyde Curry approaches such a perception in his chapter, "The Lordship of Milton's Sun," in *Milton's Ontology, Cosmogony, and Physics* (Lexington: University of Kentucky Press, 1957), 143.

112. Toni Morrison, *Playing in the Dark: Whiteness and the Literary Imagination* (Cambridge, MA and London: Harvard University Press, 1992), 43.

113. Jacques Derrida, "Women in the Beehive: A Seminar with Jacques Derrida," in *Men in Feminism*, ed. Alice Jardine and Paul Smith (New York: Methuen, 1987), 203.

114. Jonathan Richardson and Son, *Explanatory Notes and Remarks on Milton's "Paradise Lost"* (London: James, John, and Paul Knapston, 1734), 376.

115. Richard Corum, "In White Ink: *Paradise Lost* and Milton's Ideas of Women," in *Milton and the Idea of Woman*, ed. Julia M. Walker (Urbana and Chicago: University of Illinois Press, 1988), 128. On Milton's narrative strategies, see also Catherine Belsey, *John Milton: Language, Gender, Power* (Oxford and New York: Basil Blackwell, 1988), 85–105.

116. See Samuel Johnson, *An Argument Proving, That the Abrogation . . . was according to the Constitutions of the English Government, and . . . Prescribed by It* (London: n.p., 1692), 11.

117. Stanley Rosen, *Hermeneutics as Politics* (New York and Oxford: Oxford University Press, 1987), 24, 22–23, 24, 35.

118. Curry, *Milton's Ontology, Cosmogony and Physics*, [92], 103.

119. See the fine essay by Marshall Grossman, "Servile/Sterile/Style: Milton and the Question of Woman," in *Milton and the Idea of Woman*, ed. Walker, 148–68.

120. See Margaret Patterson Hannay, "Lady Wroth: Mary Sidney," in *Women Writers of the Renaissance and Reformation*, ed. Katharina M. Wilson (Athens and London: University of Georgia Press, 1987), esp. 551–52. It is possible to see in this triad of figures (Copernicus, Galileo, Urania) what (as previously noted, see note 16) Guillory sees in one of them, "a cryptic self-portrait," as well as a return of

contemporary history; that is, a return of "what is suppressed, or supposedly so, in the poem" (see *Poetic Authority*, 161).

121. Patrick Hume, *Annotations on Milton's "Paradise Lost"* (London: Jacob Tonson, 1695), 231.

122. Richardson, *Explanatory Notes and Remarks*, 291, 293–294, 327. For a contrary and compelling argument that Milton is "in the mainstream of seventeenth-century thought and method," see Harinder Singh Marjara, *Contemplation of Created Things: Science in "Paradise Lost"* (Toronto, Buffalo, and London: University of Toronto Press, 1992), 299.

123. Richardson, *Explanatory Notes and Remarks*, 293. The best recent discussion of the cosmological debate in *Paradise Lost* is provided by Barbara K. Lewalski, "The Genres of *Paradise Lost*: Literary Genres as a Means of Accommodation," in *Composite Orders: The Genres of Milton's Last Poems*, ed. Richard S. Ide and Joseph Wittreich (Pittsburgh: Pittsburgh University Press, 1983), 75–103 (a special issue of *Milton Studies*, 17[1983]). Lewalski does not interrelate the cosmological and creation narratives (as I have done), but she does elucidate the disposition of voices therein and the wily manner in which such disputes are resolved:

> Galileo's dialogue has as interlocutors three friends . . . [meeting]. . . in a spirit of friendly inquiry. Salviati, who undertakes to "act the part of Copernicus . . .". . . Simplicio . . . [who] grounds his arguments chiefly upon ancient authority and piety . . .[and] Sangredo . . . an urbane, open-minded, intelligent layman who desires to be informed about the two systems so that he may decide rationally which to credit. Galileo's dialogue leaves no question whatsoever that Salviati's arguments carry the day: the inconclusiveness of the ending and Simplicio's final appeal to the unsearchable way of God . . . were a transparent, and in the event futile, attempt to satisfy the censors. (89)

The cosmological and creation debates in *Paradise Lost* run parallel courses, although the Creation debate, in which the stakes are higher, introduces what, by Lewalski's account, is missing from the cosmological debate: "appeals to authority" and "to the need for higher illumination" (90). If the function of the latter is to establish appropriate terms and attitudes for cosmological inquiry, the function of the former is to array discrepant attitudes while advancing the terms by which one attitude may be approved over another.

124. Terry Eagleton, *Criticism and Ideology: A Study in Marxist Literary Theory* (London: Verso, 1976), 127.

125. Foucault, "What Is an Author?" in *Language*, ed. Bouchard and Simon, 121.

126. Rajan, "Milton Encompassed," 88.

127. On the former point, see esp. William B. Hunter, "The Millennial Moment: Milton vs. 'Milton,' " in *Milton and the Ends of Time*, ed. Juliet Cummins (Cambridge and New York: Cambridge University Press, 2003), 96–105.

128. Euripides, *The Bacchae*, tr. Michael Cacoyannis (New York: Meridian Books, 1982), 85.

129. Alfred Kazin, "Introduction," *The Portable Blake* (New York: Viking Press, 1946), 55.

CHAPTER 2   HORIZONS OF EXPECTATIONS: REPRESSIONS, RECEPTIONS, AND THE POLITICS OF MILTON'S LAST POEMS

1. The epigraphs are drawn from Walter Benjamin's *Illuminations*, the first paragraph of the essay entitled "The Task of the Translator" as translated by Harry Zohn and as quoted in Paul de Man's "Introduction" to *Toward an Aesthetic of Reception*, tr. Timothy Bahti (Minneapolis: Univesrity of Minnesota Press, 1982), xv, and then from Jauss's *Toward an Aesthetic of Reception*, 19, and see also 40–41.

2. William Empson, *Some Versions of Pastoral* (Norfolk, CT: New Directions, 1960), 21.

3. Hans Robert Jauss, *Question and Answer: Forms of Dialogic Understanding*, tr. Michael Hays (Minneapolis: University of Minnesota Press, 1989), 99, 101, 105. See also a series of essays by Joseph Wittreich, " 'John, John, I Blush for Thee!': Mapping Gender Discourses in *Paradise Lost*," in *Out of Bounds: Male Writers and Gender Criticism*, ed. Laura Claridge and Elizabeth Langland (Amherst: University of Massachusetts Press, 1990), 22–54; " 'Inspir'd with Contradiction': Mapping Gender Discourses in *Paradise Lost*," in *Literary Milton: Text, Pretext, Context*, ed. Diana Trevino Benet and Michael Lieb (Pittsburgh, PA: Duquesne University Press, 1994), 133–60; " 'He Ever Was a Dissenter': Milton's Transgressive Maneuvers in *Paradise Lost*," in *Arenas of Conflict: Milton and the Unfettered Mind*, ed. Kristin Pruitt McColgan and Charles W. Durham (Selinsgrove, PA: Susquehanna University Press and London: Associated University Presses, 1997), 21–40; "Milton's Transgressive Maneuvers: Receptions (Then and Now) and the Sexual Politics of *Paradise Lost*," ed. Stephen B. Dobranski and John P. Rumrich (Cambridge and New York: Cambridge University Press, 1998), 244–66.

4. Jerome McGann, "How to Read a Book," in *New Directions in Textual Studies*, ed. Dave Oliphant and Robin Bradford (Austin, Texas: Harry Ransom Humanities Research Center, 1990), 34.

5. On the other hand, individual titles at the head of each book are entirely in caps (e. g., **PARADISE LOST. / BOOK I. /** etc.).

6. Only Book 7 is missing the usual tag, "The End of . . ."—whether by calculation or oversight is uncertain (see Ee).

7. All quotations from *Paradise Lost* in this section, as well as much of the next one, both of which dwell on various states of the first edition, are from the first edition of the poem, citations for which are hereafter given parenthetically within the text of this chapter. The quotations, furthermore, correlate with two different issues of the poem, both in The New York Public Library Rare Book Room: (1) [double-ruled border] / **Paradise lost.** / **A** / **POEM** / **IN** / **TEN BOOKS**. / [bar] / The Author / *JOHN MILTON*. / [bar] / [Ornament] / [bar] / *LONDON*, / Printed by *S. Simmons*, and are to be sold by *S. Thomson* at / the *Bishops-Head* in *Duck-lane*, *H. Mortlack* at the / *White Hart* in *Westminster* Hall, *M. Walker* under / St. *Dunstans* Church in *Fleet-street*, and *R. Boulter* at / the *Turks-Head* in *Bishopsgate* street, 1668. / (this copy is identified by the New York Public Library as 1st edition, 4th title page); and (2) [double-ruled border] / **Paradise lost.** / **A** / **POEM** / **IN** / **TEN BOOKS**. / [bar] / The Author / *JOHN MILTON*. / [bar] / *LONDON*, / Printed by *S. Simmons*, and to be sold by / *T. Helder* at the Angel in *Little Brittain*. / 1669. / (this copy is identified by the New York Public Library as 1st edition, 7th title page). Cf. John T. Shawcross, *Milton: A Bibliography for the Years 1624–1700* (Binghamton, NY: Medieval and Renaissance Texts and Studies, 1984), 79, in which the first of these copies is identified as "Issue 4" and the second of them as "Issue 5."

8. Line 881 is designated line 880, and from this point on the numbering of lines for Book 10 is short by one line. Hence line 1540 is actually 1541. The longest books have also been the most forbidding. In contrast, the shortest books of the poem have registered the greatest impact and provoke still raging controversy: the 798 lines of Book 1 and the 751 (actually 742 lines) of Book 3 (again because of misnumbering beginning at line 610, actually 600, and continued when line 651 is numbered 650).

9. See John Spencer, *A Discourse concerning Prodigies . . . the Second Edition . . . to Which is Added a Short Treatise Concerning Vulgar Prophecies* (London: n.p., 1665), 55, 2.

10. Ibid., 71.

11. Ibid., 75, 110, 73.

12. See *Paradise Lost, in Twelve Books: Together with Paradise Regain'd, in Four Books* (Dublin: George Grierson, 1724). Previously, as Shawcross notes, Milton's vast design, this time embracing the final trilogy of poems, was recognized in a volume "created by adding unsold copies of the 1688 *Paradise Regain'd* and *Samson Agonistes* to the 1695 *Paradise Lost*"; see Shawcross, *Milton*, 109.

13. Jonathan Richardson, Sr., "Life of the Author," *Explanatory Notes and Remarks on Milton's "Paradise Lost"* (London: James, John, and Paul Knapton, 1734), 271.

14. As adopted and adapted from Richardson, ibid., 272.

15. Stephen Orgel, "Afterword: Records of Culture," in *Books and Readers in Early Modern England: Material Studies*, ed. Jennifer Andersen and Elizabeth Sauer (Philadelphia: University of Pennsylvania Press, 2002), 283.

16. Richardson, "Life of the Author," 239.

17. Ibid., 310. For a recent adoption of such a position, see John K. Hale, "*Paradise Lost, A Poem in Twelve Books*—or is it Ten?" in *Milton as Multilingual*, ed. Lisa Marr and Chris Ackerley, Vol. 8 (Dunedin: Otago Studies in English, 2005), 193–209, as well as the counterargument of Maren-Sofie Rostvig (reported by Hale) whose contention is that Milton mismanaged the revision of *Paradise Lost*; therefore, we should "return to the first edition as the authoritative text" (ibid., 195).

18. For this conversation, see the on-line discussion sponsored by the University of Richmond: Roy Flannagan, Joad Raymond, and Peter Lindenbaum, June 2, 1999, and Flannagan, June 9, 1999. Cf. Christopher Grose, in his conjectures concerning "the co-originality of the book proper and seeming prolegomenal apparatus, as in the proemeia of *Paradise Lost*"; see "*Theatrum Libri*: Burton's *Anatomy of Melancholy* and the Failure of Encyclopedic Form," in *Books and Readers in Early Modern England*, ed. Andersen and Sauer, 82–83. To Flannagan's remark (quoted in the text previously) should be added the insight of Sabrina A. Baron, who remarks that the unadorned, "underinformed title page . . .[is] a smoke screen behind which to conduct political and religious battles"; see Baron, "Licensing Readers, Licensing Authorities in Seventeenth-Century England," in *Books and Readers in Early Modern England*, ed. Andersen and Sauer, 224.

19. On-line conversation (see note 18).

20. Ibid.

21. Ibid.

22. Ibid.

23. "Curtis on Literary Property" (a note inserted into the New York Public Library's first edition of *Paradise Lost*, the seventh title page).

24. McGann, "How to Read a Book," in *New Directions in Textual Studies*, ed. Oliphant and Bradford, 36.

25. Adrian Johns (paraphrasing Roger Chartier), *The Nature of the Book: Print and Knowledge in the Making* (Chicago and London: University of Chicago Press, 1998), 57.

26. Thomas Newton, ed., *Paradise Lost. A Poem, in Twelve Books*, 9th ed., 2 vols. (London: J. F. and C. Rivington, 1790), 1:A2.

27. Peter Lindenbaum, "John Milton and the Republican Mode of Literary Production," in *Critical Essays on John Milton*, ed. Christopher Kendrick (New York: G. K. Hall and London: Prentice Hall International, 1995), 151.

28. Newton, ed., *Paradise Lost*, 1:A2v, A4.

29. See John Dryden, "The Authors Apology," in *The State of Innocence, and Fall of Man: An Opera* (London: T[homas] N[ewcomb], 1677), b, [bv], [c2v].

30. Nat[haniel] Lee, "*To Mr. DRYDEN, on his Poem of Paradice*," in ibid., [A4v], [A4].

31. See *Paradise Lost. A Poem in Twelve Books*, 4th ed. (London: Miles Flesher and Richard Bentley, 1688), frontispiece portrait (fig. 1.7).

32. Lindenbaum, "John Milton and the Republican Mode of Literary Production," 150. The dedication "To the Right Honourable / *John* Lord *Sommers*, / Baron of *Evesham*" first appeared in *Paradise Lost . . . The Seventh Edition* (London: Jacob Tonson, 1705), A-[Av].

33. Andrew Marvell, "On Mr Milton's *Paradise Lost*," in *The Poems of Andrew Marvell*, ed. Nigel Smith (London: Pearson Longman, 2003), 184 (ll. 43–44).

34. Heather Dubrow, "The Masquing of Genre in *Comus*," *Milton Studies* 44 (2005): 65.

35. Roy Flannagan, ed., *The Riverside Milton* (Boston and New York: Houghton Mifflin, 1998), 334.

36. See the wise remarks by Nicholas von Maltzahn, "Milton's Readers," in *The Cambridge Companion to Milton*, 2nd ed., ed. Dennis Danielson (Cambridge and New York: Cambridge University Press, 1999), 246.

37. Mark Bland, "The Appearance of the Text in Early Modern England," *Text: An Interdisciplinary Annual of Textual Studies*, ed. W. Speed Hill and Edward M. Burns 11 (1998): 101; cf. John K. Hale, "The 1668 Argument to *Paradise Lost*," *Milton Quarterly* 35, 2 (May 2001): 89.

38. "Samuel Taylor Coleridge," Entry 186, in *The Romantics on Milton: Formal Essays and Critical Asides*, ed. Joseph Wittreich (Cleveland and London: Press of Case Western Reserve University, 1970), 211. Writing his book as a corrective to Milton's representations of the devils in *Paradise Lost*, Daniel Defoe anticipates, and probably provokes, Coleridge's own complaint; see Daniel Defoe, *The Political History of the Devil, as well Ancient as Modern* (London: T. Warner, 1726), 27.

39. William Wordsworth's words from "The Recluse: Part First" are particularly apt; see *The Poetical Works of Wordsworth*, ed. Paul D. Sheats (Boston: Houghton Mifflin, 1982), 231 (l.794).

40. S. Margaret Fuller, "The Prose Works of Milton," in *Papers on Literature and Art* (New York: Wiley and Putnam, 1846), 39.

41. Both issues of the first edition from which I have been quoting (see note 7) read: "*He sends his Son to Judge the Transgressors*" (a2); another issue of the first edition also in the New York Public Library (identified as title page 8 by the New York Public Library and as "Issue 6" by Shawcross, *Milton*, 80), changes "Son" to "Angels":

"*He sends his Angels to judge the Transgressors.*" See **Paradise lost /** A / **POEM /** IN TEN BOOKS. / [bar] / The Author / *JOHN MILTON.* / [bar] / *LONDON,* / Printed by *S. Simmons,* and are to be sold by / *T. Helder,* at the *Angel* in *Little Brittain,* / 1669. This might be called "the Angel issue" of the first edition inasmuch as, unlike other title pages, the word "Angel" appears here in italic and then, mysteriously, in the Argument to Book 9.

42. In private correspondence, John Rogers, Yale University, writes: "there were Socinians, like Jonas Schlichting, who held a higher Christology than his comrades (and who were therefore much more like Milton). You could say that they flirted with the higher Christology of Arianism. Schlichting's Christ had a preexistence in heaven, and may actually have been an angel himself, who got himself promoted above the others. My book will be arguing that the semi-Arian Socinians like Schlichting were important for Milton; and in fact may have supplied something like a theological narrative that Milton would use to write the Exaltation of the Son in Book 5." To which I would add that something of this heresy may be hidden in the description of Satan (cited in the text earlier) as of the first, if not the first Archangel.

43. E. M. W. Tillyard, *The Epic Strain in the English Novel* (London: Chatto and Windus, 1958), 15.

44. Herman Melville, in *Melville and Milton: An Edition and Analysis of Melville's Annotations on Milton,* ed. Robin Grey (Pittsburgh, PA: Duquesne University Press, 2004), 187, 122.

45. Sharon Achinstein, "Milton's Spectre in the Restoration: Marvell, Dryden, and Literary Enthusiasm," *Huntington Library Quarterly* 59, 1 (1997): 8, cf. 28.

46. So one of Dryden's contemporaries seems to have thought: "the very same Spirit of Contradiction . . . seiz'd me when I undertook to clear *Miltons* Paradice of Weeds." These words derive from a conversation imagined by Thomas Brown, and the words are spoken by Mr. Bays (who is supposedly John Dryden); see *The Reasons of Mr. Bays Changing His Religion. Considered in a Dialogue between Crites, Eugenius, and Mr. Bays* (London: S.T., 1688), 18.

47. I borrow these phrases from Steven Zwicker's fine essay, "Milton, Dryden, and the Politics of Literary Controversy," in *Heirs of Fame: Milton and Writers of the English Renaissance,* ed. Margo Swiss and David A. Kent (Lewisburg, PA: Bucknell University Press and London: Associated University Presses, 1995), 284, 277. Throughout his essay, Zwicker reads the headnote (along lines drawn by David Norbrook) as a "political gesture" (272). By David Norbrook, see both *Poetry and Politics in the English Renaissance* (London, Boston, Melbourne, and Henley: Routledge and Kegan Paul, 1984) and *Writing the English Republic: Poetry, Rhetoric, and Politics, 1627–1660* (Cambridge and New York: Cambridge University Press,

1999), esp. 433–91.

48. Annabel Patterson, *Reading between the Lines* (Madison: University of Wisconsin Press, 1993), 241–42. Or as Zwicker argues, Dryden takes Milton's "theologically dense argument of Protestant radicalism, this poetic statement of republican utopianism," and then eradicates "both its politics and theology," "nervously acknowledging," while also "sidestepping" both the statement and achievement of *Paradise Lost*. See Zwicker, "Milton, Dryden, and the Politics of Literary Controversy," in *Heirs of Fame*, ed. Swiss and Kent, 284–85, 271.

49. Peter Lindenbaum, "Rematerializing Milton," *Publishing History* 41 (1997): [5].

50. R. G. Moyles, *The Text of "Paradise Lost": A Study in Editorial Procedure* (Toronto, Buffalo, and London: University of Toronto Press, 1985), 33, 157.

51. Lindenbaum, "The Poet in the Marketplace: Milton and Samuel Simmons," in *Of Poetry and Politics: New Essays on Milton and His World*, ed. P. G. Stanwood (Binghampton, NY: Medieval and Renaissance Texts and Studies, 1995), 261. Annabel Patterson's comment is apposite: "Dryden was . . . engaged in a reading of *Paradise Lost* that not only implied a straightforward political allegory—the Fall of the Angels as the Puritan Revolution—but also imposed a second level of allegory from subsequent political history—the Fall of the Angels as the Exclusion crisis, with Shaftesbury in the place of Cromwell" (see Patterson, *Reading between the Lines*, 239).

52. Anne Middleton, "Life in the Margins, or What's an Annotator to Do?" in *New Directions in Textual Studies*, ed. Oliphant and Bradford, 169.

53. Newton, ed., *Paradise Lost*, 1:[A8]. Patrick Hume and Thomas Newton represent decidedly different notions of annotation with Hume focusing on the recognition of sources (an activity emphasizing remote history) and with Newton, while sources continue to play a part in his annotation, giving attention to reception history, thus allowing his annotations at certain crucial moments to intersect with contemporary history.

54. The lines appear one way in the manuscript version of Book 1, in yet another fashion in the first edition, only to be revised again in the second edition of *Paradise Lost*.

55. *Paradise Lost*, ed. P[atrick] H[ume] (London: Jabob Tonson, 1695), [345]. Two notable yokings of Samson and Adam, before Milton's, occur in Henry Smith, "A Preparative to Mariage," in *The Sermons of Maister Henrie Smith* (London: Felix Kyngston and V. Sims, 1597), 38, and John Goodwin, *Apolutrosis Apolutroseos or Redemption Redeemed* (London: John Macock, 1651), A2. What gets highlighted in these pre-Miltonic yokings is (1) Samson and Adam letting love of woman taken precedence over love of God and (2) their failure to glorify God, or to give thanksgiving.

56. The Folger Library copy—Catalogue No. 165862—is dated 1669.

57. On titling practices with interesting attention given to Milton, see Anne Ferry, *The Title to the Poem* (Stanford, CA: Stanford University Press, 1996).

58. See Lindenbaum, "The Poet in the Marketplace," 171–86.

59. The suggestion is made by Balachandra Rajan, "The Imperial Temptation," in *Milton and the Imperial Vision*, ed. Balachandra Rajan and Elizabeth Sauer (Pittsburgh, PA: Duquesne University Press, 1999), 297. See also John Leonard, " 'Thus They Relate, Erring': Milton's Inaccurate Allusions," *Milton Studies* (a special issue entitled *John Milton: The Writer in His Work*), 38 (2000): 96–121.

60. For the modern supposition, see Hale, "*Paradise Lost: A Poem in Twelve Books*—Or Is It Ten?" in *Milton as Multilingual*, ed. Marr and Ackerley, 198; cf. Elijah Fenton, "Postscript," *Paradise Lost* (London: Jacob Tonson, 1725), 23.

61. *The Odyssey of Homer*, tr. Richmond Lattimore (New York, Evanston, and London: Harper and Row, 1967), 122–23.

62. See Marcus Walsh, *Shakespeare, Milton, and Eighteenth-Century Literary Editing* (Cambridge and New York: Cambridge University Press, 1997), 62, 74.

63. Julia Walker, "The Poetics of Antitext and the Politics of Milton's Allusions," *Studies in English Literature 1500–1900* 37, 1 (Winter 1997): 151–71.

64. See Nicholas von Maltzahn, " 'Acts of Kind Service': Milton and the Patriot Literature of Empire," in *Milton and the Imperial Vision*, ed. Rajan and Sauer, 248.

65. M. Manuel, quoting from Dryden's *Discourse on Epic Poetry* (1697), in *The Seventeenth Century Critics and Biographers of Milton* (Trivandrum: University of Kerala, 1962), 86; see also 80.

66. Anon., "Another Answer to Some Criticisms on Milton's Paradise Lost" (June 7, 1764), in *Appendix to the Memoirs of Thomas Hollis, Esq.* (London: n.p., 1780), 625, 626.

67. Mark Trevor Smith, "Introduction," *Blake and His Bibles*, ed. David V. Erdman (West Cornwall, CT: Locust Hill Press, 1990), xii.

68. See both Blake's *Milton*, 21 [23]:33, 25 [27]:22 and *The Marriage of Heaven and Hell*, 7:9, in *The Complete Poetry and Prose of William Blake*, rev. ed., ed. David V. Erdman (Garden City, NY: Doubleday, 1982), 116, 35. Milton is depicted as a star in the poem to which he gives his name: see 15 [17]:47, as well as the designs on plates 2, 17, 32, 37.

69. See Blake's *Milton*, ibid., 96.

70. Peter Levi, *Eden Renewed: The Public and Private Life of John Milton* (New York: St. Martin's Press, 1996), xi. In 1737, William Benson erected a shrine to Milton in Westminster Abbey; and by the end of the century Milton himself, his body exhumed, had become a shrine and his hair, a relic.

71. Elijah Fenton's "Life" first appeared in 1725, in *Paradise Lost . . . to Which Is Prefix'd an Account of His Life* (see note 60), [25].

72. *Paradise Lost. A Poem*, 7th ed. (London: Jacob Tonson, 1705), A-[Av].

73. Richardson, "The Life of the Author," in *Explanatory Notes and Remarks on Milton's "Paradise Lost"* (London: James, John, and Paul Knapton, 1734), cxvii–cxviii. Francis Peck comments similarly: "I need not . . . remind the reader how long PARADISE LOST itself lay neglected . . . before it could obtain its due credit in the world"; see *New Memoirs of the Life and Poetical Works of Mr. John Milton* (London: n.p., 1740), 83.

74. See John Dennis's letters to (1) Thomas Sergeant (August 27, 1717) and (2) Steele and Booth (May 25, 1719), in *The Critical Works of John Dennis*, ed. Edward Niles Hooker, 2 vols. (Baltimore: Johns Hopkins Press, 1938, 1943), 2:401, 169. Although he provides rich documentation for early receptions, John T. Shawcross comments similarly in both *John Milton: The Self and the World* (Lexington: University Press of Kentucky, 1993), 275, 278 and *Rethinking Milton Studies: Time Present and Time Past* (Newark: University of Delaware Press, 2005), 170–71.

75. For this note to Dennis's observation in what Hooker titles "Letters on Milton and Wycherley" (1721–22), see Dennis, *Critical Works*, ed. Hooker, 2:223 (for Dennis's comment) and 2:493 (for Hooker's annotation).

76. For a publication history rich in detail and laden with statistics, see Moyles, *The Text of "Paradise Lost*," 49–51.

77. Jonathan Dollimore, "Introduction: Shakespeare, Cultural Materialism and the New Historicism," in *Political Shakespeare: New Essays in Cultural Materialism*, ed. Jonathan Dollimore and Alan Sinfield (Ithaca, NY and London: Cornell University Press, 1985), 9 (my italics).

78. Jauss, *Toward an Aesthetic of Reception*, tr. Bahti, 23, 24.

79. George F. Sensabaugh contends that, during the Whig Revolution, Milton achieved "a stature commensurate with that for which he had struggled in the days of the Puritan Rebellion," even that some of Milton's positions "became fixed planks in the platform of the Whig party," and implies that the 1688 edition of *Paradise Lost* may be intended to further this new political agenda. See Sensabaugh, *That Grand Whig Milton* (Stanford, CA: Stanford University Press, and London: Oxford University Press, 1952), 125; see also 127, 134–42. Moyles is dubious; see *The Text of "Paradise Lost*," 33. See also John Walter Good on the Whig party and its espousal of Milton, in *Studies in the Milton Tradition* (Urbana: University of Illinois Press, 1915), 145–46, as well as William Kolbrener who contends that, historically, *Paradise Lost* has been a field of contention for various Whig positions, old and new: one extreme position fronts another with the Grand Whig Richard Bentley attacking the radical Whig John Toland. See Kolbrener, *Milton's Warring Angels: A Study of Critical Engagements* (Cambridge and New York: Cambridge University Press, 1997), 107–32.

80. See both Richardson, "The Life of the Author," in *Explanatory Notes and Remarks*, xcvii; and Winstanley, *The Lives Of the Most Famous English Poets; or the Honour of Parnassus* (London: H. Clark, 1687), 195. Space allotments are revealing: Milton gets a short paragraph in contrast to Roger L'Estrange's two and one half pages, which are said to be "far short" of the latter's deservings (221).

81. See Joseph Addison's "Account of the Greatest English Poets," in *Milton: The Critical Heritage*, ed. John T. Shawcross (London: Routledge and Kegan Paul, 1970), 105.

82. Marvell's dedicatory poem is discussed later.

83. Richardson, "The Life of the Author," in *Explanatory Notes and Remarks*, cxvii, cxix.

84. See William Riley Parker, *Milton: A Biography*, 2 vols. (Oxford: Clarendon Press, 1968), 2:1115.

85. Thomas Ellwood, *The History of the Life of Thomas Ellwood*, 2nd ed. (London: J. Sowle, 1714), 246.

86. Richardson, "The Life of the Author," in *Explanatory Notes and Remarks*, cxix–cxx. Later, Dryden will describe *Paradise Lost* as "one of the greatest, most noble, and most sublime POEMS, which either Age or Nation has produc'd"; see *The State of Innocence*, 62. Sir Fleetwood Sheppard has been assigned authorship of "Ad Christinam" that was often attributed to Milton.

87. Parker (quoting from Richardson's manuscript "Life" housed in the London Library), in *Milton*, 2:1116.

88. See ibid. "Fleet Sheppard . . . often told the Story" that "My Lord was in *Little-Britain*, Beating about for Books to his Taste; There was *Paradise Lost*; He was Surpriz'd with Some Passages he struck upon Dipping Here and There, and Bought it; the Bookseller Begg'd him to speak in its Favour if he Lik'd it, for that they lay on his Hands as *Wast Paper*. Jesus!"; see Richardson, "The Life of the Author," in *Explanatory Notes and Remarks*, cxix; and see also David Masson, *The Life of John Milton: Narrated in Connexion with the Political, Ecclesiastical and Literary History of His Time*, 7 vols. (London: Macmillan, 1880), 6:631–32.

89. Masson gives chief credit to Dryden: "Buckhurst [Charles Sackville Dorset, Lord Buckhurst], Roscommon, and other of the Restoration wits and critics, may have helped in the first appreciation of *Paradise Lost*; but Dryden was their leader" (*The Life of John Milton*, 6:635).

90. Patterson, *Reading between the Lines*, 243–44; also, see Gerard Langbaine, *The Lives and Characters of the English Dramatick Poets* (London: Nicholas Cox and William Turner, 1698), 47. In *Rethinking Milton Studies*, Shawcross notes Dryden's "unfortunate emphasis on the Fall only," together with his persistent "demonstration of his belief that Satan is the hero of the poem" (170). Now discussion needs to turn to Dryden's anxious rivalry with Milton, his reinflecting of Milton's poem throughout, his corrections of the poem as well as misreadings of it.

91. John Dryden, ed., *Sylvae: Or, the Second Part of Poetical Miscellanies*, 3rd ed. (London: Jacob Tonson, 1702), [a3v].

92. Dennis, "The Stage Defended," in *Works*, ed. Hooker, 2:312.

93. See Dryden, *The State of Innocence*, 40–41, 44, 45. My own observations here challenge the conclusions of Jean Gagen: "Dryden has . . . presented an Eve who is a genuine intellectual and spiritual partner to Adam and who is much more capable of 'careful questioning' and 'sober reflection' than Milton's Eve"; see Gagen, "Anomalies in Eden: Adam and Eve in Dryden's *The State of Innocence*," in *Milton's Legacy in the Arts*, ed. Albert C. Labriola and Edward Sichi, Jr. (University Park: Pennsylvania State University Press, 1988), 147.

94. See Nathaniel Lee, "To Mr. DRYDEN, on his Poem of Paradice" (1674?), in *The State of Innocence*, [A4].

95. Manuel, *The Seventeenth Century Critics and Biographers of Milton*, 44. See also William Riley Parker, *Milton's Contemporary Reputation* (Columbus: Ohio State University Press, 1940) and John T. Shawcross, *Milton: A Bibliography For the Years 1624–1700* (Binghamton, NY: Medieval and Renaissance Texts and Studies, 1984).

96. Manuel, *The Seventeenth Century Critics and Biographers of Milton*, 12, and Parker, *Milton's Contemporary Reputation*, who comments almost identically: "there seems to have been not a single printed reference to the elegy in the whole period of Milton's life" (11).

97. Humph[rey] Moseley, "The Stationer to the Reader," in *Poems of Mr. John Milton* (London: Ruth Raworth for Hymphrey Moseley, 1645), a4. On the complex typology of intertextuality that informs the Edward King memorial volume much still needs to be said. Yet discussion may begin by examining, first, the way in which the first and last of the English poems interrelate and, second, with the paradigm described by Gregory M. Colón Semenza in mind, in terms of how all the English poems in this volume interact with the first of them. See Semenza, *Sport, Politics, and Literature in the English Renaissance* (Newark: University of Delaware Press and London: Associated University Presses, 2003), 115–17. The spirit—or agon—of poetic competition that Semenza deciphers in *Annalia Dubrensia* (1636) affords an analogy for the same agon playing itself out in *Justa Edovardo King Naufrago* (1638).

98. For John Beale's correspondence on *Lycidas*, see Nicholas von Maltzahn, "Laureate, Republican, Calvinist: An Early Response to Milton and *Paradise Lost* (1667)," *Milton Studies* 29 (1992): 184. Abraham Hill's mention of *Lycidas* is cited by William Poole, "Two Early Readers of Milton: John Beale and Abraham Hill," *Milton Quarterly* 38, 2 (May 2004): 89.

99. See Levi, *Eden Renewed*, 80 and Thomas Creech, *The Idylliums of Theocritus with Rapin's Discourse on Pastorals* (Oxford: Anthony Stephens, 1684).

100. See John Langhorne, "Letter III. Waller to St. Evremond," in *Letters Supposed to Have Passed between M. De St. Evremond and Mr. Waller*, 2 vols. (London: T. Becket and P.A. de Hondt, 1769), 2:18–19, 21, as well as evidence of Milton's influence on Langhorne in *Poems on Several Occasions* (Lincoln: W. Wood [1760]), esp. "A Monody on the Death of the Author's Mother," 15. Parker corrects Good's misrepresentation of these letters; see Parker, *Milton*, 2: 1101 and Good, *Studies in the Milton Tradition*, 141.

101. Langhorne, "Letter IV. St. Evremond to Waller," in *Letters*, 2:21.

102. Christopher Hill observes: "Thirteen references to Milton's 1645 *Poems* have been noted by Marvell's editors, and many more to Milton's prose"; see "Milton and Marvell," in *Approaches to Marvell: The York Tercentenary Lectures*, ed. C. A. Patrides (London, Henley, and Boston: Routledge and Kegan Paul, 1978), 22.

103. Robert Baron, *Erotopaignion or the Cyprian Academy*, 2 vols. (London: W.W., 1647), 2:28, 45.

104. Thomas Brown, *Piscatory Eclogues* (London: n.p., 1729), 2.

105. Charles Goodall, "A Propitiatory Sacrifice, to the Ghost of J—M—by way of Pastoral," in *Poems And Translations Written upon Several Occasions, and to several Persons* (London: Henry Bonwicke, 1689). Goodall died in the very year these poems were published.

106. Ibid., 111, 112, 111, 113, 116, 115, 117.

107. Ibid., 116, 21, [A4v], 56, 86.

108. Ibid., 89, 99. See also Goodall's citation of "*Milton, Waller*, and the rest" in the poem called "Solitude," ibid., 73.

109. William Walsh, *Letters and Poems, Amorous and Gallant* (London, 1692), 110 (*Eclogue I*), 117 (*Eclogue II*), 116 (the verse is repeated eight times in *Eclogue III*). For *Eclogue IV* and *Delia*, see Walsh, *Poems on Several Occasions*, in *The Works of William Walsh, Esq.; In Prose and Verse* (London: E. Curll, 1736), 71, 81, 82, 85, 84.

110. This pseudonymous poem is reprinted in *Kissing the Rod: An Anthology of Seventeenth-Century Women's Verse*, ed. Germaine Greer, Susan Hastings, Jeslyn Medoff, and Melinda Sansone (London: Virago, 1988), 204.

111. This poem is reprinted in ibid., 250. Behn wrote under the name of "Lysidas" and in 1688 published a volume entitled *Lycidus* that one of her editors calls *Lycidas* (see 242, 269, 454).

112. Elizabeth Thomas, "*The Dream. An Epistle to Mr.* Dryden," in *Kissing the Rod*, ed. Greer, 436.

113. Ibid., 437.

114. Lady Sarah Piers, "To My Much Esteemed Friend on Her Play Call'd Fatal-Friendship," in ibid., 448, 449.

115. Ibid., 447.

116. "Philo-philippa," "To the Excellent *Orinda*," in ibid., 205, 206.

117. Ibid., 208.

118. Paul West, *Sporting with Amaryllis* (Woodstock, NY: Overlook Press, 1996), 137.

119. See West, ibid., and Peter Ackroyd, *Milton in America* (New York: Doubleday and London: Sinclair-Stevenson, 1996). Blake's *The Marriage of Heaven and Hell* and especially *Milton* are relevant here.

120. Parker, *Milton's Contemporary Reputation*, 47–48.

121. James Grantham Turner, "The Poetics of Engagement," in *Politics, Poetics, and Hermeneutics in Milton's Prose*, ed. David Loewenstein and James Grantham Turner (Cambridge and New York: Cambridge University Press, 1990), 259, 266–67. See also Lucy Newlyn, *"Paradise Lost" and the Romantic Reader* (Oxford: Clarendon Press, 1993), 92–93 and Nancy Armstrong and Leonard Tennenhouse, *The Imaginary Puritan: Literature, Intellectual Labor, and the Origins of Personal Life* (Berkeley, Los Angeles, and Oxford: University of California Press, 1992), 9–10. Armstrong and Tennenhouse resist the tendency to translate contradictions in *Paradise Lost* into contradictions within the personality of the author when, from their point of view, the contradictions are actually an aspect of Milton's culture inscribed within his poetry. In her plenary address at the Eighth International Milton Symposium, Grenoble, France, June 11, 2005, entitled "Why Is There No Rights Talk in Milton's Poetry?" Annabel Patterson argues, on the contrary, that Milton spent a lifetime resisting efforts to contaminate his poetry by reading it in terms of his prose writings.

122. That Jauss's theorizing eventually impacts upon *Paradise Lost* in a way that corroborates some of my own readings is evident in *Question and Answer*, tr. Hays, 101–05.

123. Sensabaugh, *That Grand Whig Milton*, 124.

124. Lindenbaum, "Rematerializing Milton," 11.

125. Fenton, "Life," in *Paradise Lost* (see note 71), xxvii (my italics).

126. Shawcross, *John Milton*, 93.

127. See anon., *An Answer to a Book, Intituled, the Doctrine and Discipline of Divorce* (London: G.M., 1644), 31; anon., *The Censure of the Rota upon Mr Miltons Book, Entituled, the Ready and Easie Way* (London: Paul Giddy, 1660), 6; and William Prynne, *A True and Perfect Narrative of What Was Done* (London: n.p., 1659), 50.

128. See anon., *An Answer to a Book*, F2v; James Howell (1655), in Parker, *Milton's Contemporary Reputation*, 92; and William Prynne, *Twelve Considerable Serious Questions Touching Church Government; Sadly Propounded* (London: I.D., 1644), 7.

129. Like most of his predecessors, Shawcross reports that *Eikonoklastes* and *Pro Populo Anglicano Defensio* were "burned publicly in France, again in England by order of King Charles II in 1660, and yet once more in Oxford on July 21, 1683"; see *John Milton*, 171.

130. See Roger L'Estrange, *No Blinde Guides, in Answer to a Seditious Pamphlet of J. Milton's* (London: Henry Brome, 1660), A2; Robert

South, "A Sermon Preached before King Charles the Second . . . Judges 19.30" (January 1662–63), in *Sermons Preached upon Several Occasions*, 7 vols. (Oxford: n.p., 1823), 3: 439; L'Estrange, *No Blinde Guides*, 2; Thomas Long, *Dr. Walker's True, Modest and Faithful Account of the Author of Eikon basilike* (London: R. Taylor, 1693), 2–3; Joseph Jane (1660), in Parker, *Milton's Contemporary Reputation*, 105; G. S., *Britains Triumph, for Her Imparallel'd Deliverance* (London: n.p., 1660), 15; and anon., *A Third Conference between O. Cromwell and Hugh Peters in Saint James's Park* (London: Thomas Rubb, 1660), 8; Long, *Dr. Walker's True, Modest and Faithful Account*, 2–3. Diana Trevino Benet makes the same point: "in early 1660, . . . willy-nilly he [Milton] became a member of the devil's party"; see Benet, "Hell, Satan, and the New Politician," in *Literary Milton: Text, Pretext, Context*, ed. Benet and Michael Lieb (Pittsburgh, PA: Duquesne University Press, 1994), 97. See also Sharon Achinstein, *Milton and the Revolutionary Reader* (Princeton, NJ: Princeton University Press, 1994), 195, 263.

131. See Nicholas von Maltzahn, "Laureate, Republican, Calvinist," 183.

132. Ibid., 189, 193, 194, 191, 185.

133. Beale as cited and quoted by Poole, "Two Early Readers of Milton," 82; see also 80–81.

134. For these comments by Beale and Hacket, see, respectively, Poole, "Two Early Readers of Milton," 82, 90; cf. Nicolas von Maltzahn, "The First Reception of *Paradise Lost* (1667)," *Review of English Studies*, n. s. 47, 188 (November 1996): 495, 497; and Levi, *Eden Renewed*, 237. Satan's blasphemies, as Beale understands them, are considered by Poole, "Two Early Readers of Milton," 76–88.

135. Gordon Campbell, Thomas N. Corns, John K. Hale, David I. Holmes, and Fiona Tweedie, "The Provenance of *De Doctrina Christiana*," *Milton Quarterly* 31, 3 (October 1997): 69, 80, 75, 79, 101.

136. *Poor Robin. 1666. An Almanack after a New Fashion* (London: Printed for the Company of Stationers, 1666). In *Poor Robin, 1671*, on the verso of the title page, an author's name finally appears: William Winstanley. The phrase "mock-Saints" appears in *Poor Robin, 1668* in "An Advertisement."

137. See both *Poor Robin. 1666*, "A Discourse of the Heavens," and *Poor Robin, 1669*, "The Contents of the Almanack."

138. See *Poor Robin, 1667*, A4. In *Poor Robin, 1676*, "Blind Milton" appears in connection with November 10 (in reference to Milton's possible death date?). After 1677, Milton's name disappears from *Poor Robin*, although he should probably be comprehended in the reference to "Smectymnus [*sic*]" on November 8 in *Poor Robin, 1688*.

139. Richardson, "The Life of the Author," in *Explanatory Notes and Remarks*, lxxxix.

140. What is at work in these early receptions is a process given astute explanation by Lucy Newlyn for whom Milton "is constructed by the cultural needs of his readers, being invoked or named by them, frequently in a kind of symbolic shorthand for the concepts with which he comes to be associated"; see *"Paradise Lost" and the Romantic Reader*, 24. For this reason, the key terms from various phases of Milton criticism may speak volumes even as some of the terms, remaining constant, change their valuation.

141. For Thomas Yalden's verses on Milton (1698?), see Good, *Studies in the Milton Tradition*, 59. On Milton *"evidencing* that *Devils may indue Humane Shapes,"* see L'Estrange, *No Blinde Guides*, A2, and also Masson, *The Life of John Milton*, 5:690. On Milton's contemporary reputation as a Satanic figure, see ibid., 6:636.

142. Ackroyd, *Milton in America*, 10, and see also 3, 58–59, 115.

143. John Toland, "The Life of John Milton," in *The Early Lives of Mieton*, ed. Helen Darbishire (1932; rpt. London: Constable, 1965), 180.

144. Von Maltzahn, "The First Reception of *Paradise Lost*," 487.

145. The Hobart letters are reprinted by James M. Rosenheim, "An Early Appreciation of *Paradise Lost*," *Modern Philology* 75, 3 (February 1978): 280–82. Original spellings (however eccentric) are retained throughout. Page references are given parenthetically within the text of the essay.

146. Hobart, ibid., 281–82.

147. Ibid., 281.

148. Eagleton, *Criticism and Ideology: A Study in Marxist Literary Theory* (1976; rpt. London: Verso, 1978), 56.

149. See Newlyn, *"Paradise Lost" and the Romantic Reader*, 33.

150. Masson states the case exactly: for all the confusions and uncertainties surrounding the early reported receptions, they nevertheless allow us "a glimpse of the real facts"; see *The Life of John Milton*, 6:631.

151. Von Maltzahn, "The First Reception of *Paradise Lost*," 490, 491–92.

152. Ibid., 493.

153. John Dennis as quoted in *Milton: The Critical Heritage*, ed. John T. Shawcross (London: Routledge and Kegan Paul, 1970), 134.

154. See John Norris, *Poems and Discourses Occasionally Written* (London: J. Harefinch, 1684), 2, 3.

155. For an abridged reception history of *Paradise Regain'd*, with an emphasis on that poem's fortunes in the eighteenth and early nineteenth centuries, see Joseph Wittreich, *Angel of Apocalypse: Blake's Idea of Milton* (Madison: University of Wisconsin Press, 1975), 103–08.

156. Thomas Ellwood, "Epitaph on Milton" (1675?), in *Milton: The Critical Heritage*, ed. Shawcross, 87.

157. Masson (quoting Phillips), in *The Life of John Milton*, 5:635–36.

158. Ellwood, "Epitaph on Milton," in *Milton: The Critical Heritage*, ed. Shawcross, 86.

159. Robert Graves (quoting Waller), in *Wife to Mr. Milton: The Story of Marie Powell* (1944; rpt. New York: Noonday, 1962), 364–65.

160. Samuel Johnson, "Milton," in *The Oxford Authors: Samuel Johnson*, ed. Donald Greene (Oxford and New York: Oxford University Press, 1984), 711.

161. Kevin Sharpe and Steven Zwicker, "Politics of Discourse: Introduction," in *Politics of Discourse: The Literature and History of Seventeenth-Century England*, ed. Sharpe and Zwicker (Berkeley and Los Angles: University of California Press, 1987), 2–3.

162. As reported by Levi, *Eden Renewed*, 194–95.

163. Newlyn, *"Paradise Lost" and the Romantic Reader*, 103; see also Benet who argues, in a sweeping critique, that without ever "endangering himself or marring the integrity of his poem, Milton deflates and in some respects indicts seventeenth century politics and politicians"; see Benet, "Hell, Satan, and the New Politician," in *Literary Milton*, ed. Benet and Lieb, 113.

164. Levi, *Eden Renewed*, 239, 261.

165. See Mary Ann Radzinowicz, " 'In those days there was no king of Israel': Milton's Politics and Biblical Narrative," *The Yearbook of English Studies*, 21 (1991): 242–52, and then (on *Paradise Lost*) Christopher Hill, *Milton and the English Revolution* (New York: Viking, 1978), 390–94; (on *Paradise Regain'd*) Hill again, *The Experience of Defeat: Milton and Some Contemporaries* (New York: Viking, 1984), 297–303, and (on *Samson Agonistes*), Joseph Wittreich, *Interpreting "Samson Agonistes"* (Princeton, NJ: Princeton University Press, 1986), 202–22.

166. See the title of the poem by Barrow, plus lines 1–2 and 39; see also Marvell's poem, lines 1, 2, 7, 23, 42, 44, 53.

167. The attribution of *The Transproser Rehears'd* to Samuel Butler rather than Richard Leigh was proposed initially by Paul Bunyan Anderson, "Anonymous Critic of Milton: Richard Leigh? Or Samuel Butler?" *Studies in Philology* 44, 3 (July 1947): 504–18, and has been argued lately by Nicholas von Maltzahn, "Samuel Butler's Milton," *Studies in Philology* 92, 4 (Fall 1995): 482–95.

168. Hill, "Milton and Marvell," in *Approaches to Marvell*, ed. Patrides, 9.

169. Dating from 1686–87, Benthem's comments are reported by Hill, *Milton and the English Revolution*, 391–92.

170. F[rancis] C[raddock], "To Mr. John Milton, on His Poem Entitled Paradise Lost" (1680), in *Milton: The Critical Heritage*, ed. Shawcross, 89.

171. Hill, "Milton and Marvell," in *Approaches to Marvell*, ed. Patrides, 17. Latin implies orthodoxy and thus is a way of tricking the censors, as is explained in a dedicatory note in which it is also acknowledged that writing in Latin is "especially . . . approved by most grave Censors,

to be herein most orthodox"; see Goldsmith in Hugo Grotius, *Baptizatorum Puerorum Institutio* (1647; rpt. London: n.p., 1668), A2.

172. Anon., "An Answer to Some Criticisms on Milton's Paradise Lost" from *The London Chronicle* (April 28, 1764), in *Appendix to the Memoirs of Thomas Hollis*, 623.

173. For the Earl of Roscommon's lines on Book 6 of *Paradise Lost*, dating from 1685, see *Milton: The Critical Heritage*, ed. Shawcross, 92–93.

174. Newlyn (quoting Edward Young), *"Paradise Lost" and the Romantic Reader*, 193.

175. John Spencer, *A Discourse . . . to Which Is Added . . . Vulgar Prophecies*, 2.

176. I borrow the phrase from Francis Peck, who is quoting Bishop Atterbury, in *New Memoirs*, 62.

177. Stephen Greenblatt, *Shakespearean Negotiations: The Circulation of Social Energy in Renaissance England* (Berkeley and Los Angeles: University of California Press, 1988), 65. For a discussion of how Marvell removes subversive readings of *Paradise Lost* from public discussion of Milton, see Achinstein, "Milton's Spectre in the Restoration," 1–29, as well as *Milton and the Revolutionary Reader*, esp. 212–13.

178. Greenblatt, *Shakespearean Negotiations*, 65, and Newlyn, *"Paradise Lost" and the Romantic Reader*, 261.

179. Peter Conrad, *The History of English Literature: One Indivisible, Unending Book* (Philadelphia: University of Pennsylvania Press, 1985), 244 (see also 280).

180. See Nicholas Boileau-Despréaux, *The Art of Poetry*, tr. William Soames, altered J. Dryden (London, 1683), 40–41; and cf. Harold Bloom, *Ruin the Sacred Truths: Poetry and Belief from the Bible to the Present* (Cambridge, MA.: Harvard University Press, 1989), 91–113.

181. Patterson, *Reading between the Lines*, 256, 275.

182. Edward Le Comte, *Poets' Riddles: Essays in Seventeenth-Century Explication* (Port Washington, NY and London: Kennikat Press, 1975), 146.

183. Hume, *The Poetical Works of John Milton*, [345 (first pagination)]. Similar "Tables" in later editions greatly multiply the number of similes in which Adam is implicated. The 1695 edition gives attention only to this one.

184. Hill, "Milton and Marvell," in *Approaches to Marvell*, ed. Patrides, 17.

185. Richardson, "The Life of the Author," in *Explanatory Notes and Remarks*, cxxiv. The Richardsons are not the only—and certainly not the first—critics to notice contradictions in *Paradise Lost*; see *Explanatory Notes and Remarks*, 20; see also Dennis, who likewise remarks upon inconsistencies and contradictions deriving from the

poem's Christian machinery, in "Letters on Milton and Wycherley (1721–22)," in *Critical Works*, ed. Hooker, 2:228. In *Paradise Lost*, Milton uses contradiction to develop a poetics of interrogation and disclosure. See again Kolbrener, *Milton's Warring Angels*, 107–132, in which it is argued that *Paradise Lost* captures the chief contradictions (philosophical, political, and theological) of early modern—and modern—culture. Also, see esp. Peter C. Herman, *Destabilizing Milton: "Paradise Lost" and the Poetics of Incertitude* (New York and Basingstoke, England: Palgrave Macmillan, 2005).

186. See Pamela R. Barnett who argues that in Haak's translations no allowance is made "for the internally contradictory"; see *Theodore Haak, F.R.S. (1605–1690): The First German Translation of "Paradise Lost"* (Hague: Mouton, 1962), 183.

187. Richardson, *Explanatory Notes and Remarks*, 291.

188. I am quoting from Armstrong and Tennenhouse, *The Imaginary Puritan*, 115; see also Patterson, *Censorship and Interpretation: The Conditions of Writing and Reading in Early Modern Europe* (Madison: University of Wisconsin Press, 1984), and Hill, "Censorship and English Literature," in *The Collected Essays of Christopher Hill. Volume I: Writing and Revolution in Seventeenth-Century England* (Amherst: University of Massachusetts Press, 1985), 32–71.

189. Roger L'Estrange, *A Common-Place-Book out of the Rehearsal Transpros'd* (London: Henry Brome, 1673), 36.

190. Peck, *New Memoirs*, 83–84.

191. Shawcross, ed., *Milton*, 146.

192. Newton, ed. *Paradise Lost*, 1:406; 2:384.

193. Anon., "An Answer to Some Criticisms" from *The London Chronicle*, in *Appendix to the Memoirs*, 624.

194. Ibid., 625.

195. Newton, ed., *Paradise Lost*, 2:397.

196. John Toland, "The Life of John Milton (1698)," in *Early Lives*, ed. Darbishire, 180.

197. See "An Answer to Some Criticisms" from *The London Chronicle*, in *Appendix to the Memoirs*, 621, 623 and Newlyn, *"Paradise Lost" and the Romantic Reader*, 93. Merritt Y. Hughes resists the "attribution of any topical political intention to Milton's epic plan"; see *Ten Perspectives on Milton* (New Haven and London: Yale University Press, 1965), 173. For contrary opinions, see G. Wilson Knight, *Chariot of Wrath: The Message of John Milton to Democracy at War* (London: Faber and Faber, 1942), 137 and especially Sensabaugh, *That Grand Whig Milton*, 22–23, 173, 201.

198. For Peck's various comments, see *New Memoirs*, 59–60, 85, 89, 272–74, 276–78.

199. Newton, ed. *"Paradise Regain'd" . . . to Which Is Added "Samson Agonistes"* (London: W. Strahan, J. F., and C. Rivington, 1785), 227–28, 229, 249, 256.

200. Ibid., 256, 257, 302, 303.

201. Hume, ed., *Poetical Works,* 316 (second pagination).

202. Cavell, *Must We Mean What We Say? A Book of Essays* (New York: Charles Scribner's Sons, 1969), 350.

203. Dollimore, "Introduction," *Political Shakespeare,* ed. Dollimore and Sinfield, 9.

204. See "The Preface," in *Poems on Affairs of State: From the Time of Oliver Cromwell, to the Abdication of K. James the Second* (London: S. N., 1697), [A4v].

CHAPTER 3   QUESTIONING AND CRITIQUE: THE FORMATION OF A NEW MILTON CRITICISM

1. The epigraphs for this chapter are from Yehuda Amichai, "The Shore of Ashkelon," in *A Life of Poetry 1948–1994,* tr. Benjamin and Barbara Harshav (1994; rpt. New York: Harper Perennial, 1995), 411 and Robert Scanlan, "Director's Note," *Milton's "Samson Agonistes,"* 92nd Street Y, April 21, 2003, program insert. While this chapter was written independent of the concluding chapter of Peter C. Herman's *Destabilizing Milton: "Paradise Lost" and the Poetics of Incertitude* (New York and Basingstoke, England: Palgrave Macmillan, 2005), 155–76, that chapter may be read as both complementary and supplementary to my own. Herman's entire book shimmers with new insight.

2. See Adam Engel, "*Samson Agonistes* (Confession of a Terrorist/Martyr)," from the web magazine *Counterpunch,* ed. Alexander Cockburn and Jeffrey St. Clair, November 2, 2002: <http://www.Counterpunch.com>; Christopher Shea, *The Boston Globe,* Sunday, November 3, 2002, D5 and D. D. Guttenplan, *The New York Times,* Saturday, December 28, 2002, B9. This article carries the caption, "Samson the Suicide Bomber," coupled with this remark: "More than 300 years after his death, John Milton is being accused of encouraging terrorism." In another piece, Milton is credited with having created a language for warfare; see Geoffrey Nunberg, "War-Speak Worthy of Milton and Chuck Norris," *The New York Times,* Sunday, April 6, 2003, WK 4. In yet another, its author worries over whether the borrowings of *Paradise Lost* are coming from Satan's rhetoric, see John Tierney, "Political Points: 'Paradise Lost' for the Modern Day," *The New York Times,* Sunday, August 1, 2004, A16. And in still another, the Elder Brother's words on evil (see *A Mask,* 593–99) are juxtaposed with those of George Bush on 9/11, even as Milton's portrait here appears with the legend, "Milton: A Man for Our Time" (see Daniel Henninger, "Wonder Land: 'Know Ye Not Me?': The Face of Evil Is Seen, Defeated," *The Wall Street Journal,* Friday, April 18, 2003, Opinion.

3. I borrow this phrase from Norman N. Holland, *5 Readers Reading* (New Haven and London: Yale University Press, 1975), 1 (see chapter subtitle).

4. Sharon Achinstein, "*Samson Agonistes*," in *A Companion to Milton*, ed. Thomas N. Corns (Oxford and Malden, MA: Blackwell, 2001), 414.

5. Peter Bayne, *The Chief Actors in the Puritan Revolution* (London: n.p., 1878), 345.

6. Michael Mendle (reviewing David Loewenstein, *Representing Revolution in Milton and his Contemporaries*), in *Renaissance Quarterly* 55, 2 (Summer 2002): 778. Reviewing Victoria Kahn's *Wayward Contracts* in *Renaissance Quarterly* 58, 3 (Fall 2005), Mendle continues his theme, this time complaining that Kahn never openly acknowledges that "Samson's destruction of innocent and 'guilty' alike, as well as himself, is indistinguishable from that of a suicide bomber" (1054).

7. John Carey, "A Work in Praise of Terrorism? September 11 and *Samson Agonistes*," *Times Literary Supplement*, Friday, September 6, 2002, 15. Cf. Stanley Fish, "Postmodern Warfare: The Ignorance of Our Warrior Intellectuals," *Harper's Magazine* 305 (July 2002): 33–40, and also by Fish, "Can Postmodernists Condemn Terrorism? Don't Blame Relativism," *The Responsive Community* 12 (Summer 2002): 27–31. Three recent essays by (1) Stanley Fish, "Why Milton Matters; or, against Historicism," (2) Barbara Lewalski, "Why Milton Matters," and (3) Joseph Wittreich, "Why Milton Matters," should be read within this context, each of those essays appearing in *Milton Studies* 44 (2005): 1–12, 13–21, 22–39. For a provocative response to both Carey and Fish, see Feisal G. Mohamed, "Confronting Religious Violence: Milton's *Samson Agonistes*," *PMLA: Publications of the Modern Language Association* 120, 2 (March 2005): 327–40. Cf. The "Forum" responses of Joseph Wittreich and Peter C. Herman, ibid., 120, 5 (October 2005): 1641–43, and Mohamed's reply, see ibid., 1643–44.

8. Walter Raleigh, *Milton* (1900; rpt. New York: Benjamin Bloom, 1967), 28 (and also 29).

9. H. M. Percival, ed., *Milton's "Samson Agonistes"* (London: Macmillan, 1890), xix.

10. See Ann Phillips, ed., *Samson Agonistes* (London and Cambridge: University Tutorial Press, 1974), 24, and more recently, Janel Mueller, "The Figure and the Ground: Samson as a Hero of London Nonconformity, 1662–1667," in *Milton and the Terms of Liberty*, ed. Graham Parry and Joad Raymond (Cambridge and Rochester, NY: D. S. Brewer, 2002), 146.

11. For Margaret Thatcher's op-ed piece, see "Advice to a Superpower," *The New York Times*, Monday, February 11, 2002, A27. For the supposed Samson allusion, see *Areopagitica* (YP, 2:557–58), and for Milton's injunction, see *The Doctrine and Discipline of Divorce* (YP, 2:232).

12. A. Wilson Verity, ed., quoting another commentator, in *Milton's "Samson Agonistes"* (Cambridge: Cambridge University Press, 1892), xxvii; Edmund K. Chambers, ed., *Samson Agonistes* (London: Blackie and Son, 1897), 19; E. H. Blakeney, ed., *Samson Agonistes* (Edinburgh and London: Blackwood's English Classics, 1902), xxviii (cf. xxix); Rose Macaulay, *Milton* (1935; rpt. New York: Collier, 1962), 117, and I. P. Fleming, ed., *Samson Agonistes* (London: Longmans and Co., 1876), 34, 35.

13. Adonis ('Ali Ahmad Sa'id), "Poetry and Apoetical Culture," tr. Esther Allen, in *The Pages of Day and Night*, tr. Samuel Hazo (1994; rpt. Evanston, IL: Northwestern University Press, 2000), 107, 106. In his important commentary, *The Book of Judges*, tr. P. H. Steenstra (New york: Clarles Scribner, 1872), Paulus Cassel is supremely sensitive to the force of that tradition even as he complains of "the seventeenth and eighteen century irreverence [toward Samson] too often called criticism, and [of] that frivolous insipidity . . . considered free inquiry. Aesthetic vapidness," Cassel laments, continues "to nestle in the exegesis of the Old Testament" as is strikingly evident in the Old Testament dialogues of Johann Gottfried Herder (225). On Herder, see note 34.

14. Margaret Kean, "Paradise Regained," in *A Companion to Milton*, ed. Corns, 431, 429.

15. John Calvin, *A Harmonie vpon the Three Evangelistes*, tr. Eusibius Pagit (London: Thomas Dawson, 1610), 131.

16. See ibid., 131; cf. Augustin Marlorat, *A Catholike and Ecclesiasticall Exposition of the Holy Gospel after S. Mathewe* (London: Thomas Marshe, 1570), f. 62.

17. Anon., *Christ's Temptations: Real Facts* (London: n.p., 1762), 37, 48. See also notes 35–38.

18. Joachim of Fiore, as quoted by Marjorie Reeves, *The Influence of Prophecy in the Later Middle Ages: A Study of Joachimism* (Oxford: Clarendon Press, 1969), 292.

19. I have elaborated these strategies in my book, *Shifting Contexts: Reinterpreting "Samson Agonistes"* (Pittsburgh, PA: Duquesne University Press, 2002), esp. 145–91.

20. I borrow this phrase from Walter Benjamin, the chapter entitled "Critique of Violence," in *Reflections: Essays, Aphorisms, Autobiographical Writings*, tr. Edmund Jephcott (New York: Schocken Books, 1986), 279.

21. Terry Eagleton, *Sweet Violence: The Idea of the Tragic* (Oxford and Malden, MA.: Blackwell, 2003), 118. Milton has the precedent of Peter Martyr for using of his own accord to signify of his own free will with Martyr arguing that Samson's parents made vows "of their own fre will" and follow them "of their owne accorde"; see *Most Fruitfull & Learned Comentaries of Doctor Peter Martir Vermil Florentine* (London: John Day, 1564), f203v.

22. Thomas Keightley, *An Account of the Life, Opinions, and Writings of John Milton, with an Introduction to "Paradise Lost"* (London: Chapman and Hall, 1855), 322.

23. John Upton as cited by Francis Blackburne, "An Answer to Some Criticisms on Milton's Paradise Lost," *Memoirs of Thomas Hollis*, 2 vols. (London: n.p., 1780), 2:624. For recent scrutiny of Milton's attitudes toward divine motions and commissions, see Abraham Stoll, "Milton Stages Cherbury: Revelation and Polytheism in *Samson Agonistes*," in *Altering Eyes: New Perspectives on "Samson Agonistes,"* ed. Mark R. Kelley and Joseph Wittreich (Newark: University of Delaware Press and London: Associated University Presses, 2002), 281–306 and Joseph Wittreich, *Shifting Contexts: Reinterpreting "Samson Agonistes"* (Pittsburgh, PA: Duquense University Press, 2002), esp. 268–78.

24. Andrew Marvell, "On Mr Milton's *Paradise Lost*," in *The Poems of Andrew Marvell*, ed. Nigel Smith (London: Pearson Longman, 2003), 184 (ll. 43–44).

25. M. G. Lord, "The Fourth Target," *The New York Times Book Review*, Sunday, September 8, 2002, 12.

26. In this instance, I quote from the translation of *De Doctrina Christiana* by Charles R. Sumner, CM, 14:11; cf. YP, 6:122. In this very insistence, Milton may be said to have incited, even as he continues to fuel, the controversy over the authorship of *De Doctrina Christiana*.

27. Heymann Steinthal, "The Legend of Samson," in Ignaz Goldziher, *Mythology Among the Hebrews and Its Historical Development*, tr. Russell Martineau (London: Longman and Green, 1877), 402, 446. In *The Story of Samson and Its Place in the Religious Development of Mankind* (Chicago: Open Court, and London: Kegan Paul, 1907), Paul Carus notes that Steinthal resists the idea (as developed by Gustav Roskoff) that Samson is a hero of prayer, Roskoff's chief evidence for which is that "the spirit of Yahweh comes over Samson and gives him heroic strength to accomplish his deeds" (5). Cf. Roskoff, *Die Simsonssage nach ihren Entstehung, Form und Bedeutung, und der Heracles Mythus* (Leipsig: E. Bredt, 1860), 45. On Milton's shifting idea of prayer, see Sharon Achinstein, *"Samson Agonistes,"* in *A Companion to Milton*, ed. Corns, 415–16.

28. As remarked by John Penn, *Critical, Poetical and Dramatic Works*, 2 vols. (London: Hatchard, 1796, 1798), 2:260–61. The Richard Westall illustration is reproduced by William Hayley, *The Poetical Works of John Milton. With a Life of the Author*, 3 vols. (London: W. Bulmer, 1797), 3: (opposite) 67. See fig. 3. 14.

29. Penn, *Critical, Poetical, and Dramatic Works*, 2:222.

30. John Adams, "A Defence of the Constitutions of Government of the United States of America (1787–1788)," in *The American Enlightenment: The Shaping of the American Experiment and a Free Society*, ed. Adrienne Koch (New York: G. Braziller, 1965), 258.

31. See Abram Leon Sachar, *A History of the Jews*, 5th ed. (New York: Knopf, 1965), 30; cf. *The New Testament Study Bible: Revelation*, ed. Ralph W. Harris (Springfield, Mo.: Complete Biblical Library, 1990), 115.

32. J. T., *The Spirit of Judgment: Readings and Addresses* (London: Stow Hill Bible and Tract Depot, 1932), 124, 125.

33. Cassel, *The Book of Judges*, tr. Streenstra, 224.

34. Johann Gottfried Herder, *Oriental Dialogues: Containing the Conversations of Eugenius and Alciphron on the . . . Sacred Poetry of the Hebrews* (London: n.p., 1801), 322.

35. H. Cates, *Lent Sermons: Or, An Inquiry into the Nature and Designs of Christ's Temptation in the Wilderness* (London: n.p., 1813), 125.

36. See, e. g., Joseph Hall, *Contemplations upon the Remarkable Passages on the Life of the Holy Jesus* (London: E. Flesher, 1679), 64.

37. See Jeremy Taylor, *The Life of Our Blessed Saviour Jesus Christ, with Considerations and Discourses* (Exeter, NH: Henry Ranlet, 1794), 67.

38. Hugh Farmer, *An Inquiry into the Nature and Design of Christ's Temptation in the Wilderness* (London: J. Buckland, 1761), 36; cf. 80. See, too, Hugh Farmer, *An Appendix to an Inquiry into the Nature and Design of Christ's Temptation in the Wilderness* (London: J. Buckland and J. Waugh, 1765) for a discussion of the whole temptation sequence as "a *spiritual* and mental transaction" (41). See also Thomas Belsham, *A Summary View of the Evidence and Practical Importance of the Christian Revelation* (London: R. Taylor, 1807), for whom "[t]he temptation of Christ was unquestionably a visionary scene" (14). See, too, Thomas Dixon, *The Sovereignty of the Divine Administration, Vindicated; or, a Rational Account of Our Blessed Saviour's Remarkable Temptation in the Wilderness* (London: Becket and de Hondt, 1766), 13, 18, 19.

39. Cates, *Lent Sermons*, 137; but surely Milton is similarly credited by William Blake in the poem to which Milton gives his name as well as the very conception of a visionary drama.

40. The phrase and sentiment belong to A. J. Grieve, ed., *Samson Agonistes* (London: J. M. Dent [1904]), vi.

41. Chambers, ed., *Samson Agonistes*, 16.

42. Grieve, ed., *Samson Agonistes*, v. If, as Annabel Patterson reports in *Reading between the Lines* (Madison: University of Wisconsin Press, 1993), *Paradise Lost* is "a poem dangerous to the Restoration settlement" (252), then how much more so *Samson Agonistes*. How essential, too, that Milton, in his Preface to this tragedy, should establish signals concerning how to read this poem. Again, Patterson comments importantly in *Censorship and Interpretation: The Conditions of Writing and Reading in Early Modern England* (Madison and London: University of Wisconsin Press, 1984), 47–48; and, through suggestive indexing, so too does Kenneth Burke (see notes 54 and 165). However, Milton's subterfuges were understood early in

the twentieth century, when it was argued that he focuses on aesthetic issues such as "Tragedy, Chorus, and the Unities . . . in order that the real daring of his design might escape detection and not endanger publication." A. J. Wyatt and A. J. F. Collins, eds., *Milton: "Samson Agonistes"* (London: W. B. Clive, 1911), 14.

43. J. A. K. Thomson, *The Classical Background of English Literature* (London: George Allen and Unwin, 1948), 197.

44. Elizabeth Sauer, "Milton and Dryden on the Restoration Stage," in *Faultlines and Controversies in the Study of Seventeenth-Century English Literature*, ed. Claude J. Summers and Ted-Larry Pebworth (Columbia and London: University of Missouri Press, 2002), 96.

45. See Dorothy Brooke, *Pilgrims Were They All: Studies in Religious Adventure in the Fourth Century of Our Era* (London: Faber and Faber, 1937), 304, 325.

46. So John Rogers argues in "Delivering Redemption in *Samson Agonistes*," in *Altering Eyes*, ed. Kelley and Wittreich, 83.

47. On Gregory Nazianzen and autobiography, see Georg Misch, *A History of Autobiography in Antiquity*, 2 vols. (London: Routledge and Kegan Paul, 1949–50), 2:600–24, and for a sorting and summary of his other writings, see Berthold Altaner, *Patrology*, 5th ed., tr. Hilda C. Graef (Freiburg: Herder, and Edinburgh and London: Nelson, 1960), 345–51.

48. See Gregory Nazianzen's phrase as quoted by Henry Wace and Philip Schaff, ed., "Introduction to Oration XLIII. The Panegyric on S. Basil," in *Select Orations of Saint Gregory Nazianzen*, tr. Charles Gordon Browne and James Edward Swallow, in *A Select Library of Nicene and Post-Nicene Fathers of the Christian Church . . . . Gregory of Nazianzum: Select Orations, and Letters*, 2nd series, 14 vols., ed. Wace and Schaff (Oxford: James Parker, and New York: Christian Literature Co., 1890–1900), 7:395. This volume is hereafter cited as *A Select Library*.

49. Gregory Nazianzen, "Oration III. Panegyric on His Brother S. Cæsarius" and "Oration XVIII. Funeral Oration on His Father," in *A Select Library*, 7:230 and then 7:260, 263. Also see "To his own Verses," *Gregory of Nanzianzum: Autobiographical Poems*, tr. and ed. Caroline White (Cambridge and New York: Cambridge University Press, 1996), 15, 17, and both "Oration 10 . . . on Himself" and "Oration 14 . . . On Love for the Poor," in *Gregory of Nazianzus: Select Orations*, tr. Martha Vinson (Washington, DC: Catholic University of America Press, 2003), 26, 48–49, 67, 41, respectively (hereafter cited as *Select Orations*). See also Gregory's "Oration XLIII. Funeral Oration on the Great St. Basil," in *A Select Library*, 7:408.

50. Gregory Nazianzen, "On His Brother St. Cæsarius," in *Funeral Orations by St. Gregory Nazianzen and St. Ambrose*, tr. Leo P. McCauley (Washington, DC: Catholic University of America, 1953), 14.

51. Hugh Stuart Boyd, "Preface to *Tributes to the Dead*," *The Fathers Not Papists: Or, Six Discourses by the Most Eloquent Fathers of the Church*, tr. and ed. Boyd (London: n.p., 1834), xxxiv.

52. See Gregory Nazianzen, "Oration XLII. The Last Farewell in the Presence of One Hundred and Fifty Bishops," in *A Select Library*, 7:387.

53. Verity, ed., *Milton's "Samson Agonistes,"* 163.

54. Kenneth Burke, "The Range of Rhetoric," in *A Grammar of Motives and a Rhetoric of Motives* (Cleveland and New York: Meridian Books, 1962), 552; cf. 866.

55. Verity, ed., *Milton's "Samson Agonistes,"* 63.

56. Gregory Nazianzen, "The Exordium of an Oration of St. Gregory against the Arians," in *Select Passages of the Writings of St. Chrysostom, St. Gregory Nazianzen, and St. Basil*, 3rd ed., tr. Hugh Stuart Boyd (London: John Hatchard, 1813), 181.

57. See both Merritt Y. Hughes, ed., *John Milton: Complete Poems and Major Prose* (New York: Odyssey Press, 1957), 550; and Robert J. Wickenheiser, ed., "Prose Preliminary to *Samson Agonistes*," YP, 8:135. See also G. Gregory Smith, ed., *Elizabethan Critical Essays*, 2 vols. (1904, rpt. London and New York: Oxford University Press, 1964), who thinks it a pretense—a "quasi-literary absurdity that the plays of Buchanan and the *Christus* ascribed to Nazianzen were written 'dialogue-wise' for the closet," 1:xxx; cf. 1:365–66.

58. See Francis Peck, *New Memoirs of the Life and Poetical Works of Mr. John Milton* (London: n.p., 1740), 86; Timothy J. Burbery, "Intended for the Stage?: *Samson Agonistes* in Performance," *Milton Quarterly* 38, 1 (March 2004): 35–49; H. Neville Davies, "*Samson Agonistes* in Performance: Musical Addenda," *Milton Quarterly* 39, 3 (October 2005): 180–81; and Bill Goldstein, "Samson Regained: A Play in Perpetual World Premiere," in *Uncircumscribed Mind: Reading Milton Deeply*, ed. Charles Durham and Kristin Pruitt McColgan, forthcoming in 2007.

59. The theorizing is by Lucy Newlyn, *"Paradise Lost" and the Romantic Reader* (Oxford: Clarendon Press, 1993), 33; the application is my own.

60. See Brinley Roderick Rees, *Aristotle's Theory and Milton's Practice: "Samson Agonistes"* (Birmingham, England: University of Birmingham, 1971), 9.

61. See "Gregory Nazianzen's First Invective against Julian the Emperor," in *Julian the Emperor Containing Gregory Nazianzen's Two Invectives and Libanius's Monody, with Julian's Extant Theosophical Works*, tr. C. W. King (London: G. Bell, 1888), 78; cf. 79–80. See also "Gregory Nazianzen's Second Invective against Julian the Emperor," in ibid., 117–18; and, again, "Gregory Nazianzen's First Invective," in ibid., 80.

62. Balachandra Rajan, "Surprised by a Strange Language," in *Milton and the Climates of Reading*, ed. Elizabeth Sauer (Toronto, London, and Buffalo, NY: University of Toronto Press, 2006), 56.

63. See John R. Knott, Jr., *The Sword of the Spirit: Puritan Responses to the Bible* (Chicago and London: University of Chicago Press, 1980), 22. Gregory's own project, encouraging the lowly to be wise and a tipping of the hat to a fit audience, would have caught Milton's approving attention.

64. Gregory Nazianzen, "The Exordium. Of an Oration of St. Gregory against the Arians," in *The Fathers Not Papists*, tr. Boyd, 321; and see also Gregory's "Oration XXI. Against the Arians, and Concerning Himself," in *A Select Library*, 7:333.

65. See both "Gregory Nazianzen's First Invective against Julian," in *Julian the Emperor*, ed. King, 48 and Gregory, "Oration 14," in *Select Orations*, tr. Vinson, 42.

66. See "Gregory Nazianzen's Second Invective against Julian," in *Julian the Emperor*, ed. King, 116, 86 (cf. 113); "Gregory Nazianzen's First Oration against Julian," ibid., 31; and again Gregory's "Second Invective," ibid., 113. See also Gregory Nazianzen, *Five Theological Orations*, ed. Mason, 151.

67. See also Christopher Wordsworth, *The Holy Bible, in the Authorized Version*, 6 vols. (London, Oxford, and Cambridge: Rivingtons, 1875–76), 2:138.

68. Gregory Nazianzen, "Oration XXI. On . . . Athanasius," in *A Select Library* 7:278. It has been argued that saving some of the people "mak[es] Samson's action seem more defensible"; see John Coffey, "Pacifist, Quietist, or Patient Militant? John Milton and the Restoration," *Milton Studies* 42 (2002): 168. I argue that, on the contrary, it is Milton's God, not Samson, who, from this perspective, is more defensible.

69. See Gregory Nazianzen, "Oration XXI. On Athanasius," in *A Select Library*, 7:276 and "Gregory Nazianzen's Second Invective against Julian," in *Julian the Emperor*, ed. King, 116.

70. See Gregory Nazianzen, *Christos Paschon*, tr. Fishbone, 179. For the continuation of this dramatic tradition in Milton's century, see Hugo Grotius, *Tragoedia Sophompaneas Accesserunt, tragoedia ejus dem Christus patiens et sacia argumenti alia* (Amsterdam: Ioannem Ianssonium, 1627, 1635), and then *Christ's Passion. A Tragedy. With Annotations*, tr. George Sandys (London: John Legate, 1640), as well as "Out of Grotius his Tragedy of Christes sufferinges," tr. Richard Crashaw, in *The Poems English, Latin, and Greek of Richard Crashaw*, 2nd ed., ed. L. C. Martin (Oxford: Clarendon Press, 1957), 398–400.

71. Adonis ('Ali Ahmad Sa'id), "Poetry and Apoetical Culture," tr. Allen, in *The Pages of Day and Night*, tr. Hazo, 108.

72. Matthew Jordan, *Milton and Modernity: Politics, Masculinity, and "Paradise Lost"* (New York: Palgrave, 2001), 157.

73. See "Gregory Nazianzen's Second Invective against Julian," in *Julian the Emperor*, tr. King, 105.

74. Norman Mailer, *Why Are We at War?* (New York: Random House, 2003), 23. For Mailer on Samson, see ibid., 13.

75. See "Gregory Nazianzen's Second Invective against Julian," in *Julian the Emperor*, tr. King, 105 and Gibbon, *The Decline and Fall of the Roman Empire*, 4:63.

76. See Jean LeClerc, *The Lives of Clemens Alexandrinus, Eusebius Bishop of Caesarea, Gregory Nazianzen, and Prudentius the Christian Poet* (London: Richard Baldwin, 1696), 197, 201–02, 206–07, 214. and John Duncombe, ed., *Select Works of the Emperor Julian . . . with Notes*, 2 vols. (London: J. Nichols, 1784), 2:312–13.

77. Gregory Nazianzen, from the peroration to his "Oration to the People of Nazianzum," in *Select Passages*, tr. Boyd, 148, 150. As Smith and Wace report in *A Dictionary of Christian Biography*, Gregory is adamant: it is for Christ, not man, to wield the sword (2:749).

78. Gregory Nazianzen, "Oration XLII. The Last Farewell in the Presence of the One Hundred and Fifty Bishops," in *A Select Library*, 7:390.

79. Balachandra Rajan, "The Poetics of Heresy," in *Milton and the Climate of Reading*, ed. Sauer, 54.

80. Wace and Schaff, ed., "Prolegomena. Section I. The Life," in *A Select Library*, 7:196.

81. Gregory Nazianzen, "A Selection from the Letters: Correspondence with St. Basil," in *A Select Library*, 7:447.

82. Henry Peacham, "Of Poetry," in *Critical Essays of the Seventeenth Century*, 3 vols., ed. J. E. Spingarn (Bloomington: Indiana University Press, 1957), 1:118.

83. Gregory Nazianzen, "Oration XVI: On His Father's Silence," in *A Select Library*, 7:249.

84. Gregory Nazianzen, "Oration XLV: The Second Oration on Easter," in ibid., 7:425.

85. William Empson, *Milton's God*, rev. ed. (London: Chatto and Windus, 1965), 317–18.

86. As argued by Tobias Gregory, "In Defense of Empson: A Reassessment of *Milton's God*," in *Faultlines and Controversies*, ed. Summers and Pebworth, 81.

87. See Paul Carus, *The Story of Samson*, 134–35, especially the section entitled, "Why the Resurrection of Samson was Suppressed," 152–55 and cf. Heymann Steinthal, "The Legend of Samson," who also discusses the mutilation of the Samson story, in Ignác Goldziber, *Mythology among the Hebrews and Its Historical Development*, tr. Russell Martineau (New York: Cooper Square, 1969), 392–446.

88. Thomas De Quincey, from "Dr. Samuel Parr" (1831), in *The Romantics on Milton: Formal Essays and Critical Asides*, ed. Joseph

Wittreich (Cleveland and London: Press of Case Western Reserve University, 1970), 465.

89. For Kushner's comments, see "Reflections on an America Transformed," *The New York Times*, Sunday, September 8, 2002, 15.

90. Fish, *How Milton Works*, 117.

91. Marjorie Perloff quoting Bob Perelman, "The Marginalization of Poetry," in *21st-Century Modernism: The New Poetics* (London and Malden, Mass.: Blackwell, 2002), 42.

92. For this distinction, see Janel Mueller, "Contextualizing Milton's Nascent Republicanism," in *Of Poetry and Politics: New Essays on Milton and His World*, ed. P. G. Stanwood (Binghamton, NY: Medieval and Renaissance Texts and Studies, 1995), 264.

93. See F. Calvin Parker, "Formations Lesson for August 26: Samson," *Biblical Recorder*, August 3, 2001, 1. Parker cites the example of Keito Yoshida imprisoned as a traitor by the Japanese in the aftermath of Pearl Harbor, thereupon swearing vengeance, only to discover in prison that forgiveness is superior to the way of Samson and that vengeance is God's alone. The rhetoric of terrorism is already a feature of Milton criticism in the 1990s as both Noam Flinker and Jackie Di Salvo illustrate; see Flinker, "Pagan Holiday and National Conflict: A Philistine Reading of *Samson Agonistes*," *Milton Quarterly* 25, 4 (December 1991): 160, and Di Salvo as cited by Roy Flannagan, ed., *The Riverside Milton* (Boston and New York: Houghton and Mifflin, 1998), 795. Worries about Samson, if focused by 9/11, are in the air months before: see Eric Lewin Altschuler, Ansar Haroun, Bing Ho, and Amy Weimer, "Did Samson Have Antisocial Personality Disorder," *Archives of General Psychiatry* 58, 2 (February 2001): 202–03 and Cullen Murphy, "Second Opinions: History Winds up in the Waiting Room," *The Atlantic Monthly* (June 2001): unpaginated essay.

94. Arthur E. Barker, "Calm Regained through Passion Spent: The Conclusions of the Miltonic Effort," in *The Prison and the Pinnacle: Papers to Commemorate the Tercentenary of "Paradise Regained" and "Samson Agonistes" 1671–1971*, ed. Balachandra Rajan (London: Routledge and Kegan Paul, 1973), 34.

95. See, e. g., J. J. Lias, *The Book of Judges, with Maps, Notes and Introduction* (Cambridge: Cambridge University Press, 1889), 175.

96. Eagleton, *Sweet Violence*, 210.

97. Philip Fisher, *The Vehement Passions* (Princeton, NJ and Oxford: Princeton University Press, 2002), 193, 36, and see also 10, 154. "Calm of mind," Rees reports (see *Aristotle's Theory and Milton's Practice*, 10), is a cliché of Italian criticism and, as such, reinforces the platitudinous nature of the final words of the Chorus.

98. Fisher, *The Vehement Passions*, 173. Fisher quotes from the Loeb Classical Library edition of Aristotle's *Nicomachean Ethics*, 4.5.1125b30–35.

99. Fisher, *The Vehement Passions*, 185.

100. Carey, "A Work in Praise of Terrorism," 15.
101. Ibid., 16.
102. See Cassel, *The Book of Judges*, tr. Steentra, 225, 183.
103. Rushdie, "Getting into Gang War," *The Washington Post*, Wednesday, December 25, 2002, A29.
104. Patterson, *Censorship and Interpretation*, 81; cf. 47.
105. Patterson, *Reading between the Lines*, 272. The last quotation is from *Censorship and Interpretation*, 156.
106. Empson, *Milton's God*, 12.
107. See Shafeeq Ghabra, "What Catastrophe Can Reveal," *The New York Times*, Monday, August 26, 2002, A19.
108. G. Wilson Knight, *Chariot of Wrath: The Message of John Milton to Democracy at War* (London: Faber and Faber, 1942), 83, 39.
109. Ibid., 100, 115.
110. Bayne, *The Chief Actors in the Puritan Revolution*, 299.
111. Martin A. Larson, *The Modernity of Milton: A Theological and Philosophical Interpretation* (Chicago: University of Chicago Press, 1927), viii, 171, 264.
112. As quoted by Melanie Rehak, "Questions for Derek Walcott: Poet of the Ages," *The New York Times Magazine*, Sunday, May 12, 2002, 19.
113. See the prefatory lyric to Blake's *Milton* and Wordsworth's sonnet, "London, 1802," in *The Romantics on Milton: Formal Essays and Critical Asides*, ed. Wittreich, 39 and 111, respectively.
114. Percy Bysshe Shelley, *Prometheus Unbound* and *The Cenci*, in *Shelley's Poetry and Prose*, ed. Donald H. Reiman and Neil Fraistat (New York and London: Norton, 2002), 136 (1.7) and 250 (1.3.58–61), respectively. All other citations for *Prometheus Unbound* are inserted parenthetically in the text.
115. Mary Shelley, *Frankenstein*, ed. Maurice Hindle (Harmondsworth, Middlesex, England, and New York: Penguin, 1985), 176, 207.
116. Ibid., 242.
117. Ibid., 243, 254–55, 242, 248; cf. 240, 241, 244, 251.
118. Ibid., 244, 248.
119. Mary Shelley, *The Last Man*, ed. Morton D. Paley (1994; rpt. Oxford and New York: Oxford University Press, 1998), 389. See also 32, 471–72.
120. Ibid., 356, 405.
121. Quoted from *"In the Wind's Eye": Byron's Letters and Journals—The Complete and Unexpurgated Text of All the Letters*, ed. Leslie A. Marchand, 13 vols. (London: J. Murray, 1973–1994), 9:60; cf. 53, 89, 103, 118.
122. See J. Macmillan Brown who is also quoted by Lawrence John Zillman as saying that *Samson Agonistes* "is really the tragedy not of Samson but of John Milton"; see *Shelley's "Prometheus Unbound": A Variorum Edition*, rev. ed., ed. Lawrence John Zillman

(Seattle: University of Washington Press, 1960), 70. Zillman reports further that the editors of *Poet Lore* (1897) engage Milton and Shelley under the following topics: "Grounds for Identifying the Samson with the Prometheus Story; the Lack of Correspondence of Milton's *Samson Agonistes* with the Prometheus Story" (ibid., 79). See esp. the section, "The Prometheus Stories as Treated by Aeschylus, Shelley, Goethe, Milton" (589–606) and, within that section, the subtopics of "Grounds for Identifying the Samson with the Prometheus Myth" (595), "The Lack of Correspondence of Milton's 'Samson Agonistes' with the Prometheus Story" (595–96), "The Characterization of the Heroes of Aeschylus, Shelley, Goethe, Milton, and Byron," (600–02), "The Underlying Philosophy of the Poems" (600–06), all in *Poet Lore: A Quarterly Magazine of Letters*, ed. Charlotte Porter and Helen A. Clarke (new series 1), 9, 4 (October, November, December, 1897).

123. Lord Byron, *Manfred* (1.2.27), in *Lord Byron: The Complete Poetical Works*, ed. Jerome J. McGann, 4 vols. (Oxford and London: Oxford University Press, 1986), 4:63.

124. See Abram Smythe Palmer, *The Samson Saga and Its Place in Comparative Religion* (London: Isaac Pitman, 1913), 188 and Edward Rothstein, "Shelf Life: Six Days of Confusion That Rearranged World Politics," *New York Times*, July 6, 2002, B9, who, in his Samson citation, is misquoting Levi Eshkol as his words are reported by Michael B. Oren, *Six Days of War: June 1967 and the Making of the Modern Middle East* (Oxford and New York: Oxford University Press, 2002), 18; see also 317.

125. G. H. S. Walpole, *Handbook to Judges and Ruth* (London: Rivingtons, 1901), 157–58.

126. Ibid., 159–60; cf. 158.

127. Ibid., 100.

128. Hans Robert Jauss, *Toward an Aesthetic of Reception*, tr. Timothy Bahti (Minneapolis: University of Minnesota Press, 1982), 28. Alan Rudrum complains that "the fundamental problem of most revisionist criticism" is that "it outlines what significance the poem might have for modern readers and then imputes it back to Milton as his meaning" ("Review Article," 479). On the contrary, revisionist criticism is now mapping the reception of literary works, which typically inscribes competing interpretive traditions, with those traditions, then, vastly complicated by the interplay of literary criticism (pertaining to *Samson Agonistes*) and biblical hermeneutics (for the Samson story). Traditional Milton criticism is reluctant to examine its roots and thus often denies (as does Rudrum) its own history. Witness where variorum projects of the past century and of our own commence, hence the centuries of commentary they necessarily ignore.

129. As quoted from Add. Ms 78313, letter 108, December 24, 1670, by William Poole, "Two Early Readers of Milton: John Beale and Abraham Hill," *Milton Quarterly* 38, 2 (May 2004): 81; see also 76.

130. As quoted in *Medwin's Conversations of Lord Byron*, ed. Ernest J. Lovell, Jr. (Princeton, NJ: Princeton University Press, 1966), 77–78.

131. Leigh Hunt, *Lord Byron and Some of His Contemporaries* (London: Henry Colburn, 1828), 127.

132. Jerome J. McGann, *"Don Juan" in Context* (Chicago and London: University of Chicago Press, 1976), 49. McGann gives the best account of the importance of *Samson Agonintes* to Byron's last poems. See especially Chapter 3: "Byron Agonistes," 35–50.

133. See, respectively, Andrew Marvell, "On Mr Milton's *Paradise Lost*," in *Complete Poems*, ed. Smith, 184 (see esp. lines 5–10); Samuel Johnson, "The Rambler No. 139. Tuesday, July 16, 1751," as excerpted by Ralph E. Hone, ed., *John Milton's "Samson Agonistes": The Poem and Materials for Analysis* (San Francisco, CA: Chandler, 1966), 103; Percy Bysshe Shelley, *Prometheus Unbound*, in *Shelley's Poetry and Prose*, ed. Reiman and Fraistat, 210 (1.9); Mary Shelley, *Frankenstein*, ed. Hindle, passim; James Montgomery, *The Poetical Works of John Milton with a Memoir*, 2 vols. (London: Bohn, 1843), 1:xlviii; George Gilfillan, "Critical Estimate of the Genius and Poetical Works of John Milton," in *Milton's Poetical Works: With Life, Critical Dissertation, and Explanatory Notes*, ed. Charles Cowan Clarke, 2 vols. (London: James Nichol, 1853), 2:xxx. Of Marvell's poem, it needs to be remembered that he is marking not Milton's identity with, but distinction from Samson; and of Johnson's remarks, that his harsh words come on the heels of his observation (in "The Rambler, No. 139") that Samson "declares himself moved by a secret impulse to comply, and utters some dark presages of a great event to be brought to pass by his agency, under the direction of Providence" (102) and, later (in "The Rambler, No. 140. Saturday, July 20, 1751), that his severest censure is for "the solemn introduction of the Phœnix . . . which is . . . incongruous to the personage to whom it is ascribed," hence the poet's "grossest errour" (104).

134. Bayne, *The Chief Actors in the Puritan Revolution*, 345.

135. J. Howard B. Masterman, *The Age of Milton* (London: G. Bell and Sons, 1897), 72. Cf. J. H. Hexter, *Reappraisals in History*, 2nd ed. (Chicago and London: University of Chicago Press, 1979), 248.

136. Rudrum, "Review Article," 466. Why a book addressed to "students" should be treated so dismissively needs explanation, particularly in view of the fact that the book in question is addressed to "the ordinary man . . . the intelligent reader"; see John Carey, *Milton* (London: Evans Brothers, 1969), 5.

137. Cassel, *The Book of Judges*, tr. Streenstra, 225.

138. Ibid., 208, 225.

139. W. A. Scott, *The Giant Judge: Or the Story of Samson, the Hebrew Hercules*, 2nd ed. (San Francisco: Whitton Towne and Co., 1858), 301, 305–06, 309, 253.

140. Ibid., 309–10.

141. See William Riley Parker, *Milton's Debt to Greek Tragedy in "Samson Agonistes"* (Baltimore: Johns Hopkins Press, 1937); F. Michael Krouse, *Milton's Samson and the Christian Tradition* (Princeton, NJ: Princeton University Press for the University of Cincinnati, 1949); and James L. Crenshaw, *Samson: A Secret Betrayed, a Vow Ignored* (London: S. P. C. K., 1979), the last of whom, while recognizing the negative features in Samson's character, also contends that in Milton's rendering of it Samson is depicted as driven by divine impulse (83, 89). But for other citations of Milton in Crenshaw's commentary, see 88, 95, 96, 129, 143. In "Samson," the section entitled "Postcanonical Readings of the Story," *The Anchor Bible Dictionary*, ed. David Noel Freedman, 6 vols. (New York and London: Doubleday, 1992), James L. Crenshaw concludes that "In Milton's eyes," Samson's "defeat was only a temporary tragedy" (5:954). This is not to say that there are no representations of what is supposed to be Milton's heroic Samson in the nineteenth century; see, e. g., anon., "The Samson-Saga and the Myth of Herakles," *The Westminister and Foreign Quarterly Review* 121 (April 1884): 317, 324–25.

142. See the anonymous essay, "Samson: Was He Man or Myth," *The Thinker: A Review* 4 (July–December, 1893): 294.

143. Christopher Wordsworth, *The Holy Bible, in the Authorized Version*, 6 vols. (London, Oxford, and Cambridge, 1875–76), 2:134, 139, 133, 137, 140, 144, 143–44 (my italics).

144. See Lias, *The Book of Judges*, 9, 25, 155, 165, 175. See also Lawrence Levermore, *Talks on the Book of Judges* (London: Morgan and Scott [1910]), who ends his own commentary with what he calls Milton's "thrilling lament" in *Samson Agonistes* (96).

145. Lewis Hughes and T. Boston Johnstone, *Analysis of the Book of Judges with Notes Critical, Historical, and Geographical* (Manchester and London: J. Heywood, 1884), 118.

146. See A. R. Fausset, *A Critical and Expository Commentary on the Book of Judges* (London: J. Nisbet, 1885), 4, 245, 250, 261, 262–63.

147. See Charles Simon Clermont-Ganneau, "Tour from Jerusalem to Jaffa and the Country of Samson," in *Archeological Researches in Palestine during the Years 1873–74*, tr. Aubrey Stewart, 2 vols. (London: Committee of the Palestine Exploration Fund, 1897, 1899), 2:204. See also the earlier findings of Charles Simon Clermont-Ganneau (with reference to the final catastrophe and Samson's burial ground) in *Unknown Palestines* (n. p. [1876]). This lecture has British Library shelf mark: 010057.ee.5.(3.)[.]

148. See Clermont-Ganneau, "Tour from Jerusalem," in *Archeological Researches*, tr. Stewart, 2:205.

149. Ibid., 2:205, 207, 209–10. C. F. Burney, ed., *The Book of Judges with Introduction and Notes* (1903; rpt. New York: KTAV Publishing House, 1970), 392, reports that "the place name Beth-shemesh,

'Temple of the Sun,' [is] in the immediate neighbourhood of the scene of the hero's [Samson's] exploits."

150. Palmer, *The Samson Saga*, 7, 187.

151. Ibid., 188, 232, 187.

152. Heinrich Graetz, *History of the Jews*, tr. Bella Löwy, 6 vols. (Philadelphia: Jewish Publication Socety of America, 1891–98), 1:64, 66.

153. George Foot Moore, *The Literature of the Old Testament* (New York: H. Holt, and London: Williams and Norgate, 1913), 88. If Moore is right in his conjecture that the original redactor "left out the adventure with Delilah and Samson's tragic end" (ibid., 85), then Milton's tragedy takes on even more emphatically the character of a scriptural supplement.

154. George Foot Moore, *A Critical and Exegetical Commentary on Judges* (New York: Charles Scribner's Sons, 1895), 313.

155. Burney, *The Book of Judges*, 337, 338, 339.

156. Graetz, *History of the Jews*, tr. Löwy, 5:715.

157. Luke H. Wiseman, *Men of Faith; or, Sketches from the Book of Judges* (London: Hodder and Stoughton, 1870), 281, 284.

158. Malcolm X, with Alex Haley, *The Autobiography of Malcolm X* (1964; rpt. New York: Grove Press, 1966), 185, 205–06, 185–86.

159. Ibid., 210.

160. Michael Lieb, *Children of Ezekiel: Aliens, UFOS, the Crisis of Race, and the Advent of End Time* (Durham, NC and London: Duke University Press, 1998), 155–56.

161. Malcolm X, *Autobiography*, 366, 200–01.

162. Ibid., 201.

163. Ibid., 391.

164. Ralph Ellison, *Juneteenth: A Novel*, ed. John F. Callahan (New York: Random House, 1999), 19.

165. Originally published under the title, "The Imagery of Killing," *Hudson Review* 1, 2 (Summer 1948): 151–67, Kenneth Burke's essay is reprinted under the title, "The 'Use' of Milton's Samson," in *A Grammar of Motives and A Rhetoric of Motives*, 527–44 (see note 54). For the quotations, see 528, 529, 541, 533, 527, 529, 527.

166. Ibid., 527 (my italics).

167. Ellison, *Juneteenth*, ed. Callahan, 17.

168. Ellison, *Invisible Man* (1953; rpt. New York: Signet, 1964), 212.

169. As reported by Lawrence Jackson, *Ralph Ellison: Emergence of Genius* (New York: John Wiley and Sons, 2002), 390.

170. Ellison, *Juneteenth*, ed. Callahan, 228–29, 121–23.

171. Fish, *How Milton Works*, 450.

172. Ellison, *Juneteenth*, ed. Callahan, 235 (cf. 357), 14, 17.

173. Ibid., 309 (my italics).

174. Ibid., 285, 284.

175. Hugo Grotius, *Of the Rights of War and Peace . . . in Which Are Explain'd the Laws and Claims of Nature and Nations*, tr. John

Morrice, 3 vols. (London: D. Brown, T. Ward and W. Meares, 1715), 2:465.

176. Wiseman, *Men of Faith*, 279.
177. Ellison, *Juneteenth*, ed. Callahan, 296, 310.
178. Ibid., 322, 368.
179. Toni Morrison, *Paradise* (New York and Toronto: Alfred A. Knopf, 1998), 285.
180. Ibid., 273, 87, 18, 87, 160.
181. Philip Pullman, *His Dark Materials Book III: The Amber Spyglass* (New York: Alfred A. Knopf, 2000), 408.
182. See Milton's Letter 21: To Emeric Bigot (March 24, 1656), in CM, 12: 87, and *Defensio Secunda*, in CM, 8:107. The lines from *Samson Agonistes*, once quoted by Adlai Stevenson (see Wittreich, *Interpreting "Samson Agonistes"* [Princeton, NJ: Princeton University Press, 1986], xxvii), are also, as Kemmer Anderson informs me, recorded by Thomas Jefferson, in *Jefferson's Literary Commonplace Book* (Princeton, NJ: Princeton University Press, 1989), 123, and perhaps remembered by Bill Clinton in his words to the Democratic National Convention, July 26, 2004: "Strength and wisdom are not opposing values."
183. Ellison, "Change the Joke and Slip the Yoke," *Partisan Review* 25, 2 (Spring 1958): 220.
184. See Stanley Edgar Hyman, commenting on Ellison's *Invisible Man*, in "The Negro Writer in America: An Exchange," ibid., 210.
185. Thomas Jefferson, "Notes on Locke and Shaftsbury," in *The Papers of Thomas Jefferson*, ed. Julian P. Boyd, 29 vols. (Princeton, NJ: Princeton University Press, 1950–2002), 1:548.
186. Adonis ('Ali Ahmad Sa'id), *The Pages of Day and Night*, tr. Hazo, xiv.
187. Pullman, *The Amber Spyglass*, 363.
188. Morrison, *Paradise*, 306, 318. Morrison wanted the last word of this novel (in contrast with its first word) to be lower cased, and it is in subsequent editions of the book.
189. I borrow this phrase from F. T. Prince, ed., *Milton: "Samson Agonistes"* (Oxford and New York: Oxford University Press, 1957), 16.
190. Peter Martyr, *Most fruitfull & learned Comentaries*, f202v.
191. See esp. David Crosley, *Samson a Type of Christ. Being a Sermon Preached in London July the 28th, 1691 . . . upon Judges xiv. 5*, 2nd ed. (1691; London: n.p., 1744), 3.
192. Ellison, *Juneteenth*, ed. Callahan, 14, 17.
193. As quoted by Azar Nafisi, "Words of War," *The New York Times*, Thursday, March 27, 2003, A23.

INDEX

Accedence Commenc't Grammar, 25
Achinstein, Sharon, xxiv, 81–82,
 142, 202n56, 212n45,
 220n130, 223n177, 224n4,
 228n27
Ackroyd, Peter, 112, 117–18,
 195n3, 219n119, 221n142
Adams, John (President), 154,
 228n30
Addison, Joseph, 86–87, 99,
 216n81
Aeschylus, 48, 176–77, 236n122
Aldrich, Henry, 98
Allen, William *see* Edward Sexby
Altaner, Berthold, 230n47
Altschuler, Eric Lewen, 234n93
Amichai, Yehuda, 141, 225n1
Anderson, Kemmer, 240n182
Apology against a Pamphlet, An, 2,
 20, 23, 35, 147–48
Areopagitica, 2, 23, 24, 51, 54, 58,
 64, 66–67, 68, 77, 151,
 226n11
Aristotle, 176–77, 231n60,
 234nn97–98
Arminianism, 169
Armstrong, Nancy, xviii,
 132, 196n18, 219n121,
 224n188
Art of Logic, The, 11, 13, 88
Astell, Mary, 110
Atterbury, Francis, 100
Aubrey, John, 11, 200n26
Austin, Reid, xxv
autobioghraphy, 3, 10, 22, 227n20,
 230nn47, 49

Bakhtin, Mikhail, 1, 47, 198n1,
 199n13, 205n100
Barker, Arthur E., 167, 234n94
Barnett, Pamela R., 224n186
Baron, Robert, 104–5, 218n103
Baron, Sabrina A., 201n47, 210n18
Barrow, Samuel, 29–30, 72–73,
 81–82, 84, 88, 92, 96, 100–1,
 124–29, 222n167
Barthes, Roland, 19–20, 21,
 201nn38, 41
Bayne, Peter, 143, 172, 179,
 226n5, 235n110, 237n134
Beale, John, 104, 115–16, 118,
 178, 217n98, 220nn133–34,
 236n129
Behn, Aphra, 108, 218n111
Belsey, Catherine, 206n115
Belsham, Thomas, 229n38
Benet, Diana Trevino, 220n130,
 222n163
Benjamin, Walter, 61, 208n1,
 227n20
Bensen, William, 214n70
Benthem, H. L., 27, 126
Bentley, Richard, 26, 88, 93,
 215n79
Berena, Cynthia Newton, xxv
Berger, Harry, 20
Berry, Boyd, 20
Bersani, Leo, 205n101
Bérubé, Michael, xii, 195, n8
Bible, xi, 52, 62, 75, 86, 92, 95,
 112–13, 172, 180, 186–87,
 196n16, 227nn12, 17
 annotations to, 180–86, 205n90

Bible—*continued*
Acts, 161
Corinthians, 46, 49
Genesis 1 and 2, xvii, 34, 52, 55,
56–57, 81
Hebrews, 32
Isaiah, 162
Joel, 31
Judges, 43–44, 49, 144, 152,
167, 168, 177, 188, 191–92,
234n95
Mark, 155
Numbers, 31
narrative in, 196n15
revisionist interpretation of, xviii
Blackburne, Francis, 204n86,
228n23
Blake, William, xxi, 2, 7, 36, 37, 77,
86, 96, 112, 144–45, 172–73,
187,197n30, 201nn40, 41,
208n129, 214nn67–69,
219n119, 229n39, 235n113
Blakeney, E. H., 227n12
Bland, Mark, 24, 73, 201n49,
211n37
Bloom, Harold, xi, 129, 195n2
Boileau-Despréaux, Nicholas, 129,
223n180
Bonnard, Pierre, 48
Boone, Joseph, xxv
Borges, Jorge Luis, 31, 203n64
Boros, Frank J., 21–21
Boston Globe, The, 142
Bottrall, Margaret, 22, 201n43
Boulter, Robert, 28–29, 90
Boyd, Henry Stuart, 231n51
Bradshaw, John, 117
Brahe, Tycho, 56
Briggs, Samuel, 24
Brilliant, Richard, 18, 19,
201nn34–35, 37
Bristol, James, xxv
Broadbent, J. B., 197nn32–33
Brooke, Dorothy, 230n45
Brown, J. Macmillan,
235–36nn122–23

Brown, Moses, 105
Brown, Thomas, 212n46, 218n104
Brust, Steven, xii
Bryson, Michael, xxii, 197n35
Buchanan, George, 231n57
Burbery, Timothy J., 231n58
Burke, Kenneth, 157, 189–90,
229n42, 231n54, 239n165
Burney, C. F., 185, 238–39n149,
239n155
Burton, Robert, 210n18
Bush, George (President), 225n2
Butler, Samuel, 81, 125, 222n167
Byron, George Gordon Lord, 144,
176, 178, 179, 235n121,
235–36nn122–23,
237nn130–32

Calvin, John, 36, 145, 180,
227n12
Camőens, Luiz de, 92
Campbell, Gordon, 220n135
Carew, Thomas, 92
Carey, John, 143, 168–69, 179,
180, 226n7, 235nn100–1,
237n136
Caravaggio, Michelangelo
Merisi da, 47
Cartier, Roger, 210n25
Cartwright, William, 92
Carus, Paul, 228n27, 233n87
Cassel, Paulus, 154–55, 227n13,
229n33, 235n102,
237nn137–38
Cates, H., 229nn35, 39
Cather, Robert, xxv
Cavell, Stanley, 138, 225n202
Cellini, Benvenuto, 10
Chambers, E. K., 156, 199n22,
227n12, 229n41
Chapman, Livewell, 28
Charles I, 44, 117, 148, 151
Charles II, 71, 112, 120, 123,
136–37, 205nn91, 96,
219nn129–30
Chasles, Philaréte, 200n24

Chaucer, Geoffrey, xxiii, 7
Chernick, Warren, 84
Christ Suffering, 34, 40, 48, 59, 157, 158, 160, 161, 162, 166, 231n57, 232n70
Christus Patiens see Christ Suffering
Clermont-Ganneau, Charles Simon, 238nn147–49
Clinton, Bill (President), 240n182
Coiro, Ann Baynes, 46, 205n98
Coffey, John, 232n68
Coleridge, Samuel Taylor, 1, 75, 198n1, 211n38
Collins, A. J. F., 200n23, 230n42
Comus see A Mask
Conrad, Peter, 129, 223n179
Copernicus, Nicolaus, xvii, 24–25, 51–52, 53, 55, 56, 207n123
Corns, Thomas, 220n135
Corum, Richard, 52–53, 206n115
Cowley, Abraham, 15, 116
Craddock, Francis, 222n170
Crashaw, Richard, 232n270
Creech, Thomas, 104, 217n99
Crenshaw, James L., 238n141
Cromwell, Oliver, 71, 117, 127, 148, 149, 204n78, 213n51, 225n204, 220n130
Crosley, David, 240n191
Cross, Thomas, 15
Culture Wars, 196n19, 197n27
Cuomo, Mario, 197n41
Curran, Stuart, xxv
Curry, Walter Clyde, 54, 206nn111, 118

Damon's Epitaph, 16
Dante Alighieri, 179
Davies, Neville, 231n58
DeBérulle, Pierre (Cardinal), 206n111
Decaris, Albert, xii
De Chateaubriand, Francois René, 41, 200n24, 204n84
De Doctrina Christiana See Of Christian Doctrine

Defense of Himself, 2, 18, 19, 23, 28, 36, 40, 46, 49, 115, 204n75, 205n103
Defoe, Daniel, 75, 132, 211n38
DeMan, Paul, 208n1
Denham, Sir John, 99, 100, 102, 122
Dennis, John, xxi, 98, 215nn74–75, 217n92, 221n153, 223–24n185
DeQuincey, Thomas, 166, 233n88
Derrida, Jacques, 48–49, 205n105, 206n113
DeVéricour, Louis Raymond, 10, 200n24
Diekhoff, John S., 3, 35, 198n10, 203n71
Dillon, Wentworth (Earl of Roscommon), 127, 216n89, 223n173
Di Salvo, Jackie, xxiv, 234n93
Dixon, Thomas, 229n38
Dobranski, Stephen B., 22, 201nn45, 46, 203n61
Doctrine and Discipline of Divorce, The, 24, 25, 46, 146, 226n11
Dollimore, Jonathan, 138, 225n203
Dorset, Charles Sackville, 216n89
Droeshout, Martin, 19
Dryden, John, xxi, 71, 72, 82–84, 96, 100–02, 109, 112, 122, 131, 160, 177, 202n56, 211nn29–30, 212nn45–47, 213nn48, 51, 214n65, 216nn86, 89, 217nn91, 93, 94, 218n112, 223n180, 230n44
D'Souza, Dinesh, xxi, 197n28
Dubrois, Heather, 73, 211n34
DuMoulin, Peter, 36, 45, 114–15, 205nn96, 97
Dunbar, William, 52
Durer, Albrecht, 19
Duran, Angelica, 203n64
Durling, Robert, 9, 199n17, 20
Dutoit, Uysse, 205n101

Eagleton, Terry, 58, 120, 147, 207n124, 221n148, 227n21, 234n96

Egerton, Sarah Fyge, 110

Eikon Basilike, 15, 44, 152, 220n130

Eikonoklastes, 23, 44, 45, 58, 68, 148, 149, 152, 164

"Elegy V," 147

Eliot, Charles W., 186

Ellison, Ralph, 188–93, 239nn164–70, 172–74, 240nn177–78, 183–84, 192, 194

Ellwood, Thomas, 100, 122, 123, 216n85, 221n156, 222n158

Elsevier, Daniel, 116

Emerson, Ralph Waldo, xx, 197n27

Empson, William, xxii, 62, 170, 205n99, 208n2, 233nn85–86, 235n106

Engel, Adam, 225n1

epic, 214n65

Epitaphium Damonis see Damon's Epitaph

Epstein, Edmund, xxiv

Escoiquiz, Canon Juan, 31

Eshkol, Levi, 236n124

Euripides, 48, 49, 59, 158, 160, 165, 176–77, 208n128

Evans, J. Martin, 2–3, 198n8, 201n48

Evelyn, John, 104

Fallon, Stephen M., 198n1

Farmer, Hugh, 155, 229n38

Fausset, A. R., 183, 238n146

Fenton, Elijah, 97, 214nn60, 71, 219n127

Fernandez, Troy, xxv

Ferry, Anne Davidson, 20, 196n11, 198n2, 202n59, 214n59

Figes, Eve, 195n3

Filon, Augustin, 200n24

First Defense, The, 19, 20, 28, 44–45, 68, 146, 147, 148, 201n46, 219n128

Fish, Stanley, 191, 226n7, 234n90, 239n171

Fishbone, Alan, 232n70

Fisher, Philip, 234nn97–99

Flannagan, Roy C., xxiv, 68–69, 201n49, 210nn18–22, 211n35, 234n93

Fleming, I. P., 227n12

Flinker, Noam, 234n93

Foucault, Michel, 2, 35, 48, 58, 198n6, 204n72, 205n104, 207n125

Fraser, Russell, 199n13

Frye, Northrop, 22, 145, 201n44

Fuller, S. Margaret, xx, 77, 196n22, 211n40

Fuseli, Henry, 2, 198n4

Gagen, Jean, 217n93

Gaiman, Neil, xii

Galileo, 9, 55, 206n120, 207n123

Ghabra, Shafeeq, 235n107

Gibbon, Edward, 163

Gilfillan, George, 179, 237n133

Goethe, J. W., von, 236n122

Goldsmith, Francis, 223n171

Goldstein, Bill, xxiv, 231n58

Goldziber, Ignác, 233n87

Good, John Walter, 215n79, 218n100, 221n141

Goodall, Charles, 105, nn105–8

Goodwin, John, 37, 115, 213n55

Gosson, Stephen, 160

Graetz, Heinrich, 185, 239nn152, 156

Graff, Gerald, xix, 196n19

Graves, Robert, 222n159

Greenblatt, Stephen, 129, 222nn177–78

Grieve, A. J., 156, 229nn40, 42

Griffin, Robert J., 29, 202n59

Grose, Christopher, 210n18

Grossman, Marshall, 7, 199n14, 206n119

Grotius, Hugo, 15, 43, 79, 150, 191, 205n88, 223n171, 231n70, 239–40n175
Guillory, John, 9, 199n16, 206–7n120
Gusdorf, Georges, 15–16, 200n30
Guttenplan, D. D., 225n2

Haak, Theodore, 27, 126, 131, 224n186
Hacket, John (Bishop of Lichfield), 116, 220n134
Hale, John K., 16, 200n33, 203n65, 211n37, 214n60, 220n135
Haley, Alex, 239n158
Hall, Joseph, 229n36
Handel, Georg Frideric, 136, 179, 181
Hannay, Margaret, 206n120
Harkey, John, xxiv
Haroun, Ansar, 234n93
Hayes, Tom, xxiv
Hayley, William, 34, 228n28
Henninger, Daniel, 225n2
Herder, Johann Gottfried, 155, 227n12, 229n34
Herman, Peter C., xxii, 197n35, 224n185, 225n1, 226n7
Hexter, J. H., 237n135
Hill, Abraham, 116, 217n98, 236n129
Hill, Christopher, xviii, 125, 126, 132, 134, 196n16, 202n53, 218n102, 222nn169, 171, 223n184, 224n188
History of Britain, The, 11, 12, 75, 88, 124
Ho, Bing, 234n93
Hobart, John, 118–21, 221n146
Hobbes, Thomas, 44
Homer, 84, 93, 96, 119
Holland, Joseph, xxv
Holland, Norman, 226n3
Hollis, Thomas, 204n86, 214n66, 223n172, 228n23

Holmes, David I., 220n135
Homer, 109, 214n60
Hooker, Edward Niles, 215nn74–75
Horace, 2
Horwitz, Roger, xxv
Houston, Bill, xxv
Howard, John A., 195n4
Hughes, John, 98
Hughes, Lewis, 238n145
Hughes, Merritt Y., 224n197, 231n57
Hume, Patrick, 55, 87, 98, 207n121, 213nn53, 55, 223n183, 225n201
Hungerford, Sir George, 99
Hunt, Leigh, 178, 237n131
Hunter, William B., 3, 50, 198n9, 206n107, 208n127
Huxley, Aldous, xii, 195n5
Hyman, Stanley Edgar, 193, 240n184

Ide, Richard, xxv
"Il Penseroso," 3, 7, 103
Ireton, Henry, 117
Isocrates, 160
Ivimey, Joseph, 41, 50, 204n84, 206n108

Jackson, Lawrence, 239n169
James II, 225n204
Jane, Joseph, 204n78
Jauss, Hans Robert, 61–62, 178, 208nn1, 3, 215n78, 219n124, 236n128
Jefferson, Thomas, 193, 240nn182, 185
Jenkins, Leoline, 116
Jerram, C. S., 199n22
Joachim of Fiore, 227n18
John Paul XXIII (Pope), 51, 206n110
Johns, Adrian, 9, 23, 28, 70, 199n16, 201n47, 202n54, 210n25
Johnson, Daniel, 195n1

Johnson, Samuel (17th c), 206n116, 222n160
Johnson, Samuel (18th c), 122, 179, 237n133
Johnstone, T. Boston, 238n145
Jordan, Matthew, 162, 232n72
Jortin, John, 136
Joyce, James, xx, 196n23
Justa Edovardo King Naufrago, 24, 27, 103, 105, 152, 217n97

Kahn, Victoria, xiii, 196n10, 226n6
Kazin, Alfred, 59, 208n129
Kean, Margaret, 144, 227n14
Keats, John, 76, 187
Keightley, Thomas, 228n22
Kelso, Ruth, 196n14
King, Edward, 24, 27, 217n97
King, Henry, 24, 103
King, Martin Luther, 188
Knight, G. Wilson, 170–71, 224n197, 235nn108–09
Knoppers, Laura Lungers, 195n7
Knott, John B., Jr., 232n63
Knowles, John, 198n4
Kolbrener, William, 215n79, 224n185
Krouse, F. Michael, 238n141
Kushner, Tony, 166, 234n89

Labriola, Albert C., xxiv
Laemmle, Damon, xxv
"L'Allegro," 3, 7, 103
Lang, Bernhard, 206n111
Lang, Jack, xx, 196n24
Langbaine, Gerard, 101, 216n90
Langhorne, John, 104, 218n100
Larson, Martin A., 172, 235n111
Lattimore, Richmond, 214n61
Laud, Archbishop, 133, 148
Lead, Jane, 108
LeClerc, Jean, 163–64, 233n76
LeComte, Edward, 130, 223n182
Lee, Nathaniel, 71, 102, 113, 211n30, 217n94
Leigh, Richard, 125, 222n167

Lens, Bernard, 98
Lenskiy, Vladimir, 196n21
Leonard, John, 26, 201n51, 203n65, 214n59
L'Estrange, Roger, 81, 115, 116–17, 125, 132, 204n98, 216n80, 219n130, 220n130, 221n141, 224nn189, 192, 195
Levermore, Lawrence, 238n144
Levi, Peter, 27, 97, 104, 124, 202n52, 214n70, 217n99, 222nn161, 164
Lewalski, Barbara, 10, 199n19, 200n32, 207n123, 226n7
Lewis, C. S., xxi, 196n12, 197n29
Lewis, J. D., 201n36
Lias, J. J., 182–83, 234n95, 238n144
Lieb, Michael, xxiv–xxv, 40, 44, 45, 47, 93, 94–96, 102, 187, 204n81, 205nn, 239n160
Lincoln, Abraham, xxiv, 197n41
Lindenbaum, Peter, 69, 71, 84, 210nn15–22, 27, 211n32, 213nn49, 51, 214n58, 219n124
Locke, John, 193, 240n185
London Chronicle, The, 135–36
Long, Thomas, 204n78, 220n130
Longinus, 71
Lord, M. G., 151, 228n25
Lowe, Laurence, xxiv
Luther, Martin, 147–48, 181
Lycidas, 3, 4–7, 16, 24, 26–27, 47, 64–67, 74, 76, 78, 91, 103, 104–12, 136, 151–52, 104–12, 217nn96, 98
Lycidus, 218n111

Macaulay, Rose, 227n12
Mailer, Norman, 163, 233n74
Malcolm X, xi, 158–59, 161–63, 186–88
Manning, Ann, 11, 200n25
Manuel, M., 217nn95–96
Marcus, Leah S., 198n11
Marjara, Harinder Singh, 207n122

Marlorat, Augustin, 227n12
Marshall, William, 8, 16–19, 22, 92,
  199n13
Martyr, Peter, 148, 194, 227n21,
  240n190
Marvell, Andrew, 10, 27, 29–30, 38,
  39, 41–42, 44, 72–73, 81–82,
  84, 88, 92, 96, 99, 100–1, 104,
  123, 124–29, 150, 179, 180,
  200n25, 202n56, 211n33,
  212n45, 218n102, 222nn166,
  168, 171, 223n184, 228nn22,
  24, 237n133
Mask, A., 22, 24, 36, 64, 66, 91,
  211n34, 225n2
Masson, David, 10, 27, 41, 199n21,
  202n53, 204n83, 216nn88–89,
  221nn141, 150, 157
Masterman, J. Howard B., 179–80,
  237n135
Mauger, Matthew, xxiv
McCoy, Richard, xxiv
McCloskey, Carla, xxv
McCloskey, Leigh, xxv
McDannel, Colleen, 206n111
McGann, Jerome, 63, 70, 179,
  208n4, 210n24, 237n132
McMahon, Robert, 9, 20, 199n13,
  201n39, 203n66, 204n79
Medina, John Baptist, 85, 98
Medine, Peter F., xxv
Medley, Robert, 144
Melbourne, Jane, 199n18
Melville, Herman, xxii–xxiv, 35, 81,
  197nn38, 40, 203n70, 212n44
Mendle, Michael, 143, 226n6
Menlora, Esther Khana, xxiv
Middleton, Anne, 86, 203n61,
  213n52
Milton criticism, xxii, xxiii
Milton, Deborah, 11, 51, 200n25
Milton Gallery, 2
Miltonic poetics, xviii–xx
  of incertitude, xxii
  of systematic contradiction,
    xviii–xix, xix

Miltonic Romanticism, xxi, 64, 73,
  141–42, 172–76
Miltonists, 195n3
Miner, Earl, 196n13
Mohamad, Feisal G., 226n7
Monette, Paul, xxv
Montgomery, James, 179, 237n133
Moore, George Foot, 139nn153–54
More, Alexander, 16, 18, 19, 36,
  45, 46, 115, 204n74, 205n96
More, Hannah, 34
Morrison, Toni, xi, 52, 64, 188,
  189, 192, 206n112,
  240nn179–80, 188
Moseley, Humphrey, 16, 20, 21, 22,
  84, 92, 103, 201n42, 217n97
Moyles, R. G., 202n53, 213n50,
  215nn76, 79
Mueller, Janel, 226n10, 234n92
Mulder, John, 20
Mulryan, John, xxiv
Murphy, Cullen, 234n93

Nafisi, Azar, 240n193
Naiomi, Tali, xxiv
Naylor, James, 117
Nazianzen, Gregory, 79, 155–66,
  203nn61, 69, 230–31nn47–52,
  231n61, 232nn63–66, 68–70,
  233nn73, 75–78, 80–81,
  83–84
New Historicism, xx, 215n77
Newlyn, Lucy, 123–24, 129,
  219n121, 221nn140, 149,
  222n163, 223nn174, 178,
  224n197, 231n59
New Milton Criticism, 141–94
Newton, Thomas, 10, 70–71, 86,
  93, 134–35, 136–37, 199n20,
  210n26, 213n53,
  224nn199–200
Newton, Vincent, v, xxv
New York Post, The, xi
New York Times, The, xi, 142
Norbrook, David, 212n47
Norris, Chuck, 225n2

Norris, John, 121, 221n154
Norton, Thomas, 24
Nunberg, Geoffrey, 225n2

Of Christian Doctrine, 40, 47, 49,
    50, 57, 58, 76, 95, 116, 151,
    170, 204n82, 220nn134–35,
    228n26
Of Education, 2
Of Reformation, 58
Of True Religion, 25, 51
Oldenberg, Henry, 150–51
"On Shakespear," 24, 97
"On the Morning of Christs
    Nativity," 3, 4, 7
Oren, Michael B., 236n124
Orgel, Stephen, 68, 201n50,
    210n15
Osman, E., xxv
Osman, Zeynap, xxv
Ostriker, Alicia, 187n33

Palmer, Abram Smythe, 183–85,
    236n124, 239nn150–51
Paradise Lost, xi–xx, xxv, 4, 7, 9–11,
    22, 25, 27–32, 47, 62–63,
    66–103, 104, 110–14, 150,
    154, 155, 161, 162, 164, 174,
    175–76, 178, 180, 183, 187,
    204n86, 210n26, 211nn31–33,
    211–12nn41–42, 214n71,
    215n72, 219n122,
    228nn22–24, 229n42, 231n59,
    237n133
    Adam in, xvii, 10, 33, 34, 52, 53,
        54–55, 75–76, 79, 138,
        145–46, 213n55, 217n93
    additions to, 86–97
    Angels in, xv
    annotations to, 207n121,
        209n13, 213n53, 215n73,
        216nn80, 83, 86, 220n139,
        223n185, 224n187
    and apocalypse, 77–78
    Arguments to, 29–30, 73, 75–80,
        88, 203n65, 211n37

    Beelzebub in, xvi
    Belial, 79, 87
    conscious and unconscious
        meanings in, xxi–xxii
    and consciousness, 74–77
    contradictions in, xxi, xxii, 57–58,
        80–82, 95, 131, 208n3,
        212n46, 215n79, 219n121,
        223–24n185
    controversial meanings in, xxiv
    and corrective criticism, 216n90
    cosmological discourse in, xvii,
        207n123
    critics of, 97, 197n34, 214n66,
        223n172, 224n193, 228n23
    critiques of, 81–82, 197n31
    Crucifixion in, 78, 120–21
    devils in, 75, 211n38
    duplicity in, xxi
    editions of, 68–86, 88–95, 101,
        186, 215n79
    as epic, 72–74
    Eve in, xv, 10, 52, 75–76, 76, 77,
        78, 79, 101, 110, 116, 138,
        217n93
    evolution of, 70–86
    and *felix culpa*, 32–33
    as film, 195n1
    frontispiece portrait for, 14
    and the future, xv
    gendered readings of, xvii, 208n3
    genres of, 72–73, 81, 199n19,
        207n123
    German translation of, 224n186
    God in, xv, xvi, 80, 161,
        233nn85–86
    headnote to, 64, 66, 72, 82,
        95–96, 212n47
    heroism in, 37–38, 101
    last books of, 133–37
    as a mental theater, 73
    Michael in, 145–46
    Milton as hero of, 37
    Milton's presence in, 1–3, 95–96,
        135–36
    modernity of, xxiv, 225n2

narrative strategies in, 52, 95, 206n115
narrator in, xiv–xv, xxi, 33–34, 35, 37, 54, 75, 76, 93, 138, 196n11, 199n18,
Nimrod passage in, 134–35, 136
and note to the reader, 88
and numerological design, 70
and *Paradise Regain'd*, 209n12
perspectives in, xix
poetics of, 197n35, 224n185
as political allegory, 213n51
politics in, xxiii, 31, 93–95, 97–103, 120, 122–23, 133–38, 212n47, 220n130, 222n163, 224n197
Prologues to, 35–36, 38, 55, 118, 131–32, 135, 203n71
and prophecy, 72–74, 93, 128, 130
Raphael in, 33, 53–55, 79, 127
the reader in, xv, xxi, 30–31
readers of, 34, 220nn130, 134, 221n140
reception of, 97–103, 115–23, 215n73, 216nn88–89, 217nn95, 98, 221nn145–47, 150–52
and reception theory, 208n1
revisions of, 64, 87–88
and rhyme, 29, 66, 71, 72, 128, 203n64
rival interpretations in, xvii, 78
Samson in, 34, 76–77, 87, 99–100, 130–31, 137–38, 151, 213n55
and *Samson Agonistes*, 137–38, 209n12
Satan in, xv, xvi, xxi, xxiv, 20, 35, 36, 37, 38, 54, 71, 72, 74, 79, 85, 86, 95, 101–2, 116, 135, 212n42, 220n130, 221n141
and Satanic rhetoric, 225n2
and scriptural revisionism, 66
as a secular scripture, 66
sexual politics in, xv, 87, 196n19

similes in, 87, 131, 137–38
Son in, xiv, 80, 164
Son's exaltation in, 212n42
structural center, 25, 34, 52–57, 68
structure of, 88, 89, 92, 93, 132–33, 202–3n60, 214n60
subversion in, xv–xvi, 86, 120, 129, 133
text of, 203n62, 208n5, 209nn6, 8, 213nn50, 54, 215nn76, 79
theme of awakening in, 76–77
theological narrative in, 212n42
theology in, xxiii, 136
title, 92
title pages for, 23, 24, 25–26, 27–28, 30, 32, 63–64, 88–91, 202n53, 209n7
unity of, xxi
Urania in, 206n120
Uriel in, xiv, 53–54, 79
war in, 223nn172–73
and women, 206n115
Paradise Regain'd, xviii, 3, 4, 10, 29, 34, 35, 37–38, 41, 48, 53, 62–63, 66, 67, 68, 73, 87, 110, 114, 122, 132, 144–46, 150, 155, 160, 165–66, 172, 173–74, 176–77, 178, 180, 187, 188, 194, 199n20, 205n99, 209n12, 222n165, 224nn199–200, 234n94
and Crucifixion story, 67, 121, 162
perspectives in, xix
reception history, 221n155
and religious orthodoxy, 132
rival interpretations in, xvii, 144
similes in, 87
Parker, F. Calvin, 234n93
Parker, Samuel, 125
Parker, William Riley, 41–42, 100, 102–3, 112, 114, 200n31, 204nn77–78, 85, 216nn84, 87–88, 217n95, 218n100, 219n120, 128, 220n130, 238n141

"Passion, The," 3, 74, 172
pastoral, 217n99
Patterson, Annabel, xxiv, 29, 101,
    130, 132, 169, 202n53,
    213nn48, 51, 216n90,
    219n121, 223n181, 224n188,
    229n42, 235nn104–5
Patterson, James, 195n3
Peacham, Henry, 165, 233n82
Pearl Harbor, 234n93
Peck, Francis, 132, 136, 160,
    215n73, 224nn190, 198,
    231n58
Penn, John, 152, 228nn28–29
Percival, H. M., 200n23, 226n9
Perelman, Bob, 234n91
Perloff, Joseph, xxiv
Perloff, Marjorie, xxiv, 234n91
Peter, John, 197n31
Peters, Hugh, 204n78, 220n130
Phillips, Ann, 226n10
Phillips, Edward, 39, 122, 130,
    204n80, 221n157
Phillips, John, 24, 27, 32, 36, 48
Phillips, Katherine, 106–7
Philo-philippa, 106–8, 109, 110,
    218nn116–17
Piers, Sarah, 109, 218nn114–15
Plato, 160
Poems, &c. Upon Several
    Occasions, 6, 8, 16, 18, 30,
    66, 201n36
Poems of Mr. John Milton, xiv–xvii,
    4–9, 10, 15–19, 20, 22–24, 74,
    92, 103, 105, 108, 193n13,
    218n102
Poole, William, 217n98,
    220nn133–34, 236n129
Poor Robin, 36, 116, 117,
    220nn136–38
popular culture, 195n13
Powell, Mary, 133, 136, 200n25,
    222n159
Prince, F. T., 240n189
prophecy, 203n63, 209n9–11,
    223n175, 227n18

Pro Populo Anglicano Defensio See
    First Defense
Prynne, William, 27
Ptolemy, xvii, 51–52, 56
Pullman, Philip, xi, xiii, 189, 192–93,
    195nn1, 3, 9, 240nn181, 187
Pushkin, Alexander, xix, 196n20

Radzinowicz, Mary Ann, xvii,
    196n13, 222n165
Rajan, Balchandra, 9, 164, 199n18,
    207n126, 214n59, 232n62,
    233n79
Raleigh, Walter, 226n8
Rambuss, Richard, xxiv
Rapin, Paul, 217n99
Raymond, Joad, 69, 202n56,
    210nn18–22
Readie and Easie Way, The, 25, 162
Readings, Bill, xxiii, 197n39
Reason of Church-government, The,
    24, 49, 147, 151, 171
Redman, Harry J., 200n24
Rees, Brinley Roderick, 231n60,
    234n97
Reeves, Marjorie, 227nn112, 118
Rehak, Melanie, 235n112
Rembrandt van Rign, 15–16
Renza, Louis A., 4, 198n11
Richardson, Jonathan, Sr., xxi, 11,
    35, 52, 55, 57, 68, 98, 99–101,
    102–3, 120, 131–32, 204n73,
    206nn109, 114, 207n122,
    209n13, 210nn14, 16–17,
    215n73, 216nn80, 83, 86–88,
    220n139, 223n185, 224n188
    (and Son), xxi, 52, 55, 57,
    131–32, 200n27
Riggs, William, 20
Robinson, Tancred, 100
Rogers, John, 212n42, 230n46
Romanovskaya, M., 196n20
Roscoff, Gustav, 228n27
Roscommon, Earl of see Dillon,
    Wentworth
Rose, Roland Salazar, 195n5

Rosell, Cayetano, 31
Rosen, Stanley, 53, 206n117
Rothstein, Edward, 236n124
Rousseau, Jean Jacques, 48
Rowland, John, 32
Rudrum, Alan, 236n128, 237n136
Rushdie, Salman, 169, 235n103

S., G., 204n78, 220n130
Sachar, Abram, 229n31
Sa'id, 'Ali Ahmad, 227n12, 232n71, 240n186
St. Ambrose, 33–34, 203n67
St. Evremond, M., 218n101
St. Matthew, 227n12
St. Paul, 34, 43, 49, 158, 160
Salmasius, 36, 45, 148
Samson, 19, 38, 39–48, 115, 130–31, 133, 152, 226n11, 227nn11–12, 228n27, 233n87, 234n93, 236nn122, 124, 237nn139–40, 238n142
  Milton's representations of, 151
  and New Model Army, 152, 178
  and typology, 157, 183
Samson Agonistes, xi, xii–xiii, xiv, xviii, xxv, 3, 10, 20, 29, 37–38, 40–48, 59, 62–63, 66, 73, 77, 81, 110, 114, 132–34, 136–39, 141–94, 199n20, 199–200nn22, 23, 209n12, 222n165, 224nn199–200, 225n1, 226nn4, 6–7, 9–10, 227nn12, 19, 228n23, 229n42, 230n46, 231nn53, 55, 58, 60, 234n94, 237n132, 240nn182, 189
  anger in, 168
  Argument to, 44
  as an autobiographical poem, 10, 41–48, 137
  Chorus in, 46–47, 152, 234nn97–98
  and its critics, 236n128
  and Crucifixion story, 121
  heroism in, 163, 176
  as lyrical drama, 200n24
  Messenger in, 152–53, 191
  and Milton, 10, 38, 48, 235–36n122
  and Milton's poetic career, 205n98
  modernity of, xxiv
  omissa sheet, 30, 203n61
  perspectives in, xix
  and the phoenix, 237n133
  as political allegory, 41, 134
  and politics, xii–xiii, 134–39
  and prayer, 151–55
  Preface to, 16, 44, 46, 48, 49, 121, 156, 160, 161, 164, 203n68, 229n42, 231n57
  and prophecy, 147–51
  and providence, 237n133
  and the rhetoric of inspiration, 154
  rival interpretations in, xvii, 144
  Samson as a hero, 226n10, 236n122, 238n141
  Samson as suicide bomber, 225n2
  as scriptural supplement, 167–68, 180–86, 239n153
  subterfuges in, 229–30n42
  as tragedy, 48, 87, 134, 146–47, 164–65, 166–80, 182, 205n99, 227n21, 238n141
  and terrorism, 141–94, 225n2, 226n7, 234n93
  title page for, 159
  and typology, 240n191
  violence in, 168–69
  and warfare, 225n2
Samuel, Irene, 179, 205n99
Sandys, George, 232n70
Sargent, John Singer, 18
Sauer, Elizabeth, 156, 230n44
Saurat, Denis, 37
Scanlan, Robert, 141, 225n1
Schaff, Philip, 230n48, 233n80
Schlesinger, Arthur M., Jr., xx, 196n24, 197nn25–27
Schlichting, Jonas, 212n42

Schneidau, Herbert, xviii, 196n15
Scott, W. A., 181–82, 237nn139–40
Second Defense, The, 10, 19, 23, 39,
44, 45, 68, 147, 240n182
Selvaggi, 84
Semenza, Gregory M. Colón,
195n7, 217n97
Seneca, 20, 48
Sensabaugh, George, 113, 215n79,
219n123, 224n197
September 11, 2001 (9/11), xii
Sergeant, Thomas, 215n74
Sexby, Edward, 42–43, 205n87
Shaftsbury, 213n51
Shakespeare, William, xxiii, 20, 58,
123, 129, 215n77
Sharpe, Kevin, 222n161
Shawcross, John, T., xxii, xxv, 7, 9,
20, 102–3, 114, 197n35,
198n13, 199n15, 200n31,
202–3n60, 209nn9, 12,
211n41, 215n74, 216n90,
219nn126, 129, 224n191
Shea, Christopher, 225n2
Shelley, Mary, 174–75, 179, 189,
235nn115–20, 237n133
Shelley, Percy Bysshe, 77, 173–74,
179, 200n24, 235n114,
235–36n122, 237n133
Sheppard, Fleetwood, 100,
216nn86, 88
Simmons, Samuel, 28, 29, 30, 69,
89, 202n56
Skerpan-Wheeler, Elizabeth,
199n13, 200nn28, 30
Smith, G. Gregory, 231n57
Smith, Henry, 213n55
Smith, Mark Trevor, 214n67
Smith, Nigel, xii, 44, 195n6,
196n17, 205nn92, 94
Socinianism, 80, 212n42
Sommers, Lord John, 71, 98,
211n32
"Sonnet XIX," 91
Sophocles, 48, 176–77

South, Robert, 43–44, 115,
205n91, 219–20n130
Spear, Gary, 199n13
Spencer, John, 31, 66, 203n63,
209nn9–11, 223n175
Spenser, Edmund, 21, 22, 27, 105,
119–20, 199n16
Staff, Leon, 194
Starkey, John, 29
Steadman, John, 20
Steinthal, Heymann, 152, 228n27,
233n87
Stevens, Paul, 49, 205n106
Stevenson, Adlai, 240n182
Stoll, Abraham, 228n23
Strier, Richard, 197n30
Stroehlin, Gaspard Ernest, 200n24
Stubbs, John, 27
Suckling, John, 92
Sumner, Charles R., 228n26
Swedenborg, Emanuel, 20, 96

T. J., 229n32
Tasso, 96, 179
Taylor, Jeremy, 229n37
Temptations of Jesus, 145–46,
229nn35–39
Tennenhouse, Leonard, xviii,
196n18, 219nn118–19,
224n188
Tenure of Kings and Magistrates,
The, 43, 147, 148, 149, 152
Teskey, Gordon, xxiv, 30, 197n62,
203n62
Tetrachordon, 4, 25, 34, 39
Thatcher, Margaret, 143–44,
226n11
Theocritus, 105
Thomas, Elizabeth, 108–9,
218nn112–13
Thomson, J. A. K., 230n43
Thoreau, Henry David, 84
Tierney, John, 225n2
Tillyard, E. M. W., 81, 212n43
Todd, Henry John, 41, 204n83

Todd, Janet, 198n5
Toland, John, 118, 135, 136,
    197n3, 215n79, 221n143,
    224n196
Tomkins, Thomas, 118
"To My Father," 147
Tonson, Jacob, 84, 86, 94
Treatise of Civil Power, A., 25,
    147, 152
Turner, James Grantham, 112,
    219n121
Tweedie, Fiona, 220n135
Tyers, T., 223

Upton, John, 204n86, 228n23

Van Limborch, Phillippus, 116
Vane, Sir Henry, 137
Verity, A. Wilson, 157, 199n23,
    227n12, 231nn53, 55
Virgil, 16, 18, 22, 67, 92, 93, 96,
    105, 109, 119, 132–33
Vlacq, Adrian, 28, 36, 44,
    204n74
Voltaire, François Marie Arouet de,
    197n38
Von Maltzahn, Nicholas, 28, 118,
    120–21, 202n55, 211n36,
    214n64, 217nn98–99, 220–32,
    221n144, 151, 222n167

Wace, Henry, 230n48, 233n80
Wadsworth-Booth, Susan, xxv
Walcott, Derek, 172, 235n112
Waldock, A. J. A., 197n34
Walker, Julia, 95, 214n63
Wall, Dale, xxv
Wall, Moses, 150

Waller, Edmund, 22, 92, 104, 122,
    218nn101, 108, 222n159
Walpole, G. H. S., 177,
    236n125–27
Walsh, Marcus, 214n62
Walsh, William, 105–6, 218n109
Warton, Thomas, 123
Washington Post, The, xi
Weimer, Amy, 234n93
West, Paul, 111–12, 219nn118–19
Westall, Richard, 152, 153, 228n28
Westminster Abbey, 99, 214n70
Wickenheiser, Robert J., xxiv,
    231n57
Willard, Nancy, xii
Williamson, Joseph, 116
Winstanley, William, 99, 216n80,
    220n136
Wiseman, Luke H., 186, 239n157
Wollstonecraft, Mary, 2, 37, 198n5
Wordsworth, Christopher, 232n67
Wordsworth, William, 4, 7, 173,
    182, 186, 198n12, 211n39,
    235n113, 238n143
World War II, xii
Wroth, Mary, 55
Wyatt, A. J., 199–200n23, 230n42
Wycherley, William, 215n75,
    224n185

Yalden, Thomas, 221n141
Yoseloff, Julian, xxv
Yoshida, Keito, 234n93
Young, Edward, 223n174

Zohn, Harry, 208n1
Zwicker, Steven, 212n42, 213n48,
    222n161